# THE RENAISSANCE SOCIETY OF AMERICA

*RENAISSANCE TEXT SERIES, I*

# DIARIA DE BELLO CAROLINO

Gallus interea ⸍Senas uenit:& a factiosis ciuibus in urbem exceptus est.& arcem occupauit . ~~deinde~~⸍ad Calendas Iunias Romam
uenit.Amissa opportunitate frustratus intacta
Roma , Pisas˄uenit.ubi genuenses a fide Lu-
douici ducis & quasdam trāspadanas urbes a-
uertere conatus est.ut liberam abeundi potestatem haberet . Quod cum impetrare nequi-
ret:uiam saltem sibi ferro aperiendam esse pro
posuit.Spem dabat cæleritatis fiducia:ac segni-
or (ut sperabat) sociorum expeditio.Tum Au
riliensem ducem qui haste alpium fauces custo
diebat,excitauit.ut iure hæreditario res mediolanenses turbaret opem protinus laturus. Is no
uarienses quosdam optimates ut in Ludouicum cōspirarent effecit:Forte mediolanenses
milites ad custodiendos ditionis suæ terminos
missi fuerant. Hos Auriliésis dux intercepit:
protinusq̔; in urbem Nouariam.iiii.Idus Iunias exceptus est a ciuibus quos clandestinis
consiliis sibi conciliauerat.cum eo eqtes.D.ar-
mati erant.Peditum.viii.millia.Paucisq̔; diebus arcem male munitam occupauit . Pauor
ingens Ludouicum Ducem ne iperium subito

# ALESSANDRO BENEDETTI

# DIARIA
# DE BELLO CAROLINO

## (*Diary of the Caroline War*)

*Edited*
*with Introduction, Translation, and Notes*
*by*
DOROTHY M. SCHULLIAN

*Published for*
THE RENAISSANCE SOCIETY OF AMERICA
*by*
FREDERICK UNGAR PUBLISHING CO.
*NEW YORK*

*Printed in the United States of America*

Library of Congress Catalog Card No. 66-21028

# PREFACE

This edition of Alessandro Benedetti's diary of the Caroline War attempts to serve modern historians by presenting his text in as pure a fashion as possible for those who still read Latin and by providing a faithful translation in idiomatic English for those who do not. My hope is that it will confirm for Benedetti the principle "È bello dopo il morire vivere ancora." I have tried to remember throughout that the interests of historians are varied. Some already familiar with the period of which Benedetti writes, already steeped in the wealth of source material furnished by other authors, will look to him merely for whatever additional information he may supply. But medical historians are not ordinarily so steeped in the period, and it is to them that the physician Benedetti will be of special interest. The edition therefore purposely endeavors to acquaint them in introduction and notes with the general history of the period and at the same time to stress for them the points at which Benedetti or other sources may touch on the practice of medicine. This is partly for the missionary purpose of helping to demolish through history the fence which exists between the humanities and the sciences. There was no fence in the time of Benedetti, who was humanist and physician, and as Professor Howard B. Adelmann stated in 1943, "It should never have been erected: it was illegal to begin with, and unsightly and unneighborly at best."

The edition has been long in gestation. First undertaken during World War II, and announced as in progress in 1949 and 1950 by Curt F. Bühler, it has often been laid aside as other commitments pressed, often resumed as time allowed. The final push came in 1963 and 1964 when the Renaissance Society of America expressed its interest, promised publication, and announced the project in *Renaissance News* for 1963. To the Society, to its Executive Board, and in particular to Dr. Bühler and Professors George B. Parks, Felix Gilbert, and William Nelson, my debt is very great. It is the Society which enables me, as the year 1965 approaches, to say, as did the the humanist and physician Giorgio Valla when he wrote to Jacopo Antiquari on 13 January 1494 concerning a work which he had in progress,

v

> Ex immenso pelago iam portum prospicimus; fluctus ingentes
> propemodum omnes invasimus. Hoc anno, si Deus dabit,
> in portum invehemur.

This quotation, *in Latin,* must be for the historians who still read
Latin. There will be other quotations in introduction and notes in
their original dress of Latin or French or Italian and, of course, Venetian. For I say with Agostino Sagredo, who edited Malipiero in the
original Venetian dialect,

> Avrei facilmente potuto ridurre il codice a lezione di lingua
> italiana, ma mi sarei tenuto reo di profanazione, imbellet-
> tando la fisonomia dell'autore, e togliendole la naturale
> freschezza e verità,

and with Julian Boyd,

> It has always seemed curious to me . . . that historians
> should have studiously omitted from their works the one
> ingredient capable of guaranteeing perpetuation beyond the
> generation for which they were written—that is, the dis-
> creet but extended use of quotations from the documents.

In my introduction and notes, that is, I have freely quoted in the
original languages from sources other than Benedetti in order to
impart a sense of verity, the flavor of the earlier period, and thereby
a vividness which can resurrect the people behind the documents;
perhaps also I have hoped that historians unacquainted with the
languages might begin to work in them and so acquire and enjoy
riches which no translation can bestow.

What I have quoted, however, is only a sampling of what might
be adduced from both documents and printed books. I found myself
as I worked in heartfelt sympathy with Carlo E. Visconti, who in
editing D'Atri was so embarrassed by the plenitude of supplementary
material at hand that he finally threw all his notes in the wastebasket,
and with Rinaldo Fulin, who was faced with the identical problem for
Marino Sanudo and, not wishing to "far pompa di erudizione," kept
his to the barest minimum. I have tried instead to select such sam-
plings as may induce the reader to look further and may show him
where to begin looking.

The mechanics of the edition will, I hope, be unobtrusive. Benedetti's two books have been arbitrarily divided into chapters. Abbreviations have been expanded, capitalization and punctuation adjusted
to the modern usage. Since it reflects its times the spelling of the

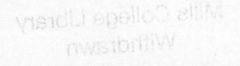

Aldine edition, even when capricious and inconsistent, has been retained wherever it does not injure the sense; the letters U and V have, however, been adjusted in the modern manner. The variants indicate differences from my text on the part of the Aldine and two later editions and a manuscript copy of one of these; insignificant variations in spelling have been disregarded. In addition, manuscript corrections made in the shop of Aldus are recorded as if made in all copies and are recorded from Dr. Bühler's pioneering article of 1949 and from additional readings which he has generously sent me. It reflects human nature in all times that the correctors of 1496 did not catch all the errors and that the corrections are not all absolutely accurate. Stop-press corrections are usually accepted silently from Dr. Bühler's article and are accepted as if made in all copies.

Dates everywhere are set down as they occur in the sources; it should be remembered that they are Old Style, that the Venetian year began on 1 March and the Venetian day in the evening, and that the various sources, being human, may err in dates as in other facts. In general, the names of modern publishers are given in the list of literature consulted but not in the notes, and titles of books cited in the notes are often provided in fuller form in the same list. Where there was not some compelling reason I have not always used either the first or the best edition of a work, preferring to save time by consulting in the several libraries and in my own the edition most readily at hand. For serials the year is given first and then the volume number; the practice is the reverse with monographs. It is hoped that the index will be helpful in the identification of individuals not discussed in the notes.

I have benefited by the continuing encouragement and sage suggestions of three stalwarts who have read portions or all of the typescript —Dr. Bühler of The Pierpont Morgan Library, who gave moral support to the project almost from its inception and performed the additional services already mentioned above; Professor Howard B. Adelmann of Cornell University, who has rallied my spirits almost daily in the final push and whose extensive experience in the art and science of translation has prodded me often and bettered my wording at many points; and Dr. Luigi Gullini, humanist and physician, who for his native Verona, for the history of medicine, and for sweet friendship's sake has devoted many hours to Benedetti during shore leave from his duties as ship's surgeon for the Home Lines. I owe a special debt to Professor R. William Shaw of Cornell University, who very graciously put at my disposal his immense knowledge of astronomy.

Among libraries I am indebted most of all to the Biblioteca Apostolica Vaticana, where for more than thirty years now, on a variety of projects, I have always met with the optimum in cooperation and in working conditions; the Biblioteca Marciana, which has assisted me generously in the three directorships of Luigi Ferrari, Pietro Zorzanello, and Tullia Gasparrini Leporace; and of course the Cornell University Libraries, their understanding director Stephen A. McCarthy, and many members of their staff. Other libraries and archives in this country and abroad have helped materially. Among individuals in and out of libraries, several of whom cannot see the finished edition, I would mention in particular Frederick L. Arnold, Rino Avesani, S. Baldelli Cherubini, Luigi Belloni, Mario Carrara, Mrs. Maud Cole, Hermann Corsten, Luigi D'Aurizio, F. Gröbli, R. Fumagalli, Teresa Guarnaschelli, Guerriera Guerrieri, Carolyn E. Jakeman, Giuseppe Mazzariol, Evaristo Menghetti, Irma Merolle Tondi, Mario Nardo, Foster M. Palmer, Donald G. Patterson, Francesco Pellegrini, Ulisse A. Pini, Francesco Reali, Giulio Sancassani, J. B. deC. M. Saunders, Hans Schadewaldt, Madeline E. Stanton, Lewis M. Stark, Bianca Strina, Mrs. Carmenina Tomassini, Roger J. Trienens, Ernst Weil, and Mrs. Nancy B. Willey.

In finishing I would not say, with Marino Sanudo and Martial before him, "Haec mala sunt, sed tu non meliora facis," but instead, with Amelot de la Houssaie and the author of the *Dialogus de oratoribus* before him (whom he believed to be Quintilian and we now accept as Tacitus), "J'avois bien la volonté de faire mieux, mais . . . mon esprit & mes forces ne répondoient pas à la grandeur de mon idée."

DOROTHY M. SCHULLIAN

*Cornell University Libraries*
*29 December 1964, N.S.*

# TABLE OF CONTENTS

# INTRODUCTION

# INTRODUCTION

On 29 December 1548, O.S., in Florence, Lodovico Domenichi [1] dedicated to his friend Giovanni Battista Pizzoni of Ancona,[2] long a resident
of Venice, the Italian translation of a well-known Latin work. It was
a work which sang the praises of Venice, in which city the translation
appeared promptly in the following year from the busy press of
Gabriel Giolito de' Ferrari.[3] Domenichi's letter of dedication [4] com-
memorated a friendship of twelve years with Pizzoni. His primary
purpose in translating, however, was not to honor Pizzoni or win
praise for himself, but, as he so frankly says, "per giovare, & piacere
in qualche modo a quegli, che cognitione non hanno della lingua
Latina." Another friend, Bernardino Daniello of Lucca,[5] had urged
him to attempt the translation, and he had performed the task with
a will during the Christmas season four years earlier in Venice.

Something of the same situation obtains more than four centuries
later with the present English translation of Alessandro Benedetti's
*Diaria de bello Carolino*. It sings again the praises of Venice, this
time in a modern language not as limpid as Domenichi's graceful [6]
and early Italian, but perhaps less rigid than Benedetti's late Latin. It
is calculated to assist readers who may have, like those of Domenichi,
no knowledge of the Latin tongue or at best an imperfect acquaintance
with it. If Curt F. Bühler did not actually suggest the translation, his
role is superior to Daniello's because he encouraged it in process, and
as friend he is easily Pizzoni's counterpart. The difference is, however,
that the present translation was not dashed off in a Christmas season
and that it carries also an introduction, a critical text of the Latin
against which the translator's English can be compared, notes, a
list of literature consulted, and an index of proper names and places—
all ponderous appendages with which Domenichi's gayer scholarship
of 1544 could readily dispense.

Both translations were made because the work of Benedetti,[7]
transferred into narrative and then print from notes hastily set down
in the field, has endured in the minds of men well beyond the year
of its publication, 1496. In accepting the Latin manuscript when
Benedetti finished it on 27 August of that year Aldus Manutius ran

3

no great risk as publisher. He was dealing not only with a man of high professional reputation, already an established author in medicine, but also with subject matter of feverish interest to every Venetian, and beyond La Serenissima to other Italians, to the French, and to a far wider Europe. Interest in the Caroline War has scarcely diminished since; it has rather spread to a continent of which Europe knew almost nothing when the war was fought, and if Fornovo was no Marathon, if we cannot speculate "Just supposing the Italians [*or* French] had won instead of the French [*or* Italians]," partisans and national pride can still argue heatedly today which side emerged victorious and how, had the battle been really decisive, the course of events in Italy and France would have been altered.

The literature began even as Charles VIII swept broadly down through Italy with his army in the fall of 1494; it marked his arrival in Rome on the last day of that year, his advance to Naples in February and his dalliance there through the Easter holidays and even into May, his forced marches back to Rome and then ever north as the league which was formed almost desperately and announced on Palm Sunday, 12 April, mustered larger and larger forces against him, the fateful meeting at Fornovo, his successful withdrawal to the French border despite the league, and Novara's hideous siege. It took the form of verse, satiric or hortatory, much of which is undoubtedly lost to us but enough of which remains to register the height to which passions rose during those months; of detailed diaries, several of which survive and among which Benedetti's is only one; of letters written home by campaigners on both sides, some of them published immediately on receipt by proud families or for motives of propaganda, others still being transcribed today as they are unearthed from archival collections; of official bulletins sometimes printed as broadsides and then posted in public places in the interest of patriotic fervor; and of letters which passed between friends removed from the actual scenes of combat. The historian's primary sources are therefore rich, so rich that he must select, remembering always, however, that the accounts will differ in details and facts and will very often be pointed toward one or the other side.[8]

Among letters we are fortunate to have many written from camp by the two principals, Charles VIII,[9] king of France, and Francesco Gonzaga,[10] marquis of Mantua and commander of the combined (if not really united) Italian forces. Several by lesser, but still eminent participants, in particular for the battle of Fornovo, are readily available in Domenico Malipiero's *Annali veneti dall'anno 1457 al 1500*[11]— letters by Daniele Vendramin,[12] for example, Angelo di Maffei,[13] the

proveditors of the Venetian forces and their staff,[14] the secretary of
Pietro Duodo, [15] and Bernardino Fortebraccio.[16] Benedetti's of 22 July
1495 is provided by Marino Sanudo.[17] They are all stirring, and those
from the French side [18] equally so, whether by combatants or by a
witness like Gilbert Pointet,[19] who in a capacity connected with the
army's finances watched the action at Fornovo from the baggage
train. These are the sources which "bear us lands [and centuries]
away," yet it is certain that they represent their age no more truly
than does Giorgio Valla when, at home in Venice, he discusses impending events on 29 September 1494 [20] with his friend Gian Giacomo
Trivulzio; or the same Valla when he mentions to the same Trivulzio,
probably on 30 October 1494,[21] the death of Giangaleazzo Sforza,
reminds him of the episode twelve years earlier when he had foretold
the death to the physician Giovanni Marliani,[22] and requests that
Trivulzio burn the letter at once; or Jacopo Antiquari when he expresses to Valla from Milan on 22 October 1495 [23] his doubts about
the recent treaty of peace, his gratitude to Venice, his apprehensions;
or Benedetti himself when he bemoans on 1 January 1507 in the
dedicatory letter to his edition of Pliny the Elder [24] the searing effect
of war on literary pursuits and the liberal arts.

Among witnesses to some or many of the events who composed
their accounts not in epistolary but in diary or other narrative form
Malipiero and Sanudo have already been mentioned. Jacopo d'Atri,[25]
who glorified the house of Gonzaga, Pietro Bembo,[26] and Girolamo
Priuli [27] are three additional representatives on the Italian side whose
wealth of material is vast. The French have a worthy historian in
Philippe de Comines; the repeated editions of his *Mémoires* from
the sixteenth century to the present day attest the popularity of his
very personal narrative, and the barbs of modern criticism can only
prick, not pierce, his facts and his presentation.[28] Around these writers
clustered others, whether contemporary or slightly later, who drew
freely on their material, sometimes in a fashion which would at once
be branded plagiaristic today—Bernardino Corio,[29] for example, writing the history of Milan and following Benedetti's so closely for the
expedition that at points his Italian is an exact translation of Benedetti's Latin and he an earlier Domenichi; Mario Equicola,[30] extolling
Mantua and accordingly D'Atri, damning Benedetti as adulator of
Venice despite the passages in which Benedetti lauds Francesco and
Rodolfo Gonzaga, and calling Corio's account a mixture of truth and
lies; Marco Guazzo,[31] mining from Sanudo but nonetheless needed
today because his text of that author was superior to the one now
available; Francesco Guicciardini,[32] composing his classical history of

Italy with somewhat greater regard for his sources. Later, toward the end of the seventeenth century, came Denis Godefroy's [33] great collection of sources, mainly French and both documentary and literary, and by the second half of the nineteenth century extensive surveys by Claude Joseph de Cherrier [34] and, in a volume so carefully prepared and sumptuously produced that it is standard in spite of its nationalistic bias, by Henri-François Delaborde.[35] The delvings continue in the twentieth—those of Francesco Reali,[36] citizen of Fornovo, for example—together with briefer allusions like that of Alfredo Panzini,[37] who visited Borgo Val di Taro and wrote of "Carlo VIII, con la lancia alla coscia, che infilzava l'Italia. Federico Nietzsche diceva: 'Benissimo.'"

Readers without a knowledge of Latin, French, and Italian, however, have been limited to accounts in English. For general background in the period they should still turn to what may seem an unlikely reference, Herman Friedrich Grimm's *Life of Michael Angelo*.[38] Accounts in *The Cambridge Modern History* summarize events in accurate fashion, that of Stanley Leathes [39] in the first edition furnishing many more details than that of Cecilia M. Ady [40] in the second. The most satisfying overall narrative in English is probably John Seargeant Cyprian Bridge's,[41] and for the engagement at Fornovo the essay of John Addington Symonds [42] endures as a piece of true literature. Fornovo, it may be added, has achieved recently a new notoriety in the somewhat racy recital by Luigi Barzini.[43]

One asks the reason for this interest through the centuries in a war which, the disaster to Italy aside,[44] really settled very little. Each party had of course its heroes, from Charles VIII and Francesco Gonzaga down through the ranks to the humblest soldier and even the most disinterested mercenary; it was natural that their deeds should be extolled both locally and nationally. But on the Italian side there was something more, what Petrarch had longed for but never encountered in his time,[45] what has been called "un soffio di italianità" [46] which moved the spirits of men even in the midst of power politics. It never aspired to the ideal which Garibaldi later personified, and it certainly fell lamentably short of the more modest goal which it had set itself, but it was nonetheless the first example since ancient Rome of Italians uniting against a foreign invader. And the breath is fresher precisely because it came in such an age, when politics was played as if on a checkerboard and power, or more power, was the primary desideratum. The great historian Lodovico Antonio Muratori surveyed human nature well before he said,[47] "Non mancarono mai nè mancheranno pretesti all'ambizione umana e all'interesse, per usurpare l'altrui, se con loro il potere si congiugne." The reader who would know exactly which position each piece occupied on the checkerboard of Italian politics may study Sanudo's analysis,[48] which is unmatched in other authors and is quoted entire below as a succinct and gripping introduction to Fornovo and to Benedetti's account.

Such, then, is the literature in which the *Diaria* of Benedetti very early took an honored place. It is an eyewitness account at least from Chapter 26 of Book I, where he begins for 18 May 1495 the actual register of events, and as eyewitness he chose and championed, as do all such witnesses, after the manner long since noted by Thucydides, whose "eye-witnesses of the several events did not give the same reports about the same things, but reports vary according to their championship of one side or the other, or according to their recollection." [49] The diary was not composed in the field and in camp in the exact form in which it has been transmitted to us, if for no other reason because its author was serving as physician to the Venetian forces and put his medical obligations first. He worked on it, however, as he could, and on 22 July 1495 he informed a friend from camp that he had "cast the history in the form of commentaries, which you may expect." [50] This friend was very possibly Giorgio Valla, for Valla wrote on 10 August from Venice a letter of friendly advice in which he counseled Benedetti to adopt instead a style patterned after Sallust and proffered his own services wherever they might advance the project.[51] The result was that on 27 August 1496, in the letter to Sebastiano Badoer and Geronimo Bernardo, counselors of the Venetian Senate, which concludes the *Diaria*, Benedetti could rightly claim to have "drawn up rather briefly and simply in writing that diary which I promised when I was in camp and which, busy as I was, I gathered together as industriously as I did cheerfully." By this time it included not only Fornovo but also Novara and the negotiations for peace.

The diary retains in its final form the vividness of the campaign. Benedetti, fully accustomed to a barren medical Latin, to the composition of tedious case histories and precise anatomical descriptions, possessed nonetheless powers of narration which, especially after the rapid summary of events up to 18 May 1495, beckon the general reader insistently on from one day to the next and keep his interest fixed and eager through both the action of Fornovo and the protracted siege of Novara. A wealth of detail which in a less skillful writer might entice at first and then repel does not cloy here. In choosing Latin, however, Benedetti was very definitely bidding for the attention of the learned few, not the general public,[52] and although the privilege at the end of the work refers to the possibility of an edition in the vernacular, there is no indication that he or Aldus ever prepared such a version.[53] Not everyone will grant that the style is actually Sallustian as Valla wanted it, much less that of Livy, whom Benedetti mentions with admiration in the dedicatory letter to Agostino Barbarigo; assuredly the Latin falters at times, as when it attempts to convert certain ecclesiastical terms which occur quite naturally in Italian, and Italianisms, whether Benedetti's or the typesetter's, occasionally betray themselves, but in general the style is correct, simple, concise, and adequate and has been so characterized by a series of competent critics.[54]

"Fide fideliores," "truer than the truth itself," said Benedetti's friend Quinzio Emiliano Cimbriaco as he introduced the diary with his hendecasyllabics. Such fulsome praise we expect in such verses. Equicola's quite contradictory opinion we have already had. The truth lies probably somewhere between. Benedetti was entirely aware of his obligations as historian. "History," he says in his dedicatory letter,

> demands a large portion of life, and in writing it such methods should be observed that truth first of all, right order, proper arrangement of the war, its causes, purposes, conferences, the outcome of events, and the course of the entire war may be accessible to those who read and the style itself seem not harsh, not listless, not too diffuse, not too abbreviated, or, finally, too studied, in order that it may the more vigorously penetrate or arouse the minds of readers. Likewise it ought to suggest sharply, persuade, provoke, impel, urge and also dissuade somewhat forcibly and sway the mind by frequent examples.

He declines to flatter for the sake of favor, to criticize too severely, and he proposes to commend the acts of the enemy when they deserve commendation, to play the role of narrator rather than censor, to practise moderation in words and thought.[55] All this is close enough to Equicola's own creed as enunciated in his prooemium [56] to Francesco Gonzaga,

> L'Istoria è da tutti universalmente commendata. Questa con piacer si scrive, & con gusto si legge. In essa si veggono varij casi di fortuna, tardi consigli, mature esecutioni, fugaci opportunità, provedimenti subiti, & improvisi assalti. Quivi la forza della virtù intrepida, & gli essempi (che molto più muovono, che le parole) impariamo.

It corresponds also to the creed of a later writer like Abraham-Nicolas Amelot de la Houssaie,[57] who believed that with his work on the government of Venice he had

> satisfait au devoir d'un Historien, qui n'aiant point d'autre but, que d'instruire, ne doit rien dissimuler, mais dire inge-nûment la vérité, sans se soucier ni d'ofenser, ni de plaire, suivant le conseil de Lucien.[58]

Where, then, if we attempt somewhat unfairly to judge Benedetti by the ideals of modern historiography, do we seem to find him wanting? Not, surely, for the speeches which he puts into the mouths of his characters and by which he enlivens his narrative; both he and the reader know that these cannot be direct quotations, no one accordingly is fooled, and the device is as useful as it was to Thucydides,[59] who realized that it was

> difficult to recall with strict accuracy the words actually spoken, both for me as regards that which I myself heard, and for those who from various other sources have brought me reports. Therefore the speeches are given in the language in which, as it seemed to me, the several speakers would express, on the subjects under consideration, the sentiments most befitting the occasion, though at the same time I have adhered as closely as possible to the general sense of what was actually said.

Not for whatever slips he, a physician, makes regarding military movements. Not for his frequent recourse to astrology, in which he was a man of his age and in particular a physician of his age, an age in which medicine had not yet emancipated itself from judicial astrology.[60] Not for any errors in chronology, topography, French surnames. No; we are troubled rather by the fact that his concluding letter belies in some degree the spirit of his dedicatory letter. "I have purposely," he says,

> passed over many points where dangers were at hand on all sides, points which could not be told without disgrace to certain individuals even though I did not doubt that they pertained to the everlasting glory of this [the Venetian] Senate. For it is very common for truth to produce hatred and often hasten death, whence in many matters that power of conscience languishes and dies and present dangers lead or incline a writer to the opposite of truth. Likewise they

think it the mark of a rash mind for a man not to excuse himself. So it was necessary to connive a little in accordance with the circumstances, until others without fear may more confidently leave things clearer to posterity, since bones and ashes scorn the frenzy of the wicked. However I do not hide my intention when somewhat sparingly I call blink-eyed someone who squints, or weak in the heel someone who limps.

He has not, in short, told the whole truth, and he could not because he was too near the events of which he wrote. He had the tact of a physician, the respect of any man of honor for the feelings of others, a fear of evil in high places which must have been all too prevalent in that age of tyranny (witness Giorgio Valla requesting Gian Giacomo Trivulzio to burn his incriminating letter concerning Lodovico Sforza), the courage to admit that he could not tell the whole truth, and the optimism to believe that writers who came after him would. We who today can deposit papers in libraries with the proviso that they be closed to historians for a discreet period can understand his position and read him fruitfully, remembering with Julian Boyd [61] that historical documents

> often contradict each other, they abound in the unspoken assumptions of the age that were too commonplace for mention, they are defective and confusing when clarity is most needed, and they can be used most effectively only by those rare spirits among us who have the gift of perceiving the evidence not there.

Benedetti is best when he is least a chronicler, when he enlarges, that is, on episodes which he himself witnessed and gives details of description not always available elsewhere—men slipping and sliding helplessly in the mire at the river Taro (I.44), Francesco and Rodolfo Gonzaga exhibiting a foolhardy courage which results in the death of the latter (I.45, 47, 51), the sky flashing and thundering with the instruments of battle (I.47), the slain lying in dignity on the field with wounds washed clean by a kindly rain (I.53), many of the living looting baggage and corpses in greed insensate (I.54, 56), Caiazzo's sister coolly waiting to flee her castle with the family's riches should need arise (I.58), Venice a prey to gnawing anxiety until finally word of victory arrives and the citizens pour forth in joy upon the Piazza (I.59), a cardinal of the Church pretending to fear treachery as he advances from the French side to confer with the Italian commanders (I.62), Charles stealthily departing while brilliant flames kindled by his men deceive the Venetians into thinking that the French are still encamped (I.65), Venice preserving as she had for centuries the purity of her coinage (I.68), the people of Novara watching from towers and walls as the Italian forces arrive before their city (I.75). Book II gives further opportunity for vivid detail—Novara succumbing to famine as mills turned by water are destroyed by the enemy and the people mash with pestles the little grain they have (II. 2, 30, 39, 51), German mercenaries and Italian allies continually bickering with one another and damaging the morale of the besieging army (II.5, 36, 38, 59), Venice gratefully conferring rewards for deeds of valor and also cannily promising them in anticipation (II.9-12, 32-33, 48), the same republic strangling a spy on the gibbet and slicing off the noses of deserters (II.8, 13), Lodovico and Beatrice Sforza inspecting the army as it passes in review through six chapters of rich description (II.18-23), a soil so fertile that it can furnish fodder for the entire army even as the abundant rivulets which course through it provide a well for every soldier (II.28), a French letter sent to Milan for decoding and translating since "talent has progressed to such a point that nothing can be hidden away in a letter which human industry will not reveal" (II.36), footsoldiers deceiving the paymasters and receiving their salary twice (II.42).

And Benedetti is best of all when these glimpses of the campaign concern that profession which was the reason for his presence with the army. The physician's eye and pride may remark what the layman overlooks. We learn of Venice's generosity in treating French as well as Italian wounded (I.56, 67); of wounded lying naked among the dead and begging for water with tongues thrust out (I.56); of men still breathing when hands and feet have been amputated, intestines collapsed, brains laid bare, "so unyielding of life is nature" (*ibid.*); of dysentery and tenesmus in camp ("none died who used the treatment of their physician"), soldiers receiving discharges for reasons of health, diarrhoea in Novara, Gonzaga himself suffering a flux (II.27, 30, 31, 39); of mighty horses dying by the hundreds as flies swarm around them and they scorn their food (II.51); of the dislocation of Niccolò Savorgnan's shoulder when his horse is frightened (II.42); and, in detail which will delight medical historians, of the wound to Niccolò Orsini, count of Pitigliano, when a lead ball strikes him under the right kidney and passes to the left scapula (II.43-45). Benedetti asks for urine, finds it clear, and so declares kidneys and bladder intact;

other military surgeons make the same pronouncement.[62] Additional
tests are made, treatment is begun, and Benedetti has a special triumph
when the advice of a quack is defeated.

He fails us in the *Diaria* on one disease, the very one on which information is most ardently desired. This was not for lack of knowledge.
His anatomical and medical works demonstrate repeatedly that he
was fully familiar with the scourge of syphilis at least a very short time
afterward.[63] Satiric poetry was circulating concerning it, its manifesta-
tions were common knowledge. For five centuries since then both
general and medical historians have discussed the place of Charles's
expedition in its history,[64] and the end is not yet. Benedetti's *Diaria*
does not help. He can give interesting detail on other things medical,
he can censure the conduct toward women of the French army in
general and of Charles VIII in particular (I.18, 29, 54, 63), he can
tantalize with "pustulas . . . epinyctidas" (I.9), which seem to desig-
nate a mild form of smallpox, and "exitialibus morbis" (II.27), which
he attributes to "the nightly fog . . ., and the heat of the sun in the
middle of the day, and the sudden change of air, and cold, and mist,
and weariness." He can, in fact, speak in the *Diaria* (I.56) of corpses
"unburied and swollen by the heat of the sun and the rain" and in his
clinical collection [65] even of swellings in the groins of these corpses
for which he says the sun and rain are responsible. But as he recounts
the daily happenings he is silent on the disease in a manner which
seems almost obdurate. This is the more surprising since by contrast
his fellow-physician in camp, Marcello Cumano,[66] who was rendering
medical services to the Italian forces at Novara, furnished a detailed
description [67] which syphilologists long thought their earliest. Did
Benedetti pass purposely over the disease? If he did, was there a
reason which we do not know, or did he simply decide that it was
more justifiably handled in his medical works? The questions will not
be answered here.

As history and as literature the *Diaria* speaks for itself without
requiring of the reader any great familiarity with the life of its
author. The definitive life of Benedetti remains to be written, and
it cannot be written without lengthy search in Italian archives and
minute acquaintance with his anatomical and medical works. The
broad strokes have already been traced by many historians.[68] He calls
himself Veronese, but Verona is a province today as well as a city,
and in the fifteenth century likewise its influence followed the course
of the Adige south to the small town of Legnago,[69] to which Scipione
Maffei [70] assigns him and which commemorates him by a portrait in
oils in its Palazzo Comunale.[71] He was born probably about 1450;

a maternal uncle Giovanni Jacopo Angelo was also physician,[72] and his father Lorenzo, he tells us, enjoyed such keen eyesight that even at the age of eighty he could dispense with glasses.[73] Benedetti's works are witness to an excellent education, humanistic as well as medical, and this education and his experience were later shared with the students whom he taught at Padua.[74] He was endowed with a sense of humor which attended him in work as well as play. We have, for example, the delightful story[75] of the medical student returning to Venice in a skiff by night after a dissection at Padua and carrying with him some bones for future examination; when he stopped at a halfway point to dine with comrades at an inn revenue officers hunting contraband discovered and confiscated the bones, which were immediately accepted and venerated by authorities as relics of saints but were later restored on the intercession of Francesco Sanudo, to the due satisfaction of the student and the immense discomfiture of the revenue officers. Benedetti's skill in dissection and his vision of what an anatomical theater should properly be are abundantly clear from his *Anatomice*[76] and have been often noted; likewise his talents as physician, exercised mainly at Venice, are amply demonstrated in his medical works.[77] Both before and after the Caroline expedition he studied or served in foreign lands—in Greece, for example, which he mentions in the dedicatory letter, dated 24 June 1493, to the treatise *De observatione in pestilentia* and often in the work *De omnibus morbis*[78]; in Crete, to which he refers in the *Anatomice* (I.14, III.9) and in the work *De omnibus morbis* (I.26, 28, 33, IX.19, XIX.40, XXI. prooem., XXV.1, 18, 34, XXVII.5, XXVIII. 12, XXIX. prooem.); and at Zadar on the Dalmatian coast, whence he wrote to Luigi Trevisan on 30 June 1499 the letter on the incursions of the Turks which is included in Marino Sanudo's *Diarii*.[79]

Such travels were not unusual for a Venetian physician in a period when the triremes of La Serenissima were carrying her commerce and interests so persistently eastward and ship's surgeons necessarily accompanied them; Gian Giacomo Bartolotti[80] is another instance. On his journeys whether abroad or in Italy Benedetti made many friends, and perhaps it is the friends, those at home as well as those far distant, who can illustrate in boldest relief his position in their political, humanistic, and medical worlds and can most heartily recommend his professional works to a later age,[81] as Valla and Quinzio Emiliano Cimbriaco have done for the *Diaria*.

Benedetti was not, of course, the only writer of his age to summon the Emperor Maximilian to an awareness of his literary activity, and the Emperor, if really an acquaintance, which seems improbable, was scarcely a friend. The *Anatomice* of 1502 was dedicated to him, on 1 August 1497, in the most flattering terms; [82] in the preface to its Book II he is invited, albeit only ceremonially and by wishful thinking, to one of Benedetti's dissections; and the work *De omnibus morbis* carries a preface to him. This is not part and parcel of the servility to actual or potential patrons which writers through many ages have been obliged to practise in order to eat: Benedetti was eating on the fees he received as physician, acclaim of those in power can have other motives, and his are not necessarily insincere.[83]

Certainly if we move to his relations with the Venetian aristocracy we find that, after the reigning doge Agostino Barbarigo (and to whom more naturally could the *Diaria*, celebrating Venice's part against the expedition of Charles VIII, have been dedicated?), they were often close and that they often ran in families. Jacopo Contarini, for example, to whom he dedicated on 24 June 1493 his treatise *De observatione in pestilentia*, had specifically requested the work, seems to have aided in its publication, and was known to Benedetti "gymnasii nostri tempore communibusque studiis," when he showed himself "in omni genere doctrinae elegantissimum, ac latinae linguae observantissimum; [84] Falleria Contarini, of the same family, is mentioned in the *Anatomice* (IV.17); Bernardo and Zaccaria Contarini are celebrated in the *Diaria*; and Maria Contarini's husband was one of the counselors to whom Benedetti sends greetings in the concluding letter of the *Diaria*. The husband's name was Geronimo Bernardo; Antonio Bernardo is one addressee of the Argument of the second book of the *Diaria*, together with Giorgio Cornelio; Antonio Cornelio, "primus apud nos philosophus," is among those invited to a dissection in the *Anatomice* (IV.1). Giovanni Marcello and Antonio Boldù are two of the decemvirs to whom the Argument of the first book of the *Diaria* is addressed; Pietro Marcello is mentioned in the *Diaria* (II.32), it was the young Marco Marcello for whom Benedetti prescribed without seeing him, and it was Boldù to whom he sent a sample of Novara's bread (*Diaria*, II.2) and whose son's dental difficulties he mentions in the *Anatomice* (III.22). Boldù is among those invited to a dissection in the preface of Book III of the *Anatomice*. Marco Sanudo is dedicatee of the *Collectiones medicinae* of 1493, Benedetti's fellow-historian Marino Sanudo is invited to a dissection in the *Anatomice* (V.1), Francesco Sanudo is credited for his sagacity in the episode of the bones. Benedetto Trevisan's services as ambassador are mentioned in the *Diaria* (I.20), Domenico Trevisan is envoy there (I.16), Melchiorre Trevisan's record as proveditor is extolled there (*passim*), to Luigi Trevisan Benedetti wrote from Zadar, and to

Paolo Trevisan he addresses on 15 May 1505 the letter which he prefixes to his edition of Giovanni Antonio Panteo's *Annotationes* . . . *de thermis Caldarianis* and in which he again lauds Melchiorre, "cuius virtutem in diariis nostris quodam breviario annotavimus." In short, we begin to discern some interplay, we begin to perceive reasons for some of Benedetti's invitations in the *Anatomice,* and we hesitate to brand him a mere name-dropper in the case of other representatives of the republic's government and nobility whom he invites to his dissections. It is not beyond belief that these invitations, fictional or not, are intended as sincere compliments and even as public expressions of gratitude.[85]

Like more than one physician in a period when the degree awarded to a successful candidate in medicine was "artium et medicinae doctor" Benedetti was at home in the humanistic world.[86] The humanist and historian Giorgio Merula had been his teacher; [87] in the dedicatory letter of 1 January 1507 to the edition of Pliny the Elder Benedetti cites his work [88] on the text of Pliny, and he is said in the *Anatomice* (III.22) to have replaced teeth for purposes of pronunciation and anchored them with gold thread, an appropriate stratagem indeed for a teacher of rhetoric. Benedetti's library alone demonstrates that the humanistic influence of his teacher persisted, for together with medical manuscripts in Greek—the *Viaticum* of Constantinus Africanus, Avicenna on winds,[89] Alexander of Aphrodisias on fevers (incomplete)— it contained manuscripts of the *Etymologicum magnum* of the Greek language,[90] Pindar's Pythian odes, and the hymns of the Neoplatonic poet Synesius.[91] This information we have from the Greek scholar and teacher Janus Lascaris, who saw the library probably when he was collecting manuscripts for Lorenzo de' Medici and whose listing is preserved in *Vaticanus graecus* 1412.[92] Janus Lascaris was the younger brother of the Greek grammarian Constantinus Lascaris, who was teaching Greek at Messina when on 15 June 1494 he in turn sent greetings to Benedetti through Giorgio Valla.[93] Benedetti, it is clear, was moving in highly learned circles, and with him moved Valla, that other humanist-physician whose influence on the *Diaria* has already been noted.

The two were bound by ties of mutual respect and affection. "Eloquio et doctrina medicus primas tenens," Valla said of his friend in the dedicatory letter, addressed to the Veronese senator Giusto Giusti, of his translation of the *Magna moralia* of Aristotle,[94] and again "nostra tempestate insignis philosophus medicusque celebris . . . qui ut est acuti ingenii, iudicii prudentis et doctrina bene armatus, ita non minus diserte quam graviter anatomicen corporis humani totam cognoscendam tradidit" when he referred the reader of his work *De expetendis et fugiendis rebus* [95] to Benedetti as authority on anatomy; "aetate nostra doctissimus," asserted Benedetti in the treatise *De observatione in pestilentia* [96] when he quoted Valla on the efficacy of a certain potion against the pest. Likewise in private letters never intended for publication a similar admiration is expressed on both sides: "Alexander Veronensis tam re quam nomine benedictus," says Valla to Antiquari on 13 January 1494,[97] "Georgius Valla in omni genere litterarum doctissimus nostrique amantissimus," affirms Benedetti to Antiquari on the same day.[98] Valla was friend in deeds as well as words,[99] sending to Antiquari in Milan sometime before 5 December 1493 [100] early publications by Benedetti, [101] discussing others on 13 January 1494,[102] concurring in Antiquari's glowing opinion of Benedetti,[103] continually spurring him in his writing of anatomical and medical works.[104] We should like to know more of Benedetti's contributions to the friendship. Certainly we can assume that he knew Valla's philosophical and rhetorical works as he knew his medical publications.[105]

Antiquari [106] made a trio. It is unnecessary to repeat the references to Benedetti which have just been cited from the Valla correspondence. The *Anatomice* of 1502 contains Antiquari's hortatory letter written from Milan 31 January 1494 to urge Benedetti to publish,[107] the work *De omnibus morbis,* another of 10 November 1508 of the same tenor on behalf of Benedetti's project on Paulus of Aegina.[108] On 13 January 1494 [109] Benedetti had laid before Antiquari, with interesting comments on his own literary activity, the projects then on the boards; these included six books *De venenis et venenatis animalibus* which Benedetti calls finished but which, if they are extant, have not been identified as his.

It is rather amazing, after so many favorable judgments, that as late as 1504 Benedetti should have found it desirable, if not necessary, to seek from another Venetian humanist an opinion on his *Anatomice* and his *Diaria.* His request can hardly have been a casual one, since the letter which he received in reply from Pietro Delfino, a patrician who had entered the Camaldolese Order and who became abbot of the monastery of San Michele di Murano, is formally worded and has almost the air of a testimonial. He and Benedetti had in common, however, not only Venice and humanism but also the expedition of Charles, during which Delfino represented Venice in Florence.[110] Although his competence to judge the *Anatomice* might be questioned (in fact, he himself apologizes for the attempt), he praises both works in the letter, and he makes special mention of Benedetti's regard for the Delfino family.

Benedetti states in a letter of 29 July 1508 [111] to the French humanist-physician Symphorien Champier that he is putting the finishing touches on his work *De omnibus morbis*, and that he will await from Champier an opinion on this and on his contribution on Paulus of Aegina.[112] The letter, which is filled with professions of admiration and affection for Champier, would seem to have been one in a series. We remember that Benedetti's *Collectiones medicinae* was republished about 1506 with works by Champier [113] and also, if we try to date the friendship earlier, that Champier had been in the service of Charles, wrote on the expedition, and may have accompanied him on it. If this was the case, the possibility that the two physicians, even though in attendance on opposing armies, met then is not inconceivable.

There was never any need for Benedetti, when one of his works was ready for the press, to search far for a poet who would introduce it with appropriate verses. Quinzio Emiliano Cimbriaco performed this midwifery on four occasions ranging in date from 1493 to 1507. A native of Vicenza and a pupil of the humanist Omnibonus Leonicenus, he spent most of his life as teacher of Greek and Latin literature in several cities in Friuli. Scholars disagree on the details of his biography [114] and even on the proper form of his name, which before he adopted the epithet Cimbriaco seems to have been Giovanni Stefano Emiliano. He wrote verses in honor of Lazzaro of Rimini, whom Benedetti mentions twice in the *Diaria;* of the emperors Frederick III and Maximilian,[115] from both of whom he received a crown of laurel and the title Count Palatine; and of the martyr St. Pantaleon, patron of physicians and midwives. His elegiacs and hendecasyllabics do not of course equal those of the Roman poets whom he emulated, but they are abundantly adequate for the purpose he intended and they support in their extravagant praise the epithet Paeantius which he applied to Benedetti. They occur in the treatise *De observatione in pestilentia,* the *Anatomice,*[116] the *Diaria,* and Benedetti's edition of the *Historia naturalis* of Pliny the Elder.

Cimbriaco, to give him the name he preferred, has therefore led us to an entire group of friends whom Benedetti, despite his long residence in Venice, never forgot. The hendecasyllabics in the Pliny sing Verona, and it is to Veronese friends that Benedetti dedicated near the end of his life, on 1 January 1507, this magnum opus of philology and textual criticism. He had honored them earlier by inviting them to a

dissection in Book II of the *Anatomice,* he commends Veronese soldiers
in the *Diaria,* and his letter to Paolo Trevisan dated 15 May 1505 is
prefixed to the edition of a work on Verona by another Veronese, the
*Annotationes . . . de thermis Caldarianis* [117] of Giovanni Antonio
Panteo, which Benedetti and Antonio Moretti had carried to publication after the author's death. In editing Pliny he was supporting the
scholars who sincerely believed that Pliny was Veronese by birth,[118]
and he was entering the lists with those several disputants on Pliny's
merits, pro and con, whose names will be found as "See also" references in the catalogues of all the great libraries—suffice it to mention
here again his teacher Giorgio Merula; Ermolao Barbaro,[119] whom he
had mentioned with approval in the dedicatory letter of the *Collectiones medicinae* and in the *Anatomice* (IV.1); and Nicolò Leoni-
ceno.[120] Benedetti's contributions to the purity of Pliny's text are large
and are especially valuable in the field of medicine.[121]

Benedetti alludes to the events of 1510 and 1511 when Pope Julius
II moved against Ferrara and the French, and he was still living when
for more than forty days beginning 1 September 1511 Italy was shaken
by a series of earthquakes.[122] Marino Sanudo [123] recorded his death
for the night of 30 October 1512. He made his last will and testament
early in his terminal illness of two months; it is dated 18 September
and is preserved in the great Archivio di Stato of Venice with the
records of the notary Hieronymus de Bossis.[124] In it he is not a
physician or humanist, but a man facing death and carefully arrang-
ing for the proper disposition of his estate. He names his wife Lucia,
a daughter Giulia, and other members of his family and circle; he
distributes his various properties, makes bequests to charity, requests
masses for his soul. The will would lead to the assumption that he
was buried in the church called by the Venetians San Pantalon, which
was founded near the beginning of the eleventh century. The present
church, however, dates from about the middle of the seventeenth
century,[125] and as yet eager historians wishing to honor him have
found no trace of inscription or tomb.

The stirring times in which Alessandro Benedetti lived are reflected
in the diary which follows. The period was one of transition, when
the old ventured into the new and could never again turn back.
Charles VIII, undertaking his expedition for a variety of reasons and
against the advice of many of his counselors, advanced triumphantly
to Naples over an Italy which from division and apathy found herself
unable to forestall him. Perhaps had Lorenzo the Magnificent lived
beyond 1492 a strong Florence could have changed the course of
events; perhaps had Venice not earlier favored France, and then in

1493 and 1494 held aloof and neutral, Charles could have been halted at some strategic point in the North. It was his artillery which brought Italy to the realization that this was a new kind of warfare, against which the strongest walls of hill town or plain city could not long stand, and to which on the open field human flesh succumbed all too readily. When Venice finally fashioned the League which met Charles at the river Taro on his return, when the League claimed the victory but failed in its purpose of preventing him from reaching his homeland, the weakness of Italy's principalities and powers was apparent to all Europe.

It was July of 1496 before the troops left behind by Charles in Southern Italy were finally dislodged. He did not live to invade again. Louis XII replaced him, to enter Milan on 6 October 1499 and hold Lodovico Sforza a wretched prisoner from 10 April 1500 until his death in 1508. All Italy was in turmoil, a prey to disunion, suspicion, jealousy, to France and Spain and Maximilian. Alliances were made and broken, Julius II succeeded Alexander VI, the League of Cambrai was formed to deprive Venice of her mainland territories, and at Ravenna on 11 April 1512 the French cavalry won out against Spanish and papal forces; a modern age was well under way.

When these events occurred Benedetti was still alive in a changing Venice. His diary of the earlier invasion, vivid in its eyewitness account and rich in detail not elsewhere recorded, is valuable both for what it tells of the past and for what it portends of the years ahead. To the physician and surgeon, and in particular the military surgeon, performing his duties almost five centuries later with knowledge and equipment far superior to Benedetti's, it has an additional and special appeal.

# NOTES TO THE INTRODUCTION

1. Lodovico Domenichi (1515-1564) of Piacenza was a polygraph much of whose time and talent went into translations commissioned by one or another publisher or patron. For brief discussions of his somewhat harried life see Girolamo Ghilini, *Teatro d'huomini letterati*, 1, Venezia, 1647, 148-149; Luigi Mensi, *Dizionario biografico piacentino*, Piacenza, 1899, 165-167, and Benvenuto Cestaro in *Enciclopedia italiana*, 13, Roma, 1932, 114. A fuller treatment, with a list of works written by him, translated by him, or "in che ebbe mano," is provided by Cristoforo Poggiali, *Memorie per la storia letteraria di Piacenza*, 1, Piacenza, 1789, 221-293.

2. A poet known to Pietro Aretino and highly recommended for his nobility of character by Lionello Pio di Carpi. See Giuseppe Colucci and Francesco Lancellotti, "Dizionario storico degli uomini illustri d'Ancona," in Giuseppe Colucci, *Delle antichità picene*, 27, Fermo, 1796, 3rd pagination, 85-86, and Vincenzo Peroni, *Biblioteca bresciana*, 3, Brescia, 1823, 55.

3. *Il fatto d'arme del Taro fra i principi italiani, et Carlo Ottavo re di Francia, insieme con l'assedio di Novara* di M. Alessandro Benedetti tradotto per Messer Lodovico Domenichi, In Vinegia, appresso Gabriel Giolito de Ferrari, 1549. Cf. Salvatore Bongi, *Annali di Gabriel Giolito de' Ferrari da Trino di Monferrato, stampatore in Venezia*, 1, Roma, 1890, 250-251.

4. Pages 2-3.

5. A poet and rhetorician who wrote commentaries on Vergil, Dante, and Petrarch. See Ghilini, *op. cit.*, 1, 32-33.

6. The adjective is used in a relative sense. Antonio Crosa and Carlo Moscotti, republishing the translation in 1863, found infelicities in it which they left unchanged because they did not have the Latin text available; see Alessandro Benedetti, *Il fatto d'arme del Taro* . . . tradotto per Messer Lodovico Domenichi, Edizione precisa alla pubblicata dal Giolito in Venezia nel MDXLIX e dedicata ai Cittadini Novaresi, Novara, 1863, 8: "A lui [Domenichi], forse pressato troppo e male rimunerato dagli stampatori assai di rado larghi e cortesi, fu tolto di dare ai suoi lavori maggiore accuratezza ed eleganza; come appare anche in questa versione, in cui talvolta sembra che zoppichi la sintassi, che a noi non fu possibile racconciare per la mancanza del testo latino."

7. Alessandro Benedetti, *Diaria de bello carolino* [Venice, Aldus Manutius, Romanus, after 27 August 1496]. See Frederick R. Goff, *Incunabula in American libraries*, New York, 1964, A-389.

8. Gratitude is due Emilie Herbst for her examination and evaluation of contemporary accounts from Florence, Venice, Rome, Milan, Naples, and the smaller Italian states in *Der Zug Karl's VIII. nach Italien im Urteil der italienischen Zeitgenossen*, Berlin und Leipzig, 1911 (*Abhandlungen zur mittleren und neueren Geschichte*, Heft 28). For a general introduction to the sources see the pertinent pages in Emmanuele Antonio Cicogna, *Saggio di bibliografia veneziana*, Venezia, 1847; Girolamo Soranzo, *Bibliografia veneziana in aggiunta e continuazione del "Saggio" di Emmanuele Antonio Cicogna*, Venezia, 1885; Auguste Molinier, *Les sources de l'histoire de France des origines aux guerres d'Italie (1494). V. Introduction générale. Les Valois (suite), Louis XI et Charles VIII (1461-1494)*, Paris, 1904; and Henri Hauser, *Les sources de l'histoire de France, XVIe siècle (1494-1610). I. Les premières guerres d'Italie. Charles VIII et Louis XII (1494-1515)*, Paris, 1906. Much work is still needed in government documents and archives, as for example in the records at the Archivio di Stato in Venice entitled Consiglio dei Dieci, Misti, Reg. 26 (1493-1495) and Deliberazioni (1494-1495), Secreta, Senato, Reg. 35.

9. The correspondence of Charles was published in five volumes under the title *Lettres de Charles VIII, roi de France*, publiées d'après les originaux pour la Société de l'Histoire de France par Paul Pélicier, Paris, 1898-1905. Volume 4, 1903, covers the period 1494-1495. Pélicier died on 27 March 1903, and Volume 5, 1905, covering the period 1496-1498 and providing the supplement and index of proper names for all the volumes, was completed by Bernard de Mandrot. For ease in citation the edition is referred to hereafter simply as Pélicier's. It is of interest that as late as 1951 one of these letters, 7 March 1494, Lyon, to Lodovico Sforza, ed. Pélicier, *4*, 25-27, was on the market; see Catalogue 29, Nouvelle Série, of C. & F. Roux-Devillas, 12 Rue Bonaparte, Paris VIe, item 267.

10. I have used letters published by Alessandro Luzio and Rodolfo Renier in their article "Francesco Gonzaga alla battaglia di Fornovo (1495) secondo i documenti mantovani," *Archivio storico italiano*, Serie 5, 1890, *6*, 205-246.

11. Ordinati e abbreviati dal senatore Francesco Longo con prefazione e annotazioni di Agostino Sagredo, 2 vols., Firenze, 1843-1844 (*Archivio storico italiano, 7*).

12. *Ibid., 1*, 1843, 356.

13. *Ibid.*, 356-358.

14. *Ibid.*, 358-360, 362-363.

15. *Ibid.*, 360-362.

16. *Ibid.*, 367-370.

17. *La spedizione di Carlo VIII in Italia* . . . pubblicata per cura di Rinaldo Fulin, Venezia, 1873, 516-517. Pages cited here for the actual text of Sanudo may be consulted in either the 1873 (Tipografia del Commercio di Marco Visentini, with facing title page *Archivio Veneto* . . . Anno Terzo) or the 1883 (same printer, with "(Estratto dall' *Archivio Veneto*, Serie I)" added on the title page and without facing title page) edition. The first contains on pp. 5-13 the "Avvertimento" of Fulin dated "Marzo, 1873." The second has following the title page a dedication to Bartolammeo Capasso signed by Fulin "Agosto, 1883" and on pp. 3-13 Fulin's introduction "Ai Lettori," which is in smaller type, longer, and fuller than the "Avvertimento" of 1873. Sanudo's text begins in both editions on p. 15 and ends on p. 677; the "Indice" follows on pp. 679-684.

18. See for example, the letter in Sanudo, *op. cit.*, 535-537 and Jacques de Thenray's account in Jules de La Pilorgerie, *Campagne et bulletins de la grande armée d'Italie commandée par Charles VIII, 1494-1495*, Nantes, 1866, 349-350.

19. La Pilorgerie, 351-361. A letter by another civil servant is provided on pp. 470-472.

20. Johan Ludvig Heiberg, *Beiträge zur Geschichte Georg Valla's und seiner Bibliothek*, Leipzig, 1896 (*Centralblatt für Bibliothekswesen*, Beiheft 16), 72-74. I owe my knowledge of this publication, on which I have leaned heavily, to Dr. Rino Avesani. Valla's survey of the situation is canny: ". . . Rumusculus ac susurus est, regem Alphonsium obnixissime pacem petere et in omnem descendere pactionem velle, Ludovicum Sfortiam non modo se appellaturum Mediolani ducem, sed et Italiae regem. Fertur etiam Maximilianus accitus venturus cum suis in Italiam copiis. Postremo quod a me exquiris, ex tanto eiusmodi gentium apparatu quid venturum perspiciam, colligam paucis. Rex Gallorum in hac sua belli expeditione non bene castra metabitur, tuorum adversariorum contundetur superbia, Ludovicus Sfortia fugiet Mediolano, eius filii occultati nec comperti tandem evadent. . . ." Heiberg published letters of Valla and his friends from *Vaticanus latinus* 3537. It is clear from film kindly sent me by Cav. Luigi D'Aurizio that letters in manuscript 2948 of the Biblioteca Universitaria at Bologna, Miscellanea Tioli, vol. 19 (cf. Paul Oskar Kristeller, *Iter italicum, 1*, London and Leiden, 1963, 22) were copied from the Vatican manuscript.

21. *Ibid.*, 74-75: ". . . Ceterum reor tibi innotuisse, quod nuper palam factum est Johannem Galeacium Mediolani ducem vita defunctum esse, et statim Ludovicum Sfortiam cum tunica aurata ducalique capitis tegmine prodiisse in vulgus et a multitudine vociferatum ducis nomine. An exciderit tibi, quod duodecimo iam anno significavi, nescio. Repetam, si forte minus meministi. Nam cum Johannes Marlianus Ducis Johannis Galeacii forte mederetur aegritudini, protuli ipsi medico fore, ut tali aegritudine e vita decederet. Id medicum sollicitum egit meque nesciente Ludovico significavit; qui statim e cubiculariis suis unum ad se me misit accitum, cumque me

htulissem, significatumque Ludovico esset in senatu, advenisse, quosdam missos fecisset, omnes alios amovit arbitros. Restitimus am.... uce quid opinarer, percunctatus est; respondi fore, ut tali langore esset e vita decessurus, futurusque dux Mediolani ipse Ludovicus; qui respondit: 'erit, ut volam.' Iteravi ego: ita fore videtur. Inde abeunti mandavit, ea apud me essent. Ego vero soli tibi omnem rem aperui. Tu respondisti: bonus profecto est Ludovicus, neque unquam crediderim, etiam si possit, se ducem effecturum. Nunc, quid sit, tenes. Post, quae in aliis litteris exposuimus, ut opinor, intuebere: non diu fore censeo, cum prorsus Sfortiarum nomen delebitur. Vale, et cum has legeris, te etiam atque etiam oro, ut eas igni immergas. . . ."

22. On Marliani see, for example, Luigi Belloni, "Storia della medicina a Milano," in *Storia di Milano* della Fondazione Treccani degli Alfieri, *11*, [Milano], 1958, 617.

23. Heiberg, *op. cit.*, 76: ". . . Quo in periculo versemur, nosti. Quid ista cum Gallis recens pax afferat, incertum; illud autem certissimum, Venetos tuos omnium hominum sapientissimos tanta gratia in vulgus propter auxilia validissima, quae in Parmensem primum, dein in agrum Novariensem miserunt, penitus descendisse, ut in suis thesauris condidisse credantur, quicquid adversus barbaros impenderunt. Et quamquam detrimentum sit acceptum non mediocre apud Tarum, neque Novariensis obsidio ex sententia cesserit, satis tamen negotii fuit restituta nobis civitate gravissimum hostem amovisse a nostris cervicibus conditionibus nescio quibus; nam perituris captata dilatio saepe salutis causa fuit. Ad eosdem rursus pertinet, quorum in amplissimum sese laus extendit, providentiae nervos in dies magis intendere, quo servetur Italia. De aris, de focis, de libertate, de iugulo agitur. Mori longe satius est quam hanc miseram foeditatem pati, quoniam eam transmittere ad posteros quoque oporteret, ubi semel barbaris herbam dederimus; verum dii melius fortasse respicient, quorum alioquin consuetudo est fortes iuvare. . . ."

24. *Historia naturalis libri XXXVII,* Venetiis, per Melchiorem Sessam, 1513, f.aalb, ". . . bellorum diuturnam iniuriam tanta studiorum ruina Italia totiens vastata cladibus secuta est, ex qua litterarum strage perniciosissima degemuere in toto orbe bonarum artium studia." Dr. Luigi Gullini calls to my attention the fact that the *Orlando innamorato* of Matteo Maria Boiardo, who died in 1494, breaks off at Part III, Canto 9, Stanza 26, "Mentre che io canto, o Dio Redentore,/ Vedo l'Italia tutta a fiamma e foco,/ Per questi Galli, che con gran valore/ Vengon, per disertar non so che loco. . . ."

25. "Croniche del marchese di Mantova," published by Carlo E. Visconti in *Archivio storico lombardo,* 1879, *6*, 38-68, 333-356, 500-513. He is mentioned by Sanudo, *op. cit.*, 90 and by Baldassare Castiglione, *Il libro del cortegiano,* a cura di Vittorio Cian, Firenze, 1947, 245. See also Alessandro Luzio and Rodolfo Renier, "La coltura e le relazioni letterarie di Isabella d'Este Gonzaga. 7. Gruppo meridionale," *Giornale storico della letteratura italiana,* 1902, *40*, where letters of his are printed on pp. 289-308; Luzio, "Una fonte mantovana del Guicciardini," *Atti della Reale Accademia*

*delle Scienze di Torino*, 1923, *58*, 284-293, who shows that he is the source termed "el Mantuano" in Francesco Guicciardini's history; and Roberto Weiss, "The castle of Gaillon in 1509-1510," *Journal of the Warburg and Courtauld Institutes*, 1953, *16*, 1-12 and 351, who publishes his description of this castle in Normandy which was erected by Cardinal Georges d'Amboise and visited by D'Atri between 20 and 26 March 1510. D'Atri, whose name was Jacopo Probo and who came from Atri in Teramo, in the Abruzzi, was count of Pianella and is so designated by the older writers.

26. *Della historia vinitiana . . . volgarmente scritta, libri XII*, Vinegia, 1552, Book II, ff. 14b-29a. This edition was translated from the Latin by Bembo himself. My copy belonged to "Il Signor Marchese di Pianella."

27. *I diarii*, a cura di Arturo Segre, vol. 1, Città di Castello, 1912-1921 (*Rerum italicarum scriptores*. Raccolta degli storici italiani dal cinquecento al millecinquecento, ordinata da L. A. Muratori. Nuova edizione, t. 24, pt. 3).

28. Cf. Bernard de Mandrot, "L'autorité historique de Philippe de Commynes," *Revue historique*, 1900, *73*, 241-257, *74*, 1-38. A specific instance of his appreciation of the lessons history may teach is the fact that about 1475 a manuscript of the French version of Valerius Maximus, *Factorum et dictorum memorabilium libri novem*, by Simon de Hesdin and Nicolas de Gonesse was executed for him with miniatures of the school of Jean Fouquet. The manuscript is *Harleianus* 4374-75 in the British Museum; its miniatures were reproduced in photogravure for Henry Yates Thompson, London, 1907, with an introduction by George F. Warner, who uses the following passage for Comines' general appreciation of the value of history: "L'ung des grandz moyens de rendre ung homme saige [est] d'avoir leü les hystoires anciennes et apprendre à se conduyre et garder et entreprendre saigement par les hystoires et exemples de noz predecesseurs. Car nostre vie est si briefve qu'elle ne suffit à avoir de tant de choses experience." See the edition of the *Mémoires* by Joseph Calmette, *1*, Paris, 1924, 129; not all the manuscripts transmit this passage. For Comines' relations with Italy see Auda Prucher, *I "Mémoires" di Philippe de Commynes e l'Italia del quattrocento*, Firenze, 1957.

29. For his biography see Filippo Argelati, *Bibliotheca scriptorum mediolanensium*, *1*, Part 2, Mediolani, 1745, coll. 466-468. In the first and best edition of his *Historia*, Mediolani, 1503, which is not foliated, the account for the years 1494-1496 occurs on ff. T6b-V7b. A summary is furnished on f. [6]b of the six unsigned folios at the beginning. When the "fratelli da Legnano librarii milanesi" some years later prepared a Repertorium for the volume, the reader was asked to foliate in accordance with the Repertorium. I quote the request here from the first f. Alb as an interesting and delightful example of early bookmaking and assistance to scholarship: ". . . historia Milanese . . . la quale essendo di volume certamente de immensa grandezza per il gran cumolo delle cose meravigliose, & gesti memorandi conchiusi in essa, e senza tavola suto impresso molti anni sono passati e per cio di

mala agevolezza non poca per volere qualcuna cosa di memoria degna ritrovare sanza leggere affatto lhistoria, Havemo noi con cotale diligentia operato, de le habbiamo nuoamente [*sic*] ritrovati, & aggiunti in modo di brevissimi elenchi, o ver argomenti, Questi repertorii sovra tutta la istessa historia contenti solo le cose meritevoli di grato conoscimento, e di palese utilitate alli leggenti. Li quali (rimossa larrogantia & il blandire) con un sol menomo rivolgimento docchio potranno discorrere, & introvedere igualmente tutta lanima della historia con quanti generosi fatti, e detti, ch ivi si contengono. Ma per non essere segnato, ne annotato il volume con li soi nomeri delle carte, ammonemo tutti li gentili lettori che non li sia molesto apporre detto nomero a foglio per foglio al volume suo, comminciando a segnare nomero vi. sovra il foglio, che comincia PRIMA PARS ove si contengono chi fossero li primeri edificatori di Milano con altre cose. Poscia seguendo di foglio in foglio con osservato nomero moltiplicando concorde col nomero del repertorio predetto. E in cotal guisa tutta la medolla: il core insiemente coi sensi dessa historia con picciolo volgimento di carte a ogni suo proposto quasi come in lucido specchio, o come picciola tavola tutto il circoito della terra dipinto vedere suolemo scorgere e comprendere apertamente potranno giocondamente leggere."

Ferdinand Güterbock, writing in *Neues Archiv der Gesellschaft für ältere deutsche Geschichtskunde,* 1898, 23, 214 of Corio's sources for the thirteenth century, states with reason that this edition "ist heute selten, hat keine Seiteneintheilung und ist daher unbequem zu citieren." I have used the copy in the Biblioteca Marciana. Editions appeared at Venice also in 1554 and 1565 and at Padua in 1646; a 3-volume edition with introduction and commentary by Egidio De Magri was published at Milan in 1855-1857. De Magri is not helpful on Corio's sources. Eduard Fueter, *Geschichte der neueren Historiographie,* München and Berlin, 1911, 47 mentions his unacknowledged indebtedness to Benedetti. Corio states quite frankly in his Praefatio to Cardinal Ascanio Maria Sforza, f. [3]a of the six unsigned folios at the beginning of the first edition, that he has "extracto da Autori viventi in ciaschuno tempo."

30. *Dell'istoria di Mantova libri cinque* scritta in commentari . . . riformata secondo l'uso moderno di scrivere storie per Benedetto Osanna, Mantova, 1607, Book IV, 199-225. His *Chronica* had appeared in 1521. Scipione Maffei, *Verona illustrata,* 2, Verona, 1731, col. 129, Apostolo Zeno, *Dissertazioni vossiane,* 2, Venezia, 1753, 45, and Giuseppe Cervetto, *Di alcuni celebri anatomici italiani del decimoquinto secolo,* Brescia, 1854, 72 mention his scorn of Benedetti. In the 1607 edition he calls Benedetti a liar on page 218, but quotes from him on page 219 without any such comment.

31. *Historie . . . ove si contengono la venuta, & partita di Carlo ottavo re di Franza,* Venetia, 1547. On the plagiarism see Fulin's preface to his 1883 edition of Sanudo, 4-13. Fulin omitted in his edition certain lists already published in Guazzo and referred the reader to Guazzo; see, for example, pages 380, 381, 404. Paolo Giovio's *Historiae sui temporis* appeared first at Florence in 1550-1552. Benedetti seems to have been among the sources which he used for his first three books; cf. the Basel edition of 1567, *1,* 1-266.

32. *La historia d'Italia,* Venetia, 1568, ff. 1-66. The first edition appeared in Florence in 1561. His dependence on Jacopo d'Atri has been mentioned above. See also his *Storie fiorentine dal 1378 al 1509,* a cura di Roberto Palmarocchi, Bari, 1931, 83-124; this work was first published in 1859.

33. *Histoire de Charles VIII roy de France,* par Guillaume de Jaligny, André de la Vigne, & autres historiens de ce temps-là. . . . Le tout recueïlli par feu Monsieur Godefroy, Paris, 1684. I cite the work by the name of the first author represented in it. I have used the copy in the Princeton University Library.

34. *Histoire de Charles VIII roi de France,* 2 vols., Paris, 1868.

35. *L'expédition de Charles VIII en Italie,* Paris, 1888. The volume was reviewed by J. Vaesen in *Revue des questions historiques,* 1889, *45,* 574-588, but not critically. It lacks an index. A comment of Luzio and Renier, *Archivio storico italiano,* Serie 5, 1890, *6,* 219 on the nationalism is refreshing: "Ma la incertezza intorno a chi fosse rimasto vincitore [at Fornovo], non fu solo una incertezza dei posteri male informati o passionati, tanto meno fu una menzogna intenzionale dei Veneziani, come oggi, in pieno secolo decimonono, vorrebbe far credere il sig. Delaborde: realmente, sinceramente, lealmente gli Italiani credettero di aver vinto."

36. In *La Gazzetta di Parma,* for example, 5 febbraio and 2 agosto 1959. For recent general accounts in Italian see Nino Valeri, *L'Italia nell'età dei principati dal 1343 al 1516,* [Milano], 1949, 717-743; Luigi Simeoni, *Le signorie,* 2, Milano, 1950, 725-747; Franco Catalano, "La crisi politica e sociale di fronte al 'barbaro,' " in *Storia di Milano* della Fondazione Treccani degli Alfieri, [Milano], 7, 1956, 415-508. For the military action and its significance see in particular Piero Pieri, *Il rinascimento e la crisi militare italiana,* Torino, 1952, 320-366.

37. *Sei romanzi fra due secoli,* [Milano], 1954, 203, in the work *Viaggio di un povero letterato.*

38. Translated by Fanny Elizabeth Bunnètt, *1,* Boston, 1906, 109-160. I owe this reference to Dr. Gullini.

39. *The Cambridge modern history, 1,* Cambridge, 1903, 104-118.

40. *The new Cambridge modern history, 1,* Cambridge, 1957, 350-355.

41. *A history of France from the death of Louis XI,* 2, 1924, covering the years 1493-1498. The account is vivid; bibliography and documentation are provided.

42. *Sketches and studies in Italy and Greece,* 2, London and New York, 1900, 180-200.

43. *The Italians,* London, 1964, 276-290.

44. Almost a century later Francesco Sansovino, the first edition of whose *Venetia* appeared in 1581, could say that the expedition of Charles "diede all'Italia quella forma che noi vediamo fino al presente, con rovina et mutatione di molti stati, et con dispositione di diversi popoli, et nationi"; see the edition of 1604, f.391a.

45. See Morris Bishop's summary, *Petrarch and his world,* Bloomington, 1963, 233-234, of Petrarch's canzone (*Rime,* 128) "Italia mia," which pleaded for Italian unity against the depredations of German mercenaries.

46. Luzio and Renier, *op. cit.,* 205.

47. *Annali d'Italia dal principio dell'era volgare sino all'anno MDCC-XLIX, 13,* Napoli, 1758, 377.

48. Marino Sanudo, *op. cit.,* 469-470: "*Digresso di l'auctore, come stava Italia in questo tempo, et li potentati.* Ben che fino questo zorno habbi narato tuto el seguito di la venuta di Carlo re di Franza, al presente esso Re volendo ritornar in Aste, sia per qual cagion si voglia, et l'exercito di la Serenissima Signoria con alquante zente de Milan, essendoli opposto contra, *unde* necessario è di far fatto d'arme; voglio qui descriver come in questo tempo Italia si ritrovava, et la conditione de li potentati *succincte,* a ciò se veda et intenda in quanto pericolo era di esser subietta et dominata da zente gallica. Alexandro romano pontifice con alcuni cardinali era in Roma tornato, dove confusione grandissime de Colonnesi et Orsini, principal parte Romane, vi era, et tra loro se molestavano. Cinque Cardinali seguiva el Re: *Vincula,* Zenoa et Samallo, et do altri. Erano pur da la so parte, ma non si partino de li soi castelli, Savello et Colonna. El Reame de Napoli dilacerato da Franzesi. Napoli, con molte terre, si teniva per esso Re, et Ferandino danizava in la Calavria, et l'armata veneta in la Puglia. La Signoria di Venetia era su grandissima spexa: *licet* fusse ligata con Papa, Re di Romani, Re di Spagna et Duca de Milano, lei sola spendeva assà quantità de danari. Havia exercito instructissimo, et za molti anni non visto tale in Italia; armata di galie zerca 40, et Antonio Grimani procurator loro capitano maritimo. Et questa Venetia sola, *ut ita dicam,* fu quella varentò Italia. El Duca de Milan, molto odiato dal populo, senza danari, et con exercito a recuperar Novara et *etiam* in Parmesana e a difender Zenoa, dubitando dil Re non li tolesse el Stado, et molto in benivolentia con Venetiani, dicendo: *Quis separabit nos?* Fiorentini, perso el dominio de Pisa, dato al Re Pietrasanta, Serzana, Serzanello et Livorno, et ancora non li erano sta restituiti. Et Monte Pulzano ribellatosi a Senesi, et quello comandava el Re, faceva; quasi havendo persa la loro libertà et teniva col Re. Senesi in confusion, et grandissima parte sottoposti a voleri gallici. Zenoa *in magno periculo;* pur Augustin Adorno teniva con il loro signor Duca de Milan; et in Riviera, per le parte de Franzesi, seguiva assà novitade. Luchesi quello ordinava el Re seguiva; et do. . . . li presentò le chiave, ma el Re non li fece alcun danno, et era de soi. Bologna et il magnifico Ioanne, conoscendo el ben suo et de Italia, era con Venetiani et Duca de Milano federati. Perosa,

su le arme, per le parte de Oddi et Bajoni. Cesena ancora in comotione, per Tiberti et Martinelli, intervenendo Guido Guerra, che pur .teniva dal Re de Franza. El Duca de Ferrara se dimostrava neutral, ma per esser cupido di nove cosse tramava col Re *occulte,* et havia mal animo a Venetiani. Duca Guido de Urbino, soldato de Fiorentini. Marchexe di Mantoa nostro Governador zeneral nel exercito, et il suo stado tutto marchescho. Sig. Iulio di Chamarin non era operato, stava a le so terre. Sig. Redolfo Malatesta di Rimano, con Venitiani soldato. Sig. Zuane Sforza de Pesaro, soldato di la liga. Madama di Forlì in amicitia con Franza, et con Milano, et nel principio si operò, ma al presente si stava a li soi Stati, et governava so fiul Ottaviano. Sig. di Piombino era casso dil soldo havia con Senesi. Vitelli, et prefato sig. de Senegaia, soldati dil Re; Mirandola, Corezo et Carpi con la Signoria et Milano. Conte di Petigliano et sig. Virginio Orsini erano contra so voja menati col Re di Franza. El sig. Prospero et Fabricio Colonna, rimasti a soi castelli, teniva dal Re. La Marchesana de Monferà et Duchessa de Savoia mostravano esser neutral tra il Re et Milano, *tamen* davano assà aiuti et lozamenti a esso Re. Sì che a questo modo era partita la povera Italia; la qual, si ben havesseno tutti considerato il danno harebbe a seguir, si Franzesi vi ponesse la mano su qualche altro Stato oltra el Reame acquistato, *sine dubio* la ragione voleva tutti havesseno seguitato el savio consiglio de Venetiani; i quali, visto el Re non si contentava di haver hauto el Reame, che voleva altro in Italia, et non più se parlava de andar contra infedeli, li puoseno le man davanti, et liberò Italia de tanto pericolo. *Sed de his hactenus.*

49. *Thucydides,* with an English translation by Charles Forster Smith, *1,* London and New York, 1928 (Loeb edition), 39. Felix Reichmann, *Library Trends,* 1964, *13,* 34 uses the translation of Rex Warner in the Penguin edition, 1954.

50. Sanudo, *op. cit.,* 517: "In commentariis historiam redegimus, quam expectabis."

51. Heiberg, *op. cit.,* 75: ". . . Habeo gratiam magnam tibi, quod patriam nostram et valere et salvere iusseris tantique mea de causa habueris. Quod autem scribis, commentarios tuos planeque de rege Gallorum historiam et legam et, si quid videatur, corrigam, ego eis, qui litteras attulerunt tuas, respondi confestim: videri mihi rem absolvendam vel saltem proximam pugnam, quam cerno cruentissimam fore maximique omnium momenti, imo equidem statuum praecipueque Mediolanensis ponderis gravissimi, esse expectandam. Itaque cum responderim illis videri mihi hoc negotium perficiendum, meam ipsi probantes sententiam tuos secum tulerunt commentarios. Nunc quod reliquum est, tamquam amicissimus frater commonebo, ut existimes imitatione aliqua te ista melius scripturum, et quemadmodum Salustius suum bellum scripsit Iugurthinum, ita tu Carolinum, mentemque tuam ad istum aut alium similem dirigas imittandum; deinde existimes fortunam laudare solam superbum esse; consilia atque iudicia apud sapientes solere vel reprehendi vel laudari; proinde non tam bellum refferendum esse, quam quo consilio regio nec non Veneto fuerit administratum, ut, si quae legationes contionesque intercesserint, nequidem supprimantur; dein quod ad doctrinam pertinere videbitur, ut acutum tuum postulat ingenium fertque

iudicium singulare, inseras historiae, quam equidem talem fore arbitror, ut sit sibi aeternitatem vendicatura. Tum si quid nos opis ferre poterimus, non detrectabimus. . . ."

52. Sanudo, by contrast, *op. cit.*, 17 preferred his native Venetian and adopted it "acciò tutti, dotti et indotti, la [gallica historia] possino leggere et intendere, perchè molto meglio è faticarsi per l'università che per rari et pochi. I quali, ancora che buona fusse, son certissimo si latina l'havessi descripta, mi harebbeno biasemato." Corio's plagiarism, the privilege which was to have endured ten years notwithstanding, has already been noted. Domenichi's Italian version of 1549 and its reprint of 1863 lack the preliminary elegiacs and hendecasyllabics of Quinzio Emiliano Cimbriaco, the dedicatory letter to Agostino Barbarigo, the summaries at the beginning of both books, the concluding letter to Sebastiano Badoer and Geronimo Bernardo, and of course the privilege.

53. The Latin *editio princeps* (A in my edition) of 1496 was issued by Aldus in a convenient format and with his customary care; I have used in the main the copy in the National Library of Medicine. The point on format which was made by Curt F. Bühler in the *Papers of the Bibliographical Society of America*, 1950, *44*, 209 can fittingly be reiterated here, that the popularity of Aldus's small, portable, convenient octavos has never declined and that "it is, perhaps, due almost as much to its handy size as to the comfortable presence of the parallel English translation that the Loeb Library [of Greek and Latin classics] has enjoyed its astonishing success"; a somewhat similar format has been deliberately adopted here. The "customary care" of Aldus was not common to all printers of his period if we are to accept as justified complaints like Valla's to Jacopo Antiquari, 13 January 1494, Heiberg, *op. cit.*, 69, when he wrote of certain works of Benedetti which "ex incude enim atque officina litteraria exierunt, scriptura convestiuntur, ne ignorarum errore imprimentium syllabarum aut vocum aliqua inquinentur labecula; quamquam id an ab his hodie impressoribus possit obtineri, haud certo scio; ita vitiari passim solent omnia" and like Benedetti's on both printers and scribes, couched in medical metaphor, in the dedicatory letter of his edition of Pliny the Elder, *loc. cit.*, "milia enim ulcerum persanavimus. . . . Relicta sunt & multa quidem: quae ad cicatricem hactenus perducere nemo potuit. Subterfugere & alia impressoris indiligentia praetermissa. Sed multo maior culpa veterum librariorum fuit: quorum ignavia in transcribendo: indies multum degenerante sorte res litterarias ruinam in ingentem traxit." Aldus, like all printers, made slips, and some remain today; the many which he corrected in various authors by stopping his presses or by adjustments in manuscript after printing was completed have recently, after more than four hundred years, been discovered and properly evaluated by Dr. Bühler from patient consultation of numerous copies; see for those in the *Diaria* the article cited, 213-214, and also the same journal, 1949, *43*, 365-373.

The second Latin edition (B) was appended to the third Latin edition, published at Strassburg in 1611, of the *Rerum venetarum ab urbe condita ad annum M.D.LXXV. historia* of Pietro Giustiniani (c. 1490-1576). It occupies folios G1b-I3a of the Appendix, which are incorrectly paginated 74,

73, 74-101, and omits the preliminary verses and the privilege. The third Latin edition (E) was included by Johann Georg von Eckhart (1674-1730) in his *Corpus historicorum medii aevi*, 2, Lipsiae, 1723, coll. 1577-1628; Eckhart was using the Aldine edition and adopted some of the manuscript corrections, but where he could not read them or did not understand them he "made no attempt to discover what Aldus had in mind and resorted to the simple expedient of printing a series of dashes" (Bühler, *op. cit.*, 369, n. 12). He omitted the preliminary verses, the concluding letter to Sebastiano Badoer and Geronimo Bernardo, and the privilege. A manuscript (F) which belonged to Filippo-Luigi Polidori (1801-1865) and is preserved in the Biblioteca Federiciana of Fano (Giuseppe Mazzatinti and Albano Sorbelli, *Inventari dei manoscritti delle biblioteche d'Italia*, 38, Firenze, 1928, 159, no. 43) contains on folios 24r-54r a nineteenth century copy of Eckhart's text. From Cervetto, *op. cit.*, 72, 76 and his *Appendice ai Cenni per una nuova storia delle scienze mediche*, Verona, 1842, 2, n. 1 it appears that Giuseppe Del Re intended to include in *Cronisti e scrittori sincroni napoletani* Benedetti's text. Only the first two volumes of this work were published, Napoli, 1845-1868. Del Re died in 1864.

54. For example, Eckhart, *op. cit.*, letter to the reader, f.b2a, "stylo . . . non ineleganti"; Zeno, *op. cit.*, 2, 44, "la eleganza, con cui [questa opera] è scritta"; Giammaria Mazzuchelli, *Gli scrittori d'Italia*, 2, Part 2, Brescia, 1760, 811, "uno stile semplice e ristretto"; Giuseppe Cervetto, *Di alcuni celebri anatomici italiani del decimoquinto secolo*, Brescia, 1854, 71, "severità ed eloquenza dello stile."

55. The reader may wish to consult also, for this general period, Bernardino Corio's views on history as expressed in the "De laudibus historiae" and "Defensio historiae" on f. [4] of the six unsigned folios at the beginning of the 1503 edition of his history of Milan.

56. *Op. cit.*, f.A2a.

57. *Histoire du gouvernement de Venise*, 1, Amsterdam, 1695, f.**9b.

58. In his *How to write history*; see pages 2-73 in *Lucian*, with an English translation by K. Kilburn, 6, London and Cambridge, Mass., 1959.

59. *Op. cit.*, 39.

60. Benedetti mentions astrology in I.2, II.35, and II.51. In only the second instance is the prediction his, when at the request of Niccolò Orsini, count of Pitigliano, for an aspect of the stars propitious to accepting terms offered by the Venetian Senate he replies that "in the judgment of the learned 22 and 23 August indicated a favorable outcome from the conjunction of Jupiter with the Moon at the twelfth degree of Libra, Venus being at the fifteenth in the same sign and Mars sixty degrees from this sign." There are also passages in his medical works which would need to be considered before deciding how thorough was his belief in astrology. Certainly Lodovico Sforza depended constantly on Ambrogio Varesi da Rosate, "suo

medico et ottimo astrologo," and would not, in fact, make a move without him; see II.51, my note I.26, Sanudo, *op. cit.*, 59, 117, 353, 412, 607, 675, and Luigi Belloni, *op. cit.*, 621-623, who states that "l'astrologia costituiva allora parte integrante dello scibile—e quindi anche della medicina— ed aveva una influenza profondissima sulla vita giornaliera dell'uomo della fine dell'evo medio e dell'inizio del moderno." Charles VIII entered Rome on 31 December 1494 "seguendo l'opinione astrologica ancora lui, vedendo esser bona hora"; see Sanudo, 163. For general discussion and bibliography the reader is referred to Don Cameron Allen, *The star-crossed Renaissance*, Durham, North Carolina, 1941, in particular the appendix on pages 247- 255 which treats of some astrological physicians and their works. See also Cervetto, *op. cit.*, 73, n.1; Cervetto, himself Medico Primario of the Ospedale Civico of Bologna, stresses the "stato politico e filosofico di quei tempi, nei quali questi studj astrologici avevansi per utili ed inconcussi, come parte integrante della filosofia naturale e della medicina, ammessa e protetta dagli stessi Principi d'Italia."

Certainly in Benedetti's period charts on favorable days for bloodletting, almanacs, horoscopes, prognostications, and zodiacal calendars, not all disreputable, were still pouring from fifteenth-century presses, and they continued far into the sixteenth and beyond. Despite the eminent voices raised even earlier against astrology it was long before its influence on the educated few passed entirely; "my inference," says Professor Allen, *op. cit.*, viii, "now is that everybody who lived during the Renaissance believed to some extent in astrology." In 1764 Voltaire had asked, "Comment donc s'est-il pu faire que, malgré la physique et la géométrie, cette ridicule chimère de l'astrologie ait dominé jusqu'à nos jours, au point que nous avons vu des hommes distingués par leurs connaissances, & sur-tout très-profonds dans l'histoire, entêtés toute leur vie d'une erreur si méprisable?" See his *Dictionnaire philosophique*, 2, Amsterdam, 1789, 140 and the review of Louis MacNeice, *Astrology*, in the *Times Literary Supplement*, 15 October 1964.

61. *The first duty.* An address delivered at the opening of an exhibition of the Arthur H. and Mary Marden Dean Collection of Lafayette at Cornell University on April 17, 1964, The Cornell University Library, 1964, 2.

62. These were Pietro Francesco of Mantua, "militia ornatus," and Andrea of Novara. In Benedetti and in other sources of the period figure many physicians. Giovanni Marliani and Ambrogio Varesi da Rosate have already been mentioned in this introduction. In the letters of Charles VIII we meet Bernard Chaussade and Olivier Laurens (Pélicier's edition, 4, 1903, 257); Jean Garcin (*ibid.*, 13; cf. Jean Astruc, *Mémoires pour servir à l'histoire de la Faculté de Médecine de Montpellier;* revus & publiés par M. Lorry, Paris, 1767, 228-229, in which work will also be found the texts of medical privileges accorded by Charles); Théodore Gaynier or Guaynier of Pavia (Pélicier's edition, 2, 1900, 430-431, 3, 1902, 137, 172, 275, Delaborde, *op. cit.*, 222, 246, 426, and my notes I.26, 132), both ambassador and physician, who at once calls to mind the more familiar Antonio Guainerio of the same city (d. 1440; his medical works were later published from the press of Antonius de Carcano there); Jean Michel de Pierrevive (my note I.12, Nicolas François Joseph Eloy, *Dictionnaire historique de la*

*médecine ancienne et moderne*, 3, Mons, 1778, 294-295, and Delaborde, *op. cit.*, 317); and the apothecary Nicolas Bourgale (my note I.12 and Jaligny, *op. cit.*, 705, where he is listed as apothecary to Charles in 1495-1496). In my notes there is mention also of Petrus de Abano (I.57, 132), Giovanni dall'Aquila (I.90, II.57 and cf. Eloy, *op. cit.*, 1, 1778, 151), Hieronymus Brunschwig (II.57), Andrea Morandini of Padua (II.17), Franciscus Pamoleus (I.132), Girolamo dalla Torre, or Turriani, of Verona (I.90, II.57 and cf. Nicolaus Papadopoli, *Historia gymnasii patavini*, 1, Venice, 1726, 293 and Eloy, *op. cit.*, 4, 1778, 447), Giovanni de Tristan of Verona (II.17), and physicians from the Signoria (I.70), Bologna (II.17), and Parma *(ibid.)*. Benedetti himself speaks of physicians from Pavia and Milan (II.45). We remark with pleasure that another physician, Georg Kloss (1787-1854), owned the copy of the Aldine *Diaria* which is preserved in the New York Public Library. Symphorien Champier will be mentioned below.

63. The *Historia corporis humani sive anatomice* (henceforth designated here simply *Anatomice* as Benedetti himself informally called it), for example, which was published at Venice by Bernardinus Guerraldus of Vercelli 1 December 1502 but is prefaced by a letter from Jacopo Antiquari to Benedetti dated from Milan 31 January 1496 and one from Benedetti to the Emperor Maximilian dated from Venice 1 August 1497, and the material for which Benedetti had been assembling at least from 1483 (III.18), contains such passages as (I.1) "Observavereque priores medici, ut si qui ignotis morbis interiissent: dissectis cadaveribus: occulta morborum initia perscrutarentur: ut pari exemplo vivis prodessent. Idem in simia sua facere Galenum non puduit ignota mortis causa sicut & nos in morbo gallico fecimus"; (I.6, in the chapter "De ossibus") "Sed abscessus innasci mirum est: ut nuper vidimus: dum mulierem quandam gallico morbo interemptam resecaremus causam morbi perquirendo: ossa sub omentis suis integris tumentia & ad medullam usque suppurata invenimus"; (II.21, in the chapter "De pene") "Ob eam causam veneno contactu novus: vel saltem medicis ignotus prioribus siderum pestifero aspectu morbus gallicus ad nos ex occidente: dum haec aederemus: irrepsit: tanta omnium membrorum foeditate: cruciatibusque nocte praesertim: ut lepram alioquin insanabilem sive elephantiosin horrore superet: non sine vitae pernicie. Haec pestis reliquas provincias iam infestavit: quae etiam praesanatis facile repululat: magna omnium medicorum ambage. Ex occidente venere emperici: qui magno quaestu urbes circumierunt: id tantum profitentes." Likewise in his vast clinical collection which was published posthumously (see the edition of Heinrich Petri at Basel, 1539, *Omnium a vertice ad calcem morborum signa, causae, indicationes & remediorum compositiones utendique rationes*, I.28) we read of the new French disease "cuius novitate aetate nostra vincuntur medicinae." This work, whose lengthy title varies from edition to edition, he himself called informally *De omnibus morbis* in his *Anatomice* (II.20) and in a letter to Jacopo Antiquari, 13 January 1494, Heiberg 89, and for convenience it will henceforth be so designated here. It was published first in Venice by Lucantonio Giunta in June, 1533; see Paolo Camerini, *Annali dei Giunti*, 1, Part 1, Firenze, 1962, 254. For additional passages on syphilis

see I.16, VI.4, VII.5, VIII.44, XIII.23, XIV.24, XXVI.1 and Cervetto, *op. cit.,* 100-103.

64. See for example Jacques de Mailles in Joseph François Michaud and Jean Joseph François Poujoulat, *Nouvelle collection des mémoires pour servir à l'histoire de France, 4,* Paris, 1837, 503, "Il y eut plusieurs gentilz-hommes qui n'apportèrent pas de grans biens de ce voyage de Naples; aucuns aussi en apportèrent quelque chose dont ilz se sentirent toute leur vie. Ce fut une manière de maladie qui eut plusieurs noms: d'aucuns fut nommée le mal de Naples, *la grosse vérole,* les autres l'ont appellée *le mal françois;* et plusieurs autres noms a eu ladicte maladie: mais de moi je l'appelle le mal de celui qui l'a"; Guicciardini, *La historia d'Italia,* Venetia, 1568, who after giving on f.66a a description of the appalling effects of the disease traces its outbreak in Europe to the sailors of Columbus and the "Isole" of the New World, where "nondimeno questo male ha prontissimo per benignità della Natura il rimedio, perche beendo solamente del sugo d'un legno, nobilissimo per molte doti memorabili, che quivi nasce, facilissimamente se ne liberano," the maxim, that is, "Unde morbus inde remedium" which is adduced by Max H. Fisch, *Nicolaus Pol Doctor 1494,* with a critical text of his guaiac tract edited with a translation by Dorothy M. Schullian, published for The Cleveland Medical Library Association by Herbert Reichner, New York, 1947, 48; Cervetto's lucid treatment in the work already cited, 98-122; Alessandro Luzio and Rodolfo Renier, "Contributo alla storia del malfrancese ne' costumi e nella letteratura italiana del sec. XVI," *Giornale storico della letteratura italiana,* 1885, *5,* 408-432; Louis Thuasne (under the anagrammatic pseudonym Hesnaut) *Le mal français à l'époque de l'expédition de Charles VIII en Italie d'après les documents originaux,* Paris, 1886; Karl Sudhoff in such contributions as *Mal Franzoso in Italien in der ersten Hälfte des 15. Jahrhunderts,* Giessen, 1912; Roberto Massalongo in *Atti del Reale Istituto Veneto di Scienze, Lettere ed Arti,* 1916-1917, *76,* Part 2, 216, 237-240; Bridge, *op. cit.,* 231-232; Francesco Pellegrini, reprint from the volume *Il contributo veronese alle scienze mediche,* edito in occasione delle Giornate Mediche Veronesi 29-31 luglio 1949, Verona, 21; Heinrich Buess in *Vierteljahrsschrift für schweizerische Sanitätsoffiziere,* 1957, *34,* 317; Belloni, *op. cit.,* 622-624.

65: XXIV.19: "Mirum est quod in castris vidimus ad Tarum in Parmensi agro, in pugna adversus Gallos, nuda erant cadavera passim per ripas fluminis iacentia, quorum inguina mire supra modum magnitudinis intenta erant, solis (ut puto) vapore, ac hesterno himbre, quo corpora perfusa fuerant." The passage is quoted by Cervetto, *op. cit.,* 110, n.1.

66. Eloy, *op. cit., 3,* 1778, 157-158.

67. See Georg Hieronymus Welsch, *Sylloge curationum et observationum medicinalium centurias VI. amplectens,* Ulmae, 1668, 30: "M-CCCCXCV in Italia, ex uno influxu coelesti, dum me recepi in castris Navarrae, cum armigeris Dominorum Venetorum, Dominorum Mediolanensium plures armigeri & pedestres, ex ebulitione humorum me vidisse attestor pati

plures pustulas in facie, & per totum corpus, & incipientes communiter sub praeputio, vel extra praeputium, sicut granum milii, aut super castaneam, cum aliquali pruritu patientis. Aliquando incipiebat pustula una in modum vesiculae parvae sine dolore, sed cum pruritu, fricabant, & inde ulcerabatur tanquam formica corrosiva, & post aliquot dies incurrebant in angustiis propter dolores in brachiis, cruribus, pedibus, cum pustulis magnis. Omnes Medici periti cum difficultate curabant. Ego cum flebotomia in saphena, aliquando in basilica, procedebam cum digerentibus, purgantibus, tandem unctionibus in locis necessariis, & durabant pustulae super personam tamquam leprosam, variolosam, per annum & plus, sine medicinis." The passage is used by many historians, as Jean Astruc, *A treatise of venereal diseases*, London, 1754, 144; Cervetto, *op. cit.*, 109; Belloni, *op. cit.*, 624.

68. For example, in chronological order, Andrea Chiocco, *De collegii veronensis illustribus medicis*, Verona, 1623, 10, reprinted in Friedrich Boerner, 1755, below; Paul Freher, *Theatrum virorum eruditione clarorum*, Noribergae, 1688, 1214; Scipione Maffei, *Verona illustrata*, 2, Verona, 1731, col. 129; Jean Jacques Manget, *Bibliotheca scriptorum medicorum veterum et recentiorum*, 1, Genevae, 1731, 281; Johann Albert Fabricius, *Bibliotheca latina mediae et infimae aetatis*, 1, Hamburg 1734, 164; Giambatista Biancolini, *Cronica della città di Verona*, 2, Part 2, Verona, 1749, 154; Apostolo Zeno, *op. cit.* and the earlier unsigned version in *Giornale de' letterati d'Italia*, 1713, 16, 468-471; Astruc, *op. cit.*, 146; Friedrich Boerner, *Noctes guelphicae sive opuscula argumenti medico-literarii*, Rostochii et Wismariae, 1755, 1-14 and the earlier edition, 1751, of these pages alone; Giammaria Mazzuchelli, *op. cit.*; Giulio Panzani, *De venetae anatomes historia*, Venetiis, 1763, 9: *Biografia universale antica e moderna*, 5, Venezia, 1822, 273; Emmanuele Antonio Cicogna, *Delle inscrizioni veneziane*, 2, Venezia, 1827, 113, n.2; Melchior Missirini, *Degli illustri italiani e loro scoperte nelle scienze nelle lettere nelle arti*, Siena, 1838, 252; J.-F. Malgaigne in Ambroise Paré, *Oeuvres complètes*, 1, Paris, 1840, CXCV-CXCVI; Cervetto, *op. cit.* and *Cenni per una nuova storia delle scienze mediche*, Verona, 1841, 16, *Appendice ai Cenni per una nuova storia delle scienze mediche*, Verona, 1842, 2, 13, *Lettera al profess. Giacom'Andrea Giacomini . . . relativa ad una orazione del prof. Francesco Cortese sul Teatro anatomico di Padova*, Verona, 1845, 8; Giambattista Giuliari, *Della letteratura veronese al cadere del secolo XV*, Bologna, 1876, 158, 177-183, 208, 212-213, 227, 305 300; Girolamo Ghilini, *Alcune biografie di medici illustri tratte dai volumi inediti del Teatro d'uomini letterati*, Venezia, 1880, 16-17; Massalongo, *op. cit.*; Francesco Pellegrini, *op. cit.* and *La medicina militare nel regno di Napoli*, Verona, 1932, 245-247; Arturo Castiglioni in "The origin and development of the anatomical theater to the end of the Renaissance," *Ciba Symposia*, 1941, 3, 831-834 and "La scuola medica di Padova," *Rivista Ciba*, 1949, 19, 613-614; the anonymous "Alessandro Benedetti, anatomo e medico militare del quattrocento," *Il giardino di Esculapio*, 1952, 21, 41-52, which used Massalongo; Andrea Bosatra and V. Candiani, "Note e commenti su Alessandro Benedetti. . . ," *Minerva medica*, 1955, 46 (2, n. 54, 7 luglio), 8 p.; Glauco De Bertolis, "Alessandro Benedetti: il primo teatro anatomico padovano," *Acta medicae historiae patavina*, 1956-57, 3, 1-13; Buess, *op. cit.*; Hans Dieter Kickartz, *Die Anatomie des Zahn-, Mund- und*

*Kieferbereiches in dem Werk "HISTORIA CORPORIS HUMANI SIVE ANATOMICE" von Alessandro Benedetti,* Diss., Institut für Geschichte der Medizin der Medizinischen Akademie in Düsseldorf, Hans Schadewaldt Direktor, 1964. My sketch is based mainly on his published works and on the portion of his correspondence which has been published. But see also footnote 124.

69. An industrial and agricultural hub today, situated 51 kilometers by rail from Verona and numbering about 24,000 inhabitants. In 1405 it came under the dominion of Venice, which in 1517 made it entirely independent of Verona. On 26 October 1953 Dr. Mario Carrara, then Vice-Director of the Biblioteca Civica at Verona, was unable to locate any manuscript of Benedetti in that library. On 2 November 1953 Dr. Giulio Sancassani, Director of the Sezione di Archivio di Stato, Verona, could find no mention of Benedetti in the Atti del Collegio dei Medici di Verona for the years 1469 through 1512, in two fiscal lists of 1473 and 1502 of the Comune di Legnago, or in various lists in the archives of the Comune di Verona.

70. *Loc. cit.*

71. Through one of the many kindnesses rendered me by Francesco Pellegrini (1883-1960), physician, lieutenant general in the medical corps, and historian, and by his wife Enrichetta Cipolla, daughter of the mediaeval historian Carlo Cipolla, I possess a photograph of this portrait. A reproduction was published by Castiglioni, *op. cit.*, 614. References to Verona and its region are frequent in Benedetti's works; cf. *De omnibus morbis,* I.4, 38, VI.18, XI.20, XIII.17, XIX.36, XXI.3, XXIII.10, XXV.20, XXVI.26.

72. See Benedetti's letter to Marco Sanudo in the *Collectiones medicinae,* appended to the Paris edition, 1514, of his *Anatomice,* 69.

73. *De omnibus morbis,* II. prooem. The passage is cited by Zeno, *op. cit.*, 2, 43. Benedetti mentions his father also in VIII.42 and XXIX. prooem. Likewise mentioned in this work are "Cornelius filius meus" (X.9), "parva Cornelia nostra" (XII.11), "Dionora nostra" (XI.10, XIII.14, XIX.33), "nobilis Veneta Dionora Georgia" (XXV.29). Sanudo, *I diarii, 16,* Venezia, 1887, col. 217, under date of 5 May 1513, includes "Bortolamio di Alexandro Benedeto, da Verona" in a list of ten soldiers "presi per li stratioti con sier Zuan Vituri provedador."

74. Papadopoli, *op. cit.*, *1,* 291 and Jacopo Facciolati, *Fasti gymnasii patavini,* Patavii, 1757, *2,* 136. From records in the Archivio della Curia Vescovile, Padua, Francesca Lucchetta in *Il medico e filosofo bellunese Andrea Alpago. . . ,* Padova, 1964, 31, n.2 sets 13 November 1478 as the date on which he took his degree "in artibus" at Padua.

75. *Anatomice,* 1502, V.23 and cf. Cicogna, *loc. cit.*

76. See I.1; the Colosseum at Rome and the Roman Arena at Verona furnished the inspiration for Benedetti's theater. Text and English transla-

tion of portions of his remarks on the ideal anatomical theater are provided by William S. Heckscher, *Rembrandt's ANATOMY OF DR. NICOLAAS TULP*, New York, 1958, 182-183. See also De Bertolis, *op. cit.*

77. He names often the patients whom he treated. Francesco Puccinotti, *Storia della medicina*, 2, Part 2, Livorno, 1859, 602, with others, accuses him of two serious mistakes, the failure to renounce judicial astrology, which as we have seen had its justifications, and his preparations for flight from the pest at Venice, when, as we are told with utter frankness in his treatise *De observatione in pestilentia*, 26 (see the collected works of 1539) he prescribed for the young patrician Marco Marcello without seeing him. For fifteenth-century attitudes on flight from the pest see my notes "The plague at Como, 1486" in *Journal of the History of Medicine and Allied Sciences*, 1946, *1*, 174 and "A manuscript of Dominici in the Army Medical Library," *ibid.*, 1948, *3*, 395-399.

78. For example, I.2, IV.20, XIII.26, XV.25, XVI.9, XXII.26, XXVI.4.

79. 2, Venezia, 1879, col. 891. Cf. for Dalmatia and Illyria *De omnibus morbis*, I.5, 29, 46, II. prooem., 29, IX.19, XIII.3, XXIV.27.

80. See Giovanni Tortelli, *De medicina et medicis*, Gian Giacomo Bartolotti, *De antiquitate medicinae*, edited and translated by Dorothy M. Schullian and Luigi Belloni, [Milano, 1954], XXV. In his treatise *De antiquitate medicinae*, XXI.1, Bartolotti states that Antonio Cittadini of Faenza was his teacher at Ferrara. An Antonio of Faenza is mentioned by Benedetti in the *Anatomice*, V.1. Bartolotti also reports, *Vaticanus latinus* 5376, f.108v, on the autopsy 21 September 1501 in Venice at which the liver of Agostino Barbarigo, who had died the day before, was found to contain a stone the size of a large olive. *Marcianus latinus* XIV.123 (4662) has on ff.95r-109v an apology of Girolamo Donato for the calumnies of Charles VIII against the Venetian Senate; the subscription reads, "Finis apologie Hieronimi Donati scrita per me Ioannem Bartholotum Parmensem Venetiis 1514, 15 aprilis." See the edition cited, XX, XXI, XXIV, XXV.

81. For lists and descriptions of the various editions see, for example, *Gesamtkatalog der Wiegendrucke*, *1*, Leipzig, 1925, nos. 862-864; British Museum, *Catalogue of books printed in the XV*[th] *century now in the British Museum*, 5, London, 1924, 344, 555; *British Museum, General catalogue of printed books*, 13, London, 1936, coll. 561-562; Bibliothèque Nationale, *Catalogue général des livres imprimés*, 10, Paris, 1902, coll. 717-719. It seems best, and somehow fairer to him, to present them here as an integral part of his life rather than in a special and isolated section. Their value was lauded by eminent anatomists and physicians in centuries before our own. Leonardo da Vinci, for example, included the *Anatomice* in a list of books from Venice of September 1508 (see *Selections from the notebooks of Leonardo da Vinci*, edited with commentaries by Irma A. Richter, London, 1953, 369 and *Leonardo da Vinci on the human body* . . . with translations, emendations and a biographical introduction by Charles D. O'Malley and

J. B. deC. M. Saunders, New York, 1952, 21); Otto Brunfels called him "medicorum omnium, quos nostra habuerunt saecula, doctissimus" in the edition of the *Anatomice* and *Collectiones medicinae* which was published at Strassburg in 1528; Giovanni Battista Morgagni included his name on 6 August 1718 in a list of "Inventori Anatomici Italiani del Sec. 16.°," later deleted it (Giovanni Battista Morgagni, *Gli inventori anatomici italiani del XVI secolo* . . . a cura di Luigi Belloni, Milano, 1953, 8), but mentioned him in the dedicatory letter, to William Bromfield, of Book II of the work *De sedibus, et causis morborum*, Venetiis, 1761. There have been also dissenting opinions, like those of Leonhart Fuchs in the "Paradoxa," III.8, 10, 11, 13, 14, 15, 16, 17 (*Opera*, 3, Francofurti ad Moenum, 1567), and Charles D. O'Malley, *Andreas Vesalius of Brussels, 1514-1564*, Berkeley and Los Angeles, 1964, 18, who believes that "his contribution to the body of anatomical knowledge was nil." Levi Robert Lind has in progress a translation of the *Anatomice*. See also Kickartz, *op. cit.*

82. Giorgio Valla mentioned him in connection with it in a letter of 13 January 1494 to Jacopo Antiquari, Heiberg, 69, and Benedetti himself, writing on the same day to Antiquari, Heiberg, 89, entitled it to him. In Antiquari's letter to Benedetti at the beginning of the work, 1 February 1494, Maximilian is called "latinorum latinissimus . . . quamquam in Germania progenitus."

83. On the subject of literary patronage see for example my dissertation, *External stimuli to literary production in Rome, 90 B.C.-27 B.C.*, Private edition, distributed by the University of Chicago Libraries, Chicago, Illinois, 1932; Karl Schottenloher, *Die Widmungsvorrede im Buch des 16. Jahrhunderts*, Münster Westfalen, 1953, who mentions on pages 53 and 223 that Marcus Hopper in 1549 dedicated to Andreas Vesalius his edition of Benedetti's *De re medica opus insigne*, Basel, Heinrich Petri; Franklin B. Williams, Jr., *Index of dedications and commendatory verses in English books before 1641*, London, The Bibliographical Society, 1962.

84. I quote from the edition in Rhazes, *De ratione curandi pestilentiam*, Parisiis, apud Simonem Silvium, 1528, f.18b. Contarini's name does not appear at the beginning of the dedicatory letter in the 1539 edition of the work.

85. On only the last statement, and in particular the word "boasting," in the following passage from Castiglioni, *Ciba Symposia*, 1941, 3, 833 would I therefore have reservations: "Very remarkable is the fact that in this book, for the first time, the anatomist cites the names of people whom he would like to have present at the dissection. It is not clear whether he gives names of people who really came to a given dissection or if he only cites the names by way of an invitation. The latter seems to be the more likely case. . . . It is hard to believe that Maximilian should have come to Padua to attend the dissection, and it seems more probable that the whole introduction [to Book II] is only the expression of the author's desire to affirm the importance of the performance itself and of his work as teacher. . . Evidently, Benedictus is boasting of his relations to important people,

above all to such as are close to the Emperor or belong to the high Venetian aristocracy." O'Malley, *op. cit.*, 441, n.5 states that if the *theatrum nostrum* mentioned at the beginning of Book V "represents more than a product of Benedetti's somewhat strong imagination, it was probably a temporary wooden structure."

86. Mazzuchelli, *op. cit.*, 812, perhaps following Zeno, *op. cit.*, 46, states that letters of Benedetti were published among those of Leonardo Bruni in Brescia in 1495. Bruni died in 1444, and Benedetti could scarcely have known him. Giuliari, *op. cit.*, 179 calls the citation false. The copy in the New York Public Library of Bruni's *Epistolarum familiarium libri VIII* [Venice, Damianus de Mediolano, de Gorgonzola, in part by Petrus de Quarengiis], 15 June 1495, Goff B-1243, contains no letters by our Benedetti; there is one, however, to Benedictus Anagninus.

87. *Anatomice,* III.22.

88. His emendations of Pliny, with dedicatory letter dated 1 March 1471, appeared with his work *In librum de homine Martii Galeotti opus* [Venice, Johannes de Colonia and Johannes Manthen, about 1474], Goff M-504.

89. The winds are discussed in the *Canon,* Liber 1, Fen 2, Doctrina 2, Summa 1, Cap. 10.

90. An *Etymologicum magnum* was published at Venice in 1499 by Zacharias Callierges, Goff E-112.

91. Giovanni Benedetto Mittarelli, *Bibliotheca codicum manuscriptorum monasterii S. Michaelis Venetiarum prope Murianum,* Venetiis, 1779, col. 1175 pointed out that the "Alexander de Verona" who in 1416 bought from the humanist Gasparino Barzizza of Bergamo a manuscript of Valerius Maximus, now no. 649 in the Hamilton Collection at Berlin, cannot of course have been Alessandro Benedetti.

92. Karl Konrad Müller, "Neue Mittheilungen über Janos Laskaris und die Mediceische Bibliothek," *Centralblatt für Bibliothekswesen,* 1884, *1,* 385; the Pindar manuscript is cited by Robert Ralph Bolgar, *The classical heritage and its beneficiaries,* Cambridge, 1954, 503. Pierre de Nolhac, "Inventaire des manuscrits grecs de Jean Lascaris," *Mélanges d'archéologie et d'histoire publiés par l'École française de Rome,* 1886, *6,* and elsewhere investigated further the activity of Lascaris in the field of manuscripts.

93. Heiberg, *op. cit.,* 63. His grammar, published at Milan by Dionysius Paravisinus in 1476, Goff L-65, has the distinction of being the first book printed wholly in Greek.

94. Zeno, *op. cit.,* 46, Cervetto, *Di alcuni celebri anatomici italiani,* 80, Heiberg, *op. cit.,* 51. The translation was published in Aristotle's *Opera,*

Venice, Joannes and Gregorius de Gregoriis, de Forlivio, for Benedictus Fontana, 13 July 1496, *Gesamtkatalog der Wiegendrucke* 2341, Goff A-966. For the life and works of Valla see Heiberg, 3-44.

95. XLVII.2; cf. Heiberg, *op. cit.*, 51. The work was published at Venice by Aldus Manutius in 1501.

96. Chapter 25; Heiberg, *loc. cit.*

97. Hciberg, *op. cit.*, 69.

98. *Ibid.*, 88.

99. "Is ego semper fui," he wrote Gian Giacomo Trivulzio on 29 September 1494, Heiberg, *op. cit.*, 72, "qui mallim opera quam verbis, ubi possim, amicis succurrere."

100. Heiberg, *op. cit.*, 68-69.

101. There are difficulties in the identification of these, cf. Heiberg, *op. cit.*, 51-52, and there is a possibility that Benedetti's larger anatomical and medical works, later published complete, were earlier printed in parts and so circulated in copies not extant today.

102. Heiberg, *op. cit.*, 69.

103. *Ibid.*

104. For example, Benedetti to Antiquari, 13 January 1494, Heiberg, *op. cit.*, 89. When on 22 October 1495, however, Heiberg, 76, Antiquari expresses a hope for another work by Benedetti ("Saltem cura, ut ab Alexandro Benedicto, cui multum debemus, aliquid eveniat, quo magis ei debere intelligamus"), Valla can only reply, 5 November, Heiberg, 77, that Benedetti is off with the army and he has not seen him: "De Alexandro Benedicto polliceri quicquam non possum; missus siquidem est medicus ab hoc senatu pridem in exercitum, ut esset, qui aegrotantibus illis mederetur; post illa ipsum non vidi."

105. It is of some interest that Benedetti possessed a manuscript of Alexander of Aphrodisias on fevers and that Valla translated this work; the translation was published at Venice by Simon Bevilaqua, 1498, Goff N-44, in an omnibus volume the first author in which was Nicephorus. A treatise *De humani corporis partibus,* which according to Heiberg, *op. cit.*, 40, is XLVII.3 of the work *De expetendis et fugiendis rebus,* was published by Eucharius Cervicornus at Köln, in 1527.

106. For his biography, see Giovanni Battista Vermiglioli, *Biografia degli scrittori perugini e notizie delle opere loro, 1,* Perugia, 1828, 58-66, and Vermiglioli's earlier publications on him.

107. F.[*]4b. Rinaldo Fulin, *Archivio veneto*, 1882, 23, 122, no. 46 cites the Notatorio del Collegio in the Archivio di Stato at Venice under date of 19 March 1496: *"Alessandro Benedetti,* 'physico', vorrebbe dare alle stampe *'la Anatomia, de febribus, de omnibus membrorum morbis, de venenis, de communibus medendi praeceptis,* et le opere *de Naturali Historia de Plinio* per lui correcte, la qual è incredibelmente depravata.' Chiede perciò ed ottiene il solito privilegio decennale; ai contraffattori, la pena che parrà al Governo."

108. Zeno, *op. cit.*, 45-56, Heiberg, *op. cit.*, 52, "Vetus nanque medicina tuam inde operam advocat, et in primis, ut e tenebris eruatur, dexteram porrigit Paulus Aegineta ante Galenum celebris, sed parum deinceps notus nisi frequenti ipsius Galeni citatione. Ad quam rem si te monuero, ineptus sum, quia ad huius laudis metam sponte curris, cum Aeginetam dicaris in manibus habere, et nisi rogavero, videbor communi causae defuisse, quoniam, ut quadrigam urgeas, multi cupiunt." This did not issue from the press; in fact, an incomplete edition of the seven books of Paulus on medicine, in Greek, appeared only in 1528, in Venice, from the house of Aldus and Andreas Asulanus, and the first Latin translation, by Albanus Torinus, in Basel, 1532, from the house of Andreas Cratander and Johannes Bebelius. The circumstance demonstrates that Benedetti in 1508 was indeed in the forefront of the philological and medical activity of his day. In the work *De omnibus morbis* he cites Paulus of Aegina often.

109. Heiberg, *op. cit.*, 88-89: "Georgius Valla . . . opuscula nostra, quae nuper praegustationis gratia edidimus, ad te familiarissime misit ductus nimia nostri affectione; unde fortasse laxato paulum diligenti examine bona esse existimavit; quae tuo quoque, vir praestantissime, cum priscis, qui de medendi ratione scripserunt, certare affirmes. Non is sum profecto ex medicorum vulgo vel postremo, qui hoc audeam, sed temporum nostrorum maxima indignatio facit, ut, qui nihil sciam, audeam scribere, ut caeteri expergefacti nostris conatibus perficere idem audeant. Non ero primus, qui medicinae rationem male prosequar; undique enim occurrit barbaries; hactenus milia errorum apparent, nec modus est; nos forte domesticam medicinam aliis diligentius excolendam dabimus; damnabantur enim, qui vineam suam habuissent derelictui. Litterae tuae ad editionem Anatomices sive historiae membrorum humani corporis ad Maximilianum imperatorem, quae libris quinque continetur, me plurimum exagitant. . . . Octo interea de omnibus morbis, qui membratim hominem invadunt, sub lima sunt, sex de venenis et venenatis animalibus perfecti; patrocinium, quod amici maxime probaverint, praestolabuntur. Triginta sex in summa volumina in plebem spargenda sunt, quae, si priusquam edita sunt, taxatorem invenerint, maturius sese ad tempestivum partum conservabunt nec ita temere aliorum exemplo in lucem exibunt." For the treatise on poisons see also his work *De omnibus morbis,* preface to Maximilian, X.10, and XI.9.

110. Cf. Sanudo, *op. cit.*, 387, *"Unde* nostri in questi zorni expedite, et si partì a dì 10 Zugno [1495], uno frate Piero Dolphin, zeneral di l'ordine camaldulense, zoè di San Michiel di Muran, et patricio veneto, homo di grande autorità, bontà et reverentia, et molto amato, a Fiorentini dove

era stato gran tempo, et tolse di andarvi in tre zorni a Fiorenza et esser con quella Signoria, et intender la volontà loro; si vogliono Franzesi siegua la vitoria usando le crudeltà usavano, o vero esserli contra et far quello hanno altre volte fatto li loro passati, che elexeno acquistar et non perder," and 405, "A dì 20 Zugno venne lettere di Fiorenza di Piero Dolfin zeneral de Camaldole narra de l'intrar dil Re." On Delfino see Joseph Schnitzer, *Peter Delfin, General des Camaldulenserordens (1444-1525)*, München, 1926 and Giovanni Soranzo, "Pietro Dolfin, generale dei Camaldolesi e il suo epistolario," *Rivista di storia della chiesa in Italia*, 1959, *13*, 1-31, 157-195. Curt F. Bühler discusses in *Renaissance News*, 1954, *7*, 95-97 the copy of Giovanni Tortelli's *Orthographia*, Venice, Nicolaus Jenson, 1471, Goff T-395, now in The Pierpont Morgan Library, which was stolen in Florence on the night of Savonarola's arrest 8 April 1498 and was later given to Delfino by Pietro Benincasa.

Schnitzer published Delfino's correspondence from the letters in the Biblioteca Nazionale of Florence. The one to Benedetti, which he knew (see p. 56, 193) is carried in draft in *Marcianus latinus* XI.92 (3828), p.1218, no. XLV and was photographed for me by the kindness of Pietro Zorzanello, director of the Marciana in 1949. It was formerly at San Michele di Murano and is mentioned in Mittarelli, *op. cit.*, col. 1175. By the kindness respectively of Carolyn E. Jakeman, Harvard College Library, and Donald G. Patterson, Library of Congress, I am informed that it is not included in the edition of Delfino's letters which was published at Venice in 1524 or in the 241 letters which were included in Volume 3 of Edmond Martène and Ursin Durand, *Veterum scriptorum et monumentorum historicorum, dogmaticorum, moralium, amplissima collectio*, Parisiis, 1724, 915-1211. It reads: "Alexandro Benedicto Veronensi. XLV. Expetisti a me litteris humanissimis iudicium meum super Anatomice atque Diaria opusculis tuis ante aliquot annos abs te editis. Quasi vero is sim ego cuius tenui iuditio standum sit et qui de magnis ac praeclaris ingeniis eorumque lucubrationibus habeam ferre sententiam. Quamobrem a me aliud requires. Spero enim te iampridem a viris doctissimis sanius super libris tuis accepisse iuditium et ab iis praesertim, qui eiusmodi litterarum studiosi aliquid nostro hoc recenti saeculo in communem latinae linguae usum ediderunt. Unum tantum modo affirmaverim utrumque mihi fuisse gratissimum tum quia per alterum mihi naturae secreta atque abdita multa reserata sunt: per alterum vero feliciter a nostris gesta adversus Gallos ad memoriam revocata tum etiam quia abs te erant qui praeter eminentem litteraturam atque doctrinam fateris te Delphinae gentis esse amantissimum. Cuius sane rei gratia debeo tibi plurimum et quantas possum pro eleganti egregioque duplici munusculo tuo tibi gratias ago. Caeterum si quid tibi duo illi nostrates patritii retulerunt de me quod maiorem tuum erga me amorem conciliaverint hac tantum de causa non aegre fero. Alioquin si iisdem haud vulgari mecum devincti benevolentia decipiuntur: ego de me ipso non fallor. Velit Dominus qui scrutatur renes et corda, quem nullius latent merita, ut vel exiguo amborum illorum testimonio atque elogio dignus sim. Vale. Ex Fonte bono die 24 Julii 1504.

111. Published on f.k4a of Symphorien Champier, *Que in hoc opusculo habentur. Duellum epistolare: Gallie & Italie antiquitates summatim*

complectens. Tropheum Christianissimi Galliarum regis Francisci huius nominis primi. Item complures illustrium virorum epistole ad dominum Symphorianum Camperium. Venetiis, Jacobus Franciscus de Jonta, 1519; cf. Paul Allut, *Étude . . . sur Symphorien Champier*, Lyon, 1859, 201-206. For extracts from Champier on the expedition of Charles see Jaligny, *op. cit.*, 285 ff.

112. "De nugis meis hec pauca subiiciam: de morbis particularibus membrorum voluminibus extremam manum imponimus, de quibus et de Egigneta in eundem pene foetura ne dicam abortione iudicium afferes. Vale ac me ama ac rescribe si per ocium licet."

113. Symphòrien Champier, *Index librorum in hoc volumine contentorum*. Libelli duo primus de medicine claris scriptoribus . . . secundus de legum divinarum conditoribus. . . . De corporum animorumque morbis. . . . Collectiones medicinales. . . . Alexandri Benedicti Veronensis Aphorismi sive collectiones. . . . Lyon, Jannot de Campis, Allut, *op. cit.*, 142-149. The treatise of Benedetti is preceded by a letter of Champier to Michel Baleoto of Novara. The volume contains also the *De febribus* of Alexander of Aphrodisias in Giorgio Valla's translation.

114. See for example Gian-Giuseppe Liruti, *Notizie delle vite ed opere scritte da' letterati del Friuli, 1*, Venezia, 1760, 382-394; Angiolgabriello di Santa Maria (Paolo Calvi), *Biblioteca, e storia di quei scrittori così della città come del territorio di Vicenza, 3*, Vicenza, 1775, LIV-LXXXII; Girolamo Tiraboschi, *Storia della letteratura italiana, 6*, Part 3, Firenze, 1809, 938-939; Vincenzo Lancetto, *Memorie intorno ai poeti laureati d'ogni tempo e d'ogni nazione*, Milano, 1839, 173-176.

115. Published in Marquard Freher, *Rerum germanicarum scriptores*, Argentorati, 1717, 2, 415-444. The encomium of Maximilian was dedicated to the Antonio Boldù whom we have already met.

116. In *Anatomice*, III.9 Benedetti mentions a son of "nostri Cimbriaci" in whose urine bloody pus was discharged "in pleuretico morbo."

117. Already mentioned in this introduction. On the work and the letter see Rino Avesani in *Italia medioevale e umanistica*, 1962, 5, 51, n.2 and Jacopo Morelli, *Operette, 2*, Venezia, 1820, 31-35. Benedetti mentions these baths in his work *De omnibus morbis*, XI.20 and XXVI.26.

118. Giuliari, *op. cit.*, 208 mentions four folios on Pliny's birthplace which were written by Benedetti to his "concivis" Matteo Ruffo and published at Brescia by Baptista Farfengus in 1496. Such a letter to Ruffo does appear on f.2a of the edition of Pliny published at Brescia by Angelus and Jacobus Brittanicus on 20 April 1496, British Museum, *Catalogue of books printed in the XV$^{th}$ century now in the British Museum, 7*, London, 1935, 977-978, Goff P-797; it is followed on f.2b by a letter of Ruffo to Giusto Giusti which seeks to prove that Pliny's birthplace was Verona, not Como.

Cf. Avesani, *op. cit.*, 54 n.2. Benedetti mentions both Ruffo and Giusti in the preface to Book II of the *Anatomice*.

119. Barbaro had his early education in Verona, where his uncle of the same name was bishop. His *Castigationes Plinianae et Pomponii Melae*, Rome, Eucharius Silber, 24 November 1492, 13 February 1493, Goff B-100, appeared after the text of Pliny in Benedetti's edition.

120. His work *De Plinii et aliorum in medicina erroribus* appeared at Ferrara, Laurentius de Rubeis and Andreas de Grassis, 18 December 1492, Goff L-168. He is mentioned in the *Anatomice*, IV.10.

121. Another famous Veronese who was engaged in editing classical texts in this period was Fra Giovanni Giocondo (c.1435-1515), whose edition of the *Epistolae* of Pliny the Younger was published by Aldus Manutius in 1508; editions of Sallust, Vitruvius, Caesar, and Cato followed. For the career of this humanist, architect, and engineer who was working in Naples in 1495, was taken from there to France by Charles VIII, and worked in Paris until perhaps 1506 see Raffaello Brenzoni, *Fra Giovanni Giocondo veronese*, Firenze, 1960, and Lucia A. Ciapponi, "Appunti per una biografia di Giovanni Giocondo da Verona," *Italia medioevale e umanistica*, 1961, *4*, 131-158.

122. Cf. *De omnibus morbis*, XXV.10, 29 and Cervetto, *op. cit.*, 70.

123. *I diarii, 15*, Venezia, 1886, col. 283: "Morite questa note domino maistro Alexandro veronese medico, qual corexe Plinio et fece la *Diaria De bello carolino*, et altre opere de observatione, in pestilentia e altro, che fo impresse. Questo è stato do mexi amalato, e *tandem* è morto." Cicogna, *op. cit., 3*, Venezia, 1830, 107, n.3 first called attention to this notice.

124. Testamenti, Busta 50, n.178. Massalongo, *op. cit.*, 227 traced the will. Its notarial hand and its abbreviations are difficult, and it is only with the gracious assistance of Dr. Bianca Strina of the Archivio that I transcribe it here, albeit imperfectly and without interpretation or commentary, in the hope that it may be more readily accessible to historians. "In nomine Dei eterni amen. Anno ab Incarnatione domini nostri Ihesu Christi millesimo quingentesimo duodecimo indictione prima die vero decimo octavo mensis septembris Rivoalti. Fragilitatis humane cursum dilligentissime considerans et ante oculos habens Ego magister Alexander de benedictis de verona physicus filius quondam domini Laurentii de confinio Sancti Pantaleonis Venetiarum sanus Dei gratia mente et intellectu licet corpore infirmus volens dum tempus datur rebus meis providere et eas debito ordine disponere ad me vocari feci Hieronymum de Bossis Venetiarum notarium ipsumque rogavi ut hoc meum scriberet testamentum ipsumque post meum obitum compleret et roboraret iuxta formam, tenorem et continentiam presentis cedule bonbicine a presente manu mea scripte et eidem notario per me presentate. Interrogatus et informatus ab ipso notario de interrogandis et informandis respondeo quod volo quod una cum commissariis meis in ipsa

cedula annotatis esse debeat commissarius meus Dominus Antonius Moretus
sororius meus et dominus vincentius saracenus ducalis secretarius et quod
misse sancti gregorii celebrentur per sacristam presentem Sancti Pantaleonis.
Item declaro quod lucia uxor mea sit commissaria mea in omni statu et quod
ea que sibi legavi intelligantur legata in omni statu. Item volo quod misse
Beate nostre Virginis Marie celebrentur per reverendum dominum magis-
trum Franciscum Colona fratrem in sancto ioanne paulo. Item quia legavi
in dicta cedula ducatos sexcentos Iulie filie mee volo quod ultra omnes vestes
extimandas et ultra tres petias terre quas sibi legavi pro computo dicte
. . . quae sunt le nogarate . . . et pergolette volo quod commissarii mei
supleant dicte iulie dictam summam ducatorum sexcentorum de terris meis
quas habeo in villa sancti bonifacii intra . . . Veronensem Item dimitto
praefato domino vincentio saraceno ducatos decem quos sibi dare debeo ex
causa mutui Tenor autem dicte cedule bonbicine talis est et infra sequitur
de verbo ad verbum videlicet testamentum mei Alexandri Benedicti veronensis physici et cetera MDXI die ut in eo. In christi nomine Amen. Individue
trinitati comendo spiritum meum et Marie virgini In nomine Dei eterni
Amen Anno domini MDXI Die primo Iulii primum testamentum quod alias
Iadre Condidi obliteratum volo ac irritum. Deinde fateor quod Iulia habeat
de bonis quae nunc possideo que fuere domine Dionore . . . primum ducatos
ducentos quinquaginta que sunt pro venditione facta in eximium legum doc-
torem dominum Bartolomeum . . . civem civitatis Austrie pro possessione
in contrata de Kriliono [?] ut patet instrumento domini Ioannis . . . de
. . . ut in eo. Item quod ducatis ducentis septuaginta quod pretium fuit
pro domo habitata per me in presentiarum reliquum vero quod exbursavi
sit pro computo meo ut apparet ad officium consulum mercatorum et cyro-
grapho manu ser Ioannis Francisci may . . . Cum hoc tamen pacto quod
si fuerit contenta de summa supradicta hoc est in duabus partitis ducatos
quingentos et viginti . . . tot posessiones de . . . hoc est in castro cruce
totum quod ibi possideo pro ducatis centum triginta hoc est tres petias
terre hoc est nogarete . . . et le pergolette cum quella pocha pension che
paga a la giesia de Illasi et altri fiti et campi che ascenda a la dicta summa
de ducati de ducati cinquecento et venti computando i soi vestimenti di
dosso extimadi per persone idonee sia per conto de sua dota et del mio li
lasso tanto de i mei mobili che ascenda a la summa de ducati 600 doro. Et
non volendo star quieta volio et ordeno che la casa comprada a nome de
sua madre ma per me compidamente pagada ut supra cum li melioramenti
fati per me sia messo a conto de la sua dote zoe de sua madre cum sit che
in libro meo computum sia nota tutto quello ho speso in dicta casa Et
morendo senza fioli legitimi volio che il dicto superhabundante sia de li
altri fradelli over sorelle Et per che Marin per me novamente legitimado
cum intention che volesse clericare et non volendo li lasso di mei beni
mobili tanto per summa de ducati cento de esser stimadi per. . . . Item per
lanima mia lasso dei beni mobili sia fatto uno incanto et se venda per ducati
50 zoe cinquanta da esser dati a la schola di san marco ducati diexe a la
scola del spirito santo ducati diexe a la scola di santa maria formosa ducati
cinque li altri ducati venticinque per la mia sepultura et spese del obito da
esser partiti come parera al mio infrascripto commissario. Item el resto che
sonno ducati 300 doro posti in tanti beni stabeli in san bonifacio sonno per
conto de lucia mia consorte. Et lei habia a tuor dove li piace segondo el

precio che sonno compradi. Et li soi fiti compradi per essa dispona a sua a sua voglia. Di beni mobili per so conto portadi per essa per ducati 300 li romagna per suo conto cum honesta stima ut sopra. El resto veramente siano de Cornelia et Livia egualmente Et se una more vada in laltra. Et se tutte doe vada la meta in dicta Iulia et laltra in dicta lucia mia consorte Et se tutte tre morisseno senza heredi per la parte che io le don del mio volio sia ducati 200 zoe duxento de marin ultra li dicti ducati 100. El resto de dicta lucia. Item volio che si faci inventario dele mie robe quale se habi a vender al publico incanto per el mio commissario infrascripto El qual volio habi del mio non per merito ma per segno de dilection ducati X Et volio sia anchora commissaria in omnibus cum esso dicta lucia mia donna Et sia mio commissario messer benedetto Calbo quondam magnifici domini petri el qual habi quam citius poterit adempido ogni cosa al qual recomando la-nima mia et far dir che de bonis meis le messe de san gregol et de la ma-donna. Item per che intendo esser morta Faustina sua sorella in ongaria et se quella havesse fato altro testamento per el qual essa lasasse la soa parte ad altri che a la dicta Iulia in questo caxo intendo lhabia tanto de la parte soa quanto dicta faustina havesse ordinato azo che non seguita qualche . . . error in la quantita de essa dote da esser disegnada a la dicta Iulia per che se convegnicra lassar dove essa faustina havesse ordenado Et questo volio sia fermo e rato et questa la mia ferma et constante volunta ultima in omnibus et per omnia da esser observada Ego Iohannes Alex-ander benedictus physicus veronensis Artium et medicine doctor corpore et mente sanus manu propria hoc testamentum annotavi die et anno ut supra quod meis sigillis roboravi et signavi clausumque dedi lucie uxori mee servandum Preterea plenissimam virtutem potestatem et auctoritatem do et confero suprascriptis commissariis meis post mei obitum commissariam meam intromittendi regendi gubernandi et administrandi pecunias res et bona petendi exigendi et recuperandi et de exactis habitis et receptis quietandi liberandi et absolvendi et pro ea in omni iuditio comparendi agendi defen-dendi petendi et respondendi, lites contestandi, Iura producendi, probandi, in animam meam iurandi, sententias et acta quaelibet fieri faciendi apellandi et appellationem prosequendi usque in finem ac omnia et singula alia faciendi et exercendi quae egomet facere possem si viverem Si quis igitur contra hanc mei testamenti cartam ire temptaverit componat cum suis here-dibus huic mee commissarie auri libras quinque et nihilominus haec mei testamenti carta in sua permaneat firmitate signum manus suprascripti domini magistri Alexandri benedicti. Io antonio agnello spicier quondam ser agnello da Lonigo testis subscripsi. Ego Hieronymus de Bossis quondam domini Bartolomei Venetiarum notarius complevi et roboravi.

125. Cf. Alfonso Bisacco, *La chiesa di S. Pantaleone in Venezia,* Venezia, 1933.

# DIARIA DE BELLO CAROLINO

# DIARY OF THE CAROLINE WAR

## QUINTII HAEMILIANI CIMBRIACI POETAE
### SCHEDION IN GALLOS

Cedite ab Oenotriis, Galli, iam cedite terris,
　　Dum licet innocuis serta referre domum.
Nam si quae properat vos hic deprehenderit aestas
　　Non erit ad reditum tam via lata iugis.
Laeta modo, versis lugebit Gallia fatis
　　Ni male tentata ceditis Italia.
Scilicet Ausonidum vestris ditata triumphis
　　Tellus Gallorum barbara gesta feret?
Quae quondam Cimbros, quae saevis Teutonas armis,
　　Quae potuit Poeno sub duce ferre minas;
Quaecunque Italiam gentes movere tumultu
　　Eventus olim non habuere bonos.
Quas ego non ferrem nostris cecidisse sub armis?
　　Sed non tam longam teximus historiam.
Et iam finitimi feriunt nova foedera reges
　　Et fit dictator exul et arma parat.
Non Leo bellipotens non Gallica sceptra, Quirites,
　　Non feret expertas Herculis Hydra manus.
Vos igitur moniti veterumque exempla secuti
　　Discite quid fronte Ianus utraque ferat.

## EXTEMPORANEOUS LINES OF THE POET QUINZIO EMILIANO CIMBRIACO AGAINST THE FRENCH

Depart, O ye French, depart now from Oenotrian lands while as yet unharmed you may carry your garlands home. For if the hastening summer finds you still here the road back will not be so broad for your teams. France, which now rejoices, will mourn her reversed fortunes if you depart not from an Italy which you have wickedly attacked. Will the land of the Ausonians, enriched by your triumphs, suffer forsooth the barbarous deeds of the French? She once survived the Cimbrians, the Teutons and their cruel arms, the threats of the Carthaginian leader, but whatever peoples have caused an uproar in Italy have not once found success. What tribes could I mention that have not fallen under our arms? But I am not spinning so long a tale. And now the neighboring kings are forging new compacts, and the exile becomes a dictator and prepares for war. The Lion of Venice, O ye citizens, is mighty in war and will not suffer the French domination, nor will Hydra suffer the hands of Hercules she once has felt. Warned then and following the example of the ancients, learn what two-faced Janus discloses.[1]

QUINTII HAEMILIANI CIMBRIACI POETAE
IN DIARIA ALEXANDRI PAEANTII BENEDICTI
VERONENSIS PHYSICI EPOS HENDECASYLLABICON

Si te nosse iuvat seorsum ab ore
Vulgato Venetis modo sub armis
Res gestas, atavis nihil minores
Quamvis historias diu exoletas
Iam longam repetes per aevitatem,
Quum Galli Ausonia quasi subacta
Ad Tarrum furerent novum furorem,
Rem factam arbitrio diu arbitrati,
Paeanti legito Diariorum
Libros. Hosce fide fideliores
Dices, ac subito videbis esse
Nullam nunc Venetis potentiorem
Gentem, Strymonios sequi furores.
Testis dissidium Novariorum
Quum movit Leo fortior Libyssis
Et Gallos retudit diu vagatos.

### HENDECASYLLABICS OF THE POET
### QUINZIO EMILIANO CIMBRIACO
### ON THE DIARY OF
### ALESSANDRO BENEDETTI OF VERONA,
### PHYSICIAN, CALLED PAEANTIUS

If apart from what the herd relates you would learn about the deeds recently performed by Venetian arms (deeds in no wise inferior to those of our ancestors, though you review them over an extended period of time in histories long obsolete), when with Ausonia almost subdued the French were piling rage upon rage at the Taro and had long thought the thing accomplished by the decision to accomplish it, read the *Diaria* of Paeantius. Truer than the truth itself you will call it, and you will see at once that no people is now more powerful than the Venetians and that the Strymonian rage takes second place; testimony thereof is the contest at Novara when the Lion of Venice, stronger than those of Libya, drove and beat back the far roving French.

## ALEXANDER BENEDICTUS VERONENSIS PHYSICUS AUGUSTINO BARBADICO ILLUSTRISSIMO VENETORUM PRINCIPI SALUTEM PERPETUAM DICIT

Bellum quod hoc anno, Illustrissime Princeps, tuis sanctissimis auspiciis cum Carolo octavo Gallorum rege pro tuenda sociorum libertate gessisti Francisco Gonzaga marchione Mantuanorum imperatore tuo felicissimo duobus duntaxat voluminibus, altero pugnam Tarrensem altero Novariensem oppugnationem, complexus sum, quibus Diaria inscripsimus. Causam enim belli huius et primum Galli adventum plerique copiosius scripsere, quae transcursu quodam delibavimus; reliqua, quae vidimus vel quaecunque nobis tradita sunt, incorrupta protulimus.

Nudam enim materiam, rudem ac pene indigestam, inter annales tuos reponendam coacervavimus. Erunt ex posterioribus qui collatis undique historiis hanc simplicitatem nostram, quae fortasse nunc fastiditur quod sit arida et exanguis, suaviorem uberioremque reddent quod inter veteres Titus Livius miro successu eo modo adimplevit. Historia magnam quidem vitae partem expostulat,[1] in qua modus servandus est ut veritas imprimis ordo digestio belli causae consilia contiones rerum eventa et totius belli progressus legentibus in promptu sit, atque ipsa oratio [2] non salebrosa non languens non nimium diffusa neque succincta nimium neque affectata denique videatur ut legentium animos vividius penetret aut excitet. Acriter item proponere debet,

SIGLA

A [Venice, Aldus Manutius Romanus, after 27 August 1496]

B Pietro Giustiniani, *Rerum venetarum ab urbe condita ad annum M. D.LXXV. historia,* Argentorati, 1611, Appendix, ff.G1b-I3a. This edition omits the preliminary verses.

E Johann Georg von Eckhart, *Corpus historicorum medii aevi,* 2, Lipsiae, coll.1577-1628. This edition omits the preliminary verses and the concluding letter.

F Fano, Biblioteca Federiciana, MS.43, Polidori, 19th century, ff.24r-54r. This manuscript omits the preliminary verses and the concluding letter.

[1] postulat EF [2] orõ A, om. EF

ALESSANDRO BENEDETTI OF VERONA, PHYSICIAN,
SENDS CONSTANT GREETINGS TO
AGOSTINO BARBARIGO,[2]
MOST ILLUSTRIOUS DOGE OF THE VENETIANS

In only two books, Most Illustrious Doge, one on the battle of the Taro
and the other on the siege of Novara, I have covered the war which
you fought under your very sacred auspices this past year with
Charles VIII, king of the French, to protect the freedom of your allies,
and in which Francesco Gonzaga, marquis of the Mantuans, was your
very fortunate general. I have entitled these books *Diaria.* A great
many have written more profusely on the reason for this war and the
first arrival of the Frenchman, but I have touched on these points
merely in cursory fashion; the other events, those which I saw myself
or any which have been related to me, I have presented accurately.[3]

For it is indeed naked material, rough and almost without order,
which I have assembled to be stored among your annals. This simple
style of mine perhaps awakens scorn now as being dry and bloodless,
but there will be those among posterity who, when they have compared various histories, will pronounce it more agreeable and rich
because among the ancients Titus Livy discharged his task in this way
with wondrous success. For history demands a large portion of life,
and in writing it such methods should be observed that truth first of
all, right order, proper arrangement of the war, its causes, purposes,
conferences, the outcome of events, and the course of the entire war
may be accessible to those who read and the style itself seem not
harsh, not listless, not too diffuse, not too abbreviated, or, finally, too
studied, in order that it may the more vigorously penetrate or arouse

vehementius persuadere irritare urgere suadere item [3] et dissuadere, exemplis frequentibus animos inflectere. Haec omnia iis [4] praeponenda [5] sunt qui imperii tui gesta veluti Romani nominis reflorescentis descripturi sunt.

Ego simplicius quaedam quae in dies gesta sunt annotavi minime in gratiam adulator vel in damnando nimis severus. Res hostiles debita commendatione non defraudo ut magis narrator quam censor acer et tetricus esse videar. Verbis et sensu restrictus incedo. Scio etiam quosdam ieiune hanc historiam tetigisse vel pauca vera demonstrasse, alios copiosiores ad vanitatem redegisse.

Haec enim, Humanissime Princeps, nitidiora melioraque fieri curabis, qui in rebus publicis Marcum fratrem tuum optimum principem imitatus es, qui non minus intestinam quietem quam foris bella cum opus est foves et civitatem miro studio uberiorem reddis pater patriae appellatus. Leges sanctissimas condis, munera in Senatu amplificans Quadraginta Viros tertios addidisti, imperatoribus statuas publicare coepisti, palatium miro ornamento [6] extruis [7] et universam urbem exornas. Tuo demum ductu et optimis auspiciis rabies Gallica perdomita [8] est, tuo consilio ingenio et armis Gallorum truculentia ultra Alpes coercita saevit, quam [9] natura sagax (dicere id solitus es) Alpium mirabili septo et inexuperabili [10] munimento [11] a mitiori orbis parte diduxerat,[12] ut pacem quam tantopere amas cum sanctissimo Senatu tuo amplectereris.[13] Tu in hoc flagrantissimo bello imperii terminos longius protraxisti. Iam Apulus te et Senatum tuum voti compos summissus adorat et colit. Haec enim faciunt ut te magis ad principatum divina ratione quam senatorum suffragiis delectum fuisse posteritas admiretur. Vale. Venetiis duodecimo Kalendas Apriles anno MIIIID.

---

[3] idem EF    [4] his B    [5] proponenda B    [6] ornamentis B    [7] om. F
[8] predominata F    [9] quem EF    [10] inexpugnabili F    [11] monumento EF
[12] deduxerat EF    [13] amplecteris EF

the minds of readers. Likewise it ought to suggest sharply, persuade, provoke, impel, urge and also dissuade somewhat forcibly and sway the mind by frequent examples. All these points ought to be considered of first importance by those who would set forth the events of your rule as if Rome's glory were blossoming again.

Certain things which have occurred from day to day I have noted down somewhat simply, for I am not at all a flatterer for the sake of favor, nor am I too severe a critic. When the acts of the enemy deserve commendation I do not deny it, so that I may seem to be a narrator rather than a fierce and harsh censor. I practise moderation in words and thought.[4] I know also that some writers have touched upon this history in jejune fashion or have set forth only a few truths, while others who are more prolix have reduced it to something untrustworthy.

You will see to it, Most Humane Doge, that these acts are rendered brighter and more comely, you who in public affairs have emulated that excellent doge, your brother Marco; who support quiet at home no less than wars abroad when necessary; and who with wondrous zeal enrich the state and are called father of your country. You establish most sacred laws. You enlarge the duties of office in the Senate and have added a third group of Forty.[5] You have started to erect statues to generals,[6] you heap the palace with marvelous decoration,[7] and you adorn the entire city. Finally, under your leadership and excellent auspices the French fury has been vanquished; by your purpose, ability, and forces the savagery of the French has been restricted to rage on the other side of the Alps. Wise nature, as you were wont to say, had separated that savagery from the more gentle part of the world by a marvelous fence and insurmountable barrier, the Alps,[8] so that with your most sacred Senate you might embrace the peace which you love so dearly. In this most searing war you have extended the bounds of your sway, and now even the Apulian,[9] his wish fulfilled, pays humble reverence and court to you and your Senate. The result is that posterity will marvel at your having been selected for the rule by divine wisdom rather than by the votes of the Senators. Farewell. From Venice, 21 March 1496.

# BOOK I

## ARGUMENTUM PRIMI LIBRI
## AD ANTONIUM BOLDUM EQUITEM CLARISSIMUM,
## IOANNEM MARCELLUM ET ALOISIUM MOLINUM
## DECEMVIRORUM PRAESIDES PRAESTANTISSIMOS

Carolus Gallorum [14] rex ab Italis principibus in Italiam ducitur, qui Tusciam protinus occupat, Romam superat, Pontificem parere cogit, expulso Alphonso et Ferdinando regibus Neapolim sine praelio subigit regnat imperat triumphat.[15] Icto inter Pontificem Alexandrum [16] Maximilianum [17] Imperatorem Ferdinandum [18] et Elisabetham Hispaniae reges Senatum Venetum et Ludovicum ducem Mediolanensem foedere onustus praeda rediens capta Novaria ad Mediolanum occupandum anhelat. Insurgunt Veneti et ad Tarrum subito milite illum aggrediuntur et tentoria et impedimenta regia non incruenta victoria corripiunt. Gallus impetratis induciis turpi fuga ad extrema Italiae confugit.

---

[14] om. B    [15] regnat—triumphat om. F    [16] om. EF    [17] Max. A, Maximum EF    [18] Alphonsum ABEF, Ferdinandum A by MS. correction

ARGUMENT OF THE FIRST BOOK
TO ANTONIO BOLDÙ, MOST EMINENT KNIGHT,
GIOVANNI MARCELLO, AND LUIGI MOLINO,
MOST EXCELLENT LEADERS OF THE COUNCIL OF TEN

Charles, king of the French, is lured into Italy by Italian princes. He immediately seizes Tuscany, conquers Rome, forces the Pope to submit. When the kings Alfonso and Ferdinand have been driven out, he subjugates Naples without a battle, reigns, governs, celebrates a triumph. Pope Alexander, the Emperor Maximilian, Ferdinand and Isabella the rulers of Spain, the Venetian Senate, and Lodovico duke of Milan make an alliance. Charles returns laden with booty, and since Novara has been taken he is eager to seize Milan. The Venetians rise up, attack him suddenly at the Taro with their forces, and seize the royal tents and baggage in a victory which is not bloodless. After obtaining a truce the Frenchman escapes in disgraceful flight to the borders of Italy.[10]

ALEXANDRI BENEDICTI PHYSICI
DIARIORUM DE TARRENSI PUGNA
LIBER PRIMUS [19]

1. Carolus octavus Gallorum rex vigesimum quartum aetatis annum
agens regnandi cupidine ductus, ut fidem rebus faceret, simulata
religione bellum contra Turcas parare ubique vulgavit et quaedam
vaticinia de se ipso augurari confidentius professus est, ita ut eius
auspiciis Hispania Germania et Italia perdomita facile Graecia Asia
Syria ac [20] Egyptus illum tanquam deum venerarentur [21] et adepta
Hierosolyma deposita humi corona sepulchrum Christi veneratus victor
triumphans suprema die in coelum raperetur. Nocturna praeterea
quaedam visa animum [22] ut aiunt commovisse iactaverat quibus facile
universum orbem occupaturus esset si religiosi cuiusdam monitis [23]
paruisset. Ea de se dici vel praesens patiebatur, cumque de Neapolitano regno animo plura volutaret id haereditario iure ad se pertinere
non veritus est dicere ac proximo Andegaviensium quorum fuerat id
regnum sibi convenire, bene gerendarum praeterea rerum duntaxat
occasionem non imperium quaerere, plurimumque ad bellum locorum
vicinitatem et rei frumentariae opportunitatem prodesse commemo-
rabat.

2. Eo tempore calamitatem ingentem in Italiam venturam astrorum
periti praedixerunt Ferdinandumque Regem imperium sine cruore
sed sola fama [24] amissurum, Saturno oeconomo Marte adverso sole
horoscopo incipientis anni siderumque defectibus praeteritis auguran-
tes. Elementa quoque non sine praesagio fuere. Auctis supra modum
in tota Italia fluminibus anno MVIID Octubri mense Athesis inter
caetera flumina aquarum impetu ingentem pontis molem ad imum
devolvit, qui ingentes externarum gentium copias Italis urbibus

---

[19] LIBER PRIMUS om. F   [20] atque EF   [21] veneraretur ABEF
[22] om. B   [23] moniti F   [24] fame BF

## THE DIARY OF THE PHYSICIAN ALESSANDRO BENEDETTI.
## BOOK I, THE BATTLE AT THE TARO

1. Charles VIII, king of the French, was seized in the twenty-fourth year of his life with a desire for power, and to lend credence to the affair he feigned religious motives [11] and let it be known everywhere that he was preparing a war against the Turks. He even avowed with still greater boldness that certain prophecies were prophecies concerning himself, so that when Spain, Germany, and Italy had been vanquished under his auspices Greece, Asia, Syria, and Egypt would without hesitation worship him as a god, and that when he had acquired Jerusalem, and laid his crown on the ground, and venerated the tomb of Christ, he would be borne off to heaven a triumphant victor on his last day. Moreover he had boasted, as the story goes, that certain visions had stirred his mind by night, according to which he was destined easily to lay hold of the entire world if he followed the advice of a certain religious man.[12] Such things he allowed to be said about himself even in his own presence. And while he was turning over in his mind many things concerning the kingdom of Naples, he did not hesitate to assert that it belonged to him by hereditary claim [13] and that dominion over it was his right because he was next in line of the house of Anjou, under whose rule it had already been. He added moreover that he was seeking only an opportunity for successful accomplishment, and not power, and he mentioned that in war proximity of bases and convenience of grain supply are of the greatest benefit.

2. The astrologers predicted that a mighty calamity would befall Italy at that time and that King Ferdinand would lose his realm without bloodshed and through public opinion alone. This they prophesied from the solar horoscope of the year which was beginning, Saturn being uppermost and Mars beneath, and from previous deviations of the heavenly bodies.[14] Nor were the elements free from foreboding. In October of the year 1493 rivers throughout Italy were immoderately swollen, and among these the rushing waters of the Adige tumbled the huge mass of a bridge right down to its foundations [15] and furnished thereby a portent that huge numbers of foreign peoples would in the

undique sese superfusuras augurium dedit. Religiosus praeterea quidam pari modo ieiuniorum tempore sequenti anno cum Novariae pro
more praedicaret civibus ingentem cladem imminere, Hispanos Gallos
Elvecios Suevos Teutones Dalmatas Macedones Graecos Turcas in-
numerasque alias nationes prope moenia audituros praedixit verissima
quidem praedivinatione. Maiora quoque in Graecia Constantinopoli
praesertim a vulgo iactabantur ruinam hoc tempore religionis Maumet-
tanae finemque [25] imperii Othomannorum magis minitantibus. Ea
omnia a [26] plerisque ita verisimilia videbantur specie religionis sa-
lutari omnium fere animis caligatis ad rabiemque non aviditatem
populis adactis ut pro publico veluti bono vota ubique [27] solverentur
victoriamque Christianissimo Regi priscos omnis [28] gloria superaturo
praecarentur.

3. Carolus itaque concepto regnandi desiderio dissidentibusque in
Italia varias ob causas principibus a Ludovico Sforcia qui guberna-
tionis a Mediolanensibus primatibus imperium acceperat facile ad
bellum invitatur ac Hercule Ferrariensi duce Iuliano cardinale Sancti
Petri in Vinculis Laurentinoque Medice Florentino Ianuensi altera
factione. Nam et Pontificis Alexandri VI invisum quibusdam cardinalibus nomen de pontificatu mutando occasionem dabat.[29] Haerebant
praeterea lateri perpetui regulorum qui proscripti fuerant aculei
plebeiusque [30] totius regni Neapolitani favor. Ludovicum nanque con-
citaverant Ferdinandi Regis importuna imperia ut Ioanni Galeacio
adolescenti nepoti suo qui ducis nomen duntaxat haberet guberna-
tionem restitueret, alioqui armis eum exterminaturus esset. Herculem
vero nota veneni ut quidam dicunt suspicio vel Rhodigii amnicae
insulae ut alii ferunt repetendae spes quam pridem [31] inter pacis
conditiones cum Venetis amiserat praecipue impulerat. Nam priori
anno ad Regem Gallum filium promissae fidei obsidem praemisit, ipse
vero ad Ludovicum se contulit generum cum quo animi sui consulta
retexit. De belli summa diutius egit, Ludovici itaque nomine ducenta
millia nummum aureorum ad milites alendos Regi per legatos polli-
cetur, classem item validam, DC equites armatos.[32]

4. Rex igitur Gallus his incitamentis invitatus [33] convocatis Galliarum principibus varias de bello suscipiendo contra Ferdinandum

---

[25] -que om. EF    [26] om. EF    [27] om. EF    [28] omnes BEF    [29] om. B
[30] plebis eiusque EF    [31] primum EF    [32] classem—armatos om. B
[33] om. B

same way pour from every quarter upon the cities of Italy. Moreover, during the Lenten period in the following year [16] a certain religious man, when he was preaching as usual at Novara, predicted in like manner (and with the most genuine divination as it turned out) that an awful disaster was threatening the citizens and that they would hear Spaniards, French, Swiss, Swabians, Teutons, Dalmatians, Macedonians, Greeks, Turks, and countless other peoples about their walls. Even greater disasters were commonly predicted in Greece and especially in Constantinople, with the soothsayers threatening the downfall of the Mohammedan religion at this time and the end of the Ottoman empire.[17] All these things seemed so probable to most persons (for the minds of nearly all of them were befogged by the beneficial pretext of religion and peoples were being urged on to frenzy and not just vehement desire) that vows were made everywhere as if for the public good and victory was invoked for the Most Christian King who would surpass all earlier rulers in glory.

3. And so Charles, because he had been seized with a longing for power and because the rulers in Italy were at variance for a number of reasons, was easily incited to war [18] by Lodovico Sforza, who had received control of the government from the aristocrats of Milan; by Ercole, duke of Ferrara; by Giuliano, cardinal of San Pietro in Vincoli; by Lorenzo de' Medici of Florence; and by one of the two Genoese factions. Then too the fact that the name of Pope Alexander VI was hateful to some of the cardinals presented the occasion for changing the pontificate. Moreover constant goads from rulers who had been exiled kept spurring him on, as did also the popular favor of the entire kingdom of Naples. For the importunate commands of King Ferdinand had urged Lodovico to restore the rule to the young Giangaleazzo, his nephew, who had merely the name of duke; otherwise he would drive him out with arms. Ercole, however, was impelled especially by the well-known suspicion of poison, as some say, or, as others put it, by the hope of recovering the lowland at Rovigo which he had lost earlier as a condition of peace with the Venetians.[19] For in the previous year he despatched his son to the French King as a pledge of the good faith which he had promised; [20] he himself went off to his son-in-law Lodovico, to whom he revealed the plans which he had in mind. He discussed with him for a long time the issue of the war, and so in the name of Lodovico he promised to the King through envoys two hundred thousand pieces of gold for maintaining the soldiers and likewise a powerful fleet and six hundred armed horsemen.

4. Accordingly the French King, encouraged by these inducements, called together the barons of France and began to give ear to their

sententias audire coepit. Alii victoriam, alii difficultatem ostendere, nonnulli pericula ingentia Gallorum in Italia frequentem stragem vel hac nostra aetate indicantes. Ille silentio facto sese in Italiam ire decrevisse,[34] divinam quidem occasionem sibi oblatam sequi velle respondit, ceterum ut ipsi quae bello necessaria essent in medium proferrent. Primum itaque pacis foedere[35] principes totius fere Europae iungendos esse proposuit, alios condonatis civitatibus, alios pecunia conciliavit, quosdam redimendae rei publicae Christianae spe vel veteri amicitia stabilivit, nonnullos amplificandi imperii gratia Elvecios[36] et Cimbros sibi certa fide confirmavit. Omnes iure iurando foedera iniere.[37]

5. Ea fama Ferdinandum perterruit,[38] qui Apuliae principes variis de causis consilii inops ad unum sustulerat ut solus imperitaret.[39] Omnes igitur populos concitavit in sui odium et eos praesertim qui veteris Andegaviensis factionis studiosissimi erant atque pristinae libertatis memores. His omnibus labefactare imperium coepit. Tum Rex consiliorum Galli haud inscius flammam ingentem quam ipse totiens in Italia aluerat in se ipsum converti senserat, et quo numine vel furore praeditus esset nescio Gallorum adventum et praesentem ruinam Venetosque ad ultima incredulos palam iam praedixerat.

6. Cum igitur Gallorum Regem per exploratores bellum parare intellexisset Venetum Senatum supplex litteris ac legatis perpetuis socium sibi petere non cessavit, in quo salutis imperii sui praesidium omne locaverat. Sed iam Gallorum Rex litteris a Senatu fidem acceperat ut manus quoquomodo a bello abstineret fidemque veteris amicitiae servaret sua duntaxat sine alicuius iniuria repetiturus. Pontificis et Ferdinandi ac Florentinorum legati aderant qui Venetos a fide Galli revocare conantes totius Italiae praesentem ruinam et imminentem populorum stragem ante oculos preponebant[40] et Italiam quondam rerum dominam predam barbaris brevi futuram. Ferdinandus spem denique omnem in Pontificis et Florentinorum copias transtulit et

---

[34] decrevisse? A by MS. correction   [35] foedera AEF, foederae A by MS. correction, faedera B   [36] Suecios B   [37] inire B   [38] praeterruit B   [39] imperaret EF   [40] proponebant BEF

varied opinions about undertaking the war against Ferdinand. Some prophesied victory, others pointed out the difficulties, still others reminded him of the enormous dangers and the repeated ruin which the French had undergone in Italy even in our own day. He called for silence and then replied that he had determined to go into Italy and that he wished to take advantage of this really providential opportunity which had been offered to him, and that for the rest they themselves should bring forward whatever was necessary for war. And so he resolved first that the princes of almost all Europe must join in a peace treaty; some he won over by presenting cities to them, others by money, certain ones he secured by the hope of redeeming the Christian state or by the ties of ancient friendship, and some, such as the Swiss and the Cimbrians, he confirmed in fixed loyalty to himself on the plea of increasing their power. All entered into sworn compacts.

5. The report of these developments terrified Ferdinand, who had displayed his poor judgment by removing to a man the princes of Puglia on various pretexts, so that he might rule alone. In this way he incited all the people to hatred of himself, and especially those who had been very devoted to the old faction of Anjou and remembered the earlier freedom. Because of all these things his rule began to totter. Moreover the King was by no means unaware of the purposes of the Frenchman; he realized that the mighty flame which he himself had so often fed in Italy was now directed against himself, and, endowed I know not with what divination or frenzy, he had already openly predicted the arrival of the French and the ruin which was now at hand and had prophesied that the Venetians would be incredulous to the very end.

6. So when he had learned through spies that the King of the French was preparing war, he repeatedly endeavored to win the Venetian Senate as an ally, beseeching its members in a continual stream of letters and envoys; on this he depended entirely for the protection and preservation of his rule. But already the King of the French had received by letter a pledge of good faith from the Senate: it would refrain altogether from the war and would preserve the bond of ancient friendship, since it intended to claim only what was its own without injury to anyone else. Envoys of the Pope [21] and of Ferdinand and of the Florentines assisted in trying to recall the Venetians from their pledge to the Frenchman, pointing out that the ruin of all Italy was even then at hand and that the destruction of her peoples impended: Italy, mistress formerly of the world, would in a short time be a prey to barbarians. Ferdinand finally transferred all his hope to the forces of the Pope and of the Florentines, and believing that he had been

Venetorum auxiliorum spe, ut sibi videbatur, destitutus moerore ut dicunt obiit.

7. Alphonsus filius malis auspiciis regnum init. Copias undique et classem comparat seque aperto Marte cum Gallorum Rege dimicaturum iactat nec se inter angustias saltus ritu ignobilium ferarum vel in silvarum latebris occultare magnificentius quam verius dictitat. Gallus interea Venetis legatum miserat qui [41] promissorum fidem rursus acciperet persuaderetque pro rei publicae Christianae salute in fide permanerent.[42] Venturum eum non credentes vulgarant [43] ingentibus Gallorum copiis alimenta non sufficere, divisis vero discrimen [44] imminere. Sed plurimos ea opinio fefellit.

8. Gallus itaque classem Genuae parari iubet alimentaque per statuta Alpium loca distribuit sub variisque ducibus per intervalla ob rei frumentariae inopiam in Liguriam praemittit. Ita sensim Alpium radices sine tumultu militibus complet.[45] Putant quidam ad XXV millia hominum venisse,[46] inter quos V millia equitum armata erant, Cymbrorum vero et Elveciorum XV millia, reliqua peditum varii generis turba erat. Ad hanc quoque expeditionem et milites Italos coegit, Mediolani Bononiaeque ac Ferrariae conscripsit. Inter principes vero Franciscum Gonzagam marchionem Mantuanum magnis oblatis stipendiis a fide Venetorum per nuncios revocare conatus est. Ille vero se Veneto Senatui quam acceptissimum esse [47] respondit militiaeque fidem acceptis conditionibus servaturum.

9. Tandem Rex Gallus ex Alpium angustiis praeter omnium fere opinionem Hastem III Idus Septembres MVID pervenit, ubi mutato coelo febre acutissima correptus est pustulasque [48] quas epinyctidas vocant, nostri variolas, extulit,[49] ac adepta tandem valitudine Ticinum [50] venit, ubi copias divisit, partem alteram in Flamminiam alteram Florentiam versus praemittit accepta a Ludovico Sfortia ingenti pecunia. Tum Petrus Medices ut gratiam Regis iniret oppida obtulit, quibus acceptis et praesidio firmatis contendit Lucam, deinde [51] Pisas [52] et a civibus in urbem receptus est. Rex vero Alphonsus Ferdinandum filium Calabriae ducem Cesenam [53] praemittit ut hostium copiis occurreret quas Hercules Dux in agrum Ferrariensem contraxerat, ut divisis viribus facile a Gallo superaretur. Patefacta igitur

---

[41] quod EF    [42] permaneret EF    [43] vulgarunt B    [44] alimenta EF
[45] complent EF    [46] cecidisse EF    [47] fore EF    [48] -que om. EF
[49] extrusit EF    [50] Tranum B    [51] om. EF    [52] om. EF    [53] Caesariam B

robbed of any expectation of Venetian aid he died, according to the popular view, of grief.

7. His son Alfonso entered upon the rule under evil auspices. From all sides he collected troops and a fleet [22] and boasted that he would fight with the King of the French in open battle; he asserted repeatedly, and more grandly than truly, that he would not hide himself in a narrow pass or in some den in the woods after the manner of lowly beasts. Meanwhile the Frenchman had sent an envoy to the Venetians to receive confirmation of their promises and to persuade them to abide by their pledge for the salvation of the Christian state. Believing that he would not come they had spread the word that the provisions were not sufficient for the vast forces of the French and that danger threatened if they were divided; a great many held this mistaken opinion.

8. And so the Frenchman ordered a fleet to be prepared at Genoa and distributed provisions at appointed places through the Alps, and because of the scarcity of the grain supply he sent men ahead at intervals under various leaders into Liguria. Thus gradually and without commotion he filled the foothills of the Alps with soldiers.[23] Some believe that about twenty-five thousand men made the journey, among whom were five thousand armed horsemen and fifteen thousand Cimbrians and Swiss; the rest of the throng of infantry were of various peoples.[24] In addition, he assembled Italian soldiers for this expedition, and he recruited at Milan, Bologna, and Ferrara. As for the rulers, he tried through messengers to draw Francesco Gonzaga, marquis of Mantua, from loyalty to the Venetians by offering huge stipends, but Gonzaga replied that he had ties of the greatest understanding with the Venetian Senate and that, since the terms had been accepted, he would maintain the pledge of service.[25]

9. At last, contrary to the prediction of almost everyone, the French King successfully traversed the passes of the Alps and arrived at Asti on 11 September 1494; there a very acute fever laid hold of him because of a change in the weather, and he developed the pustules which the French call night-blains and we call variola.[26] At length he recovered his health and came to Pavia, where he divided his forces, sending one part ahead into Romagna and the other in the direction of Florence. A large sum of money was received from Lodovico Sforza. Then Piero de' Medici offered towns in order to obtain the favor of the King,[27] who took them over and strengthened them with garrisons and then hurried on to Lucca [28] and next to Pisa,[29] where the citizens welcomed him into the city. But King Alfonso sent his son Ferdinand, duke of Calabria, ahead to Cesena [30] to meet the troops of the enemy which Duke Ercole had assembled in the territory around Ferrara; the result

alia via Gallus has copias revocavit Florentiamque contendit.

10. Magnitudo namque instantis belli universam Europam concitaverat, quum facile Pontificis Ferdinandi et Florentinorum vires inter tantas viarum praesertim angustias Gallorum copiis resistere posse existimarent [54] in bienniumque bellum protrahi non dubitarent.[55] His diebus Ioannes Galeacius Maria Mediolanensis dux Ticini moritur. Ludovicus patruus imperium accipit rogantibus optimatibus urbis, quem paulo post Maximilianus Imperator privilegio confirmavit. Appropinquante Gallorum Rege Florentinorum res publica a primatibus urbis Petro Medice ac Laurentino destituta pugnae discrimen mutata sententia subire noluit et oblatas a Gallo conditiones accepit, et Carolum Regem cives patrem patriae salutarunt et CXX [56] millia aureorum obtulerunt et in urbem ovantem acceperunt. Hic Rex arbiter paucos post dies Pisas libertate donavit invitis Florentinis. Horum legati qui Venetiis erant accepta tantae rei publicae clade sponte missionem accepere, Pontificis vero et Alphonsi Regis ad ultima permansere.[57]

11. In Pontificis igitur [58] atque Alphonsi Regis virtute spes omnis relicta est, unde robur omne in Urbem receptum est. Tum Hostia oppidum obsesso flumine Romam fame premebat Sancti Petri in Vinculis cardinale Pontificis hoste, unde ad rerum omnium inopiam Romani pervenere. Pontifex vero, cum antea Romanorum numero et virtute fretus securus esse videretur, appropinquante Gallorum rege adeo territus est ut vi illa ac magnitudine animi elanguescente ad oblatas Regis quoque per legatos conditiones protinus descenderet. Tum populus omnis ex summa tristitia in plausum ac laetitiam convertitur. Pontifex invitus regias copias quae in auxilium venerant [59] extra urbem excludit. Ipse vero in arcem se contulit formidinis plenus. Carolus Calendis Ianuariis cum universo exercitu Romae exceptus in Palatio Divi Marci sedem [60] locavit ubi cum Pontifice compositis rebus inter mutuos complexus Maclodiensem unum ex baronibus Regi

---

[54] extimarent E    [55] dubitaret F    [56] 12,000 EF    [57] Pontificis—permansere om. EF    [58] vero EF    [59] non erant B    [60] se sedem A, sedem A by MS. correction

was that the Frenchman even with forces divided easily defeated him. Accordingly, since a second route had been opened, the Frenchman recalled these troops and proceeded to Florence.

10. The magnitude of the impending war had indeed aroused all Europe, since men thought that the troops of the Pope, of Ferdinand, and of the Florentines could easily withstand the forces of the French especially at the many defiles on the roads and did not doubt that the war could be drawn out for two years. At this time Giangaleazzo Maria, duke of Milan, died at Pavia.[31] His uncle Lodovico assumed the rule at the request of the aristocrats of the city, and a little later the Emperor Maximilian confirmed this appointment with a privilege.[32] As the King of the French approached, the republic of the Florentines, since it had been abandoned by the heads of the city, Piero and Lorenzo de' Medici, changed its opinion, decided against undergoing the risk of battle, and agreed to the terms offered by the Frenchman. The citizens even greeted King Charles as father of their country, presented him with one hundred and twenty thousand pieces of gold, and welcomed him joyfully into the city.[33] Here a few days later the King as arbiter bestowed freedom upon Pisa against the will of the Florentines, and when their envoys, who were at Venice, heard of this disaster to the great republic, they terminated their duties of their own accord, but the envoys of the Pope and of King Alfonso remained to the end.

11. Accordingly all surviving hope was anchored in the courage of the Pope and of King Alfonso, and all strength was concentrated in Rome. At that time Rome was held in the grip of hunger by the town of Ostia, for the river was blockaded because the Cardinal of San Pietro in Vincoli was an enemy of the Pope, and the result was that the Romans suffered scarcity of all things.[34] But the Pope, even though he had earlier thought himself safe because he relied on the numbers and courage of the Romans, now as the King of the French approached was so terrified that the usual strength and greatness of his spirit weakened and he also forthwith yielded to the terms which were offered by the King through envoys. Thereupon all the people turned from the very depths of woe to applause and joy. The Pope against his will sent outside the city the royal forces [35] which had come to his assistance, and he himself, filled with fear, took refuge in his stronghold.[36] Charles entered Rome on the first day of January [37] with his entire army and established quarters in the Palace of San Marco; [38] there, after having settled affairs with the Pope amid mutual demonstrations of affection, he obtained the cardinalate for the Bishop of Saint-Malo, one of his

charissimum mentitae amicitiae auctorem cardinalem designat.

12. Subiugata deinde rerum quondam [61] domina Roma quinto Calendas Februarias rex Gallus Roma [62] discessit et invito Pontifice Zizimum imperatoris Turcarum fratrem, virum maximae virtutis et strenui animi, ut omnia in Turcas moliri videretur secum abstulit. Eius causa Pontifex XL [63] millia nummum aureorum singulis annis data taxatione a fratre accipiebat,[64] traduntque eam ob causam hactenus Turcas extra Italiam coercitos fuisse.

13. His successibus commoti Hispaniae reges naves XL [65] Siciliae insulae praesidio miserunt rerum eventum expectantes. Hyems eo tempore adeo secunda adeo prospera Regi fuit ut de stativis [66] Rex non cogitaret; teporarium [67] enim ver vel autumnus videbatur [68] clemens. Eius temporis clementiam sine nive sine pluvia a Deo [69] opportune sibi dari iactabat. Per hyberna enim castra metari Gallis [70] perquam facile erat, Italis insuetis praesertim difficillimum. His commodis invitatus Rex in regnum Neapolitanum dirigere exercitum statuit tanto successu laetus. Sed insidias Pontificis metuens Caesarem cardinalem Valentianum obsidem et urbes Neapolitano regno proximas [71] iam acceperat. Interea Alphonsus Rex omnibus destitutus cognito etiam perenni populorum odio salutis viam prosperam sibi invenisse ratus deposito diademate regno sponte se abdicavit filioque Ferdinando a populo dilecto imperium dedit, qui studiis rei militaris disciplina clementia pietate iustitia liberalitate [72] qui [73] nec manus quidem sanguine imbuisset [74] ardentius colebatur.

14. Hic quietum regnum polliceri proscriptis parcere et iniurias omnes privatas et publicas abolere coepit. Milites quoque recognoscit, urbes oppidaque novis firmat praesidiis. At pater relicto regno omnem supellectilem thesaurumque secum abstulit et Siciliam versus navigavit. At Gallus Pontificis urbes Terracinam Carpentum Campaniam et maritimas oras occupavit diruitque, Iacobum Comitem ac Fundorum Principem sedibus expulit. Ferdinandus adventante hoste pugnam protrahere decrevit et angustias tantum locorum tueri sibi proposuit Nicolao Ursino Petiliano comite imperatore suo et Ioanne Iacobo

---

[61] q. A, -que B, om. EF    [62] Romam F    [63] XXI EF    [64] accepit EF
[65] XVI EF    [66] statutis A    [67] temporarium AEF, teporarium A by MS. correction    [68] videbantur EF    [69] adeo AEF, a deo A by MS. correction
[70] Galli F    [71] proximos EF    [72] excellebat add. EF    [73] om. EF
[74] imbuisse EF

barons who was very dear to him and had promoted the pretended friendship.

12. And now that he had subdued the city which was once mistress of the world, the French King left Rome on 28 January, and in order that he might seem in everything to be making plans against the Turks he took with him, though the Pope did not approve, Zizim, brother of the Sultan of the Turks,[39] a man possessed of very great courage and a vigorous mind. Because of him the Pope was receiving from the brother forty thousand pieces of gold a year in fulfillment of a contract,[40] and for this reason, it is generally believed, the Turks had thus far been kept outside Italy.

13. Aroused by these events the rulers of Spain sent forty ships to defend the island of Sicily [41] and awaited the outcome of affairs. The winter that year was so favorable and propitious for the King that he gave no thought to fixed quarters; indeed it seemed like a gentle spring or a mild autumn, and he boasted that this good weather, without snow and without rain, was fitly given to him by God. For the French, in fact, it was very easy to pitch camp in winter, but for the Italians, who were quite unaccustomed to it, it was extremely hard.[42] The King, tempted by these favorable conditions and rejoicing in such great success, decided to direct his army into the kingdom of Naples. But because he feared treachery on the part of the Pope he had already taken as hostage Cesare, cardinal of Valencia,[43] together with the cities which were nearest to Neapolitan territory. King Alfonso, meanwhile, abandoned by all and recognizing also the everlasting hatred of the populace,[44] thought to find a favorable way of safety for himself by laying down his crown, and so of his own accord he abdicated his power [45] and gave the rule to his son Ferdinand, who was beloved of the people and esteemed for his learning, knowledge of military tactics, mercy, devotion to duty, sense of justice, and generosity, and the more warmly because he had not dipped his hands in blood.

14. Ferdinand began his reign by promising a quiet rule, sparing the proscribed, and abolishing all public and private outrages. In addition he reviewed the soldiers and strengthened the cities and towns with new guards. But his father on abdicating carried off with him all the royal goods and the treasury and sailed toward Sicily. The Frenchman seized the cities of the Pope, Terracina and Carpineto; [46] he invaded and devastated Campania and the strip along the seacoast and drove from their territory Jacopo Conti and the Count of Fondi.[47] As the enemy drew near Ferdinand decided to prolong the struggle and proposed to defend only the narrow passes: in this he was following the advice of his general Niccolò Orsini, count of Pitigliano, and his com-

Triulcio duce suadentibus ne pugnando fortunae imperium commit-
teret, sed cunctando Gallorum Regem ad rerum inopiam deinde
famem perniciosam cum universo exercitu perduceret. Ita enim
evenit, neque opinio fefellit. Nam annonae caritas deinde fames protinus in Gallicis castris secuta est, et equis pro pabulo vitium sar-
menta [75] erant.

15. In tanto rerum discrimine Gallus modum invenit in celeritate
et regnum Neapolitanum subito milite ingreditur et Aquilam [76]
copiarum parte praemissa cives sponte sese dediderunt, deinde quaedam oppida in deditionem accepit, alia quae portas praecluserant
protinus diripuit. Campani Regem Gallorum laeti excipiunt. Ferdinandus vero, qui Neapolim confugerat, cognito populorum odio amisso
levi momento regno collectis pariter impedimentis praesidiis arcibus
duabus firmatis triremes conscendit et in Prochytam insulam VII
triremibus omni cum familia se recepit.

16. Carolus his auditis relicto Capuae praesidio Neapolim contendit,
quem cives ingenti plausu suscipiunt et de regno adepto in sequentes
dies triumphum amplissimum pollicentur. Arcem Novam paucis
diebus cepit, at In Ovo sitam scopulo paulo post ad conditiones
compulit. Hinc Caieta munitissima urbe accepta arcem expugnavit.
Nicolaum Ursinum comitem Petilianum et Ioannem Iacobum Triulcium, qui [77] ad Nolanos confugerant, captivos habuit. Sed hunc ob
res Mediolanenses statim liberavit, illum sub custodiis tenuit. Taren-
tum Salernum usque ad extrema Italiae omnia in eo successu sibi XIII
diebus vendicavit. Quaedam maritimae urbes in fide Ferdinandi
permansere. Legati Veneti Antonius Lauredanus et Dominicus Trivisanus equites tantarum rerum magnitudine attoniti Regem parva
manu ea omnia paucis diebus confecisse admirabantur Fortunam
ipsam Regi ancillam factam esse putantes paucisque diebus discessere.

17. Hac [78] victoria fama incredibili universam Europam ad Asiam
usque concitaverat Gallus, unde Baisetus Turcarum imperator ac
Egypti deinde Rex de bello iam cogitare caeperunt. Iam littora Turcae
et insulas in continentem fugientes destituerant. Chalcidis praefectus
in Euboea suos omnes [79] Constantinopolim miserat. His diebus Zizi-
mus Baiseti frater indiligentia Regis rheumatismo moritur non parva

---

[75] ramenta EF     [76] aliqua EF     [77] quod EF     [78] Haec B
[79] in add. EF

mander Gian Giacomo Trivulzio not to entrust his power to fortune in
an open battle, but by delaying the King of the French to reduce him
and his entire army first to scarcity of supplies and then to ruinous
hunger; so it turned out, and they were not mistaken in their opinion.
For first a dearth of grain and then in a short time actual famine was
visited upon the French camp,[48] and grape branches became the fodder of the horses.

15. At so great a crisis of affairs the Frenchman found a way out in
speed; he quickly entered the kingdom of Naples with his army and
sent on part of his forces to L'Aquila, where the citizens voluntarily
surrendered.[49] He then accepted additional towns in surrender and
straightway ravaged others which had shut their gates. The Campa-
nians welcomed the King of the French joyfully. But Ferdinand, who
had taken refuge in Naples, recognizing the hatred of the populace and
realizing that in a fleeting moment the kingdom had been lost, likewise
gathered his goods together, strengthened the two citadels with garrisons, and then boarded ship and with seven triremes sailed with his
entire household to the island of Procida.[50]

16. On hearing this news Charles left a garrison at Capua [51] and proceeded to Naples, whose citizens greeted him with thunderous applause and in the days which followed promised him a glorious triumph
for his acquisition of the kingdom.[52] In a few days he took the Castel
Nuovo and a little later reduced to terms the Castel dell'Ovo, set on
a crag. Thereupon, having received in surrender the very well fortified
city of Gaeta,[53] he stormed its citadel. He took prisoner Niccolò Orsini,
count of Pitigliano, and Gian Giacomo Trivulzio, who had fled for refuge to the people of Nola.[54] But Trivulzio, because of his Milanese
connections, he straightway released; Orsini he continued to keep
under guard. Within thirteen days he laid claim in his advance to
Taranto,[55] Salerno, and all the territory right up to the very limits of
Italy. Some maritime cities remained loyal to Ferdinand. The Venetian envoys, knights Antonio Loredan and Domenico Trevisan, were
astounded at the magnitude of events and marveled that the King with
a small army had accomplished all this in a few days; opining that
Fortune herself had been the handmaid of the King, they departed
after a short time.[56]

17. By this victory the Frenchman had stirred with his incredible
reputation all of Europe right up to Asia, where Bajazet, sultan of the
Turks, and then the Sultan of Egypt now began to reflect upon war.
Already the Turks had abandoned the shores and the islands and fled
to the mainland. The ruler of Chalcis in Euboea had sent all his people
to Constantinople. During this period Zizim ,brother of Bajazet, died [57]

rei Christianae iactura. Gallus superbia tumens intermortuam in toto fere orbe militarem disciplinam arbitratus praecipuum ex praesentibus adiudicavit magis movendam esse Fortunam quam expectandam. Post tantam victoriam a Pontifice per legatos diadema regni Neapolitani petiit censum quotannis persoluturus, quod cum Pontifex cum universo concilio recusasset de Hierosolyma nihil cogitans de Italiae imperio deque Pontificis statu mutando in animo volvere coepit.

18. Interea milites per Campaniam Apuliam Calabriam Brutiumque distributis magistratibus securi vagabantur, domos privatas diripiebant, fana spoliabant, nec a sacris virginibus abstinebat dira libido. Principales foeminae stupra perpessae corporum ludibria deflebant. Itaque nulla in parte cessavit luxuria ebrietasque atque rapinae quae invisum Gallorum nomen protinus effecerunt.[80] Incolae magna ex parte mutata sententia iam pro Ferdinando vota nuncupare coeperunt, vulgata oppidi Montisfortini truculenta caede ac Sancti Ioannis Caietae item ac Tuscanensis civitatis eversione.

19. His cognitis Alexander Pontifex sibi timens deposita spe quam in Romana turba rei militaris experte posuerat Urbe extrema inopia laborante cognito Caroli Regis odio ac Valentiani Cardinalis fuga instantem ruinam reformidans incerta consilia volvebat. Statuit convocato patrum concilio de summa rerum deliberare, in quo haec pauca elocutum accepimus: "Videtis," inquit, "filii,[81] Carolum [82] Gallorum Regem [83] Italiae magnam partem subegisse et eam armis virisque implevisse. A pontificia sede oppida urbesque ademisse [84] iam penitus Ecclesiam eversurum videmus; multos enim proditores, multos sedis apostolicae hostes cernitis. Nemo nostrum in reditu tutus erit; hinc profecto mea sententia discedendum est."

20. His dictis confusae voces fuere aliis alia iudicantibus. Tandem visum est in tanto rerum praesentium discrimine nutantes Italiae res principum foedere posse contineri, ad id Maximilianum Romanorum [85] regem et Hispaniae reges Senatum Venetum ac Mediolanensem princi-

---

[80] fecerunt EF      [81] om. EF      [82] om. EF      [83] Carolum add. EF
[84] emisse EF      [85] Romanum B

as the result of a cold because of the negligence of the King, and his loss was no small one to the Christian cause. The French King, swelling with pride and believing military prowess extinct in almost the entire world, judged that under the circumstances he ought to set Fortune in motion rather than await her. After so great a victory he requested of the Pope through envoys the crown of the Neapolitan kingdom, with the promise that he would send his tribute every year,[58] and when the Pope along with his entire college had refused, Charles stopped thinking about Jerusalem and began to turn over in his mind the transformation of the entire realm of Italy and of the papal position.

18. Meanwhile his soldiers, since the civil magistrates had been dispersed, were wandering at will through Campania, Puglia, Calabria, and the Abruzzi,[59] ravaging private homes, despoiling churches, and abstaining not even from nuns in their terrible lust. Eminent women who were raped bewailed the mockery shown their bodies.[60] And so on no side was there any cessation of the excesses, the drunkenness, and the plundering which straightway made the name of the French a hated one. The natives in large part soon changed their opinion and began to offer vows for Ferdinand.[61] At the same time came the report of a cruel massacre in the towns of Montefortino [62] and Monte San Giovanni [63] and the fall of Gaeta and Ferentino.

19. On learning of these matters Pope Alexander, fearing [64] for himself, abandoned the hope which he had placed in the Roman troops, who were devoid of military experience; the city was suffering extreme want, he was aware of the hatred of King Charles and knew of the flight of the Cardinal of Valencia, and in dread of approaching ruin he began to ponder dubious plans. He decided to call a consistory of the cardinals and deliberate on the crisis, and at the consistory I understand that he made the following brief remarks: "You see, my sons," he said, "that Charles, king of the French, has subdued a great part of Italy and filled her with arms and men. We observe that he has snatched towns and cities from the pontifical domain, and it is clear that he will soon overthrow the Church utterly, for you realize that there are many traitors and many enemies of the apostolic foundation. No one of us will be safe on his return, wherefore, in my opinion, we must certainly depart." [65]

20. At these words there were confused utterances, some men pronouncing one judgment and others another. At length it seemed that in so great a crisis of events the tottering affairs of Italy could be supported by a league of princes and that Maximilian, who was king of the Romans, the rulers of Spain, the Venetian Senate, and Lodovico

pem Ludovicum Sphortiam idoneos esse. Missis igitur legatis nova foedera inter hos principes circiter Calendas Aprilis icta sunt, ad quae Dux Mediolanensis invitus trahi videbatur. Eum tamen Sebastianus Baduarius eques et orator clarissimus Veneti Senatus legatus mortuo Benedicto Trivisano collega adeo constanter stabilivit ut imperium omne pro Italiae et Ecclesiae salute facile expositurus esset.

21. Eo tempore fama huius victoriam iam [86] Imperatoris Turcarum aures impleverat, qui ad Senatum Venetum legatum misit ut in comune rebus consuleret. Is pollicitus est exercitum et classem ingentem sibi magis quam Senatui Veneto timens. In Senatum supervenerat Philippus Argentonus regius legatus, qui cum audiret ut fit Turcarum superbas minas illos Regem suum in Italia [87] malle experiri quam in Graecia vel Thessalia respondit. Hic sequentibus diebus patefacto principum foedere ita supra [88] modum excanduit ut quae in Senatu a Principe dicerentur non perciperet, respondit tandem [89] audito novo foedere impium sibi videri Regem suum periculose in extrema Italiae [90] occludi. Ad quem Princeps foederis summam [91] his paucis aperuit: "Scito hanc societatem non in Regis tui perniciem excogitatam sed pro Ecclesiae salute ac Italiae tutela initam esse."

22. His acceptis solicitudinis plenus discessit et Regi per nuncios omnia significavit, qui simulato [92] metu sibi ampliora foedera superesse iactabat, verum qua ratione liberum in Galliam recessum habere posset turbatus in contionem processit, in qua discriminis ratio habita est et qua posset [93] via Genuensium studia a fide Ludovici Ducis evocare perquisivit. Verum Pontificem ad obsequia facile revocare posse sperabat; alioqui obiectis criminibus nec purgatis convocato patrum concilio a pontificia sede perturbaret vel invitum in Galliam duceret. Urgebat instantis pudoris dolor quod rex summus devictis regibus ac subito amisso regno praeceps discedere cogeretur. Decrevit tandem relictis in Apulia et universo regno praesidiis subitis itineribus magna copiarum parte Romam contendere, ut rei festinatione socii novi foederis opportune militem cogere non possent.[94] Haec cum intellexisset Pontifex

---

[86] om. EF  [87] Italiam B  [88] super F  [89] tamen B  [90] Italia EF  [91] summa EF  [92] dissimulato EF  [93] nesciens add. EF  [94] posset B

Sforza, duke of Milan, were suitable members for this. Accordingly envoys were sent and a new compact was made between these princes on about 1 April,[66] to which the Duke of Milan was a party apparently against his will. Nevertheless the knight Sebastiano Badoer, a very brilliant orator and ambassador of the Venetian Senate on the death of his colleague Benedetto Trevisan,[67] steadied him so firmly that he was fully ready to risk his entire realm for the safety of Italy and the Church.

21. At that time the renown of this victory had already filled the ears of the Sultan of the Turks, who sent an envoy to the Venetian Senate to consider affairs for the common good.[68] He promised an army and a large fleet, fearing more for himself than for the Venetian Senate. Philippe of Argenton, the royal ambassador,[69] had come to the Senate, and when he heard, as it happened, the haughty threats of the Turks, he replied that they preferred to test his King in Italy rather than in Greece or Thessaly. When in the days which followed the league of the princes was disclosed, he became so immoderately enraged that he did not take in what the Doge was saying in the Senate, but when at length he did hear about the new compact, he replied that to him it seemed wicked for his King to be dangerously barred at the confines of Italy. The Doge revealed the substance of the league to him in these few words: "Know that this league was not devised for the destruction of your King but for the safety of the Church and the defense of Italy." [70]

22. On hearing this Argenton departed filled with anxiety and notified the King of everything by messengers. And the King, concealing his fear, boasted that stronger treaties remained to him, but, since he was disturbed as to how he might have an unrestricted withdrawal back to France, he called a meeting in which the matter of danger was considered and he searched for a way in which he might lure the inclinations of the people of Genoa away from their devotion to Duke Lodovico. He hoped, however, that he could readily recall the Pope to compliance; otherwise, on the ground of faults committed and not atoned for, he thought that he might call a consistory of the cardinals and remove him from the pontifical throne [71] or take him against his will into France. He was beset by the anguish of the threatening disgrace, that the greatest of kings, after defeating other kings, should suddenly lose his power and be compelled to depart in haste. He decided at length to leave garrisons behind in Puglia and over the entire land [72] and to hurry to Rome in forced marches with a large portion of his troops, so that because of the very speed of the undertaking the allies in the new league would be unable to gather their soldiers to-

cum universo concilio V Calendas Iunias Roma egressus Hieronymo Georgio equite Veneto legato suadente militibus quos Venetus Senatus ad eius tutelam paulo ante miserat circumseptus [95] in Urbem Veterem primum secessit. Deinde Perusia decreverat Anconam adire et Venetias postremo navigare si opus fuisset.

23. Rex Gallus interea ad Calendas Iunias Romam venit. Amissa opportunitate frustratus intacta Roma Senas venit et a factiosis civibus in urbem exceptus est et arcem occupavit. Pisas deinde venit,[96] ubi Genuenses a fide Ludovici Ducis et quasdam Transpadanas urbes avertere conatus est ut liberam abeundi potestatem haberet. Quod cum impetrare nequiret viam saltem sibi ferro aperiendam esse proposuit. Spem dabat caeleritatis fiducia ac segnior ut sperabat [97] sociorum expeditio. Tum Auriliensem Ducem qui Haste [98] Alpium fauces custodiebat excitavit ut iure haereditario res Mediolanenses turbaret, opem protinus laturus. Is Novarienses quosdam optimates ut in Ludovicum conspirarent effecit. Forte Mediolanenses milites ad custodiendos ditionis suae terminos missi fuerant; hos Auriliensis Dux intercepit protinusque in urbem Novariam IIII Idus Iunias exceptus est a civibus quos clandestinis consiliis sibi conciliaverat. Cum eo equites D armati erant, peditum VIII millia, paucisque diebus arcem male munitam occupavit.

24. Pavor ingens Ludovicum Ducem ne imperium subito amitteret attonitum animoque haerentem reddidit, qui cum haec tristia accepisset ex arce summa ad haedes [99] Hieronymi Leonis legati Veneti descendit paucis comitantibus amotisque arbitris allocutus est orans ut titubanti imperio nutantibusque rebus subveniret, Novariam urbem ditissimam misere amissam esse, utque Senatui rem ordine [100] significaret statumque illi commendaret obsecravit. Legatus vero omnia se facturum promisit, illum semper Veneto Senatui carissimum fuisse nec socia arma pro eius salute defutura idque propediem re ipsa cogniturum.

25. Unde Venetus Senatus cognito sociorum discrimine pacis alioqui studiosissimus a Pontifice et Ludovico Duce ad redimenda loca quae amiserant ad arma capessenda sociali iure in dies magis atque magis

---

[95] circumspectus F      [96] interea Senas venit et a factiosis civibus in urbem exceptus (receptus EF) est et arcem occupavit. Deinde ad Calendas Iunias Romam venit. Amissa opportunitate frustratus intacta Roma Pisas venit AEF, as above A by MS. correction B (deinde Pisas)      [97] sperabant B      [98] om. EF      [99] aedes BEF      [100] ordinem F

gether in time. When the Pope realized this, he went out from Rome on 28 May with his entire consistory. On the advice of the knight Geronimo Giorgio, who was Venetian envoy,[73] he withdrew first to Orvieto, accompanied by the soldiers whom the Venetian Senate had sent a little while before for his protection.[74] Then from Perugia he had decided to go to Ancona and to sail finally to Venice if necessary.[75]

23. The French King meanwhile came to Rome on 1 June;[76] frustrated there by the lost opportunity he left Rome unharmed and came to Siena, where he was welcomed into the city by seditious citizens and took possession of the stronghold.[77] He then came to Pisa,[78] where he tried to turn the people of Genoa and certain cities beyond the Po from their loyalty to Duke Lodovico in order that he might have unimpeded opportunity for departure. When he was unable to accomplish his purpose he determined that he had to open a way at least by the sword. His trust in his own speed, and, as he anticipated, the slower campaign of the allies gave him hope. He next incited the Duke of Orléans,[79] who was at Asti guarding the passes of the Alps, to disturb the Milanese situation by hereditary claims, saying that he would bring assistance at once. The Duke got certain nobles of Novara to plot against Lodovico. As it happened, Milanese soldiers had been sent to protect the bounds of their territory; these the Duke of Orléans intercepted, and forthwith on 10 June he was received into the city of Novara by the citizens whom he had won over to his cause by secret measures. With him were five hundred armed horsemen and eight thousand foot soldiers, and in a few days he seized the citadel, which was poorly fortified.[80]

24. A mighty dread of suddenly losing his power made Duke Lodovico frantic and hesitant of mind, and on receiving this bad news[81] he went down from the citadel with a small escort to the house of Geronimo Lioni,[82] the Venetian envoy, dismissed the witnesses, talked with him, and begged him to come to the aid of his faltering rule and tottering circumstances; he declared that he had wretchedly lost the very wealthy city of Novara, and he beseeched him to make an orderly report of these events to the Senate and to commit his affairs to it. The envoy promised that he would do all this and said that Lodovico had always been highly esteemed by the Venetian Senate, that allied arms would not be lacking for his deliverance, and that he would recognize this shortly from events.

25. Thereupon the Venetian Senate, when it had learned of the peril of its allies, though in other respects it was very desirous of peace was more and more incited by the Pope and by Duke Lodovico as the days went by to take up arms according to the compact of the league and

excitatur. Constitutionibus enim foederis pro sociorum auxiliis quisque proportione virium et [101] fortunae taxatus fuerat. Subito igitur Graecos milites stratiotas MCC navibus longis onerariis iussit acciri, ex quibus [102] DC [103] Bernardo Contareno duci designat.[104] Is protinus Novariam contendit [105] cum Galeatio Severinate omnium Mediolanensium copiarum praefecto cum DCC equitibus armatis Teutonum peditum VIII milibus, et Auriliensem Ducem obsidione premere coeperunt.

26. In Italia nihilominus Senatus militem cogere coepit, et XIIII Calendas Iunias,[106] ut Diariorum nostrorum rationem exordiar, Melchiorem Trivisanum exercitus legatum delegit. Interea Carolus praeclusis undique viis maris pericula subire nolens eventum belli ancipitem tentare maluit et Pontremolum subito milite venit. Id oppidum sub Appennino est angustiasque montium praecludit quibus Parmam itur, idque captum quod sine ullo fere [107] praesidio esset [108] protinus cremavit. In hac re Ludovicum Mediolanensium Duce non probarunt, qui in tanta rerum expectatione ita oppidum misere deseruerit.[109]

27. Tum Melchior Trivisanus IIII Calendas Iunias Patavium venit, ubi milites qui in stativis erant collegit. Idem mira celeritate Veronae Brixiaeque effecit. Interea Senatus Venetus suadente Augustino Barbadico Principe Francisco Gonzaga Mantuano marchioni socio Rhodulpho patruo praefecturam exercitus designavit, qui [110] summam rei cum legatis gubernaret. Dum hi militiae se accingunt et milites cogunt Melchior Trivisanus consilio Comitis Rhanucii Phrenesii [111] ac aliorum ducum de belli apparatu deliberavit. De numero equitum ac peditum deque tormentorum ratione ac numero quae bigis vehi possent recensere coeperunt. VI Idus Iunias equitibus levis armaturae stratiotis qui pridem DC numero Venetias venerant longis navibus advectis [112] Petrus Duodus praeficitur. Melchior Trivisanus legatus a Senatu petiit ut longiora ad se tormenta quae serpentinas, vulgus passavolantes, vocant XII mitterentur, quibus Gallus uti maxime solet. IIII Idus nunciatum est Germanorum liberas quasdam civitates quae Bovis [113] Sociae dicuntur in Mediolanensem Ducem arma movisse Regis Gallorum causa, ad quem furorem sedandum praemissae pecuniae fuere.

---

[101] om. B    [102] contendit ad. B    [103] ducenta EF    [104] signat EF
[105] om. B    [106] Iulias ABEF    [107] om. F    [108] quod—esset om. B
[109] deseruit EF    [110] quae B    [111] Pharmesii E Pharnesii F    [112] advecti EF    [113] nobis EF

to win back the places which they had lost. For by the provisions of the league each state had been appraised according to its strength and wealth for the sake of assisting its allies. Accordingly the Senate straightway ordered twelve hundred Greek soldiers, called stratiotes, to be fetched in warships and transports, out of whom it assigned six hundred to the command of Bernardo Contarini.[83] He immediately pressed on to Novara with Galeazzo Sanseverino, leader of all the Milanese forces, together with seven hundred armed horsemen and eight thousand Teutonic foot soldiers, and they began to blockade the Duke of Orléans.

26. In Italy no less the Senate began to assemble soldiers, and on 18 May, to begin the register of my *Diaria*, it appointed Melchiorre Trevisan proveditor of the army.[84] Meanwhile Charles, since routes by land were closed to him on all sides and since he was unwilling to risk the dangers of going by sea, preferred to try the doubtful expedient of war and came directly with his army to Pontremoli.[85] That town is in the foothills of the Apennines and controls the pass through those mountains in the direction of Parma, and when he had captured it (for it was almost without defense) he immediately burned it. At this point opinion turned against Lodovico, duke of Milan, because at such a crisis he had so wretchedly abandoned the town.

27. Then Melchiorre Trevisan came on 29 May to Padua,[86] where he assembled the soldiers who were in quarters. He did the same thing with wondrous speed at Verona and Brescia. Meanwhile the Venetian Senate on the advice of Doge Agostino Barbarigo put Francesco Gonzaga, marquis of Mantua, in charge of its army [87] and gave him as associate his uncle Rodolfo; he was to manage the whole matter together with the proveditors. While these were preparing for the campaign and assembling the soldiers, Melchiorre Trevisan on the advice of Count Ranuccio Farnese and the other leaders took counsel on the equipment for war, and they began to reckon on the number of horsemen and foot soldiers and the type and number of hurling machines which could be transported in two-horse wagons. On 8 June Pietro Duodo was put in command of the light-armed and mounted stratiotes,[88] six hundred of whom had already arrived at Venice in warships. The proveditor Melchiorre Trevisan asked the Senate to provide him with twelve longer engines which are called serpentines and commonly *passavolanti;* the Frenchman was in the habit of using these especially. On 10 June it was reported that certain free cities of the Germans which are called Allies of the Ox had taken up arms against the Duke of Milan on behalf of the King of the French; money was sent on to quiet this madness.

28. Idibus Iuniis legatus Venetus collectis undique magna ex parte militibus ad Olium flumen pervenit Senigaeque constitit expectaturus Senatus imperia. Interea Franciscus Gonzaga Mantua cum delectis equitibus peditibusque Rhodulpho patruo socio Senigam contendit, ubi legatus XI Calendas Iulias constructo ponte Olium flumen superat. Tum praefectus copiarum equites mille [114] armatos peditum X millia collecta recensuit. Deinde castrorum praetores creavit VI qui ius militi dicerent alimentisque pretia darent, Phaebum Mantuanum Comitem Aloisium Avogarium Comitem Ioannem Franciscum Gambariensem Marcum Martinengum Tutium Constantinum Iulianum Codonoliensem, et copias demum traiecit X Calendas Padum constructo ponte transit. VIII Calendas per agrum Parmensem ad Tarri pontem IIII millia passuum a Parma urbe distantem pervenere ibique castra locarunt copias militum Mediolanensium expectantes duce Comite Ioanne Francisco Acaiazano. Huc Lucas Pisanus alter legatus a Veneto Senatu designatus venit. Convenerant Italae [115] acies CXL [116] peditum XII millia.

29. Quinto Calendas vallem versus qua Gallus transiturus esset castra moverunt [117] in Opianoque [118] vico consederunt a Foronovo circiter III millia passuum a Parma VIII millia, ubi vix fides de adventu Gallorum habebatur. Itaque IIII Kalendas speculatores praemissos explorare iubent, qui ex incolis Gallorum copias adventare acceperunt numerumque hostium circiter XX millia per Appenninas valles duci alii XV millia [119] duntaxat significarunt, nam inutilis plebs calones lixae foeminarum grex impedimentorum ingens numerus maiores hostium copias ostentabat. Latinorum vero numerum suo recensebimus loco adventantibus singulis diebus militibus.

30. Iamque Carolus Rex ad vallis extremas angustias pervenit supraque montis vertice II millia passuum a Foronovo castra metatus est. Interea Senatus Venetus, qui a rebus divinis semper exordium sumere consuevit, publicas supplicationes pro pugna ineunda decrevit, nec cessarunt ab oraculis pia sanctorum virorum vota ac sacrarum virginum apud Deum deprecationes quibus Deus Optimus Maximus Venetum Senatum Divo Marco praeside procurante servaret. Post haec variae in Senatu sententiae fuere. Alii in pugna spem posuerant

---

[114] milites B     [115] Italiae B     [116] XI EF     [117] moverant E     [118] Opinianoque EF     [119] per—millia om. F

28. On 13 June the Venetian proveditor, after having assembled his soldiers in large part from all sides, arrived at the river Oglio and halted at Seniga to await the commands of the Senate. Meanwhile Francesco Gonzaga proceeded with select horsemen and foot soldiers and in company with his uncle Rodolfo from Mantua to Seniga, where the proveditor on 21 June crossed the Oglio River on the bridge which had been erected there. Then the commander of the forces reviewed the thousand armed horsemen and ten thousand foot soldiers which had been assembled. Next he created six magistrates of the camp who were to sit as judges over the soldiers and set prices on food, and these were Febo of Mantua, Count Luigi Avogadro, Count Gianfrancesco of Gambara, Marco of Martinengo, Tuzio Costanzo, and Giuliano of Codogno.[89] Finally on 22 June [90] he sent his forces across the bridge which had been built over the Po,[91] and on 24 June they arrived by way of the country around Parma at the bridge over the Taro which is four miles distant from the city of Parma.[92] There they pitched camp and awaited the forces of the Milanese under command of Count Giovanni Francesco of Caiazzo. To this spot came Luca Pisani,[93] the other proveditor appointed by the Venetian Senate. Italian battle-ranks to the number of 140 and twelve thousand footmen had come together.

29. On 27 June they moved camp in the direction of the valley through which the Frenchman would pass, and they halted at the village of Oppiano about three miles from Fornovo and eight miles from Parma,[94] where there was scarcely any assurance concerning the arrival of the French. And so on 28 June they sent scouts ahead with orders to reconnoiter, and these learned from the natives that the forces of the French were approaching.[95] Some pointed out that the number of the enemy being led through the valleys of the Apennines was about twenty thousand, others put it at only fifteen thousand, on the ground that a useless group of people—servants, camp-followers, a throng of women—and a great mass of baggage swelled the numbers of the enemy. But at the proper place I shall reckon the number of the Latins,[96] whose soldiers were arriving every day.

30. And now King Charles reached the last pass of the valley [97] and pitched camp beyond the summit of the mountain two miles from Fornovo.[98] In the meantime the Venetian Senate, which was always wont to attend to religion in initiating its undertakings, decreed public supplications for the beginning of the struggle.[99] Saintly men offered their vows continuously at the shrines, and nuns prayed in the churches that Almighty and All Merciful God might defend the Venetian Senate through the mediation of its protector St. Mark. After these religious rites various opinions were aired in the Senate. Some members, influ-

copiarum numero incredibili hostiumque formidine et rerum omnium inopia moti, fugientium tergis inhaerere facile persuadentes praesertim cum auri argentique cupidine milites traherentur, alii pugnam protrahendam esse ostendebant dubiumque belli eventum [120] esse: victum Gallum exercitum duntaxat amittere, victore [121] vero universam Italiam in maximo discrimine versari. Vicit tandem sententia ut fortunae [122] pugna [123] committeretur.

31. Famaque vulgaverat Venetos nullo pacto cum Gallis pugnaturos. Propterea iam Hercules dux Ferrariensis ad Regem litteras dederat [124] quibus Venetos legatos nullam prorsus pugnandi auctoritatem habere a [125] Senatu [126] significavit.[127] Eius fides ac auctoritas apud Regem mira habebatur quandoquidem filium obsidem reliquerat. Optabat [128] hic ut Gallus potito regno totius Italiae arbiter fieret. Gallus nihilominus sollicitudinis plenus Venetorum exercitum incredibili celeritate praeter spem comparatum [129] esse ab exploratoribus audivit ac in dies augere cognovit. Accedebat et militum fames et intra Appenninum exigua pabula. De fuga pace vel induciis cogitare coepit, cum nulla supplementorum certa spes esset: [130] ex Gallia rei festinatio milites [131] prohibebat acciri. Verebatur ne divina iustitia illam ipsam fortunam quae totum orbem polliceri antea videbatur praecipitem ex alto rerum fastigio in imum subito devolveret. Itaque ut solet fieri cum ultimi discriminis tempus appropinquat in solicitudinem solita confidentia, in metum prior audacia, in humilitatem tumens superbia vertitur.

32. Tandem cum pugnandi necessitatem videret in virtute paucorum militum [132] Suevorumque robore ac tormentorum mirabili magisterio omnem spem contulit, spem vultu simulans aspectu admodum laeto similis et in armis promptae audaciae videbatur. Totis tamen viribus omnique consilio pacem vel inducias primum tentare, alioqui belli discrimen subire statuit, cogitavitque praecipue Ioannis Iacobi Triulcii consilio victoriam facile successuram si titubantes Parmenses sibi adiungeret idque facile fieri posse si Venetorum copiae ultra Tarrum castra collocarent. At contra legati Veneti suspecta Parmensium fide Opianum clivum [133] occuparunt Galloque spem ademere ne Parmenses deficere auderent. Cognita hac re Gallus animum alioqui ferocem ad

---

[120] bellique eventum dubium F      [121] victorem EF      [122] fortuna EF
[123] pugnae EF      [124] dedit EF      [125] om. EF      [126] om. EF      [127] significaverat EF      [128] optarat EF      [129] compertum EF      [130] om. F      [131] om. EF      [132] paucorum militum virtute EF      [133] vicum EF

enced by the incredible number of the enemy's forces and their fear of
them and the scarcity of all supplies, had put their hope in battle and
urged that it would be easy to press upon the backs of those who were
fleeing especially since soldiers are lured by love of gold and silver;
others declared that the battle ought to be postponed and that the
outcome of the war was dubious: the Frenchman if defeated lost only
his army, but all Italy was plunged into the greatest peril if he was
victorious. At length the opinion prevailed that the battle should be
entrusted to fate.

31. Already the report had gone around that the Venetians would by
no means fight with the French, and therefore Ercole, duke of Ferrara, had sent a letter to the King in which he declared that the Senate
had as yet not authorized the Venetian proveditors to fight.[100] He had
great credence and authority with the King, since he had left his son
as hostage, and he wanted the Frenchman to acquire the rule and become arbiter over all Italy. Nonetheless the Frenchman was filled with
anxiety when he learned from spies that contrary to expectation the
army of the Venetians had been assembled with tremendous speed and
was increasing in numbers daily. The hunger of his soldiers and the
meager fodder in the Apennines [101] added to his anxiety, and he began
to deliberate on flight, or peace, or a truce, since there was no fixed
hope of reinforcements: the need for haste prevented the summoning
of soldiers from France. He feared that divine justice might suddenly
plunge down from the loftiest heights to the lowest depths that very
fortune which earlier seemed to promise the entire world. And so as
is wont to happen when a time of crisis draws near, his usual assurance
changed to anxiety, his earlier daring to fear, his swollen pride to
humility.

32. At length, when he saw that it was necessary to fight, he put all
his trust in the courage of a few soldiers, in the strength of the Swabians, and in the wonderful mastery of his engines, and feigning hope on
his countenance he seemed like a man entirely happy and of ready
daring in arms. Yet he decided to seek for peace or a truce first with
all his powers and with every device, and otherwise undergo the risk
of war, and he reflected in particular, on the counsel of Gian Giacomo
Trivulzio, that the victory would be readily assured if he brought over
to his side the vacillating citizens of Parma, and that this could easily
be done if the forces of the Venetians pitched their camp beyond the
Taro. But on the contrary the Venetian proveditors, suspecting the
loyalty of the people of Parma, took Oppiano and dashed the hopes of
the Frenchman that the people of Parma might dare to desert. When
the Frenchman heard of this he turned a mind which was fierce in

pacem tentandam magis convertit caduceatoremque ad Venetos legatos Lucam Pisanum et Marchiorem Trivisanum mittit.[134]

33. Hunc patrio nomine araldum [135] vocant Galli. Is intromissus (aderant enim et reliqui duces) pallio lineo [136] cyaneo aureis distincto liliis inquit Regem suum novum exercitum Veneti Senatus vias praeclusisse non parum admirari semperque rei publicae Venetae amicum fuisse non esse qui nesciat nihilque aliud desiderare quam in Galliam abeundi potestatem alimentaque pro exercitu velle aequo pretio.[137] Dimisso in aliud cubiculum caduceatore consultisque rebus eidem rursus intromisso sic legatum alterum locutum esse accepimus, nullam pacis neque [138] induciarum [139] auctoritatem a [140] Senatu [141] sibi esse, verum si pacem velit depositis armis Ludovico Duci socio Novariam et quae Pontificis sunt urbes et oppida vi sublata prius restituat. Caduceator vero respondit Regem suum liberum aditum [142] velle, alias super Italorum cadavera cruentum transiturum. Illi superbia Gallica indignati id actutum velle experiri dixerunt, nec Latinos omnis imbelles ac effoeminatos existimari debere, nec virtutem militarem in Italia penitus esse deletam, nec Florentinos Romanum Pontificem ac Alphonsum Regem vel filium Ferdinandum hostium fortitudine superatos fuisse sed putandum id fortunae ostentatione accidisse.

34. Dimissus caduceator haud imprudens lustrato [143] Venetorum exercitu (ita enim evenire solet) quae audiverat videratque Regi renunciavit, Venetorum copias ingentes adesse qui hylari animo pugnam expectarent quique potius ultima passuri essent quam liberum commeatum praestarent. His auditis IIII Nonas Iulias in summum montis iugum se contulit ex quo ut copias Venetorum ingentes prospexit, ingenti suspirio [144] sese deceptum fuisse acclamavit. At Ioannes Iacobus Triulcius et Franciscus Seccus cum optimatibus Regis animum large exhortati sunt, quod solo regio nomine hostes in fugam verti non dubitaret. Itaque cum pugnandi necessitatem videret belli discrimen subire constituit militesque circiter XL speculatum praemisit.

35. Ab exploratore [145] Gallos primum adventare in Venetorum castris nunciatum est; omnes fere ad capessenda arma prosiliere laeti militesque levis armaturae quos stratiotas vocant circiter DC primi obviam venientibus hostibus cursu [146] citatiores iere. Galli cum duce venientis

---

[134] mittit Trivisanum EF      [135] cocaldum B      [136] linteo EF      [137] comparare add. EF      [138] om. EF      [139] induciarumque EF      [140] om. EF [141] om. EF      [142] abitum EF      [143] a EF      [144] respirio B      [145] ubi add. EF      [146] cursibus EF

other respects rather to suing for peace and sent a herald to the Venetian proveditors, Luca Pisani and Melchiorre Trevisan.

33. This messenger the French call in their own tongue *héraut*. He was admitted (other leaders were present also) wearing a blue linen mantle decorated with gold lilies; he stated that his King was no little astonished that the new army of the Venetian Senate had blockaded the roads: he had always been a friend of the Venetian state; everyone knew this, and he desired nothing else than the right to withdraw into France, and he wanted provisions for his army at a fair price.[102] The herald was conducted to another room and the matter was considered, and I heard that when he was admitted again one proveditor said to him that they had no authority from the Senate to make peace or a truce, but that if he wished peace he should first lay down his arms and return Novara to their ally, Duke Lodovico, and restore the cities and towns of the Pope which he had taken by violence. The herald however replied that his King wanted free passage and that otherwise he would cross in blood over the dead bodies of the Italians. They were enraged at the French arrogance and said that they were willing to test this at once, and that he need not think all Latins unwarlike and effeminate, or that military courage had been blotted out over all Italy, or that the Florentines, and the Roman Pope, and King Alfonso and his son Ferdinand had been conquered by the bravery of the enemy: rather should it be reckoned that this happened by a trick of fortune.

34. The herald, who was no ignorant man, was dismissed after observing the army of the Venetians (this is indeed the usual practice [103]), and he reported to the King what he had seen and heard, that vast forces of the Venetians were at hand awaiting battle with joyful spirits and ready to endure to the end rather than afford free passage. On hearing this, the King went on 4 July to the highest point of the mountain, and when he saw from it the vast forces of the Venetians, he exclaimed with a deep sigh that he had been deceived. But Gian Giacomo Trivulzio and Francesco Secco,[104] together with the nobles, freely encouraged the spirits of the King, saying that he need not doubt that the enemy would be turned to flight by the royal name alone. And so when he saw that he had to fight, he decided to undergo the risk of battle and sent about forty soldiers ahead to reconnoiter.

35. A scout reported that the French were now approaching the camp of the Venetians; almost all the men sprang up eagerly to grasp their arms, and since they were swifter footed light-armed soldiers (who were called stratiotes) to about the number of six hundred were the first to go and meet the approaching enemy. The French with their

exercitus speciem tribuentes anteibant, quos Graeci milites statim ex improviso aggressi sunt; partim in fugam convertere, partim trucidavere. Stratiotae victores prima dimicatione laeti affixis lanceis velitaribus [147] hostium capitibus castra ingressi sunt ac magno plausu excepti. Quidam eorum ne vacuus ex praelio redire [148] videretur obtruncato crudeliter cuiusdam incolae presbyteri capite de quo statim conquestum est militum ordini se adiunxit.[149]

36. Hoc parvae rei successu summae indicabatur [150] eventus. Qui fugerant Regi terrorem incusserunt et cum copias contrahere non posset tertio Nonas in extrema valle constitit et robur omnium virium recensuit. MCCC equites fortissimos armatos delegit, sagittariorum equitum duo millia et septingentos, Suevorum Germanorum peditum sex millia qui bipennibus securibus hastis ac minoribus [151] tormentis armati sunt, pedites sagittarios CCCC, milites levis armaturae ducentos, tormenta quae pilas imanis [152] ponderis ferreas ac plumbeas emittunt XLII magisterio incredibili instructa. In his salutis spem omnem locavit nec diutius famem expectandam sed belli discrimen subire decrevit.

37. Vallis ipsa a Foronovo ex angusto in patentes campos duobus utrinque collibus extenditur in destram et sinistram, illa in Opianum vicum versus, haec in Medesanum Tarro flumine per mediam fere planiciem decurrente. Veneti enim, ut dictum est, in destro clivo consederant Parmensibus obiecti. Gallus vero peracto divino sacrificio sinistram omnium optimatum consilio petere constituit Medesanum versus locum tutissimum. Pridie Nonas Iulias primum milites curare corpora, deinde armari iussit. Per locum enim tutissimum transiturus erat, hoc est, per collis decliva, quae lacunae coenosae voragines Tarrus fluvius riparum altitudo arbusta praeterea virgultaque hostibus praetereuntibus tutissima etiam reddebant, ad quae sine magno incommodo hostes pervenire non poterant, qui si praecipites ac pervicaci animo adoriri velient sua lassitudine dissipati vincerentur. Ea ratio salubris consilii visa est, ut inter eas angustias saltus [153] hostes Venetos tuto opperirentur, qui ubi dimicaturi essent nescio quo animo furore aut praecipite mente planum locum non reddiderant. Alii repentinae et tumultuariae pugnae, alii mercenarii militis inopia, qui nondum in castra venerant, id attribuunt. Erant in hostili exercitu

---

[147] velitariis EF        [148] redire ex praelio EF        [149] addixit EF        [150] judicabatur B        [151] minaribus EF        [152] imani A immani BEF        [153] -que add. EF

leader were in the front and gave the appearance of an advancing army. These the Greek soldiers at once attacked unexpectedly, turning some to flight and killing others. The victorious stratiotes, exulting over the first clash, affixed the heads of the enemy to their light lances, entered camp, and were welcomed with great enthusiasm.[105] One of them, so that he might not be seen returning from battle empty-handed, cruelly cut off the head of a priest of the area, a deed which was straightway lamented, and joined the ranks of the soldiers.[106]

36. This success in a small sally indicated the outcome of the whole affair. Those who had fled struck fear into the King, and since he could not draw in his troops he halted on 5 July at the edge of the valley and reviewed the strength of all his forces. He selected thirteen hundred very brave armed horsemen, two thousand seven hundred arrow-bearing horsemen, six thousand Swabian and German foot soldiers armed with axes, hatchets, spears, and small missiles, four hundred arrow-bearing foot soldiers, two hundred light-armed soldiers,[107] and forty-two artillery pieces constructed with incredible skill which hurl forth iron and lead balls of immense weight. In these he put his entire hope of safety and resolved not to await hunger longer, but to undergo the risk of battle.

37. The valley itself extends beyond Fornovo [108] from a narrow passageway into the open plains with two hills on either side, to the right and to the left; the former direction is toward Oppiano, the latter toward Medesano, and the river Taro flows almost through the very middle of the plain.[109] The Venetians, as we have already said, had taken their position on the right slope opposite the Parmesans. But when mass had been said the French King [110] decided on the advice of all his nobles to keep to the left in the direction of Medesano, a very well-protected place. On 6 July he ordered his soldiers first to care for their bodies and then to arm themselves. He intended indeed to pass through a very well-protected place, that is, along the slopes of the hill, which were rendered fully secure from passage of the enemy also by ditches, muddy depths, the river Taro, the height of the banks, and moreover the shrubs and thickets. Here the enemy could not arrive without great trouble, and even if they wanted to attack precipitately and obstinately they would be overcome and routed by their own weariness. This seemed a wise way of planning, that between these narrow passes they might safely await the Venetian enemy, who through some folly or rashness of mind had not leveled the ground where they were to fight. Some ascribe this lapse to the suddenness and confusion of the battle, others to the scarcity of mercenary soldiers, who had not yet come to the camp. In the opposing

Parmenses agricolae qui locorum rationem noverant. Himber item plurimus campos lubricos et inequitabiles effecerat.[154]

38. Rex interea tria agmina ingentia digerit. Primo Ioannem Iacobum Triulcium praeficit, in quo CCC equites erant ac ducenti leviter armati, peditum hastatorum Germanorum duo millia, quos qui parva tormenta manibus gestabant et bipennibus et securibus armati circuibant. Exiguo intervallo antequitabant soli Comes Nicolaus Petilianus ac [155] Franciscus Seccus (hic ductor ille captivus erat) de rerum eventu inter se colloquentes. Paulo post secundum agmen sequebatur cui Rex ipse [156] praeerat. Sexcentis equitibus constabat; id pugnam vocant Galli altissimo vexillo conspicuum.[157] In eo equites sagitarii erant omnes quos enumeravimus et Germanorum peditum [158] robur fere omnium virium Regis. Postremum agmen pari spatio succedebat in quo quadringenti equites erant, pedites circiter mille. Reliqui hastati pedites agmen unum vel phalangem ingentem constituebant quae non longe ab equitum aciebus incedebat. Tormenta a fronte primum agmen et secundum Tarrum versus tuebantur. Adeo disciplina militari recte composita erant ut nihil ordine excederet neque miles neque pedes vagus aciem exiret.

39. Rex ipse duobus cardinalibus tergo inhaerentibus [159] agmina obequitabat et quanta inter indoctos poterat esse eloquentia (principes enim Galli litteras negligunt) duces omnis ac equites peditesque ad pugnam hortabatur. Nihil infractus ferox [160] Regis animus ununquenque nominatim excitabat. Galli vero, qui mira quadam religione regem suum colunt protinus his vocibus secuti sunt: "Omnes vel viventes vel mortui ultima vi victoriam tibi hodie daturi sumus ante conspectum tuum." Mox iubet Rex ne quis vagus agmen exeat neve quis praedae [161] intentus socios deserat aut gradum referat ad [162] vexillaque respiciant memoresque sint admonuit tantae et divinae victoriae qui Italiae magnam partem sola [163] fama [164] subegissent et inveteratae virtutis qua Occidentis populos domuissent militesque Italos tyrones militumque praefectum iuvenem sine rei militaris experientia cum illis certaturos cognoscerent. Ludovici Ducis milites imbelles, nullam praeterea in fuga spem sed in victoria tantum esse edocuit. "Spolia

---

[154] effecerant B    [155] om. B    [156] om. B    [157] conspicuam EF    [158] agmen add. EF    [159] imminentibus EF    [160] -que add. EF    [161] pede B    [162] om. EF    [163] om. EF    [164] ferme EF

army there were farmers of Parma who knew the terrain. Likewise a great deal of rain had made the fields slippery and impassable for the cavalry.[111]

38. Meanwhile the King drew up three enormous battle groups. He put Gian Giacomo Trivulzio in charge of the first, which consisted of three hundred horsemen, two hundred light-armed soldiers, and two thousand German foot soldiers equipped with spears, who were surrounded by men carrying small hand-machines and armed with axes and hatchets. After a short space Count Niccolò of Pitigliano and Franceso Secco rode alone in front, the first one the prisoner, the second the leader, and they were talking with one another about the outcome of affairs. A little after them followed the second group, of which the King himself was in command. It consisted of six hundred horsemen, and this group the French call the real line of battle; it was conspicuous for its very lofty standard, and in it were all the mounted bowmen which I have enumerated and of the German foot soldiers the flower of almost all the troops of the King. After a like space came the last group, in which were four hundred horsemen and about a thousand foot soldiers. The rest of the spear-bearing foot soldiers made up one line or vast phalanx which advanced not far from the lines of the horsemen. Machines protected the first line from the front and the second toward the Taro, and they were drawn up properly and with such military discipline that nothing was out of the right order and neither soldier nor footman wandered off from the line.

39. The King himself was riding up to the lines with two cardinals close behind, and with as much eloquence as was possible among those who are untaught (for French princes neglect letters) he was urging on all his commanders and horsemen and foot soldiers to the battle. With his bold spirit entirely unbroken he incited each one by name, and the French, who regard their king with a certain wondrous reverence, straightway replied in these words: "All of us, alive or dead from our last effort, promise to bring you victory today before your very eyes." Then the King gave orders that no one should stray from the line or desert his fellows for the sake of booty or turn back; he admonished them all to watch the standards, to remember the great and divine victory by which they had conquered a large part of Italy by their reputation alone and also the old courage by which they had subdued the peoples of the West, and to realize that fighting against them would be Italian soldiers who were mere tyros and a commander who was young and without experience in warfare. He pointed out that the soldiers of Duke Lodovico were unfit for war and that there was moreover no hope in flight but only in victory. "Moreover," he added, "the

item quae vobiscum affertis ex hostibus vestra sunt; omnia auro argentoque fulgent. Venetos nihil aliud quam arma gestare video." His dictis equites cruce obsignata fronte, Cymbri pedites deosculata tellure omnes ordine incedebant. Interequitabant tubicines qui regio nomine milites ad hostium iugulos et oculos hortabantur.

40. Interea Franciscus Gonzaga praefectus socio Rhodulpho patruo qui castra in tutissimum locum intulerant vallo fossaque munierant, etsi magna ex parte arduo clivo Tarrum versus suapte natura tuta erant. Audito Gallorum adventu et perfecto Deo Optimo [165] sacrificio in cubiculum legatorum intromissi sunt cum ducibus omnibus, primusque Melchior Trivisanus annuente collega pauca in medium protulit. "Certa," inquit, "hodie, principes ac duces optimi, a Deo Optimo [166] Divoque Marco urbis nostrae praeside victoria nobis parata est. Certus tibi, Francisce Gonzaga, triumphus est vobisque [167] caeteris ducibus ac militibus [168] omnibus [169] opima spolia oblata sunt. Hostis Gallus qui divinis humanisque rebus non pepercit [170] inopia fameque quali clausi solent laborat multisque itineribus praeruptisque saltibus defatigatus est; hostibus circumquaque septus sine auxiliorum spe adeo divino fato derelictus est ut qui induciarum praeposita [171] specie fugae locum non invenit in summa rerum desperatione versatur gladio salutem quaeret,[172] ferro sibi viam faciet.[173] Etsi nobis ingentes copiae sunt et veteranorum militum promptiores animi tyronumque feroces et quisque pugnandi desiderio tenetur consilio tamen atque disciplina militari opus est, quae omnia etiam sine obsequio irrita sunt. Spolia illa Neapolitani regni ingentia quae secum ducit vestra sunt si hodie Gallos praelio domueritis."

41. Subito tota contione manavit laeticia. Verebantur duces ne Senatus Venetus bellum protraheret. Tum Franciscus Gonzaga praefectus "Patres," inquit, "optimi, si fata nobis hodie propitia erunt Veneto Senatui vel universae magis Italiae si non disciplinae militaris exemplum fidei tamen periculum in conspectu omnium vestrorum ostendam, et quo maius discrimen erit, relicto huic patruo meo imperandi officio, ipse pilo ac ense cum delecta manu viam inter hostes faciam. Nec rerum magnitudo nec Gallorum summa desperatio animum perturbat."

---

[165] primo B  [166] Maximo EF  [167] -que om. E  [168] est—militibus om. B  [169] om. EF  [170] percepit F  [171] proposita EF  [172] quaerat EF  [173] faciat EF

spoils which you carry off with you from the enemy are yours; all gleam with gold and silver. I see that the Venetians carry nothing but arms." At these words the horsemen made the sign of the cross on their foreheads, the Cimbrian foot soldiers kissed the ground, and then they all advanced in order. The trumpeters rode in their midst, encouraging the soldiers in the name of the King to aim at the throats and eyes of the enemy.

40. Meanwhile the commander Franceso Gonzaga with his colleague, his uncle Rodolfo, had set his camp in a very safe spot and fortified it with a rampart and ditch, although it was already secure in large part by its very nature because of the steep hill in the direction of the Taro; on hearing of the arrival of the French, and after mass had been said to All Merciful God, they were introduced into the room of the proveditors with all the leaders. And first Melchiorre Trevisan with the approval of his colleague said a few words in their midst. "Today," he said, "O chiefs and good leaders, a sure victory has been prepared for us by All Merciful God and St. Mark, guardian of our city. A triumph is assured for you, Francesco Gonzaga, and for you other leaders, and to all the soldiers rich spoils have been offered. The French enemy who has not spared divine and human affairs labors under scarcity and hunger, as is usual in a blockade; he is weary from many marches and steep passes; surrounded on all sides by the enemy and without hope of aid, he has been so wholly forsaken by divine fate that after failing to find an occasion for flight under the preferred guise of truce he is plunged into utter desperation at events and will seek safety by the sword and make a way for himself by force.[112] Even though we have mighty forces, the readier spirits of veteran soldiers and the fierce spirits of fresh soldiers, and each one is possessed of a longing for battle, there is nevertheless need of sagacity and military discipline, all of which things are also useless without obedience. Those huge spoils of the Neapolitan kingdom which he carries with him are yours if you overcome the French today in battle."

41. At once joy pervaded the entire assembly. The leaders feared that the Venetian Senate might postpone the war. Then the commander Francesco Gonzaga said, "Good fathers, if the fates are propitious to us today, before you all I shall display to the Venetian Senate, or rather to all Italy, if not an example of military discipline, at least a proof of faith. Wherever the danger is greater, I shall leave the duty of commanding to my uncle here and will myself with javelin and sword and a chosen band cut a path among the enemy; neither the magnitude of the enterprise nor the utmost desperation of the French disturbs my spirit."

42. Post haec agmina duces et eorum ordo constitutus est. Numerus omnium copiarum in acies novem more Gallico divisus est eo consilio, ut prima Gallorum acies ac media duabus Italis attentius pugnando vexaretur [174] ita ut postremi agminis oblitae [175] gradum referre nequirent, ipse vero praefectus ac eius patruus cum Rhanucio Phrenesio [176] in postremum agmen hostium ab utroque latere irrueret, dissipato eo agmine priora facile a fugientibus perturbarentur, et caeterae acies in promptum datae subito imperata facerent. Prima acies Graecos milites levius armatos continet DC [177] Petro Duodo duce, cui imperatum est ut summum montis iugum a tergo caperet, hostes lacesseret ordinemque [178] disturbaret. Secunda quae ex Italis equitibus cataphractis constabat quingentis decem Rhanucio Phrenesio [179] Aloisio Avogario sociis, tertia peditum phalanx cui Gorlinus Ravennas et alii duces praeerant IIII millia continebat. Huic, ne magno intervallo a praefecti agmine distaret, locum designavere [180] ut titubantibus protinus subveniret. Comes Bernardinus Fortebracius Vincentio Corsico Ruberto Strocio Alexandro Beraldo Patavino Iacobo Savorgnano Utinensi Aloisio Vallaresso patricio Marco Martinengo Comitibus Brandolinis sociis cum equitibus CCCLXX cataphractis quartum agmen ducit, cui ut postremum quoque Gallorum agmen adoriretur imperatum est. Ioannes vero Franciscus Acaiazanus Comes sociis Galeacio et Antonio Maria Palavicinis Hannibale Bentivolo Bononiensi et Galeotti Mirandulensis filio cum equitibus cataphractis DLXXX ut secundam Gallorum aciem aggrederetur iussa accepit. Inter haec duo agmina duo millia peditum distributa sunt. In sexto agmine CCLV [181] milites ducit cum Thadeo Motella socio Alexander Coleonus, quibus iussere ut fluctuanti ubi opus esset aciei suppetias ferrent,[182] ob id parvo intervallo distarent. Comes Antonius pariter Urbinas ut pari spatio sequeretur admonitus est. Hunc ex ducibus sequebantur Comes Ioannes Franciscus Gambarensis Carolus Seccus Antonius Pius Ioannes Rippa Veronensis et [183] Anguillarenses Ioannes Gradenious patricius Lazarius Ariminensis Petrus Chieregatus Tutius Cyprius Philippus Macedo cum CCCCLXV [184] equitibus cataphractis. Postremum vero cataphractorum Carolus Melitensis regit Taliano Carpensi Angelo de Sancto Angelo [185] ac Iacobatio Veneto sociis ducibus equitibus [186] CCLXXX, cui imperarunt ut castra servaret; cum eo Nicolaus Savorgnanus cum peditibus mille aderat. Nonum equitum leviter armatorum erat, inter quos et scorpionum milites erant, in summa CCCC Ioanne

---

[174] vexaret B    [175] om. EF    [176] Pharnesio EF    [177] om. EF    [178] ordineque A ordinesque EF    [179] Pharnesio EF    [180] subjugavere EF [181] CCIX EF    [182] ferret EF    [183] om. EF    [184] CCCLXV EF    [185] Angelo Sancti Angeli A, Angelo de Sancto Angelo A by MS. correction [186] equitum EF

42. Thereupon the ranks, their leaders, and the arrangement were determined.[113] The entire force was divided into nine lines, according to the French practice, the purpose being to harass the first and middle line of the French by two Italian lines in closer fighting, so that they could not forget the last group and turn back; the commander himself and his uncle along with Ranuccio Farnese would thus attack the rear of the enemy on both sides, and when that group had been scattered those in front would easily be thrown into confusion by the fugitives, and the other lines, standing in readiness, would at once carry out the commands given them. The first line consisted of six hundred lightly armed Greek soldiers commanded by Pietro Duodo, who had been ordered to seize the highest point of the mountain from the rear, provoke the enemy, and throw them into disorder. The second was composed of 510 Italian mailed horsemen under Ranuccio Farnese and Luigi Avogadro; the third, a phalanx of infantry, numbered four thousand, with Gorlino of Ravenna and other leaders in charge. To this, so that it might not be far distant from the line of the commander, they assigned a place from which it might bring aid at once if those in front wavered. Count Bernardino Fortebraccio, together with Vincenzo Corso, Roberto Strozzi, Alessandro Beroaldo of Padua, Jacopo Savorgnan of Udine, the noble Luigi Valaresso, Marco of Martinengo, and the Counts Brandolini led the fourth group with 370 mailed horsemen, and he was ordered to attack also the last line of the French. And Count Giovanni Francesco of Caiazzo, together with Galeazzo and Antonio Maria Pallavicino, Annibale Bentivoglio of Bologna,[114] and the son of Galeotto della Mirandola,[115] received orders to attack the second line of the French with 580 mailed horsemen. Between these two lines two thousand foot soldiers were distributed. In the sixth line Alessandro Colleoni and Taddeo dalla Motella led 255 soldiers, and they had orders to assist wherever a wavering line needed help, and to take their stand accordingly a short distance away. Count Antonio of Urbino also was told to follow at a like distance. After him came the leaders Count Gianfrancesco of Gambara, Carlo Secco, Antonio Pio, Giovanni Riva of Verona and those from Anguillara, the noble Giovanni Gradenigo, Lazzaro of Rimini, Pietro Chieregato, Tuzio of Cyprus, and Filippo of Macedonia with 465 mailed horsemen. The last group of the mailed horsemen was commanded by Carlo of Pian di Meleto with Taliano of Carpi, Angelo of Sant'Angelo, and Jacopaccio of Venice, with 280 horsemen; his orders were to protect the camp, and Niccolò Savorgnan and a thousand footmen were with him. The ninth line consisted of light-armed horsemen, among whom were also soldiers equipped with scorpions; these totaled four hundred and were

Graeco et Soncino Benzono ducibus. Tormentorum item [187] ordo ac ratio habita est.

43. Dimissa deinde contione dum se curarent milites speculatores hostium adventum nunciant triaque agmina haud procul abesse obfirmantes,[188] quod ubi in tota castra pertulit rumor repente tubicinum clamor ad arma milites excitavit pugnandi avidos, qui partim ieiuni partim recreati in equis stetere agminaque milites haud impigre secuti sunt. Legati Veneti eventum rei iuxta postrema agmina expectabant, ut si opus esset imperatoris officio fungerentur. Verum inter se ex dubio pugnae eventu perniciosum Italiae immo fere [189] totius orbis discrimen pensitabant: Regem si superari contigerit nihil praeter exercitum et impedimenta amissurum, verum amisso Venetorum exercitu totam protinus Italiam ad extrema venturam. Sed instantem pugnam necessario ineundam esse fatebantur.

44. Interea Gallus Rex agmina per collis decliva ducens cum plueret miro modo compacta per aequa intervalla impedimenta universi exercitus quae innumera erant et mulierum gregem summo colle servabat; pedites tormentaque agmina circuibant. Appropinquantibus itaque Venetis Galli in hostium agmina primi [190] tormenta emiserunt,[191] quae magis pavorem ordinumque perturbationem novo praesertim militi quam stragem intulerunt. Tum Veneti incredibili pugnandi desiderio audito tubarum [192] signo et exorto per agmina ingenti clamore ex quocunque agmine strenui [193] iussi sunt procedere, qui hostium acies agressi sunt. Franciscus Gonzaga postremum Comite Bernardino Fortebrachio cum altero agmine medium Acaiazanus eodem ferme momento omnes in hostes irruunt qui obiecta fossa aggere inaccesso flumine Tarro interiectis virgultis spinetisque ac imbre dissipati proni in hostium agmina magno impetu irrumpunt.[194] Impigre pedites quidam sequuntur, sed equites fere soli pugnam complent. Multi fossa coenosa involuti cadunt, alii flumen non transeunt, quidam lubrico aggere [195] prolabuntur in coenum. Multi loci iniquitatem timentes citra flumen constitere, sed qui strenui [196] pugnam inierant iam discordes nec ad unum intenti imperium vario tumultu gladios miscent;

---

[187] idem EF     [188] affirmantes EF     [189] vere EF     [190] prima B     [191] immiserunt EF     [192] turbarum B     [193] strenue EF     [194] qui—irrumpunt om. B     [195] agmine EF     [196] strenue EF

led by Giovanni Greco and Soncino Benzoni. In like manner the arrangement and method were fixed for the artillery.

43. Then, when the assembly had been adjourned and the soldiers
were caring for their bodies, scouts announced the arrival of the
enemy, asserting that three companies of them were not far distant.
When this report had been carried throughout the camp, straightway
the sound of trumpets aroused the soldiers to arms; they were eager
to fight, and they took their stations at their horses, some still hungry,
others refreshed, and the soldiers quickly fell into their companies.
The Venetian proveditors awaited the outcome of the affair near the
last ranks, so that if there was any need they might perform the duty
of the general. But between themselves, since the result of the battle
was dubious, they weighed the deadly peril for Italy and indeed for
almost the whole world: if it happened that the King was defeated, he
would lose only his army and his baggage, but if the army of the
Venetians was lost, all Italy would at once approach her end. They
agreed nonetheless that the impending battle must be fought.

44. In the meantime the French King was leading his troops over
the hillside, and he kept the baggage train of the entire army, which
was endless, wondrously compact and evenly spaced in spite of the
fact that it was raining, and the host of women he kept at the top of
the hill; the infantry and artillery surrounded the lines. And so as the
Venetians approached the French were the first to hurl their artillery
at the lines of the enemy, producing more fear and disorder in the
ranks especially among the new recruits than they did destruction.
Then the Venetians, who were unbelievably anxious to fight, raised a
mighty shout through the lines as soon as they heard the signal of
the trumpets; they were ordered to advance zealously in the ranks to
which they had been assigned, and they attacked the forces of the
enemy. Francesco Gonzaga along with Count Bernardino Fortebraccio
and another company assaulted the last line, the Count of Caiazzo the
middle one, all rushing at almost the same moment against the enemy
who because they were confronted with a ditch, an inaccessible rampart,
the river Taro, and the thickets and shrubbery which lay between,[116]
and because it was raining, scattered and rushed headlong against the
ranks of their enemy in a vast assault. Some of the infantry followed
quickly, but the cavalry almost alone completed the battle. Many fell,
rolling in the muddy ditch, others did not cross the river, and some slid
from the slippery rampart into the mire. Many, fearing the difficulties
of the terrain, halted this side of the river, but those who had zealously
entered upon the struggle were soon in disorder and, not governed by
one command, wielded their swords in varied confusion; the slaughter

caedes undique increscit, nec victus a victore dignosci potest.

45. Quidam ex Venetis relictis agminibus formidantibus ducibus in hostes irruunt morae impatientes ad virtutis et animi ostentationem, alii imperium frustra exequebantur angustiis retenti. Comes Antonius Urbinas agminis dux loci iniquitate gradum non intulit. Veneti quidem animo maiore Galli maiore industria pugnant; nanque non mediocris formido eorum animos incesserat ac hostium multitudo perterruerat. Franciscus Gonzaga praefectus magis hic militem agens [197] quam [198] imperatorem infesto pilo primo concursu confosso hostis pectore agmen perturbavit gladioque exinde acriter pugnando multa caede ad interiora agminis penetravit confossumque mutaturus equum ad suos rediit. Tum Rhodulphus equites peditesque cruentus quoque ad pugnam hortabatur et inveteratae virtutis nominatim admonebat viros. Tota enim postrema Gallorum acies pavore fluctuabat. Tum Galli Latinique palantes manus conserunt adeoque implicantur adeo impigre utrinque gladios stringunt [199] ut qui victores victique essent a nemine dignosceretur [200] et ita omnes cohaerebant ut armis arma pulsarent.

46. Impedimenta statim novo furore perturbantur ab equitibus leviter armatis qui [201] prius Gallos pedites retro ferre pedem coegerant. Hos secuti Graeci milites qui cuncta ex iugo despexerant [202] tanquam aquilae decurrerunt. Hi hostes et suos trucidando ea diripiunt, quos et Latini pedites plerique ob avaritiam relictis ordinibus contra militiae iura sequuntur valido ruinae incitamento. Ingens igitur rapina nullo ordine miscetur.

47. In hoc tumultu Rhodulphus Gonzaga in medio hostium agmine memorabili edita pugna aperta galea in facie graviter vulneratur ac protinus concidit. Rhanucius pariter a pluribus simul Gallis post multas caedes opprimitur. Comes Bernardinus Fortebrachius vir strenuissimus iniquissimo loco et periculi non ignarus Gallorum aciem dissipato agmine aggreditur. Tum hostis compositis alis confusos milites excipit; hi mutuis vulneribus pugnant a pluribusque [203] pauci oppressi interficiuntur. Alii palude involuti necantur, quidam aggere ac flumine arcentur retroque cedunt. Ipse ductor Vallaresso acriter pug-

---

[197] agebat EF   [198] qua B   [199] fringunt EF   [200] dignoscerentur B
[201] quae B   [202] conspexerant EF   [203] -que om. B

increased on all sides, and the victors could not be distinguished from the vanquished.

45. Some of the Venetians broke ranks when the leaders were terrified and rushed against the enemy in their impatience at delay, displaying courage and bravery. Others were cramped by the narrow quarters and tried in vain to carry out their orders. Count Antonio of Urbino, leader of one line, failed to advance because of the difficulties of the terrain. The Venetians indeed fought with greater spirit, the French with greater industry, for a fear far from moderate had invaded their minds and the huge numbers of their enemy terrified them. The commander Francesco Gonzaga, acting more as soldier than general,[117] pierced the chest of an enemy with a deadly javelin in the first charge, disturbed the ranks, and then fighting keenly with his sword penetrated with much slaughter inside the lines and returned to his men to replace his horse which had been hit.[118] Then Rodolfo, though covered with blood, also encouraged the cavalry and infantry to fight and called upon the men in the name of their ancient courage. For the entire rear line of the French was wavering in fear, and wandering French and Latins joined in hand-to-hand struggle; they became so entangled and drew their swords so readily on both sides that no one could distinguish who was victor and who vanquished, and all were so massed together that arms beat upon arms.

46. Soon the baggage train was disturbed in a new onset by light-armed horsemen who had first compelled the French infantry to withdraw. Upon these followed Greek soldiers who had looked down upon the whole proceeding from the top of the hill and swooped down like eagles; butchering the enemy and also some of their own side they plundered the baggage train,[119] and after them came a great many Latin foot soldiers [120] who, contrary to military law, had left their ranks because of greed and were bent on destruction. So pillaging was vast and chaotic.

47. During this confusion Rodolfo Gonzaga, who had fought a memorable battle in the midst of the enemy lines, opened his helmet, was seriously wounded on the face, and straightway fell. Several of the French together overcame Ranuccio too after he had killed many. Although his company was scattered Count Bernardino Fortebraccio, a most zealous man, attacked the French line in a most unfavorable spot and with clear knowledge of the danger. Then the enemy by bringing together its wings trapped the disordered soldiers; they fought wounding one another, and the few were overcome by the many and killed. Some were bogged down in the swamp and slain there, some were confined by the rampart and river and drew back. The leader

nanti opem laturus a pluribus hostibus circumseptus [204] opprimitur; collisa galea in capite graviter malleo vulneratur moribundusque equo concidit. Agmen cui Ioannes Franciscus Acaiazanus praefectus est dissipatur bombardarum terrore magis quam caede. Solus dux cum paucis strenue pugnam init, in qua [205] Ioannes Picininus [206] avitae gloriae studiosus occubuit ac Galeacius Corrigiensis; ex caeteris equitibus XIIII [207] desiderati sunt. Reliqui milites abiectis lanceis et armis leviores foede terga vertunt Parmamque pecorum modo [208] fugientes contendunt. Quidam Carolus cognomento Ingratus omnes duci ad macellum ducem obiurgando clamabat. Crebris undique ignibus caelum micat, tormentis [209] tonat, ploratibus clamoribusque completur. Pilae ferreae aeneae plumbeae sibilantes sublimes feruntur quae sine caede militum et peditum ordines disturbant.

48. In eo pugnantium tumultu Comes Nicolaus Petilianus, qui hostium agmina antecedebat, nacta occasione sponte sese Venetis dedit, qui suo adventu animos multorum titubantes erexit et agmina nutantia cohortando [210] stabilivit. Hic legatis Venetis Gallos in summa trepidatione esse primus denunciavit eosque haud dubio terga daturos, ob id persequendos esse quibus satis non [211] est hostes depulisse contentosque esse sola fuga. Pedites qui inter utraque agmina dispositi erant inter quos plurimi ex Veneta plebe ancipiti pugna manus miscent, nec Gallus nec Venetus dignoscebatur.[212] Ex his circiter CC Hieronymo Genua [213] duce desiderati sunt solique in ea parte pugnam sustinuere. Ductor in iugulo vulneratur et manu [214] inutilis redditur. Parva utrinque tormenta irrita fuere pulvere inflammabili hymbre madefacto. Magno tormento Iacobus Salernus [215] Veronensis in postremo agmine colliditur. Alter miles sublato equo in pedes stetit illaesus.

49. Ex hostibus nemo singulari certamine audet concurrere sed plures singulos aggrediuntur protinusque ad vexilla redeunt. Nulla enim Gallorum acies est vel peditum phalanx quae sine vexillo manus conserat. Sciunt enim quo redeundum sit dissipati milites. Ex Graecis pauci pugnant, inter quos Petrus Busichius et Nicolaus Nonensis vulnerantur; reliqui impedimenta corripiunt. Ex Gallis plerique amissis

---

[204] circumspectus F    [205] quo ABEF    [206] picinius B    [207] XLIII EF
[208] more EF    [209] tormentorum EF    [210] hortando EF    [211] om. ABEF
[212] dignoscebantur B    [213] Genuam B    [214] manus B    [215] Adernus EF

himself, when about to bring aid to Valaresso, who was fighting savagely, was surprised by several of the enemy and overwhelmed; with his helmet shattered he was severely wounded on the head by a hammer and fell in agony from his horse. The line over which Giovanni Francesco of Caiazzo had command was scattered by fear of missiles rather than by actual carnage. Only the leader and a few men zealously entered the battle, and in it perished Giovanni Piccinino, who was mindful of ancestral glory, and Galasso of Correggio; of the other horsemen fourteen were lost. The rest of the soldiers cast away lances and arms and lightened of this load disgracefully turned their backs and like sheep fled to Parma. A certain Carlo by the name of Ingrato kept shouting out that they were all being led to slaughter and that the commander was at fault. On every side the sky repeatedly flashed with fire and thundered with artillery and was filled with wails and cries. Iron, bronze, and lead balls sped hissing aloft, and these threw the ranks of cavalry and infantry into turmoil even without slaughter.

48. In the confusion of those who were fighting Count Niccolò of Pitigliano, who was in the van of the enemy ranks, found an opportunity and voluntarily surrendered himself to the Venetians.[121] His arrival cheered the wavering spirits of many, and his encouragement strengthened the tottering lines. He was the first to report to the Venetian proveditors that the French were greatly terrified and would doubtless turn their backs, and that therefore those should pursue for whom it is not enough to rout the enemy and to be satisfied with flight alone. The infantry, which was arranged between the respective lines of cavalry and in which there were a great many from the Venetian populace, joined in the uncertain struggle. French and Venetian soldiers could not be distinguished from one another. Of the latter about two hundred led by Geronimo Genova, the only ones to sustain the battle in that sector, were lost. Their leader was wounded in the throat and a hand was rendered useless.[122] Small artillery was of no effect on either side because the gunpowder had been drenched by rain. In the last line Jacopo Salerno of Verona was struck by a large ball. Another soldier stood uninjured on his feet after his horse had been killed under him.

49. None of the enemy risked fighting in single combat, but in greater numbers attacked single individuals and straightway returned to the standards. For there is no French line or infantry phalanx which joins battle without a standard; thus soldiers who have been scattered know where to return. A few of the Greeks fought, and among them Pietro Busichio [123] and Niccolò of Nin were wounded; the rest plundered the baggage train. Many of the French, when they had lost

armis supplices annulos pecunias monilia offerunt, deinde ad suos redeunt.

50. Legati Veneti iuxta [216] castra obequitantes fugientes milites ignavos prae nimio pavore nullo hoste persequente (terror nanque plerosque invaserat) coercent graviterque vano metu increpant; sese inermes ostendebant, ut sisterent fugam et secum essent adhortantur. Comes Nicolaus Petilianus agmina inferre subsidio pedem [217] suadere non cessabat nec tantam tamque divinam victoriae occasionem oportere negligere acclamabat: victos fugatosque Gallos esse, si agmen unum auxilio gradum intulerit. Ductores discrimen timentes cunctando certamen differunt. Interea dum acriter pugnatur quidam peditum duces, qui nec nomine digni sunt, sive dolo sive avaritia legatis denunciant Italos bello fractos cogique militem novo stipendio oportere. Alter item Melchiorem Trivisanum obvium ut fuga se redimat hortatur, cui legatus sine intermissione respondit nequaquam victoribus fugiendum esse. "Nam etsi ab hostibus vinceremur [218] satis esset in praelio trucidari quam ob male res gestas a Veneto Senatu capite puniri." Fortasse ille exercitus ruinam optabat.

51. Interea multum sanguinis [219] funditur, nec timido nec ignavo qui pugnam trans Tarrum inierat cessare nunc licet. Galli paulatim pugnando gradum referunt per collis decliva, Veneti vel saucii insequuntur. Franciscus Gonzaga praefectus mutato equo eminens militem rursus cogit et delectis militibus pluribus interfectis hostem persequitur instatque maiore conatu Barbontemque nothum regiae stirpis cepit et Miolensem Principem aliique milites nobiles a Venetis capti [220] sunt, plures interfecti. Rex Gallus nec crista nec armis minus item sublimitate equi a caeteris dignoscebatur ne hostibus ad incessendum incitamentum daret, sed in agmine humilis delitescebat et regia insignia deposuerat ne in praelio proderent.[221] Gallos tandem cedentes Veneti pauciores insequuntur. Illi statim praecipites in collem abeunt contra Venetorum castra; direpta [222] tandem per se pugna Latini ad socia agmina redeunt, deinde omnes in castra se recipiunt.

---

[216] vix B      [217] peditum EF      [218] convinceremur B      [219] sanguis B
[220] capte A capti A by MS. correction      [221] proderetur B      [222] dirempta E

their arms, offered in supplication rings, money, and necklaces and then returned to their own men.

50. The Venetian proveditors, riding toward the camp, forced back the fleeing soldiers whom excessive fear had made cowards even though no enemy was pursuing (for terror had taken possession of most of them) and reproached them severely for their vain anxiety; they pointed out that they themselves were unarmed and urged them to stop their flight and stay with them. Count Niccolò Pitigliano continued to urge the squadrons to bring aid and kept shouting that they should not neglect so great and so providential an opportunity for victory: the French were defeated and put to flight if one squadron alone brought help. The leaders, fearing the risk, delayed and prolonged the battle. Meanwhile, with the fighting still keen, certain heads of the infantry, unworthy even to be named, reported to the proveditors whether through treachery or greed that the Italians were defeated in battle and that soldiers ought to be assembled at new salaries. Another likewise met Melchiorre Trevisan and urged him to save himself by fleeing. To him the proveditor replied on the instant that there was no need for victors to flee. "For even if we were conquered by the enemy," he said, "it would be better to be slain in battle than to be executed by the Venetian Senate because we had been defeated." Perhaps that one wanted the ruin of the army.

51. Meanwhile much blood was shed, nor was it allowed those who in fear or cowardice had begun fighting on the other side of the Taro to stop at this time. Gradually the French retreated as they fought over the slopes of the hill and the Venetians, though wounded, followed them. The commander Francesco Gonzaga, standing out above the others on a fresh horse, pulled his soldiers together again, and with a selected group pursued the enemy after killing a number of them, and pressing on with greater effort he captured the Bourbon bastard of royal blood [124] and Marshal Miolans; other noble soldiers were taken by the Venetians and many were killed. The French King was distinguished from the others neither by his helmet nor by his arms, and much less in the height of his horse, lest he give incentive to the enemy to attack; instead he was hiding away as a humble soldier in the line, and he had removed his royal insignia, so that they would not betray him in battle. A lesser number of Venetians pursued the French who were finally yielding, and the latter straightway went off hastily to the hill opposite the camp of the Venetians, and at last, when the fighting had broken off of itself, the Latins returned to the lines of their allies, and then all betook themselves to camp.

52. Haec pugna intra horae spatium peracta est, in qua tot nobiles duces interiere. In Gallorum exercitu circiter mille desiderati sunt, in Italo vero ad [223] duo millia. Ex Gallis item calones lixaeque qui interfecti fuere numerum caesorum auxere. Ex optimatibus XII caesi sunt, ex quibus Vardus Aristeus dux sagitariorum Dasonus et Semplensis natalibus praenobiles Torsuensis [224] Chandensisque pecuniae locuples Benonensis Lemerlensis Chetensisque barones. Frater Turonensis principis graviter vulneratus est dux vigilum regius. Amprutensis [225] equitum sagittariorum dux tormento contritus est. Hi [226] atris avibus dimicavere. Capti fuere praeter quos diximus Cherensis nothus principis filius Bonnionensis [227] nothus regius Borsensis ditissimus Foretensis patricius valde opulentus, ex nostris vero circiter CC equites. Ubi hostium agmina fuerant similis ruinae strages visa est a nobis [228] nobilium ducum et Gallorum et Italorum; illos calceorum deformis magnitudo ad miram levitatis ostentationem vel in armis ipsis discernere dabat, quos et scalae ab equorum sellis dependentes iusta latitudine excipiunt, unde equorum pari argumento ingens numerus dignoscebatur.

53. Ex Latinis vero praeter quos supra diximus Vincentius Corsicus honestis vulneribus concidit, Rubertus item Strocius et Alexander Beraldus socii in mediis hostium cadaveribus reperti sunt. Petrus Mapheus et Hieronymus Recalchus Veronenses [229] Ioannes Malumbra Venetus strenui in interiore hostium agmine cecidere. Hi egregia morte ante oculos [230] iacebant sine cruore; oscula enim vulnerum imber colluerat. Omnes in ora proni sicut [231] dimicantes adverso corpore vulneribus pluribus in iugulo acceptis qui [232] acrius quam [233] cautius inter hostes dimicaverant quibusque prospera fuerit pugna strenue dimicantibus nemini fere certum fuit. Equites Latini cathaphracti graves per iniquas campi angustias fluminis mobilem glaream ripasque inaccessas aegre subvenire potuerunt. Galli expeditiores leviusque armati ex declivo collis subsidio compacto agmine procurrebant. Verum neque Gallus neque Venetus in pugna cruentissima persistere voluit. Veneta [234] tamen ingentia agmina quae infra teli iactum immota manebant veluti imperia expectantia metum Gallis incutiebant. Avaritia item ad praedam Graecorum militum procurrentium pugnandi suspitionem attulerat.

---

[223] om. EF    [224] Tornensis B    [225] Amputrensis B    [226] his B    [227] Pronniovensis B Bononiensis EF    [228] a nobis visa est EF    [229] Veronensis BE    [230] actos B    [231] sunt B    [232] quod B    [233] qui EF    [234] Veneto EF

52. This battle [125] lasted for one hour, and during it many noble leaders perished; in the army of the French about a thousand were lost, but in the Italian about two thousand.[126] Among the French likewise the servants and camp-followers who were killed increased the number of the slain. Of the nobles twelve perished,[127] among them Varde Aristé, leader of the archers, Doyson and a seigneur from Chambly, both of high birth, one from Torcy and another from Candes who was very wealthy, and barons from Béon, Limerlé, and Chécy. The brother of the prince of Tours, captain of the King's guard, was seriously wounded. The leader of the mounted archers, from Amplepuis, was blown to bits by artillery. These fought under evil omens. In addition to those I have mentioned the following were captured: [128] the bastard son of the prince of Chères, the royal bastard from Boulogne, a very rich seigneur from Bours, an exceedingly wealthy noble from Forez, and of our forces about two hundred horsemen. Where the lines of the enemy had been I saw ruinous slaughter of noble leaders both French and Italian. The former could be recognized by the unusual size of their shoes in comparison with the wonderful display of lightness even in the arms they bore; stirrups of the proper width to fit the shoes hung from the horses' saddles,[129] and so the horses gave equal evidence of the vast numbers of the French.

53. Of the Latins in addition to those I have mentioned above Vincenzo Corso perished of honorable wounds; likewise Roberto Strozzi and Alessandro Beroaldo were found together in the midst of enemy corpses. Pietro Maffei and Geronimo Recalco of Verona and Giovanni Malombra of Venice fell valorously within the lines of the enemy. These lay in a noble death before my eyes, and there was no blood, for the rain had bathed their gaping wounds. All lay prone, just as they had fought, body to body, and most of the wounds were in their throats, since they had contended more eagerly than carefully in the enemy's midst and almost no one knew for which of the zealous warriors the battle was going well. It was difficult for the heavily armored Latin troops to bring assistance over the uneven defiles of the field, the shifting gravel of the river, and the inaccessible banks. The French, less encumbered and more lightly armed, hastened down the hill in a dense mass to help. But neither Frenchman nor Venetian wanted to continue the very bloody fight. However, the vast Venetian lines which stood immovable beyond the reach of the weapons, as if waiting for commands, struck fear into the French. Likewise the avarice of the Greek soldiers who were rushing forward to plunder had sapped their confidence in fighting.

54. In ea pugna Gallorum impedimenta innumera omni opulentia ditia amissa sunt, in quibus auri argentique [235] pondus ingens repertum est. Gemmae, monilia, vestimenta et maximus luxuriae apparatus a Veneto milite direptus est, et illa ingens regia praeda quam ex Neapolitano regno exultans Rex in Galliam triumphans asportabat inter milites divisa est Graecos et pedites Latinos. In hunc enim diem totius anni discrimina fortuna accumulavit, cumque plus milites raperent passim [236] strata erant loca vilioribus [237] sarcinis quas in comparatione meliorum priorum [238] militum avaritia calonibus lixis rusticisque contemnendo reliquerant, et tabernaculum Regis omni luxu et opulentia instructum ad vilissimos milites pervenit. In summa praeda omnis sequenti [239] die inter socios Graecos nequiter divisa fuit, quae ducentis [240] milibus aureorum aestimata est. Vexilla quedam ducum peditum in manus Venetorum pervenere. Equorum mulorumque infinitus pene numerus in castra perductus [241] est. Inter ipsos victores dum dimicaretur hostis erat qui pretiosiorem occupasset praedam. Dolabris pretiosae artis vasa argentea concidebant. Ex regio apparatu abacus omnis ex auro argentoque cubiculi [242] scrinia rapta sunt in quibus vestimenta stragulae [243] peristromata et vasa convivalia quae reges longa imperii possessione cumulaverant, sacelli sacri libri pretiosi, tabella gemmis ornata et sacris veneranda, annuli praeterea gemmis pretiosi. In ipsa praeda librum vidimus in quo pellicum variae formae sub diverso habitu ac aetate ex naturali depictae erant prout libido in quaque urbe ac [244] vesanus [245] amor eum traxerat [246]; eas memoriae gratia pictas secum deferebat.

55. Interea Rex Gallus postquam castra locaverat de fuga incerta consilia volvebat periculoso ac longo itinere Hastem versus obvio.[247] Metus Regem turbabat ne ab utraque parte hostibus occluderetur tot urbibus oppidis fluminibusque [248] interiacentibus. At pro sepeliendis cadaveribus [249] induciae datae sunt. Rex protinus caduceatorem misit qui sine tubicine Veneto ingredi castra [250] non ausus est. Is comitatus ad Franciscum Gonzagam praefectum et legatos venit, a quibus cum inducias trium dierum peteret hi ad meridiem [251] duntaxat sequentem cessationem [252] pugnae pacticiam [253] aegre permiserunt.[254]

56. Interea mixti sparsim Latini et Galli suos quisque quaeritans quos noverat [255] pacem funeri pro more dabat. Vidimus corpora for-

---

[235] -que om. B      [236] om. EF      [237] viliorum F      [238] priorum meliorum EF
[239] sequente EF      [240] ducentibus EF      [241] productus B      [242] cubiculique
EF      [243] stragula B      [244] om. EF      [245] vesanusque EF      [246] trajecerat
B      [247] om. EF      [248] -que om. EF      [249] caveribus A      [250] castra ingredi EF      [251] meridiam B      [252] secessionem EF      [253] om. EF
[254] pactitiam add. EF      [255] noverant EF

54. In that battle countless baggage piles of the French, abounding in all riches, were lost; [130] in them was found a great weight of silver and gold. Gems, necklaces, clothing, and the grandest furnishings of wealth were snatched by the Venetian soldiers,[131] and that vast royal booty which the exulting King was carrying in triumph from the Neapolitan realm to France was divided among the Greeks and the Latin infantry. Indeed fortune heaped the hazards of an entire year upon this day, and as the soldiers continued their looting, on every side the ground was strewn with bundles of cheaper wares which the avarice of the first soldiers had scornfully abandoned to servants, camp-followers, and peasants in favor of better booty. And the tent of the King, equipped with every luxury and evidence of wealth, fell to the lowliest soldiers. In short, all the plunder on the following day was wickedly divided among the Greek allies, booty which was worth two hundred thousand ducats. Certain standards of the infantry leaders fell into the hands of the Venetians, and an almost countless number of horses and mules was brought into camp. Among the victors themselves during the course of the battle he was an enemy who had seized the more valuable plunder. With pickaxes they cut up silver vessels of wondrous craftsmanship. From the royal effects a table entirely of gold and silver was carried off together with bedroom chests containing the clothing, rugs, tapestries, and banquet vessels which the kings had accumulated in their long possession of power. There were also precious books from the holy chapel, a plaque inlaid with gems and deserving of reverence for its sacred relics, and rings loaded with jewels. In that plunder I saw a book in which were painted various nude images of his mistresses, differing in appearance and age as his lust and insane love had impelled him in each city; these pictures he carried with him as souvenirs.[132]

55. Meanwhile after the French King had pitched camp he weighed a dubious plan to flee toward Asti, a route dangerous and long. He was disturbed by the fear that he might be shut off by the enemy on both sides, since so many cities, towns, and rivers lay between. But a truce was granted for burying the dead. The King straightway sent a herald who did not dare enter the camp without a Venetian trumpeter. He came under escort to the commander Francesco Gonzaga and the proveditors to request of them a truce of three days. These allowed reluctantly a stipulated cessation of hostilities only until noon of the following day.

56. Meanwhile the Latins and the French together were searching here and there, each one for those whom he knew, and were observing the customary truce for burial. I saw corpses of brave men protruding

tium virorum exerta [256] ex intervallis a pluribus spoliata; primi cariora ornamenta [257] vel vivis detraxerant [258] milites Graeci ac Latini, deinde rusticorum incolarum greges e [259] summis montium iugis pugnae eventum spectantium arma sustulere, ac postremo calonum [260] lixarumque qui nudos tunica intima detracta passim mortuos et semivivos reliquere. Nec equorum corporibus invitamento minimo [261] vis ac libido pepercit; sellas equorum tegumenta tergora et soleas denique revulsas vidimus, lancearum fasces laceratos alibi integros tela innumera sagittas pilas ferreas aeneasque et alia humi coniecta videbamus. Saucii plurimi nudi inter cadavera reperti sunt, partim opem petentes partim semimortui fame sanguinis profluvio confecti ac solis vapore siti exerta lingua fatigati aquam poscentes. In ea re nulla crudelitatis facies deesse [262] visa est. Hi circiter CXV fuere, inter quos et Galli mixti erant confoedata [263] cruore limoque facie servitutem mentientes,[264] qui sine delectu in castra Veneta delati a vulnerum medicis curabantur impensa publica. Quidam amputatis manibus pedibusque [265] collapsis intestinis nudo cerebro spirabant, adeo vitae contumax natura est. Plurima cadavera Tarro flumine in Padum devoluta sunt, reliqua [266] plus quam [267] duo millia quingenta [268] feris relicta sunt inhumata solis ardore et imbre tumentia quae [269] punctim fere [270] omnia sub iugulo vel in facie vulnerata erant, tormentis vero pauca contrita.

57. Galli plurimi primo concursu prolapsi concidere. Pila enim breviora gestant, ob id priores ictus sensere; verum Galli gladio aptiores videbantur, nam quo brevior est, eo aptior habetur. Arbitrantur plerique Gallos exigua manu Italos fugare potuisse si ausi fuissent ultro gradum inferre, quos locorum angustiae coarguunt. Compacto enim agmine Latinos loci iniquitate lacessere non potuissent qui pari conditione per angustias paludesque dispalati fameque domiti quinque Venetorum agmina integra minime profligassent, nec latius extendi acies patiebantur angustiae.[271]

58. Verum Comes Acaiazanus rem dubiam esse ratus pugnam sequenti die expectans perpetuos nuntios ad oppidum Colurnum iuxta Padum miserat, ubi soror sarcinas quae in arce erant collegerat, ut si Latinis male pugnare contigisset litteris admonita divitias omnis in naviculam in promptum datam protinus deportaret. Nec ea nocte

---

[256] exuta E excuta F    [257] ornamento B    [258] detraxerunt EF    [259] a EF
[260] calorum B    [261] minime B    [262] deest EF    [263] confaedato B
[264] metientes EF    [265] -que om. E    [266] reliqui E reliquis F    [267] -que B
[268] quingenta om. EF    [269] qui B    [270] ferme EF    [271] angustias B

at intervals which had been despoiled by many; the Greek and Latin soldiers had been first and had removed the more precious ornaments even from those still living, and then crowds of native peasants who had watched the issue of the battle from the summits of the mountains carried off the armor, and finally groups of servants and camp-followers removed the underclothing and left naked everywhere soldiers who were dead or half-alive. Nor, if there was the least inducement, did violence and greed spare the horses' bodies; I saw saddles, coverings, hides, and finally shoes of horses torn away, and I saw bundles of lances, some torn, others whole, innumerable darts, arrows, iron and bronze pikes and other instruments scattered over the ground. Very many wounded were found naked among the corpses, some begging aid, some half-dead. They were weakened by hunger and loss of blood and wearied by the heat of the sun and thirst; with tongues thrust out they begged for water. In this affair no form of cruelty seemed to be lacking. There were about 115 of these; some Frenchmen were mingled among them, begrimed with mud and blood and looking like slaves, and these without distinction were brought into the Venetian camp and attended by the surgeons at public expense. Some still breathed after hands and feet had been amputated, intestines collapsed, brains laid bare, so unyielding of life is nature. The river Taro carried very many corpses to the Po; the rest, more than twenty-five hundred, unburied and swollen by the heat of the sun and the rain, were left to wild beasts. Almost all of these had a piercing wound in the throat or on the face, but a few had been lacerated by artillery.

57. A great many French fell and perished at the first onrush, for they carry shorter javelins, wherefore they felt the first blows; however, the French seemed better suited to the sword, for as it is shorter, it is on that account considered better. Very many think that the French with a small band could have routed the Italians if they had dared advance freely, but the narrowness of the field refutes them. For by means of a compact line, because of the difficult terrain, they could not have harassed the Latins, and in like manner scattered over the defiles and the swamps, and subdued by hunger as they were, they could by no means have crushed five whole Venetian lines, nor did the narrow quarters permit the lines to be spread out more widely.

58. But the Count of Caiazzo, thinking the outcome indecisive and expecting a battle on the following day, had sent messengers repeatedly to the city of Colorno near the Po, where his sister had assembled the luggage which was in the stronghold, so that if the battle went poorly for the Latins he could advise her by letter and she could at once put all these riches into a skiff readied for this purpose. Nor on that night

scribendi defuit cura ut de rebus certior fieret. Eius milites plurimi hac die confugere nec vulpem oblatam venari [272] voluerunt novo castrensi adagio. Vesperi itaque cum legati Veneti se in castra [273] recepissent dispositis a praefecto excubiis de pugnae eventu Senatui significarunt. Litterae quae citius quam credibile sit crebris per iusta intervalla tabellariis Augustino Barbadico Principi sapientissimo redditae sunt, quae maxima totius urbis expectatione in populum effusa omni civitate in frequentissimo Senatu lectae sunt, quarum summa erat exercitum cum hoste conflixisse collatis signis, plurimos utrinque concidisse, salvum denique exercitum esse. Eventum nanque praesentis pugnae in tantis rerum perturbationibus adhuc non satis sibi esse perspectum nunciarunt, verum sequenti se epistola rem ad unguem significaturos. Hi victoriae ignari conversis partim militibus ad sua tentoria ut dividerent spolia partim ob insuetam armis [274] multitudinem in fugam concitam varioque castrorum tumultu quique hostium damna non cognoverant vix ea significare potuerunt.

59. Senatus igitur Venetus ac universa civitas deteriorem fortunam existimans lectis litteris in summo discrimine rem versari arbitrabatur,[275] quandoquidem nihil specialius ex iis intelligi potuisset. Suspitionem teterrimae fortunae auxere litterae quae Ferraria [276] eadem die delatae sunt, quibus simulato moerore Venetos bello fractos fuisse denunciabatur. Eadem ferme Ludovicus Mediolanensis Dux a Comite Acaiazano litteris acceperat non sine magna animi perturbatione quarum exemplum ad Senatum miserat. Vario igitur tumultu universa civitas [277] fluctuabat donec Senatus sequenti die de rerum omnium [278] statu particulatim litteris certior factus desperatam victoriam omnibus patefaceret. Exorta est praeter spem per totam urbem laetitia perspecta victoria cognita magna ex parte praeda ac hostili metu, qui pugnare non auderent sed modo inducias modo pacem supplices peterent. His ordine acceptis Senatus decreto Deo Divoque Marco praesidi publice [279] gratiae aguntur, et civitas genus omne laetitiae offusim [280] celebrat.

60. Interea igitur Gallus convocatis in contionem primoribus, "Ecce," inquit, "proceres, multa caede multoque sanguine perfusi in hac cruentissima pugna hostes post terga tandem, etsi perquam infortune [281] reliquimus [282] pluribus impedimentis amissis. Satis tamen fuit

---

[272] venari oblatam EF      [273] in castra se E      [274] annis B      [275] arbitrabantur B      [276] Ferrariae EF      [277] om. B      [278] omnium rerum EF      [279] publicae EF      [280] effusum B      [281] importunae B      [282] relinquimus EF

did he fail to write and inform her of events. A great many of his soldiers wished to flee that very day and not, as a new byword of the camp puts it, hunt the flushed-out fox. And so that evening when the Venetian proveditors had returned to camp and watches had been posted by the commander, they reported to the Senate concerning the outcome of the battle, and the letter, carried with incredible swiftness in regular relays by bearers stationed at equal intervals from one another, was given to the very wise Doge Agostino Barbarigo, and amid the greatest expectation on the part of the whole city, for all the citizens had flocked forth, it was read to the people in a very crowded Senate. The gist of it was that the army in close array had fought with the enemy; very many had perished on both sides and the army was at length saved. And they announced that the outcome of the present battle, in view of such a confused state of things, was not yet sufficiently clear to them, but that they would report everything in detail by a letter to follow. They were uncertain of victory partly because the soldiers had returned to their tents to divide the spoils, partly because the crowd which was unaccustomed to arms had turned to flight, and also because of the great confusion in camp. Since they did not yet know the losses of the enemy, they could scarcely indicate them.

59. Accordingly after the letter had been read, and especially because it gave no particulars, the Venetian Senate and the whole city thought that their fortunes had worsened and that the enterprise was in the greatest peril. A letter which came from Ferrara on the same day increased the suspicion of a very grim outcome, since it stated with pretended sorrow that the Venetians had been defeated in war. Lodovico, duke of Milan, had had almost the same report in a letter from the Count of Caiazzo, and his mind was greatly disturbed; he had sent a copy of this letter to the Senate. So the entire city was a prey to varied turmoil, until on the following day the Senate was informed in a detailed letter concerning the state of everything and revealed to all the victory of which they had despaired. The whole city was surprised and joyful when it realized that it had triumphed and recognized the extent of the plunder and the fear that had seized the enemy, who dared not fight but as suppliants sought now a truce, now peace. When this news had been duly received, thanks were given publicly by decree of the Senate to God and their defender St. Mark, and the citizens poured forth demonstrating every kind of joy.[133]

60. Meanwhile the Frenchman called his leaders into conference and said, "Behold, nobles, after great slaughter and much bloodshed in this very cruel battle we have at length left the enemy behind us, yet we have been very unfortunate, for we have lost most of our bag-

parva manu tantum evasisse discrimen. Summa enim foelicitas esset, si omnia prospera evenirent, sed ferendum est si fortuna totius anni mala omnia in hunc diem congesserit quae atra nobis praenunciata fuerat, ita ut fame coactus magno periculo amissa gloria amisso regno amisso triumpho relictis in Apulia Calabriaque militibus parvis copiis domum mihi redeundum sit. Sed hoc uno laetor, quod milites nostri summa virtute, vera militari disciplina pugnaverunt, paucique ex nobilibus et caeteris militibus non multi desiderati sunt, pauciores saucii. Nihil quidem sub coelo diuturnum,[283] cedendum est quandoque fortunae. Bellum cum Alphonso Rege et filio sine cruore confecimus. Sed omnia Veneti nobis immutarunt. Id regnum non mihi, sed vobis omnibus partum est; nos regno amplissimo longa successione fruimur. Reliquum est ut quanta maxima potest [284] celeritate universus exercitus in tuto collocetur. Sed tu, Triulci, praefectum castrorum iuvenem puerumve [285] sine disciplina militari praedicabas. Malus puer mihi eo die visus est, quod [286] si in plano pugnare contigisset longe pessimus fuisset."

61. Dimissa contione coenavit, eaque nocte in alieno quievit tentorio.[287] Excubiae duplicatis ordinibus in maxima [288] rerum trepidatione [289] imperatae sunt, ignes perpetui in castris erant, magna noctis pars a ducibus in consultatione consumpta [290] est. Summa consiliorum fuit ut sub induciarum specie hostis deciperetur et ipsi fugam corriperent. Rex Nonis Juliis caduceatorem ad Venetos legatos mittit, qui intromissus coram praefecto castrorum et caeteris ducibus nuntiavit Argentonum nomine regio colloquia desiderare. Assensere dictis legati. Dum discedere vellet caduceator a praefecto exercitus interrogatus est quot ex Gallis optimatibus caesi fuissent in pugna; ille [291] circiter XIIX vel mortuos vel [292] captivos [293] deflevisse Regem respondit. Praefectus [294] duos vivere indicavit, nothum magnum Barbontem et Principem Miolensem nonnullosque equestris ordinis saucios servari, reliquos mutua vicissitudine trucidatos esse.

62. Dimisso caduceatore cum legatis exercitus praefectus Comite Acaiazano ac Nicolao Petiliano Argentonum legatum regium ad Tarrum expectaturi devenere; fluvius enim utriusque exercitus arbiter erat. Argentonus cum primum venisset nuntiavit Maclodiensem Cardinalem statim venturum, qui cum in planum venisset constitit et

---

[283] diurnum EF     [284] possit B     [285] puerumque EF     [286] qui BEF     [287] tentorio quievit EF     [288] maximo EF     [289] discrimine EF     [290] consumata F     [291] idem EF     [292] om. EF     [293] om. EF     [294] praefecto EF

gage. Yet it was sufficient to have escaped so great peril with a small band. It would indeed have been the height of felicity if all had turned out well, but we must endure it if fortune has heaped on this one day all the evils of a whole year, a fortune which had been predicted to us as black, so that now, driven by hunger amid great danger, with glory and a kingdom and a triumph lost, with soldiers left behind in Puglia and Calabria, I must return home with a few forces. But in this one fact I rejoice, that our men fought with the utmost courage and true military discipline, and only a few of our nobles, and of the other soldiers not many, are missing, and even fewer are wounded. There is indeed nothing lasting under the heavens, and we must yield sometimes to fortune. The war with King Alfonso and his son we fought without bloodshed. But the Venetians have changed everything for us. This kingdom was not acquired for me, but for all of you; I enjoy a very extensive kingdom in a long succession. It remains to establish the whole army in safety with the greatest possible speed. But you, Trivulzio, proclaimed that the commander of the camp was a young man, or a boy, without military training. An evil boy he seemed to me on that day, but if the fight had taken place in the open he would have been far worse."

61. Then he adjourned the conference and dined, and that night he slept in another's tent. Because the greatest fear prevailed over the state of things two lines of sentinels were ordered posted, fires were kept burning in the camp, and the leaders spent a great part of the night in consultation. The gist of their deliberations was this, that to deceive the enemy a truce should be pretended and that they themselves should flee. On 7 July [134] the King sent a herald to the Venetian proveditors; he was brought before the commander of the camp and the other leaders and reported that Argenton desired an audience in the royal name. The proveditors agreed to the request. When the herald wanted to depart he was asked by the commander of the army how many of the French nobles had been killed in battle; he replied that the King mourned eighteen dead or taken prisoner, and the commander revealed that two of these were alive, the great Bourbon bastard and Marshal Miolans; that some of the knightly order who had been wounded were safe; and that the rest had been slain in exchanges with their assailants.

62. When the herald had left, the commander of the army with the proveditors, the Count of Caiazzo, and Niccolò of Pitigliano went to the Taro to await the royal envoy Argenton,[135] for the river was the boundary for the two armies. As soon as Argenton arrived he announced that the Cardinal of Saint-Malo would come at once, but when the Cardinal

insidias timere simulavit, nec ad colloquia ut veniret audere visus est. Interea diutina cunctatione Argentonus strenuos Venetorum militum animos summopere laudavit, qui [295] omni incommodo neglecto pugnare voluerint, et utrumque exercitum parvo [296] momento cruentissimam pugnam confecisse. Legati vero multa adversus Regem protulere, illum fidem non servasse, oppida Pontificis diripuisse et urbes plurimas sociorum occupasse et Mediolanensis postremo Ducis Novariam cepisse.[297] Praefectus vero se egregium facinus tentasse inquit, Barbontem ducem pro Rege cepisse vestimenti similitudine deceptum; nec aliud in ea pugna optasse quam Regem equo sublimem dignoscere, ad quem tota acie [298] neglecto omni discrimine irrupisset. At Argentonus inquit non facile posse Gallorum Regem capi nisi deleto omni [299] exercitu quem omnes summa veneratione et colunt et tuentur. His dictis infecta re utrique in castra rediere. Vesperi cum in coena legati essent idem regius caduceator supervenit, ingressus nunciat Argentonum regio nomine [300] colloquia desiderare et eadem quae [301] Cardinalis statuerat dicturum. Illi respondent horam suspectam esse militibus furore percitis, sed summo mane opportunum fore; ille non priusquam victa fame discessit.

63. Legati percognita Gallorum trepidatione visa denique praeda victoriam omnem exactius Veneto Senatui, ut dictum est, significavere. Per id ferme tempus Senatus Venetus classis imperatori Antonio Grimanno litteris imperavit ut statim Corcyra solveret stratiotasque traiiceret in Apuliam, ut urbes quas Galli possiderent omni nixu expugnaret. Hic depositis equitibus et omni milite Monopolim urbem vi [302] protinus occupavit, in qua pugna Petrus Bembus dux triremis fortiter pugnando bombardae ictu contritus est et praedae civitas data est, salvis sacris aedibus et muliebri sexu qui in templis [303] imperatoris iussu custoditus est, arcemque deinde [304] sub conditionibus a praefecto quodam Gallo in deditionem accepit impositoque praesidio Neapolim versus navigavit.

64. VIII Idus Rex Gallus ducibus omnibus assentientibus post primas vigilias frenatos equos stare et universum exercitum in armis esse iubet, idque per tubicinem totis castris significavit, simulans se idem per exploratores ab hoste Veneto fieri accepisse ne tumultu et [305]

---

[295] quod B   [296] pravo EF   [297] cepisset EF   [298] acies EF   [299] om. B
[300] nomine regio EF   [301] quam EF   [302] in B   [303] templo EF   [304] denique EF   [305] ac EF

advanced into open view he stopped and pretended to fear treachery, and seemed not to dare to come to the conference. Meanwhile during the long delay Argenton praised highly the active courage of the Venetian soldiers who were willing to fight despite every disadvantage and the fact that both armies had finished the very bloody battle in a short time. But the proveditors cited many things against the King, that he had not kept the faith, had destroyed the towns of the Pope, had seized many cities of the allies, and lastly had taken Novara which belonged to the Duke of Milan. The commander however said that he himself had attempted a brilliant action but had captured the Bourbon leader in place of the King, since he was deceived by the similarity in dress: he had wanted nothing more in that battle than to distinguish the King high on his horse and rush against him with his entire line, disregarding all peril. But Argenton said that the King of the French could not be readily captured except by destroying the entire army, since all cherish and protect him with the greatest veneration.[136] At these words they returned each to his own camp with the matter unsettled. In the evening when the proveditors were at dinner the same royal herald arrived, and when he was introduced he announced that Argenton desired a conference in the King's name and would report what the Cardinal had decided. They replied that the hour was dangerous since the soldiers were aroused by the noise, but that it would be convenient early in the morning; he departed after eating.

63. The proveditors, having recognized the alarm of the French and having finally seen the plunder, reported the entire victory in great detail to the Venetian Senate, as has been related. At about this same time the Venetian Senate by a letter ordered Antonio Grimani,[137] admiral of the fleet, to set sail at once from Corfù and carry stratiotes over to Puglia in order that he might storm in an all-out effort the cities which the French held, and he, landing cavalry and all his soldiers, straightway seized the city of Monopoli by force.[138] In this battle Pietro Bembo,[139] captain of a trireme, was hit by a ball and killed while fighting bravely, and the city was given over to plunder. The sacred shrines, however, were respected, and also the women, who on order of the admiral were kept in the churches.[140] Then when terms had been agreed upon he accepted the citadel in surrender from the Frenchman in command and after setting a garrison over it sailed to Naples.

64. On 8 July the French King, with the approval of all his leaders, ordered that the horses stand bridled after the first watch and that the whole army be under arms; this he announced to the entire camp by a trumpeter, pretending, in order to prevent the camp from waver-

pavore castra fluctuarent, vigiliasque intentiore cura servari iussit. Ergo ignibus perpetuis solito maioribus tota regia castra fulgebant. Ipse cum ducibus quam [306] acceptissimis agmina laeto similis circuibat et ad pugnam omnes parari suadebat et sarcinas colligi ut pugnando discederent. Solicitudo vero Venetos vigilandi [307] duntaxat tenebat secundam sequenti die pugnam expectantes, nec defuere ex iis qui vigilias custodirent quin [308] significarent tumultus in Gallorum castris et equorum hinnitus exaudiri, unde ad arma milites excitarunt ex tabernaculis horrido tympanorum pulsu,[309] qui exinde nihil aliud exaudientes quieti rursus corpora dedere; suspitio, quae non vana erat, per se resedit.

65. At post primas vigilias Gallus collectis sarcinis territus sine tubae signo precatus ut prospere et inscio Veneto aufugere posset, ac pervigil ea nocte ad fugam tantum se accingebat. In tentorio quodam [310] modo [311] noctis horam quaerebat, modo [312] vigilias recte servari iubebat.[313] Circumstabant tentorium ordinum duces sine somno ad accipienda imperia. Ille tandem ut equos conscenderent imperavit et Trebiam versus Triulcio duce iter facere iubet. Milites ubi Regis fugam tandem deprehendere exustis tentoriis quibusdam et tegumentis equorum aureis concisis [314] quorum frusta humi cernebantur sepultisque quibusdam tormentis ac vasis militaribus iugulatisque equis in praelio sauciis quicquid gravissimum onus erat igni tradidere, alioqui hostium esse confitebantur, unde collucentium ignium vis illa erat qua eos adhuc castra tenere credebant Veneti. Traditum est illos quosdam saucios alios invalidos qui agmen sequi non poterant truculentia barbara necasse.

66. Legati Veneti cognita tandem hostium fuga convocatis ducibus eos fugientes persequi statuerunt [315] miseruntque ad incessendos a tergo remorandosque Petrum Duodum praefectum militum Graecorum levis armaturae cum equitibus suis ac Comitem Acaiazanum cum Italis leviter armatis. At illi praedae intenti in sequentem diem rem distulerunt. Ob id legatus Melchior Trivisanus excandescens e tabernaculo plerosque excitavit, qui hostes segniter persecuti [316] sunt. Tradunt in hac Gallorum nobili fuga Acaiazanum Comitem [317] ac Fracassium fratres Regem Gallum fugientem salutasse magna totius exercitus suspitione et praetereuntibus Gallis fame marcescentibus incolas

---

[306] om. EF      [307] vigilandi Venetos EF      [308] qui EF      [309] impulsu B
[310] quotam A      [311] om. EF      [312] om. EF      [313] iubebant B      [314] conciscis B      [315] statuebant EF      [316] prosecuti B      [317] om. EF

ing in confusion and fear, to have learned through spies that the Venetian enemy was doing the same thing, and he ordered also that the watches be kept with even greater care. So the whole royal camp was agleam with fires which were continuous and larger than usual. He himself with his favorite leaders rode around his lines as if in joy and urged everyone to be ready for battle and to collect the baggage so that they might depart fighting. But the desire only to keep careful watch lay hold of the Venetians, for they expected a second battle on the next day. And some of those who stood guard reported hearing confusion in the camp of the French and the neighing of horses, wherefore the soldiers were aroused to arms from their tents with a fearful beating of drums; then, hearing nothing more, they gave themselves over to rest again, and the suspicion, which was not vain, subsided of itself.

65. But after the first watch the Frenchman waited terrified, with his baggage collected and without a trumpet signal, praying that he could flee successfully and without the knowledge of the Venetians; all during the night he was wakeful and girding himself only for flight. In his tent he would now ask the time, now order the watches to be carefully kept. The leaders of the ranks stood around the tent without sleep to receive orders. At length he commanded them to mount their horses and journey to the Trebbia under the leadership of Trivulzio. When the soldiers finally understood that the King was fleeing, they burned some tents, cut to pieces the golden trappings of the horses, fragments of which were seen on the ground, buried some of the artillery and military objects, slew the horses which had been wounded in battle, and set fire to whatever was hardest to carry, conceding that the rest belonged to the enemy. It was the bright light from all the fires which led the Venetians to believe that the enemy was still encamped. The report is that they killed with barbarous cruelty some wounded and sick men who could not follow the lines.[141]

66. The Venetian proveditors, when they finally realized that the enemy had fled, called the leaders together and decided to pursue them in their flight, and they despatched Pietro Duodo, leader of the Greek light-armed soldiers, with his cavalry and the Count of Caiazzo with the Italian light-armed soldiers to assault them in the rear and delay them.[142] But these troops were concerned with plunder and postponed the assignment to the following day. Therefore the proveditor Melchiorre Trevisan became enraged and from his tent incited a great many who followed the enemy slowly. They say that during this celebrated flight of the French the Count of Caiazzo and his brother Fracasso greeted the French King as he was fleeing, arousing great dis-

alimenta obtulisse ne fugientes famis desperatione vicos et oppida cremarent.

67. Interea tormentorum supplementa CC bigis onerata Verona in castra sero missa sunt, quae castrorum magnam partem munierunt, ac tormentorum magistri quo pugnae tempore desiderarunt duces. Verum in eo pugnae furore nec pulvis accensibilis nec tormentorum periti reperiebantur, itaque vis omnis in dextera posita fuerat. Hac die dum sarcinae colliguntur Melchior Trivisanus legatus exercitus saucios omnis qui castra sequi non poterant Parmam misit, quibus Senatus nomine pecunias effusim ipse elargitus est et medicos vulnerum adhibuit non parva mercede. Lectulos hilaris senex classis quondam proimperator circuibat beneque sperare [318] omnes hortabatur; inter hos et Galli saucii cogniti sunt. Demirabantur Parmenses Senatus Veneti clementiam ac miram erga subiectos pietatem.

68. Senatus interea cum de persequendis hostibus litteras legatorum accepisset eorum sententiam large probavit, qui singulis diebus equitum et peditum supplementa [319] sine intermissione mittebat. Legati amotis castris impedimentorum tedio tormenta eadem Veronam remisere, verum Senatus alia singulis diebus assidue [320] conflabat, nec cessabant ab opere tormentorum artifices qui tum mari tum terra omnia subministrabant.[321] Senatus impiger totius belli onera solus substinebat;[322] in Germania Suevia equitum peditumque delectum habebat, item in Illyria Delmatia Graecia Transpadana regione. Omito Romam, Bononiam, Mantuam, Flaminiam omnem, in quibus Venetorum pecuniae diffundebantur. Classis quoque numerosa sine sociorum auxilio levi momento parata est; quo [323] magis mirum est, ad belli necessitatem cives omnes aurum argentumque laeti aerario deferebant, nullusque seculo nostro princeps est aut res publica quae puriorem monetam spargat adulterantesque saevius puniat. Ea pecunia nil [324] apud omnes nationes carius est, quam nemo respuit, punit et qui alienam monetam adulterant, in signanda pecunia idem pondus eandem metalli sincaeritatem quae multis saeculis servata est mire custodit; purissimo Senatui puro ac mundo metallo uti convenit.

---

[318] proimperator—sperare om. F      [319] supplenta B      [320] om. EF
[321] administrabant EF      [322] sustinebat BEF      [323] quod EF      [324] nihil EF

trust in the entire army,[143] and that as the French passed by wasted with hunger the natives offered food lest the fugitives, driven to despair by hunger, burn their villages and towns.[144]

67. Meanwhile additional engines loaded on two hundred two-horse wagons were sent late from Verona to the camp; these fortified a great part of the camp, and with them were the masters of the artillery, whom the leaders had missed at the time of the battle. But in that. frenzy of fighting neither powder for firing nor those experienced in artillery were available, and so all the power depended on their own right hands. On this day as the baggage was being collected Melchiorre Trevisan, proveditor of the army, sent to Parma all the wounded who could not follow the camp and himself gave them a generous amount of money in the name of the Senate. At no small expense he provided wound-surgeons, and the merry old man who was formerly vice-commander of the fleet went around to their beds and encouraged them all to have good hope; among them were also recognized some French wounded. The people of Parma marveled at the clemency of the Venetian Senate and its wondrous mercy toward the defeated.[145]

68. In the meantime the Senate, when it had received the letter of the proveditors concerning the pursuit of the enemy, freely approved their opinion, and every day in succession it kept sending without interruption supplementary forces of cavalry and infantry. The proveditors after breaking up camp sent that artillery back to Verona because of the difficulty with baggage, but for several days continuously the Senate kept procuring more, nor did the masters of the artillery, who at that time managed all things on land and sea, stop working, and the energetic Senate all alone actively supported the burdens of the entire war. In Germany and Swabia it held a levy of cavalry and infantry, likewise in Illyria, Dalmatia, Greece, and the region beyond the Po, not to mention Rome, Bologna, Mantua, and all Romagna, among which the money of the Venetians was poured forth. In a short time also a large fleet was made ready without the help of the allies, and, far more to be wondered at, all the citizens joyfully brought their gold and silver to the treasury for the necessities of war, and there is no prince in our time, no state which circulates purer money or punishes counterfeiters more severely. Nothing is more precious among all nations than that money, which no one rejects. It punishes also those who counterfeit the money of others, and in coining money it maintains marvelously the same weight, the same purity of metal which it has preserved for many centuries; it is fitting for this very pure Senate to use pure and unadulterated metal.

69. IIII [325] Idus Iulias legati speculatores primum, agmina deinde [326] praemisere, ipsi postremo secuti sunt. Opportune enim ex Opiano [327] vico discessere ingruentibus morbis quos odor cadaverum totis iacentium campis ardente Syrio excitabat. Ad Sanctum Doninum oppidum imbre fere perpetuo ac lubrica via pervenere qua impedimenta difficulter sequi poterant, unde ea nocte legati in foeno incommode iacuere. Hic accepere Gallorum agmina bidui intervallo magna itineris spatia citato exercitu confecisse, unde legati Senatui significavere [328] frustra hostes persequendos esse, Ludovicusque Mediolanensis dux Novariam a Gallis captam reddi iure foederis requirit traiiciendasque ob id trans Padum copias esse. A Senatu igitur litteras de traiiciendis copiis legati accepere quibus fidissimo praefecto exercitus commendabatur. VI [329] Idus legati Placentiam venere qui sine exercitu in urbem recepti sunt. Quinto Idus Trebiam superarunt,[330] Romanorum exercituum et cladium testimonium, ac [331] ad Sanctum Ioannem oppidum pervenere cum omnibus copiis, unde ex Venetis militibus circiter duo millia ad Dertonam [332] Alexandriamque Statiliensem praesidio firmandam mittuntur ne Galli praetereuntes iniuriam foederatis [333] urbibus inferrent neve [334] cives [335] titubantes ad deditionem excitarent.

70. Hic audivimus Gallos praetereuntes nimia famis impatientia semicoctos profluente adhuc sanie commanducasse sues atque in emendis rebus ab incolis praeter opinionem omnium [336] mira abstinentia usos fuisse etsi rustici in plerisque locis fluviorum pontes diruerant ad remorandam hostium fugam. Alii vero illos reliquerant pro cuiuslibet animo et studio. At Galli mira celeritate ripas fluviorum [337] altissimas ubi pontes diruti iacebant prostraverant.[338] Saucii vel itinere fatigati Galli qui interierant secundum viam sepulturae dabantur tumulorum frequentium indicio. In hac fuga frater Turonensis principis [339] obiit ac sine feralibus officiis terrae datus est.

71. Quarto Idus ad Clastigium [340] vetustissimum oppidum castra perducta [341] sunt. Hinc sequenti die Casotum [342] ubi ponte Padi ripas Mediolanenses iunxerant. In eo exercitus praefectus ordinem praetereuntium disponebat ne impedimenta equitibus peditibusque mixta

---

[325] quarto B   [326] om. EF   [327] Appiano B   [328] significare EF
[329] sexto B   [330] superabant EF   [331] atque EF   [332] Tortonam ABEF, Dertonam A by MS. correction   [333] soederatis A foederatis A by MS. correction faederatis B   [334] eius add. EF   [335] om. EF   [336] om. B
[337] ffuviorum A   [338] prostraverat B   [339] principis Turonensis EF
[340] Clastichium EF   [341] producta B   [342] Cassetum EF

69. On 12 July the proveditors first sent the scouts ahead, then the lines, and then they themselves followed later. Indeed they departed opportunely from the village Oppiano, for diseases were breaking out because of the stench of the corpses lying over all the fields as the Dog-Star blazed. They arrived at the town of San Donnino in almost continual rain and by a slippery road over which the baggage trains could scarcely follow, wherefore on that night the proveditors slept uncomfortably in the mud. Here they heard that the ranks of the French had hurriedly traversed long stages of their journey in a period of two days, and therefore the proveditors notified the Senate that it was useless to pursue the enemy,[146] and Lodovico, duke of Milan, demanded that Novara, which had been captured by the French, be returned in accordance with the conditions of the league, and that forces be sent across the Po for this purpose. So the proveditors received from the Senate a letter concerning the crossing of the forces; by it the matter was entrusted to the most faithful commander of the army. On 10 July the proveditors arrived at Piacenza and were received into the city without the army. On 11 July they crossed the Trebbia, witness to the destruction of Roman armies, and arrived at Castel San Giovanni with all their forces. From there about two thousand Venetian soldiers were sent to Tortona and to Alessandria to strengthen those places with a garrison, lest the French as they passed by inflict some injury on the allied cities or incite the wavering citizens to surrender.

70. I heard here that the French as they went by, being unable to endure hunger any longer, had devoured pigs half-cooked and with blood still flowing and that in buying supplies from the inhabitants [147] they had contrary to everyone's expectation used great restraint, even though the peasants at very many points had destroyed the bridges over the rivers in order to delay the enemy's flight. Others however had left the bridges standing, according as each one willed or desired, but the French with wondrous speed had leveled the very high banks of the rivers where the bridges lay destroyed. Those of the French who were wounded or worn out from the journey and who had died were buried along the road, as the many graves show. On this flight the brother of the prince of Tours died and was committed to earth without funeral services.

71. The camp was brought on 12 July to Casteggio, a very old town. From here on the following day they reached Caseto, where the Milanese had thrown a bridge between the banks of the Po. The troops crossing this bridge were disposed by the commander of the army in such a way as to prevent the baggage train from becoming mixed with the

celeritatem perturbarent fustibusque temeritatem coercebat. Itaque paucis horis universum exercitum miro ordine traiecit, summoto protinus ponte ad Sanctum Georgium oppidum castra locata sunt. Hic sequenti die Laurentius Avogarius sanguinarius alioqui miles et in patria pluribus caedibus cruentus lanceis a pluribus in media via confossus iacuit. Sed nulla lex est contra priscorum observationem quae in castris homicidam insidiatorem seditiosumque puniat, pudet nostri saeculi. Qui sanguine propinquiores erant insidiarum libellum dedere, inimici scelerum poenas merito luisse responderunt, legati homicidii causam ad Senatum retulere.

72. Hic nuntiatum est Gallorum Regem Hastem pervenisse ad Italiae terminos ibique fessum militem magnis itineribus vires [343] recolligere [344] iussisse. Hic convocatis copiarum ducibus ac caeteris principibus in contionem processit. "Parva," inquit, "manu tot tantisque itineribus confectis Appenninas angustias tabescentibus fame fere militibus Venetorum manus et sociorum tandem evasimus; Deo igitur Optimo Maximo gratias ingentes debemus. Superest ut hic collatis auxiliis recreato milite fesso Novariam urbem longa obsidione tandem liberemus nisi Venetus alia quoque auxilia miserit, alioqui maiora copiarum supplementa quaerere opus est quae [345] a Germanis attiguis regionibus largiore pecunia conducenda sunt. Ex Gallia frustra opem expectaturi sumus loci distantia et pluvioso autumno instante." Universa contio assensa est, deinde silentio facto haec pauca retulit: "Scio plerosque vestrum amissis impedimentis vel diutina foris militia in patriam redire [346] velle, qua nihil carius habetur. His redeundi liberam potestatem damus eorumque desiderio optemperamus laeti. De infirmis ac sauciis pariter taceo, qui per se liberam et [347] causariam [348] missionem habent. Sed hoc unum animum excruciat,[349] Apulorum et Calabrorum levitas et Neapolitanorum facilis rebellio, qua praefectum nostrum cum omnibus copiis in maximo versari periculo videtis. In classe spes omnis sita est. Divi bene vertant; omnia perturbari video. Neapolitani cives agrum feracissimum depopulari non patientur. Arces tamen et totius provinciae oppida munitissima longiorem obsidionem, si viri sunt, sustinebunt. Utinam vel pacis vel belli viam Deus nobis

---

[343] om. EF       [344] ecolligere B quiescere EF       [345] om. B       [346] ire EF
[347] om. EF       [348] om. EF       [349] excruciat animum EF

cavalry and infantry and slowing the speed of march, and with whips
he curbed any rashness. And so in a few hours he got his entire army
over in wonderful order, and at once destroyed the bridge and pitched
camp at the town of San Giorgio. Here on the following day Lorenzo
Avogadro, for the rest a bloodthirsty soldier and already stained with
several slayings in his native town, was stabbed by lances at the hands
of numerous assailants and lay dead in the middle of the street.[148] But
contrary to the observance of our ancestors there is, to the shame of
our own century, no law which punishes a homicide or waylayer or
seditious person in camp. His closest relatives charged treachery, his
enemies replied that he had rightly expiated his crimes, and the proveditors reported the case of homicide to the Senate.

72. It was announced here that the King of the French had arrived
at Asti at the border of Italy and there had commanded his soldiers,
weary from the long marches, to gather up their strength again. Here-
upon, when the leaders of the forces and other heads had assembled,
he advanced before the gathering and said, "With a small band, even
though our troops are almost wasted away by hunger, and after making
so many and such long marches, we have left behind the passes of the
Apennines and also the Venetian troops, and finally those of their
allies; accordingly we give great thanks to Almighty and All Merciful
God.[149] It remains, when we have assembled auxiliary forces here and
refreshed our weary soldiers, to free the city of Novara at last from its
long siege, if the Venetian enemy does not also send additional forces.
Otherwise we must seek greater complements of troops which must
be hired at greater expense from the adjoining German districts. In
vain shall we await aid from France, which is far off, and besides, the
rainy autumn season is at hand." The whole assembly gave its approval,
and then, when there was silence again, he made these few statements: "I know that a great many of you who have lost your baggage
and served a long campaign abroad want to return to your country,
than which nothing is more dearly cherished. To these I give full
opportunity of returning, and I happily submit to their desire. I give
the same opportunity to the sick and the wounded, who have free
discharge for themselves for this reason. But this one thing tortures
my mind, the fickleness of the populace in Puglia and Calabria and
the ready rebellion of the Neapolitans, which you see has plunged our
commander with all his forces into the greatest danger. All hope rests
with the fleet. May the gods look with favor; I see everything in confusion. The Neapolitan citizens will not permit their very fertile land
to be ravaged. Yet the citadels and the very well fortified towns of the
entire province will support a longer siege if they are men. May God

ostendat. Maximilianus ac Hispaniae reges (non enim dubito) sacra foedera servabunt, unde Italia universa vobis praedae exposita erit, urbes omnes iugum subiturae sunt nostrum, quas vobis condonabimus. Ego nihil aliud quam victoriae nomen volo et cogito." Post haec plurimi domum abiere labores et incommoda pertesi.

73. Eo die litterae in castra delatae sunt quae [350] militibus omnibus laetitiam attulerunt. Nuntiatum est Ferdinandum Regem Neapolim subinde ingressum summo omnium civium studio Gallosque intra arces obsideri et urbes omnes quae in propinquo sunt Ferdinandi vexilla extulisse. His cognitis Franciscus Gonzaga exercitus praefectus Regi Gallorum per nuntium significavit ut de bello quid [351] speraret facile conciperet, cui Gallus respondit nec id perpetuum esse, plurimum interesse muros an parietes vel arces possidere. XVII [352] Calendas Augustas [353] Virgilius Ursinus Romanus factionum princeps Nolae a Gallis captus ad Venetos legatos venit [354] a Rege dimissus. XVI [355] Calendas [356] copiae omnes ad Vespellum oppidum ductae sunt. Tum nuntiatum est classem regium a Genuensibus captam fuisse, quod non sine gaudio omnes audivere congestis in unum ferme tempus in Gallos tot malis. Ioannes Franciscus Comes Acaiazanus Mediolanensium rerum studiosus copias a Venetis legatis ad praesidium caeterorum oppidorum rursus petiit. Illi subirati ex suis mitti oportere responderunt, hic enim exercitum Venetum sua custodire oppida gaudebat. E diverso legati Veneti qui totius Senatus robur ultra Padum intulerant [357] milites non sine magno periculo dispergere posse arbitrabantur sua et sociorum incommoda gnari: satis esse Dertonam [358] Alexandriamque Statiliensem praesidio suo firmasse.

74. XV [359] Calendas [360] LXXX millia nummum aureorum ad militum stipendia a Venetis missa sunt. Mussitabant plerique Mediolanensium milites ex quibus pedites denarios ternos duntaxat acceperant, equites vero duplum, nec id sine Veneti Senatus laude, qui mercenario militi semper ignoscit. Eo die de collocandis castris inter duces verba facta sunt pro Novariae urbis obsidione. In eam contionem [361] venerat Bernardus Contarenus patricius stratiotarum praefectus, qui obsidione cum Galeatio Severinate, Ludovici Ducis omnium copiarum praefecto, Novariam urbem, ut dictum est, premebat perpetuisque incursionibus

---

[350] qui B      [351] quod EF      [352] septimamdecimam B      [353] Augusti BEF
[354] nenit A      [355] sextadecima B      [356] Calendarum B      [357] transtulerant EF
[358] Tortonam AB Dirtonam EF      [359] quintadecima B      [360] Calendarum B
[361] contentionem EF

show us the way either of peace or of war. Maximilian [150] and the rulers of Spain will (I doubt not) keep the sacred compact, and as a result all Italy will be laid before you for plunder; all her cities are due to submit to our yoke, and I shall present them to you. I want and plan nothing else than the honor of victory." After this a great many who had wearied of the toils and inconveniences of camp went home.

73. On that day a letter was brought to the camp which gave joy to all the soldiers, for it announced that King Ferdinand had forthwith entered Naples amid the greatest eagerness of all the citizens, that the French were besieged within the strongholds, and that all the towns in the vicinity had raised aloft the standards of Ferdinand.[151] At this news Francesco Gonzaga, commander of the army, indicated by a message to the King of the French that he could readily comprehend what he might hope from the war, and to this the Frenchman replied that this was not enduring and that there was a very great difference between holding city or house walls and holding strongholds. On 16 July Virginio Orsini of Rome, leader of factions, who was captured at Nola by the French, was released by the King [152] and came to the Venetian proveditors. All the forces were conducted on 17 July to the town of Vespolate. Then it was announced that the royal fleet had been captured by the Genoese,[153] a report which all heard not without joy, since so many misfortunes were heaped upon the French at almost the same time. Giovanni Francesco, count of Caiazzo, who was zealous in the interests of Milan, again requested forces from the Venetian proveditors for the protection of the other cities, but they angrily replied that these should be sent from his own forces. He rejoiced indeed that the Venetian army protected its own towns. On the other hand the Venetian proveditors, who had advanced the might of the entire Senate beyond the Po, thought that soldiers could not be scattered without great danger, though aware of the disadvantages to themselves and their allies: it was enough, they said, to have strengthened Tortona and Alessandria with their aid.

74. On 18 July eight thousand ducats were sent by the Venetians as salary for the soldiers. A great many of the Milanese troops grumbled, since their foot soldiers had received only three denarii apiece, and the cavalry double that, and this was not done without praise of the Venetian Senate, which always excuses the mercenary soldier. On that day the leaders discussed pitching camp for the siege of Novara. To this conference had come the patrician Bernardo Contarini, captain of the stratiotes, who was blockading the city of Novara, as has been said, together with Galeazzo Sanseverino, prefect of all the forces of Duke Lodovico, and he was ravaging everything in repeated incur-

cuncta vastabat. Hic ab omnibus in concione maxime laudatus est ac
militum ipsius virtus quod [362] uno duntaxat congressu LXX Gallos
milites ceperit equosque quinquaginta in castra duxerit neminemque
ex sociis amiserit.

75. XIIII [363] Calendas [364] Augustas ad Tiliam oppidulum castra con-
tulere, duobus milibus passuum ab urbe Novaria Vercellas versus,
ubi pabuli et lignorum et aquae suppetebat copia, etsi tuto minime
collocata erant vicino hoste circumdante. Novarienses ex altis turribus
et moenibus victricia agmina venientia spectabant ad pugnam instructa. Acceperat Auriliensis Dux apud Tarrum Gallos suos fuisse
victores, quos laetus in urbem excepturus esset, sed suorum fraude
nuntiorum se deceptum fuisse cognovit quandoquidem Rex iam Haste
a fuga sese [365] contineret ubi vexatos fame itinereque milites firmabat;
unde Gallus cognito Venetorum adventu Ducem Auriliensem auxilia
expectantem litteris ad sustinendam paucorum dierum obsidionem
hortatus est, sese propediem venturum pollicitus est ingentibus copiis.
Unde manavit [366] tota urbe laetitia de Regis adventu. Tum [367] cives
qui proditione urbem Gallis dederant ac plebeii qui Gallorum rebus
studebant ultima pati potius statuerant quam rursus [368] Ludovici Ducis
ferre imperia. Munimenta igitur ante portas construere coeperunt
cespite vimine fronde luto atque ante ipsa suburbia vallum et fossam
obiicere quae omnium militum mansionibus sinistra sunt et audenti-
bus periculum afferunt.[369]

Finis libri de Tarrensi pugna.

---

[362] qui EF    [363] quartadecima B    [364] Calendarum B    [365] se EF
[366] in add. EF    [367] tamen EF    [368] om. EF    [369] affuerunt F

sions.[154] He and the courage of his soldiers were highly praised by all in the assembly because in only one clash he had captured seventy French soldiers and brought fifty horses to camp and lost none of his comrades.

75. On 19 July they encamped at the little town of Tiglia, two miles from Novara in the direction of Vercelli, where an abundance of food, wood, and water was at hand, although the position was not at all safe, since the enemy nearby encircled them. The people of Novara watched from their lofty towers and walls as the victorious lines arrived drawn up for battle. The Duke of Orléans had heard that his French had been victors at the Taro, and he expected to receive them joyfully into the city, but he realized that he had been duped by the deceit of his messengers, since the King had now stopped his flight at Asti and was refreshing his soldiers who were wearied with hunger and the journey. Therefore the Frenchman on hearing of the arrival of the Venetians wrote a letter to the Duke of Orléans, who was awaiting aid, and encouraged him to endure the siege for a few days, with the promise that he himself would come shortly with vast forces. Joy spread through the whole city at the news of the coming of the King. The citizens who had treacherously handed over the city to the French and the people who favored the French cause had already decided to suffer to the end rather than endure again the rule of Duke Lodovico. Accordingly they began to build fortifications before their gates with turf, brushwood, leaves, and mud, and to throw up before the approaches to the city a rampart and a ditch, which are a hindrance to the stationing of all troops and bring danger to those who risk them.

End of the book on the battle of the Taro.

# BOOK II

### ARGUMENTUM SECUNDI LIBRI
### AD ANTONIUM BERNARDUM ET GEORGIUM CORNELIUM
### EQUITES CLARISSIMOS ET ALOISIUM VENERIUM
### DECEMVIROS PRAESTANTISSIMOS

Veneti a pugna superato Pado ad Novariam expugnandam cum exercitu contendunt, at Ludovicus Dux obsidione cogere statuit. Gallus interea Rex Haste recreato milite Novariae fame laboranti opitulaturum se promittens simulata dimicandi promptitudine Vercellas venit ubi seditionem in castris Venetis ortam esse audivit, qua sedata clam de pacis conditionibus cum Ludovico Duce agere coepit Venetis longae obsidionis taedio arctius urbem prementibus. Tum Franciscus Gonzaga a Veneto Senatu imperator creatus est, et milites qui strenue cum eo pugnarant maiora stipendia accepere. Novus interea miles perpetuis excubiis et laboribus tyrocinium exuit et promptior aptiorque redditus est. Comes Nicolaus Petilianus dum muros tormentis quateret pilula plumbea lethaliter confossus. Gallus Rex tandem et Ludovicus Dux variis de causis praecipites pacis conditiones complectuntur; ille Novariam restituit et spe redeundi in Galliam discessit incertos fortunae [1] eventus et ancipites lusus accusando. Veneti defenso tandem Insubre restituto Regi Ferdinando regno liberata Roma et universa pene Italia domum laeti rediere et triumphum imperatori suo Francisco Gonzagae Mantuanorum principi ob res bene foeliciterque gestas decrevere.

---

[1] belli EF

### ARGUMENT OF THE SECOND BOOK
### TO ANTONIO BERNARDO AND GIORGIO CORNELIO,
### MOST EMINENT KNIGHTS, AND LUIGI VENIER,
### ALL MOST EXCELLENT DECEMVIRS

After the battle the Venetians cross the Po and hurry along with the intention of storming Novara with their army, but Duke Lodovico decides to force it by a siege. Meanwhile the French King has refreshed his soldiers at Asti, and promising to bring aid to Novara, which is suffering from hunger, he comes to Vercelli as if ready to fight, when he gets news that sedition has sprung up in the Venetian camp. After this has been quelled he begins to treat secretly with Duke Lodovico about terms of peace as the Venetians blockade the city more firmly with a long and tedious siege. Then Francesco Gonzaga is appointed general by the Venetian Senate, and the soldiers who had fought strenuously with him receive higher stipends. Meanwhile new recruits have cast off their inexperience in constant watches and labors and have become readier and more adept. Count Niccolò of Pitigliano is critically wounded by a lead ball while storming the walls with artillery. At length the French King and Duke Lodovico for varying reasons hastily accept terms of swift peace: the King returns Novara and departs with the expectation of going back to France; he complains of the uncertain issues and doubtful gambles of fortune. The Venetians at length, having defended the Insubrian Duke, restored his kingdom to King Ferdinand, and freed Rome and almost all Italy, joyfully return home and decree a triumph for their general Francesco Gonzaga, marquis of the Mantuans, in appreciation of deeds well and successfully accomplished.[1]

## SECUNDUS LIBER DE OBSIDIONE URBIS NOVARIAE [2]

1. Franciscus Gonzaga Mantuanus princeps exercitus praefectus pulsis ad extremos Italiae terminos Gallis in armis laetus et equo sublimis XIIII Calendas Augustas equitum ingentia agmina peditumque phalanges in conspectum [3] Novariensium ad Tiliam, ut diximus, castellum locavit, quod eadem ferme hora Mediolanensium exercitus praefecto Galeatio Severinate adventante Venetorum exercitu expugnaverat, cuius existimatione Galli qui oppidum in potestate tenebant ad arbitrium hostium deditionem protinus fecere. Ii pridie suburbana concremari passi fuerant [4] auxilia ab Auriliensi Duce singulis momentis [5] expectantes. Legati oppidum occupavere, praefectus foris tentoria haud procul locavit. Reliqui duces cum suis equitibus veluti per vicos pariter tabernacula et tuguria posuere.

2. Tum Auriliensem Ducem perterruit novus hostis ac Gallorum fuga instantis [6] item famis quam propediem civitas passura esset periculum reformidabat. Fruges enim perexiguas vixque in calamo maturas collegerat arcemque tribus mensibus duntaxat munire potuerat.[7] Ante oppidum forum constitutum est atque alterum in sociorum castris erat; in illo annona cara erat ac praecipue vinum, reliqua usui necessaria primis fere diebus abundare coeperunt. XIII Calendas [8] praecluso unde descendit fluminis alveo Venetus miles alio cursu dato ab urbe avertit molasque frumentarias quas versabat aqua VI stadiis iuxta urbem ferro ignique demolitus est. In urbe molae trusatiles perpaucae, asinariae nullae. Plebs frugem pilo [9] pinsebat et panem semicontusum sine cribro conficiebat, cuius indicaturam nos magnifico equiti Antonio Boldo Venetias ut inopiam urbis clausae cognosceret misimus. Frugum protinus incommoda Novarienses sensere; noctu [10] enim Vercellis alimenta aegre mittebantur militum metu. Illi ante [11] urbis portas munimenta quaedam construxere, ut dictum est, muri

---

[2] SECUNDUS—NOVARIAE om. B    [3] conspectu B    [4] passa sunt EF
[5] diebus EF    [6] instans EF    [7] poterat EF    [8] Calendarum B    [9] pilo
frugem EF    [10] nocte EF    [11] autem B

## BOOK II, THE SIEGE OF THE CITY OF NOVARA

1. When the French had been driven to the farthest borders of Italy, Francesco Gonzaga, marquis of Mantua and commander of the army, rejoicing in his arms and proudly riding his horse, on 19 July stationed his mighty forces of cavalry and phalanxes of infantry in sight of the people of Novara at the fortress of Tiglia, as I have said.[2] At almost the same hour the army of the Milanese, with Galeazzo Sanseverino in command, had stormed this fortress as the army of the Venetians was approaching. Because of their reputation the French, who had the town in their power, straightway granted surrender on the enemy's terms. The day before they had tolerated the burning of the suburbs as they awaited aid from the Duke of Orléans at every moment. The proveditors seized the town and the commander pitched camp not far outside. The rest of the leaders as well, with their cavalry, put up tents and huts in villages as it were.

2. Then a new enemy terrified the Duke of Orléans, and he was frightened both by the flight of the French and also by the danger of impending hunger which the city was shortly to endure.[3] For he had gathered together very little grain and that scarcely ripened on the stalk, and he had been able to stock the citadel for only three months. A market place was set up before the town and another in the camp of the allies; in the former grain was expensive, and wine was especially dear. Other things necessary for use began to be plentiful almost on the first day. On 20 July the Venetian soldiers shut off the channel where the river comes down and gave the river another course, turning it away from the city,[4] and with sword and fire they destroyed for six stades around the city the grain mills which the water turned.[5] In the city there were a very few mills turned by hand, and none turned by asses. The people mashed their grain with a pestle and made bread with half-ground unsifted flour; I sent a sample of this to the magnificent knight Antonio Boldù in Venice so that he might comprehend the want that prevailed in the besieged city. Straightway the people of Novara felt the scarcity of food; in fact with great difficulty, because of the fear of the soldiers, was food sent from Vercelli by night. They had erected some fortifications before the gates of the city, as has been

duplici fossa muniti erant, nullis fere propugnaculis dispositis. Perquam [12] rara item in urbe tormenta habebantur.

3. Auriliensis Dux qui se inani nomine Mediolanensem principem dictitabat detractis a portis prioribus Sfortiadum insignibus sua iam imposuerat convocato Principe Salucensi et caeteris acceptissimis amicis haec pauca protulit: "Maximum strenuissimi duces discrimen nobis adesse video regia auxilia a Tarrensi pugna diu expectantibus qui nescio [13] quo furore Hastam recto itinere concesserit. Eius auspiciis obsidioni [14] nos liberatum iri sperabamus. Longam famem sustinere non possumus; oppugnationem tanti Venetorum exercitus ferre difficillimum est. Vinum in urbe non esse non [15] ignoratis, quo Suevorum [16] praesertim copiae [17] magis quam auro et argento tenentur, nec habendi spes ulla relicta est. Certum periculum instare video si hos amiserimus; facile enim ad hostes transfugient si modus non erit. Ea omnia Regi nuntio significanda sunt; narrabimus rem in difficili esse, famem instare, ac militum seditionem, vini praecipue inopiam summam esse, et nisi suppetias protinus miserit desperatione oblatas conditiones accepturos."

4. Probata ab omnibus sententia fuit. Dimissa contione noctu nuntius per invia [18] et occulta itinera ad Regem pervenit, qui lectis litteris ita paucis respondit, se novum militem expectare et fessum itineribus recreare ac propediem Ioannem Iacobum Triulcium cum magna copiarum parte Vercellas missurum. Nuntius tutus castra Veneta subit et egressus Novariam contendit. Litterae coram omnibus militibus lectae sunt, quae [19] omnium animos expectatione erexere.

5. Eadem die in sociorum Mediolanensium castris Germani cum Latinis dissedere; ea enim a Venetis intercedente via [20] Vercellina XII stadiis distabant. Vinum enim in maximo diei [21] aestu furorem incusserat et insuetis ocyus mentes solverat, et nisi Bernardus Contarenus cum Graecis leviter armatis praesto fuisset maior strages secuta fuisset. XL Teutones caesi sunt ac statim ob tumultum humati, ex Latinis IIII desiderati. Hoc fuit ob scortum [22] ignobile seditionum primum [23] seminarium. Idem demum furor ad Venetorum castra penetravit in quibus

---

[12] -quae EF   [13] vestro B   [14] obsidione BEF   [15] om. B   [16] Sueviorum A Suevorum A by MS. correction   [17] copiae praesertim infima EF   [19] qui B   [20] die EF   [21] om. EF   [22] scortorum B   [23] om. B

said, and the walls were defended by a double ditch, but almost no ramparts were constructed. There was likewise very little artillery inside the city.

3. The Duke of Orléans, who vainly kept calling himself the Duke of Milan,[6] had already removed the earlier insignia of the Sforza family from the gates and put up his own. He called into conference the Marquis of Saluzzo and the rest of his dearest friends and spoke briefly as follows: "I see, O most zealous leaders, that very great danger is at hand for us who have now for a long time, ever since the battle of the Taro, been awaiting aid from the King. But he, possessed by I know not what madness, has retreated straight to Asti. We hoped to be freed from siege under his auspices. Long hunger we cannot endure; assault by so large an army of Venetians is very hard to bear. You are not unaware that there is no wine in the city, and it is by wine, rather than by gold and silver, that the forces of the Swabians in particular are retained. Nor does any hope remain of having some. If we lose these men I see inevitable danger impending; certainly they will readily desert to the enemy unless a way of procuring wine is found. All these things must be reported by messengers to the King; we shall say that we are in difficult circumstances, that hunger threatens together with mutiny of the troops, that there is especially the greatest scarcity of wine, and that unless he sends help at once, we shall in desperation accept the terms offered."

4. This judgment was approved by all. The assembly was adjourned, and a messenger travelling by night over pathless and hidden ways reached the King, who read the letter and replied in these few words, that he was expecting new recruits and was refreshing the soldiers who were worn out from the journey, and that shortly he would send Gian Giacomo Trivulzio to Vercelli with a large part of the forces. The messenger reached the Venetian camp in safety, and passing beyond it proceeded to Novara. The letter was read in the presence of all the soldiers, and it encouraged the spirits of them all in expectation.[7]

5. On the same day in the camp of the Milanese allies the Germans had a quarrel with the Latins; this camp indeed was twelve stades from the Venetians, with the road to Vercelli intervening. For during the hottest part of the day wine had excited frenzy and had the more quickly unbridled their minds because they were unaccustomed to it, and if Bernardo Contarini had not been at hand with his light-armed Greeks, greater carnage would have ensued. Forty Teutons were slain, and they were buried at once because of the uproar; four Latins were lost. This first seedbed of sedition was over a worthless harlot, and

et Teutones erant.

6. Hac die quidam ex Novariensibus militibus legatos edocuit Venetos D milites armatos in urbe esse peditumque circiter VIII millia, et in iis sagittariorum duo millia contineri, reliquos hastatos et parvorum tormentorum magistros. Legati vesperi litteras a Senatu accepere qui summopere eorum diligentiam laudavit quod labores perennes aestus ingentes sitim famem [24] vigilias in persequendis hostibus pro rei publica salute indefesse passi fuerint ipsisque de re publica bene meritis pollicebatur [25] se gratias aliquando relaturum. XII Calendas Augusti Novaria [26] turmae Gallorum egressae cum Latinis prima [27] tumultuaria pugna dimicavere. Ex Latinis VIII desiderati sunt, XII saucii, ex Gallis pauciores. Legatorum iussu pro distribuendis militibus stipendiis copiarum numerus equorum notae peditum nomina recognita sunt. Plurimi enim ex peditibus acceptis pecuniis per Appenini invia distributorium [28] fefellerant, nec ulla lex est quae hoc tempore huiusmodi furta [29] puniat deleta prisca militandi disciplina. Vidimus pedites duces ab equitibus militum calones lixas ac famulos bis in die invicem supponi. Teutones duces die recognitionis CCCC interdum ab aliis mutabantur [30] magno [31] distributorii muneris damno, nec modus in tanta fraude inventus est.

7. Duo Galli capti fuere [32] qui retulerunt Auriliensem Ducem quartana laborare, equo tamen per urbem vehi, suos hortari, excubias noctu tentare, et saepe queri se segnem esse damnareque fortunam suam, nobilitatem vero ac plebem direptionem domorum rapinas coniugum et filiarum stupra universaeque [33] civitatis ruinam famem et ultima denique omnia passuros quam Ludovicum Ducem pati et eius iugum subire. Verum sese Veneto Senatui et eius fidei facile dedituros ea in urbe iactari certior fama erat. XI Calendas alii pariter capti fuere qui litteras ad Regem Gallorum deferebant, inter quos presbyter quidam Gallus erat qui simulata aegrotantis cuiusdam desperatione remedia et potiones litteris petere videbatur, alioqui aegrum a medico deploratum esse. Is non multis post diebus custodiarum taedio dimissus est. Sed

---

[24] famem sitim EF     [25] pollicebantur B     [26] Novariae B     [27] primo EF
[28] diributorium AEF distributorium B     [29] om. B     [30] mutabantur EF
[31] magna EF     [32] facere B     [33] -que om. EF

next the same madness penetrated to the camp of the Venetians in which also there were Teutons.[8]

6. On this day one of the soldiers of Novara told the Venetian proveditors that there were five hundred armored soldiers in the city and about eight thousand infantry, and that among these were included two thousand archers; the rest were armed with spears or were masters of light artillery. In the evening the proveditors received a letter from the Senate which praised their diligence highly because they had tirelessly endured constant toil, excessive heat, thirst, hunger, and loss of sleep in pursuing the enemy for the safety of the republic, and it promised that to them all, deserving well of the republic, it would later render official thanks. On 21 July squadrons of the French came out from Novara and fought with the Latins in a first, confused battle. Of the Latins eight were lost and twelve wounded, of the French fewer. On order of the proveditors the number of troops, the brands of the horses, and the names of the foot soldiers were reviewed for the purpose of distributing salaries to the soldiers. For a great many of the foot soldiers had deceived the distributing office when salaries were received in the pathless regions of the Apennines, and there is no law which punishes thefts of such a nature at such a time, since the discipline formerly prevailing during campaigns has been destroyed. I saw foot soldiers, leaders of the cavalry, servants, camp-followers, attendants paid twice in one day. On the day the review was made four hundred of the Teuton leaders interchanged with one another, with great loss of the money distributed, and no way out was found for such deceit.

7. Two Frenchmen were captured who reported that the Duke of Orléans was suffering from quartan fever,[9] but was nonetheless carried on his horse through the city, encouraged his men, attempted night watches,[10] and often accused himself of being lazy and condemned his own fortune. And they declared that nobles and populace would endure the pillaging of their homes, the rape of their wives and violation of their daughters, the destruction of the entire city, famine, and every extreme rather than suffer Duke Lodovico and submit to his yoke. However, according to a definite rumor they claimed in the city that they would readily surrender themselves to the Venetian Senate and to its good faith. Some more were captured on 22 July also; [11] they were carrying letters to the King of the French, and among them was a French priest who pretended that some patient was desperately ill and appeared to be asking in the letters for remedies and potions: otherwise the sick man was given up by his physicians. Not many days later this priest was released because the guards became bored, but

Venetorum nimia clementia ad subeundos huiusmodi labores ex hostibus plurimos invitabat nullo vix obiurgato nedum fustibus caeso.

8. X [34] Calendas Gallus Rex ut aliquid moliri videretur quasdam
copias Tortonam versus submovit [35] ad perturbandos civium animos,
unde legati rursus Carolum Melitensem ducem equitum cum militibus
armatis CL peditibus delectis D ex Venetorum copiis Tortonam misere,
eadem de causa pedites D equites C Taliano [36] Carpensi duce militum
Alexandriam Statiliensem praemiserunt. IX et VIII Calendas [37] equitum supplementa novorum castra ingrediuntur Pandulphus Malatesta [38]
Ariminensis ac Ioannes Paulus Mamphronus cum equitibus et [39] CL [40]
leviter armatis C.[41] VII Calendas exercitus omnis et Ludovici Ducis
socii constructis aciebus ad pugnae imaginem ante oculos Novariensium
ducitur. Id et [42] hostibus terrori fuit et tyronibus perquam utile; ignavia
eo modo rumpebatur. VI Calendas ad terrendos Gallorum exploratores
altissimum in castris patibulum erectum est quod a Novariensibus
facile conspiceretur; in eo Gallorum explorator Boninus revelare secreta quaestione coactus strangulatus est. Tormenta XV Mediolano in
castra evecta sunt, quae librarum XL pilas emittunt pro oppidi Bryoni
expugnatione, quod paulo ante defecerat. Ad id expugnandum Franciscus Crassus cum D peditibus ac equitibus C sub Taliano duce a
praefecto missus est, quod sequenti die oppidanis ad foedera venientibus in deditionem nec prius nisi admotis tormentis accepit.

9. V Calendas Virgilius Ursinus Romanus qui Regem Gallorum se-
cutus fuerat a Venetis legatis missionem accepit. Eo die litterae a
Senatu missae sub tentorio Francisci Gonzagae Mantuanorum principis castrorum praefecti omnium [43] militum exemplo palam lectae sunt
ut fidem et virtutem eorum qui in [44] Tarrensi pugna acriter dimicassent
dignam praemiis laudem consequi constaret et viventes inter alios
gloria eminerent, mortui fama et meritis laudibus in coelum referren-
tur, et posteritati exemplo essent honesta morte defuncti qui in pugna
mori quam capti expectare Gallorum arbitrium maluissent,[45] ut de
caetero sua quisque dextra Venetorum nomen ac patriae salutem acrius
defenderent memoresque essent omnes Romanorum decoris qui totius

---

[34] VIII EF      [35] submonuit B      [36] Talio B      [37] Calendarum B      [38] Mo-
natasta B      [39] om. B      [40] et add. B      [41] om. EF      [42] et id EF
[43] omni B      [44] om. F      [45] maluerunt EF

the excessive clemency of the Venetians invited a great many of the enemy to attempt tasks of this nature, and scarcely anyone was rebuked or beaten with rods.

8. On 23 July the French King, so that he might seem to be planning something, sent off certain forces in the direction of Tortona in order to disturb the minds of the citizens. Thereupon the proveditors sent Carlo of Pian di Meleto, leader of the cavalry, to Tortona again with 150 armed soldiers and five hundred foot soldiers chosen from the forces of the Venetians, and for the same reason they sent ahead to Alessandria five hundred foot soldiers and a hundred cavalry under command of Taliano of Carpi. Supplementary forces of new cavalry entered the camp on 24 and 25 July, Pandolfo Malatesta of Rimini and Giovanni Paolo Manfrone with 150 cavalry and a hundred light-armed soldiers. On 26 July the entire army and the allies of Duke Lodovico, with the lines drawn up as if for battle, were paraded before the eyes of the people of Novara. This was for the purpose of awakening terror in the enemy and was very useful for the new recruits, since by such means listlessness was ended. On 27 July a very high gibbet which could be seen easily by the people of Novara was erected in the camp to terrify the French spies. On it Bonin, a French scout, was strangled after being forced by torture to reveal secrets.[12] Fifteen pieces of artillery which discharge balls weighing forty pounds were brought to the camp from Milan; these were for storming the city of Briona which had revolted a little earlier.[13] Francesco Crasso was sent by the commander to storm this city with five hundred footmen and a hundred horsemen under the command of Taliano, and on the following day the citizens came to terms and he received it in surrender, but not before artillery was used.

9. On 28 July Virginio Orsini of Rome, who had followed the French King, received a discharge from the Venetian proveditors,[14] and on that day a letter sent by the Senate was publicly read in the tent of Francesco Gonzaga, marquis of the Mantuans and commander of the camp, as an example to all the soldiers so that it might be clear that the faith and courage of those who had fought fiercely in the battle of the Taro acquired praise worthy of rewards, and so that during their lifetime they might tower above the rest in glory and after death be lauded to the skies in deserved renown and praises; likewise so that those who had died an honorable death and had preferred to perish in battle rather than await as captives the judgment of the French might be an example to posterity; for the rest, so that each one might defend more zealously with his own right hand the reputation of the Venetians and the safety of his country and be mindful every one of

Occidentis regna tot saeculis memorabili laude tenuerint et Gallos stipendia quondam [46] Italiae tulisse et de iis ingentia trophaea, itaque ut qui magno animo pugnassent et quibus non contigisset vel ignavia maiores et condignos spiritus caperent et simili animorum constantia dimicando laudem et gloriam adipiscerentur et quicquid deinde sors tulisset pari exemplo et sibi et suis Senatus Venetus grata retributione pensitaret.

10. Imprimis igitur Francisco Gonzagae ex castrensi praefectura sine imperatorio nomine, quod maxime optaverat, sponte Senatus imperatoris vexillum ac sceptrum rerum [47] omnium quae in continenti habentur merito elargitus est. Huius enim ductu auspiciis virtute et consilio qui modo miles modo imperator fuerat Galli ferocia perdomita est: Carolum Regem alioqui cavillantem de Italis audivisset universus orbis qui [48] invita pene tota Italia sine cruore trophaeum intra Alpes de Italiae primo imperio miro imo [49] divino, ut putabant, successu celebrasset. Huic uni merito imperatoris nomen etiam iuveni debet, qui multo maiora in ea pugna fecisset si agminum ductores ac peditum duces paruissent. Illi praeterea Senatus maiores copias dedit singulisque annis III millia nummum aureorum praeter stipendia pro convivali [50] lance, X millia item aureorum pro reparando milite qui in praelio perierat vel equos amiserat. Is cum haec audisset [51] legatos praesentes summo gaudio [52] amplexus est gratiasque immortales [53] in conspectu omnium ducum Senatui egit.

11. Comiti Bernardino Fortibrachio, qui fortium virorum more pericula et mortem contempserat duplicatam militiam dedit CCL equitum [54] armatorum aureosque nummos praeter stipendia D singulis annis. Catharinae vero Gonzagae uxori et filiis Rhodulphi qui forti animo occubuerat mille aureos singulo [55] quoque anno elargiri decrevit ac oppida praeterea in patrocinium accepit. Rhanucii Phrenensis filiis paterna militia designata est filiasque nubiles [56] a Senatu maritari [57] grata dote, intereaque pro victu CCCC aureos ab aerario eis elargiri decretum est. Vincentii Corsici filio egregia morte nobilitati paternam militiam dedit sororemque in aede sacrarum virginum ad coniugii tempus servari iussit, exinde singulis annis XL aureos pro victu donare constituit. Alexandri Beraldi fratri milites et stipendium eandem con-

---

[46] quae B -que EF    [47] om. B    [48] quod EF    [49] om. B    [50] provinciali B [51] audivisset B    [52] om. B    [53] mortales B    [54] militum EF    [55] singulos B    [56] -que add. B    [57] om. B

the honor of the Romans, who for so many centuries held sway with memorable praise over the whole Western world, and remember that the French had formerly paid tribute to Italy and that from them had come mighty trophies; finally so that those who had fought with courage and had no part in cowardice might take on even greater and very worthy courage and with like steadfastness of spirit win praise and glory in battle and, whatever lot befell them, receive in like manner from the Venetian Senate gratcful recompense for themselves and their families.[15]

10. Therefore first of all to Francesco Gonzaga, commander of the camp without the title of general, which he had especially hoped for, the Senate of its own accord justly presented the standard of general and authority over all land forces.[16] For under the leadership, auspices, courage, and wisdom of this man who had been both soldier and commander the ferocity of the Frenchman was curbed. Otherwise the whole world might have heard King Charles deriding the Italians, since by wondrous and even, as they thought, divine good fortune he had in his early sway over Italy celebrated a triumph this side of the Alps against the will of almost all Italy and without bloodshed. To that one man, even though he was young, the title of general was deservedly due, for he would have accomplished far greater things in that battle if the leaders of cavalry and infantry had obeyed his command. Moreover, the Senate gave him greater forces, and each year three thousand ducats over and above his salary for table expenses, and likewise ten thousand for replacing soldiers dead in battle or horses lost. When he had heard this he embraced with the greatest joy the proveditors who were present and before all the leaders gave enduring thanks to the Senate.

11. To Count Bernardino Fortebraccio, who as is usual with brave men had scorned danger and death,[17] the Senate gave a double allotment of 250 armed cavalry and five hundred ducats each year beyond the usual salary. To Caterina Gonzaga, widow of Rodolfo,[18] who had died courageously, and their sons it decreed a thousand ducats each year, and it took their lands under protection. To the sons of Ranuccio Farnese the father's stipend was assigned, and it was decided that his maiden daughters were to be married with a dowry given in gratitude by the Senate and that meanwhile for living expenses four hundred ducats were to be bestowed upon them by the treasury. To the son of Vincenzo Corso, renowned for a glorious death, it gave his father's stipend, and ordered that his sister should be protected in a convent until the time of her marriage, and it appointed that from then on forty ducats a year be given her for living expenses. To the brother of

ditionem Carolo Strocio concessit Ruberti fratri, Nicolao Nonensi Delmatae milites levius armatos XXX pacis tempore, bello C et stipendium auxit. Iohannis demum Aethiopis uxori viduae animo non ingrato vel in minimis Senatus aureos LXXII singulis annis ex aerario elargitur[58] ac perpetuam domum.

12. Lectis litteris et strenui et ignavi animum ad res bene gerendas erexerunt fortium virorum praemia ac laudes audientes, et ad exequenda imperia periculaque subeunda excitarunt. Qui segniter pugnarant tum sese purgabant. Incitabat virtutem et ignominiae demendae cupido Graecis militibus qui in Tarrensi pugna dimicare noluerunt sed impedimenta duntaxat diripuerant, quapropter militia se amoveri plurimum verebantur, quod maxime caeteri optabant Graeci qui sub Bernardo Contareno apud Novariam[59] meruerant[60] magna gloria.[61] Indiscreto enim genere ii quoque turpi ignavia damnabantur timebantque ne aliena culpa damnum ac dedecus subirent. Invidia quoque praedae odium auxerat, illi vaecordiae conscientia ne a caeteris dignoscerentur socia et mixta tuguria optabant.

13. IIII Calendas exploratores denuntiarunt Regem Gallorum nova militum supplementa expectare, tum traditum est (verum fuerit necne incertum habeo) Regem[62] a Regina subita auxilia petentem litteras duntaxat accepisse in quibus sese non milites sed tristes viduas missuram respondebat orabatque ut tandem in regnum suum rediret: satis illi imperii esse. Non vana fama fuit Regem Teutones sub vexillo Bovis conscripsisse qui in Mediolanensem agrum statim sese superfunderent. Eam Teutonum incursionem[63] Ludovicus Dux oblatis ducibus pecuniis retroegit. Tertio Calendas legatus Ludovici ducis Mediolanensis in castra venit nuntiavitque ab exploratoribus accepisse Gallorum Regem cum omnibus copiis Taurinum venisse, ubi militem sine intermissione conscribit. Eo die pedites quidam qui[64] acceptis pecuniis[65] e Venetis castris aufugerant Mediolani capti sunt, qui sub aliorum nomine missionem dolo quaesierant, de quibus rebus legati Veneti admoniti scripsere eos[66] abscisis naribus et inusta facie sine armis dimittendos.

14. Interea imperator ut si qua via posset urbem capere circuivit longiorem obsidionem pertesus qua Ludovicus Dux urbem capi posse

---

[58] largitur EF   [59] Novaria B   [60] meruerunt B   [61] magnam gloriam EF
[62] et add. B   [63] concursionem EF   [64] om. B   [65] om. B   [66] om. B

Alessandro Beroaldo it granted soldiers and salary, and the same terms to Carlo Strozzi, brother of Roberto. To Niccolò of Nin, in Dalmatia, it granted in time of peace thirty light-armed soldiers, in time of war one hundred, and it increased his stipend. Finally, since it was not without gratitude in the smallest matters, the Senate presented to the wife of Giovanni the Moor,[19] now a widow, 72 ducats each year from the treasury and a home forever.

12. When the letter had been read both the courageous and the cowardly lifted up their spirits to high achievement as they heard the rewards and praises given brave men, and they were anxious to carry out the commands and undergo dangers. Those who had fought lazily then excused themselves. A desire to remove disgrace incited bravery also in the Greek soldiers who were unwilling to fight at the battle of the Taro and had only plundered the baggage train; for this reason they feared very much being removed from the fighting. This was what the other Greeks who had served with great glory at Novara under Bernardo Contarini especially wanted, for with no distinction they too were accused of disgraceful cowardice, and they feared that by the fault of the others they might undergo condemnation and dishonor. Envy over the plunder had also increased their hatred, but the others in a realization of their folly wanted allied and joint encampment so that they would not be distinguished.

13. On 29 July scouts reported that the King of the French was awaiting fresh supplies of soldiers, and then it was related (I know not whether truly or not) that the King, requesting immediate aid from the Queen,[20] had received only a letter in which she replied that she would send not soldiers but sad widows and asked that he return at last to his kingdom, since he had enough power. It was no idle rumor that the King had enrolled Teutons under the standard of the Ox who straightway poured into the Milanese territory. Duke Lodovico by offering money to the leaders drove back this incursion of Teutons. On 30 July an envoy of Lodovico, duke of Milan, came to camp and reported having heard from scouts that the King of the French had come with all his forces to Turin, where he was recruiting soldiers without interruption.[21] On that day certain foot soldiers, who on receiving their pay had fled the Venetian camp, were captured at Milan. These under assumed names had deceitfully requested discharge. On being advised of these facts the Venetian proveditors wrote that their noses should be cut off and their faces burned and that they should be dismissed without their arms.

14. Meanwhile the general went around to see if there was any way of capturing the city, since he was tired of the long drawn-out siege

protinus [67] sperabat, ut fame coacti sese dederent neve misere ab exercitu civitas [68] diriperetur [69] sed ea integra incolumisque iugum sponte subiret [70] magno Venetorum damno. Hoc enim bello in stipendia C millia aureorum singulis mensibus a Venetis militiae numerabantur. Hac longa obsidione hyemis inclementia imbreque plurimo paludosum solum tutum ab hoste reddebatur, unde infecta re dissolutum iri castra sperabant. Sed quis in hoc bello doctior fuit? [71] Nullam enim rationem in rebus attulit [72] sive propinquitas sive vicinitas, sed una tantum [73] irrationabilis libido principes in sui commodum trahebat. Haec omnia igitur diuturnioris obsidionis causa fuere. Scio his diebus Acaiazanum Comitem in contione affirmasse Novariam propediem sine cruore nullis tormentis ad manus Mediolanensium venturam: ob id ab oppugnatione contra Senatus Veneti studia abstinendum esse. Nec defuere in castris qui ea consulto fieri iactarent quandoquidem sola militari disciplina et stipendio plerique vivant.[74] Bellum igitur consulto protrahi [75] credidere.

15. His diebus Helias eques Foroiuliensis ac [76] Aloisius Turris equitum levius armatorum supplementa in castra duxere. Pridie Calendas imperatorem contione convocata dixisse accepimus se urbem circuisse quam palude silva caedua duplici fossa et [77] arce munitissimam esse [78] animadvertit, praeterea Gallorum exercitum haud dubio adventare, ob eam causam supplementa mitti oportere. Ea item dies moestum exercitum reddidit perpetuo imbre,[79] unde rerum inopiam protinus [80] milites senserunt, verum sequentibus diebus uberiora castra fuere. Calendis Augusti explorator quidam Gallorum Regem Novariam pro [81] militibus pecunias noctu [82] missurum significavit. Milites leviter armati constructa acie Galeacio Mediolanensium copiarum praefecto ad intercipiendas pecunias obviam iere, qui nihil [83] invenientes in tabernacula rediere.[84] At nocte [85] sequenti vigilum negligentia vel viarum inscitia urbem cum pecuniis [86] hostes [87] ingressi sunt.

16. His diebus [88] tabella quaedam famosissima [89] quae in Tarrensi pugna a milite quodam correpta fuerat Veneto Senatui dono data est Melchioris Trivisani legati suasu, ut inter donaria Divi Marci collocaretur.[90] Per id ferme tempus fides certior facta est Turcarum Imperatori Gallorum Regem illum quem a Deo missum esse audiverat unica

---

[67] serotinus B    [68] civitatis EF    [69] diriperentur EF    [70] subiret sponte EF    [71] fuerit B    [72] in—attulit om. B    [73] tam EF    [74] juvant B [75] protracti B    [76] om. EF    [77] om. B    [78] om. EF    [79] om. B    [80] om. EF    [81] om. F    [82] om. F    [83] om. B    [84] iere EF    [85] noctu B [86] pecunia B    [87] om. EF    [88] diedus A    [89] formosissima B    [90] collocent EF

by which Duke Lodovico constantly kept hoping that it could be taken, that is to say, kept hoping that the inhabitants would be forced by hunger to surrender and the city would not be wretchedly plundered by the army but would voluntarily pass under the yoke intact and unharmed, though at great loss to the Venetians. Indeed in this war the Venetians spent a hundred thousand ducats every month in salaries for the campaign. In this long siege because of the bad winter weather and the great amount of rain the marshy soil was rendered secure from the enemy, and they hoped therefore that the campaign could be ended indecisively. But who was wiser in this war? For neither kinship nor nearness brought any reason into events; on the contrary irrational greed alone impelled the leaders to act in their own interests. All these things, therefore, caused the longer siege. I know that during these days the Count of Caiazzo affirmed in the assembly that Novara would shortly come into the hands of the Milanese without bloodshed and artillery; therefore against the wishes of the Venetian Senate they should abstain from storming it. Nor were those lacking in the camp who claimed that this was done on purpose since very many exist on military discipline and stipend alone. Accordingly they believed that the war was prolonged purposely.

15. At this time Elia, a knight of Forlì, and Luigi Torre brought to the camp reinforcements of light-armed soldiers. I heard that the general called an assembly on 31 July [22] and said that he had made a circuit of the city and noted that it was very well fortified by a swamp, a forest ready for cutting, a double ditch, and a stronghold; moreover, that there was no doubt that the army of the French was approaching and for that reason reinforcements ought to be sent. The continuous rain that day cast the army into gloom, hence the troops immediately felt the scarcity of supplies, but in the days which followed the camp was better supplied. On 1 August one of the scouts indicated that the King of the French would send money to Novara by night for the soldiers. A group of light-armed soldiers led by Galeazzo, commander of the Milanese forces, was drawn up and went to intercept the money; finding nothing they returned to their tents. But on the following night through carelessness of the sentinels or ignorance of the roads the enemy entered the city with the money.

16. In these days a certain very renowned plaque, which had been taken at the battle of the Taro by one of the soldiers, was presented to the Venetian Senate as a gift at the instigation of the proveditor Melchiorre Trevisan, so that it might be put among the presentation gifts to St. Mark. At almost the same time it was reported to the Sultan of the Turks that the King of the French, who he had heard had been

pugna ex Italia foede [91] propulsum. Ille summo gaudio ad caelum manus [92] tendens Deo gratias egit exinde [93] Veneto Senatui cuius armis et consilio hostis qui Neapolitanum regnum XIII diebus occupaverat, qui Delmatiam Macedoniam Graeciamque iam turbaverat metumque usque Constantinopolim incusserat, qui sibi imperii terminos Hierosolimae animo posuerat nunc victus terga vertisset. Laetus Turca legatum rursus Senatui misit qui vires omnes large polliceretur quandoquidem et sua et Veneta communi consilio et auxilio servata fuerint.

17. III Nonas Augustas [94] Ludovicus Mediolanensis princeps in castra venit et equitum supplementa secum duxit Germanos D peditum duo millia. Cum eo legati erant Ferdinandi [95] et Helisabeth regum [96] Hispaniae [97] Regis Neapolitani Veneti Senatus ac [98] Ducis Ferrariae, nam hostem Gallum adventare cognoverat. Ob id in tabernaculo convocata contione imperator exercitus et legati Lucas Pisanus Melchior Trivisanus et Nicolaus comes Petilianus venerant, aderant et alii accepti duces. Iussi [99] considere silentio facto Ludovicus Dux de rerum summa loqui coepit, de castris mutandis et campo aequando aggeribusque [100] construendis. Alii in Vespello oppido exercitum servandum esse, alii Vegevenis, alii [101] ad Monticellos occupandos maioribus copiis, alii tanti exercitus roboris existimatione nullo modo discedendum esse suadebant. Hinc [102] alimenta, hinc loci debilitas adversabatur. Disceptarunt diu inter se duces, verum huic sententiae universa fere contio assensa est, castra non esse mutanda ne turpi fuga adventante Gallorum exercitu cedere viderentur. Existimatione enim bellum constare maxime certum est. Tandem munimenta [103] quatuor ad tutanda castra construi statuere. Objectum tamen est et [104] id periculosum esse, ne rerum inopia invitus exercitus ad dimicandum ab hoste traheretur pugnandoque semper exercitus nutrimenta quaereret. Inter has difficultates Ludovicus Dux hac in re viam invenit tutiorem, etsi in suo quisque negocio soleat hebetior esse quam in alieno. Turbida facta fuere omnium [105] consilia [106] qui mutanda esse castra suaserant. In mensa omnia descripta erant urbes viae paludes silvae flumina fossae oppida. Alios naturalis amor eorum quae [107] excogitaverant ad disceptationis pertinaciam trahebat. Vicit tandem principis sententia ut

---

[91] sede  B    [92] manum  B    [93] deinde  B    [94] Augusti  B    [95] Alphonsi ABEF    [96] om. B    [97] om. B    [98] om. EF    [99] justi EF    [100] -que om. B [101] om. B    [102] hic B    [103] monumenta EF    [104] om. B    [105] aliorum E [106] turbida—consilia om. F    [107] qui B

sent by God, had been disgracefully driven from Italy in a single battle. In the greatest joy he raised his hands to heaven and gave thanks to God and then to the Venetian Senate, by whose arms and wisdom the enemy who had seized the Neapolitan kingdom in thirteen days, who had already thrown into confusion Dalmatia, Macedonia, and Greece and had produced fear as far as Constantinople, and who in his mind had set the bounds of his empire at Jerusalem, that enemy had now been defeated and had turned his back. Joyfully the Turk sent an envoy again to the Senate to promise generously all his power, since his own affairs and those of Venice had been preserved by their combined wisdom and aid.

17. On 3 August Lodovico, duke of Milan, came to the camp and brought with him reinforcements of cavalry, five hundred Germans, and two thousand infantry. With him were legates of Ferdinand and Isabella, the rulers of Spain, of the King of Naples, of the Venetian Senate, and of the Duke of Ferrara, for he had heard that the French foe was approaching. Accordingly a conference was called in the pavilion to which came the commander of the army, the proveditors Luca Pisani and Melchiorre Trevisan, and Niccolò, count of Pitigliano. Others recognized as leaders were also present, and when they had been asked to take their seats and silence had been obtained Duke Lodovico began to speak on the state of events—on changing camp, and leveling the field, and constructing ramparts. Some urged that the army should be kept safely at Vespolate,[23] others at Vigevano, others that Monticelli ought to be occupied with greater forces, others that in view of the strength of so great an army they ought in no wise to withdraw. On the one hand the food supply, on the other the weakness of the position was urged in objection. For a long time the leaders argued among themselves, but almost the entire assembly approved the decision not to change camp lest they appear to be withdrawing in disgraceful flight at the approach of the army of the French. For it is certain above all that war is dependent upon reputation. At length they decided to erect four works of defense to protect the camp. The objection was made, however, that this also was dangerous, since from scarcity of supplies the army might be induced by the enemy to fight against its will, and it might always seek its food by fighting. In these difficulties Duke Lodovico found the safer way in this matter, even though each one is usually duller about his own affairs than about those of someone else. The plans of all those who had urged that the camp ought to be moved had become confused. On the table were drawn all the cities, roads, swamps, forests, rivers, ditches, towns. A natural love of what they had planned made some stubborn in argu-

ex binis castris una fierent quae praeter munimenta quae diximus flumen ac fossa tuerentur. De pugna pauca dicta fuere nondum lustrato exercitu. Propterea Ludovicus Dux Venetorum robur et suum pariter in armis lustrare [108] sequenti statuit die [109] atque contio protinus dimissa. Tum edixit imperator ut duces cum omnibus copiis in armis summo mane essent locumque et ordinem agminum [110] praescripsit.

18. Pridie Nonas Augustas universus exercitus ad imaginem pugnae instructus est, ad cuius conspectum Ludovicus Dux Beatricem uxorem duxerat quae una acierum ordinem conspiceret. Primus itaque exercitus imperator Franciscus Gonzaga agmen suum ducit, quem antecedebant equi plurimi velocitate praestantes ephippiis Phrygionica arte insignibus sericis pictis vel Attalicis auro argentoque intertexto. Post hos equi magnitudine sublimes maximo luxu cataphracti quibus insedebant pueri ingenui galeas cassidesque cristas habentes tubicinum turba comitante. Hos sequebantur peditum duo millia qui [111] scuta hastas manubalistas secures parva tormenta gerebant,[112] modico intervallo deinde Ludovicus Dux ac [113] imperator ipse Franciscus Gonzaga Comes [114] Nicolaus Petilianus rei militaris scientissimus; armati in equis eminentes erant aureis ephippiis instratis.

19. Post hos septem ingentia militum armatorum agmina per intervalla antecedentibus suis doctoribus in statutam planiciem ducebantur. Singula enim [115] nova pugnantium instituto XX supra CCCC equites habebant ac pedites mille. Inter hos tubarum [116] clangor caelum complebat, tormenta parva aures torpentes reddebant. Equites in armis conspicui in nucis pineae modum constipati equis cataphractis ephippiisque ornatis pro cuiusque luxu ac fortuna lanceis armati depictis ferro praelongo acutissimo praefixo duplicem thoracem saepe penetrante. Post hos peditum quoque circiter duo millia erant iisdem armis instructi ordine [117] suum quique locum [118] servantes tympanis sonoque suo vel segnes animos excitantes. Proxime erant militum Latinorum [119] levis [120] armaturae [121] agmina tria lanceis velitaribus scorpionibus armata numero mille trecentorum, alterum agmen Graecorum stratiotarum mille ducentorum lanceis ense clypeo lorica pauci thorace armati erant qui equo citatissimo cuncta percurrunt sericis pro more

---

[108] lustrari B     [109] die statuit EF     [110] agminum ordinem EF     [111] om. B
[112] om. AB     [113] om. BEF     [114] om. EF     [115] etiam B om. EF     [116] turbarum EF     [117] ordinem EF     [118] locumque EF     [119] om. EF     [120] om. EF     [121] armatorum EF

ment. At length the opinion of the leader prevailed, that of two camps one be made which, in addition to the fortifications which we have mentioned, the river and a ditch would protect. Little was said about the battle because the army had not yet been reviewed. So Duke Lodovico decided to review on the following day the strength of the Venetians in arms and likewise his own, and the assembly was forthwith dismissed. Then the general proclaimed that the leaders with all their forces should be under arms early in the morning, and he appointed the position and order of the ranks.

18. On 4 August the whole army was drawn up as if for battle, and for its inspection Duke Lodovico had brought his wife Beatrice to review with him the order of the ranks.[24] And so first of all the general Francesco Gonzaga led his own company. Before him went a great many horses excelling in swiftness, their caparisons brilliant with Phrygian embroidery, painted silks, or Attalian stuffs interwoven with gold and silver. After these came horses of extraordinary height; they were mailed in the greatest luxury, and on them rode noble youths wearing helmets and crested headgear. They were accompanied by a crowd of trumpeters and were followed by two thousand footmen equipped with shields, spears, hand-ballistas, axes, and light artillery, and then after a short space by Duke Lodovico, the commander himself, Francesco Gonzaga, and Count Niccolò of Pitigliano, who was very expert in military science. These were armed and were mounted on horses covered with golden caparisons.

19. After these seven huge lines of armed soldiers were paraded over the appointed area at intervals, with their leaders preceding them. These lines according to the new arrangement of soldiers were composed each of 420 horsemen and a thousand foot soldiers. The clash of trumpets among them rose to the sky, and light artillery numbed the ears. Horsemen outstanding in arms were arranged in the manner of a pine-cone, with horses adorned with mailed coverings and caparisons in accordance with the luxury and fortune of each one. They were armed with painted lances which had very long and sharp points of iron; these would penetrate even double breastplate. After them came about two thousand foot soldiers provided with the same arms, each keeping his own place in the line and exciting even sluggish minds by their drums and noise. Next followed three companies of light-armed Latins equipped with lances adapted to skirmishing and with scorpions; these were thirteen hundred in number. Another line of Greek stratiotes came next, twelve hundred in number; these were furnished with lances, swords, shields, leather corselets, and a few of them with breastplate, and they ran along everywhere on very swift horses and

et aureis tegminibus ornati duce Bernardo Contareno. Alterum CCC agmen sequebatur equestre manubalistis Italorum more leviter armatorum quibus nec ensis [122] nec pugio deerat. Tertium quoque CC leviter armatos continet; hi hastati erant duce Alexio.

20. Haec agmina per iusta intervalla comitabatur [123] Ludovicus Dux, et in dextrum latus agminis ductorem excipiebat in conspectumque carissimae uxoris suae in rheda sedentis agmina ducebat. Hos sequebatur Galeatius Severinas copiarum Mediolanensium praefectus veste Gallica virgata [124] armis superinduta more Gallico Attalica ac serica consuta multiplici virga, qui cum in conspectu uxoris esset a Ludovico Duce graviter obiurgatus est Gallici habitus imitatione iussusque [125] ne de caetero veste Gallica indutus in conspectum suum prodiret. Hunc vexillarius ac pueri in equis galeis cristati antecedebant, sequebatur autem agmen CCC equitum. Sed vexillum paululum contemplatus est quidam; in eo enim imagines depictae erant contra Mediolanensium ducum vetera [126] instituta, Maurus scilicet niger manu dextra aquilae alas aversas continens, sinistra draconem strangulans. Iudicium [127] voluntarium [128] sit. Ab eo agmine proximi erant Fracassius et Antonius Maria fratres Severinates,[129] qui non minori studio agmen CCC equitum armatorum agebant. Haec sequebatur agmen Germanorum equitum D qui non minus in armis conspicui erant; levius enim armati sunt quam Latini, sine cataphractis [130] equis pileo magis quam galea tecti.

21. Ab his phalanx una peditum Germanorum erat [131] quae omnium oculos in se convertebat quadratae figurae quae VI millia peditum continebat, Georgio Petroplanensi duce integerrimo in equo eminente.[132] In ea acie tympanorum multitudo audiebatur Germanico more quibus aures rumpebantur; hi [133] pectore tantum armato incedebant per ordines primo a posteriore parvo intervallo. Primi longiores [134] lanceas [135] humeris deferebant [136] infesto mucrone, sequentes lanceas erectiores portabant, post hos bipennibus et securibus armati, ab his signiferi erant ad quorum inclinationem totum agmen [137] acsi una rate veherentur, in dextrum levum ante [138] retro ingrediuntur.[139] A tergo pilularii dicti parvorum tormentorum, hos a leva et sinistra scorpionum magistri sive manu balistarii sequuntur. Hi in conspectu Beatricis Ducis [140] quadratum agmen uno signo in cuneum subito commutavere,

---

[122] recensis EF    [123] comitabantur B    [124] jurgata B    [125] justusque EF
[126] veterum E    [127] ludicium A    [128] volantarium A    [129] Severinitates B
[130] et add. EF    [131] erant EF    [132] emittente F    [133] in B    [134] longiorem
B    [135] in add. EF    [136] ferebant EF    [137] agmen totum EF    [138] om.
EF    [139] regrediuntur EF    [140] ducissae B

were decked according to custom with coverings of silk and gold. Their leader was Bernardo Contarini. Another equestrian line of three hundred followed, lightly armed with hand-ballistas in the manner of the Italians and carrying also swords and daggers. Then came a third line consisting of two hundred men also lightly armed and carrying shields, and their leader was Alessio.

20. Duke Lodovico accompanied these lines at appropriate intervals, and on his right he had the leader of the line, and he conducted the companies in the sight of his beloved wife who was seated in a carriage. Galeazzo Sanseverino, commander of the Milanese forces, followed these, wearing over his armor according to the French custom a French striped cloak which was stitched with numerous bands of cloth of gold and silk,[25] and when he was in sight of his wife Duke Lodovico reproached him for this imitation of French dress and ordered him for the future not to appear before him again in French costume. A standard bearer and youths with crested helmets on horses preceded him, and a company of three hundred cavalry followed him. But the standard attracted one's attention for a short space, for on it were painted figures contrary to the ancient practice of the Milanese leaders, namely a black Moor holding in his right hand an eagle with wings pinned back and strangling a serpent in his left. Draw what conclusion you will. Next after that line came Fracasso and his brother Antonio Maria Sanseverino, who with no less zeal were leading a squadron of three hundred armed horsemen. These were followed by a company of German horsemen, five hundred of them, and they were no less conspicuous as regards arms, for they were more lightly armed than the Latins, their horses were not mailed, and they wore caps instead of helmets.

21. After these there was one phalanx of German foot soldiers in square formation which attracted the eyes of all. It comprised six thousand footmen, and its very virtuous leader was Georg Ebenstein, who stood out on his horse. In this line, according to the German custom, a host of drums was heard which deafened the ears, and these men advanced in order one just a little distance behind the other, with breasts alone clad in armor. The first ones carried on their shoulders longer lances with deadly points, those who followed lances which were more upright, and those next axes and pikes. Behind these were the standard-bearers, at whose signal the whole line was turned as if it were a single ship and proceeded to the right or left, forward or back. After these followed the so-called *pilularii* of light artillery and on these at left and right the masters of the scorpions and those equipped with hand-ballistas. Before Duchess Beatrice at one signal they sud-

paulo post in alas sese divisere, demum in rotundum, altera tantum parte levi motu altera cursim movebatur [141] prima parte circumacta postrema immota ita ut unum corpus esse videretur. Post haec agmina tormentorum robur ingens sequebatur curribus oneratum numero XVII quae inflammato pulvere pilas in Novariam emitebant [142] tonitrua sonitu aequantia. Post haec minora tormenta quae serpentinas vulgus passavolantia vocat bigis vehebantur, minora quoque his alia plura erant quas sphingardas vocant ob similitudinem, puto, appellatas.

22. Reliqui vero equites et pedites ac tormenta item alia castra servabant, nec omnia ad hanc praelii imaginem exposita fuere gubernatore Carolo Melitensi. In eo exercitu XLV millia hominum collecta erant. Miro enim honore Ludovicus Dux agmen Comitis Bernardini Fortebrachii veneratus est veluti pectora in maximo discrimine experta et bonae spei capacia. Terribilior namque universi exercitus species [143] visa est tubarum clangore tympanorum tinnitu virorum clamore armorum strepitu equorum hinnitu bombardarum tonitru frequenti, ita ut aures horrido sono fatigarent. Agmina cohortes phalanges auri argenti armorumque nitor varius equitantium motus tela pila lanceae commotae oculorum aciem turbabant, nec quicquam [144] nisi ordine videri potuit. Laetitiam pavorem spem metumque intuentibus incutiebant. Nemo enim aetate nostra veteranorum asseveratione parem exercitum in Italia vidit, in quo nihil aliud quam fortuna desiderari potuit.

23. Conspecto omnium virium [145] robore Ludovicus Dux cum Gallis rursus [146] maximam dimicandi fiduciam concepit frequenterque [147] uxoris currum et virginum comitantium spei plenus adibat quaerebatque subinde quid illi videretur de tanto exercitu; illa multitudinem laudavit ac ornatum. Inter equitandum equus Ludovici Ducis quatuor pedibus in terram collapsus est, malo omnium circunstantium augurio. At Dux protinus in bonum vertens omen illud esse supremum quod in eo bello passurus esset respondit. Paulo post exercitum in castra remisit. Vesperi convocato imperatore et legatis Venetis ac caeteris ducibus in concionem processit. "Miram pugnandi spem cum Gallo Rege [148] hodie," inquit,[149] "concepi, principes vosque, Veneti legati, non satis admirari possum qui in Tarrensi agro longe paucioribus copiis collatis signis cum Gallorum Rege dimicare voluistis maximoque rerum omnium

---

[141] movebant EF    [142] emittebat EF    [143] spes EF    [144] quisquam EF
[145] virorum EF    [146] rursus cum Gallis EF    [147] -que om. B    [148] om. EF
[149] pugnandi EF

denly changed their square formation to a wedge. A little later they
divided themselves into wings, and finally formed a circle, one part in
a light movement only, the second moving quickly as the first part
turned around, and the last immobile, so that it seemed one body.[26]
On these followed squadrons of artillery, a mighty force, loaded on
seventeen wagons, and when they fired their powder they hurled balls
at Novara with a roar like thunder. After these came lighter artillery,
called serpentines or commonly *passavolanti,* on two-wheeled chariots,
and there were many others smaller than these which are called spin-
gards, because of the resemblance, I suppose.

22. The rest of the horsemen and foot soldiers and the other artillery
likewise continued to guard the camp, nor was everything brought out
for this make-believe battle of which Carlo of Pian di Meleto was over-
seer. In that army the total was forty-five thousand men. Duke Lodovico
accorded unusual honors to the company of Count Bernardino Fortebraccio, as to one whose courage was tested in the greatest peril and
from whom much could be expected. The appearance of the entire
army seemd more horrendous because of the clanging of trumpets, the
din of drums, the shouting of the men, the noise of arms, the neighing
of horses, and the frequent detonation of bombs, so that ears grew
weary of the awful sound. Companies, cohorts, phalanxes, flash of
gold and silver and arms, the varied movements of the riders, brandish-
ing of weapons, javelins, lances stirred the pupils of the eyes, nor could
anything be seen out of order. In the onlookers it all awakened joy,
fear, hope, and terror. For no one in our age, according to veterans,
saw a like army in Italy, in which nothing other than good fortune
could be desired.

23. When he saw the strength of all his forces the greatest confidence
in fighting with the French once more was kindled in Duke Lodovico,
and he went often, filled with hope, to the carriage of his wife and her
attending maidens and kept asking what she thought of so great an
army, and she praised its size and equipment. While Duke Lodovico
was riding his horse fell with all four feet to the ground, an evil omen
in the opinion of those standing around. But the Duke straightway
turned it to a good one by countering that this was the last thing
which he would suffer in the war. A little later he sent the army back
to camp. In the evening, when the commander and the Venetian proveditors and the other leaders had been summoned he advanced before
the assembly and said, "Today I have conceived a wondrous hope of
fighting with the French King, and I cannot marvel enough, O princes
and you, Venetian proveditors, that you who with far fewer forces
and at the greatest disadvantage in all things were willing to bring

incommodo nunc vero pugnam nisi Senatus prius consulto protrahendam ducitis ultroque [150] hostem lacessere timetis. Nonne duode-
cim fere ingentia agmina vidistis? Vim Germanorum peditum equitum [151] ac tormentorum robur quae Gallorum ferociam domare
possunt?"

24. Facta dicendi potestate Melchior Trivisanus legatus haec pauca
protulit, hostium numerum exiguum spernendum non esse, nec in re
militari maiorem numerum semper victorem esse, dubium esse eventum
belli, pugnam cunctando protrahendam esse in qua certa victoria est,
Gallis salutare esse summam [152] rerum experiri qui nihil si male pugnassent [153] imperii amittere possent.[154] "Temeritate vero, si quid nobis
adversi evenerit, imperium amissum iri quis non videt? Verum urbis
expugnatio hactenus nobis invitis et Senatu nostro summo utriusque
exercitus dedecore dilata est."

25. Ludovicus Dux legatum Venetum sapientia clarum summopere
laudavit. Statuerunt igitur principes [155] hostem nullo modo provocan-
dum sed venturum aequa planitie expectandum Novariamque urbem
interea oppugnare, agros penitus devastare, moenia urbis tormentis
maioribus ad imum concutere.[156] Lodovicus Dux quam [157] primum
bombardas ingentes Mediolano crates scalas testudines et expugnationi
reliqua necessaria mittere [158] statuit ne inani obsidione fatigatus exercitus maximarum rerum opportunitatem amitteret. VIII Idus Augustas
citra [159] Camarianum oppidum [160] quod inter Novariam et Vercellas
situm est latissima planities reddita est. Id oppidum paucis ante diebus
omnibus hostibus trucidatis crematis aedificiis [161] nam et igne in suburbia quoque saevitum est a Venetis militibus.

26. At Gallorum Rex cognito Venetorum consilio sine praelio Novariensibus opitulari invitis hostibus miro ingenio cogitavit. Relicta via qua
Vercellis Novariam itur ad dextram operariorum ingenti multitudine
aliam sibi viam facere eamque fossa aggereque munire statuit miro
invento. Interea cum audivisset Venetos forti [162] animo pugnam expectare Ioannem Iacobum Triultium ut aliquid moliri videretur cum copiis
praemisit ut exercitus Venetus pugnae expectatione ab oppugnatione
desisteret donec imbribus a pabulo milites arcerentur alimentaque
aegrius in castra deferrentur cogerenturque hostes re infecta ad stativa

---

[150] utroque EF    [151] equitum peditum EF -que add. B    [152] summa EF
[153] pugnaverit EF    [154] potest EF    [155] milites EF    [156] jussus est add.
EF    [157] qui EF    [158] om. EF    [159] extra B circa EF    [160] oppidum
Camarianum EF    [161] ⚹ add. E    [162] ingenti EF

your standards together at the Taro and fight with the King of the French now consider that the battle should be postponed unless the Senate is first consulted and moreover fear to challenge the enemy. Have you not seen twelve mighty companies? The force of the German infantry and cavalry and the strength of the artillery? These can tame the ferocity of the French."

24. When permission to speak was granted, the proveditor Melchiorre Trevisan said these few things, that they should not make light of the small numbers of the enemy, that in military affairs the greater number was not always victorious, that the outcome of war was doubtful, that the battle in which victory was certain ought to be postponed by delaying, and that it was advantageous to the French to test the crisis, since if they fought poorly they would lose nothing of their empire. "But who does not see," he said, "that if anything went wrong for us we would by our rashness lose our empire? But the storming of the city has been postponed up to now against our will and that of the Senate and with very great dishonor to both armies."

25. Duke Lodovico praised greatly the Venetian proveditor who was outstanding in wisdom. So the leaders decided that in no wise should a challenge be issued to the enemy, but that they should await his arrival on the level plain and should meanwhile storm the city of Novara, devastate the fields, and raze the walls of the city to the ground with heavy artillery. Duke Lodovico resolved to send mighty bombs, coverings, ladders, tortoises, and all the other things necessary for storming as soon as possible from Milan,[27] so that the army would not grow weary of the vain siege and lose the opportunity for great events. On 6 August a very wide level stretch was made on this side of the town of Cameriano, which lies between Vercelli and Novara. This town a few days before had been ravaged by Venetian soldiers; all the enemy were slain and all its buildings burned, and fire raged also in the suburbs.

26. But the King of the French, when he learned of the plan of the Venetians, plotted with wondrous sagacity to help the people of Novara without a battle and against the will of the enemy. Abandoning the road which leads from Vercelli to Novara, by an astonishing device he decided to make another road on the right for himself with a great mass of workmen and to fortify it with a ditch and rampart. Meanwhile since he had heard that the Venetians bravely awaited battle, he sent Gian Giacomo Trivulzio ahead with forces so that he might seem to be planning something, his purpose being that the Venetian army in expectation of a battle might desist from the siege until the soldiers would be kept from fodder by the rain and the food situation become

redire.

27. His diebus equites peditesque magna ex parte nocturna caligine quae tabernacula et tentoria ut fumus ad secundam diei horam complebat meridie vero solis vapore mutata subito aeris qualitate frigore ac vapore lassitudineque [163] pariter defatigati exitialibus morbis periclitari coepere; plurimi [164] febribus correpti dysenteria tenasmoque ex Latinis pauci ex Germanis multi interiere. Vino enim ea gens in febris ardore non abstinet. Qui medici officio usi sunt nulli prosus interiere. Multi itaque ex peditibus e castris missionem causariam accepere, ex equitibus vero perpauci. Ex Graecis V ad hostes transfugerunt.

28. Novarienses eo die urbem egressi in Venetos impetum fecere. In eo subitario praelio XXX desiderati sunt ex Latinis, XXX capti. Novarienses cives in urbe conquerebantur quod Cymbrorum asperitatem et feram [165] petulantiam ferre non possent: cuncta ii ceu communia possidebant. Hac die male obsessis viis in urbem panis currus IIII armenta XXVIII recepta sunt. Mediolanensibus secure praetereuntibus pectoralia quae pectus tantum tegunt D eripuere, qua iniuria universum agrum exinaniendum esse mandarunt, eam rem seditionis in urbe causam facile esse posse existimantes. Ager enim Novariensis campestris est tam uberi et pingui solo ut pabula effusim [166] universo exercitui large hoc tempore suppeditaret, nec defuit in ea perpetua obsidione in agris panicum milium ac melica quae ab hostibus colligi non poterant. Causa fertilitatis humor est quo omnis ager abundat, toto fere solo per venas aquarum resudantibus rivulis. Primo enim die quo castra locata sunt unus duntaxat puteus in castello inventus est qui singulis diebus exhauriebatur. Alioquin a militibus aquatum extra castra ire opus [167] erat.[168] Puteum igitur [169] quisque ante tabernaculum sibi [170] fecerat, quare paucis diebus ad MD puteos vel scrobes magis milites confodere.

29. Gregarii milites peditesque VII Idus Augustas [171] agri magnam partem ferro ignique devastarunt; contra Novarienses pertinaciore animo resistebant. Eo die legatus inclytae Ducis Allobrogum ad legatos venit nuntians non sine parvo Principis suae [172] moerore Gallos invita Domina Vercellas occupasse nec potuisse eorum viribus resistere: studiosam semper fuisse Veneti Senatus bonique consulerent si ipsa

---

[163] -que om. EF          [164] plurimum EF          [165] om. EF          [166] effusum B
[167] alioquin militibus—opus add. A          [168] om. EF          [169] itaque EF          [170] sibi
ante tabernaculum EF          [171] Augusti E          [172] sui BEF

more difficult in camp and the enemy be compelled to return to permanent quarters with the affair unfinished.

27. At this time horsemen and footmen in large part began to be imperiled by deadly diseases, exhausted as they were by the fog which nightly filled huts and tents just like smoke to the second hour of the day, and the heat of the sun in the middle of the day, and the sudden change of air, and cold, and mist, and weariness; a great many were laid low by fevers, dysentery, tenesmus, and a few of the Latins and many of the Germans perished. Indeed that race in the heat of fever does not abstain from wine. Certainly none died who used the treatment of their physician. And so many of the foot soldiers received discharges from camp for reasons of health, but of the horsemen very few. Of the Greeks five deserted to the enemy.

28. The people of Novara went out from the city on that day and attacked the Venetians. In that sudden battle thirty of the Latins were lost, thirty captured. The citizens of Novara within the city complained that they could not endure the harshness and rude impudence of the Cimbrian mercenaries, who seized everything as if it were common property. On this day, since the roads were poorly blockaded, four wagons of bread and twenty-eight cattle were received into the city.[28] From the Milanese, who were passing by freely, they snatched five hundred breastplates which cover only the chest, at which insult the Milanese ordered that the entire territory be devastated, thinking this could easily be a reason for sedition in the city. For the level country round about Novara has soil so fertile and rich that during this period it bountifully furnished fodder for the entire army, and in that continual siege there was no dearth in the fields of panic-grass, millet, and melic, which could not be gathered by the enemy. The reason for the fertility is the dampness in which the whole territory abounds, since rivulets of water seep out in courses over almost the entire region. For on the first day when camp was pitched one well only was found in the stronghold, which was exhausted every day. For the rest, the soldiers had to go outside the camp for water, and accordingly each one had made a well before his tent for himself, and in a few days the soldiers dug fifteen hundred wells or rather trenches.[29]

29. The common soldiers and foot soldiers devastated a great part of the fields with sword and fire on 7 August; in spite of this the people of Novara resisted even more stubbornly. On that day an envoy of the illustrious Duchess of Savoy came to the proveditors announcing that with no small anguish on her part had the French seized Vercelli against her will and that she was unable to resist their force: she had always been friendly to the Venetian Senate and they should take it

foemina armis impotens hostes coacta in urbem accepisset, orabatque ut ab incursionibus abstinerent, igni ferroque parcerent. Haec [173] elocuto Melchior Trivisanus et Lucas Pisanus legati haec pauca respondere, Allobrogum amicitiam Venetum Senatum semper magni fecisse amicitiaeque complura extare exempla, verum bellum id Veneti Senatus causa non geri sed pro Mediolanensis Principis statu ea fieri commemorarunt, Principem ob eam causam adeundum esse. Interrogarunt praeterea plura de Gallorum Rege deque principum consilio. Respondit ille procerum diversa studia esse: plures belli incommoda pertaesos [174] domum abiisse, quosdam pacis studiosos, tres vero superesse concordiae plurimum adversantes, eos [175] tamen pecuniarum avidiores facile corrumpi posse. Numerum hostium retulit. Regem pecuniam universam et mulctaticiam [176] quoque ad stipendia impendisse [177] nec existimare illum aperto Marte cum Venetis dimicaturum mutata fortunae vicissitudine, verum Novariam urbem maxime cordi esse auxiliaque propediem noctu missurum.

30. His dictis legatus ad [178] sese purgandum ad Ludovicum Ducem [179] contendit. Quinto Idus stratiotae Graeci milites Vercellas recto cursu petiere et milites IIII Ioannis Iacobi Triulcii captos in castra duxere, octo vero trucidatos reliquere. Vitellius autem Neapolitanus dux fere captus est. Captivi seorsum interrogati de hostium numero, quidam se torquendos [180] existimantes [181] prae metu secreta revelabant, XV millia Gallorum tunc Hastae Taurini Vercellisque esse referebant. IIII Idus Bulgarum oppidum iuxta Vercellas Ludovicus Dux consensu crematum est ne in manus hostium deveniret.[182] Hoc die ex Teutonibus D qui Regis stipendia secuti fuerant ad Venetos transfugere. Nuntius Ioannis Iacobi Triulcii ad imperatorem venit nuntians mentita [183] promptitudine bellandi illum propediem hostiles vires armis tentaturum.[184] Pridie Idus viis male custoditis tormentorum genus quoddam quod arcus perforatos vocant militari verbo CC in urbem recepti sunt. Idibus Novarienses furfureo pane uti [185] coeperunt in maxima annonae inopia; ob id Auriliensis Dux paupertatem omnem ac inutilem plebem exclusit. Plurimi malo cibo [186] et aquae [187] potu febre ventrisque proluvie laborabant.

---

[173] Hoc B     [174] pertaesi B     [175] om. B     [176] mulctationem B     [177] adhibuisse EF     [178] om. EF     [179] ad Ludovicum Ducem sese purgandum EF     [180] torquentes EF     [181] existimabant EF     [182] veniret EF     [183] merita EF     [84] temptaturum EF     [185] frui EF     [186] cibi A     [187] aqua A

in good part if a woman who was powerless in arms had received the enemy into the city under compulsion. And the envoy asked that they desist from attacks and abstain from fire and the sword. When he had said this the proveditors Melchiorre Trevisan and Luca Pisani replied in these few words, that the Venetian Senate had always considered the friendship of the Savoyards of great value and that there were many examples of this, but they reminded him that the war was not being waged for the sake of the Venetian Senate but that these things were being done for the state of the Duke of Milan and that therefore the Duke should be approached. Moreover they asked several questions about the King of the French and the plan of the leaders, and the envoy replied that the wishes of the nobles differed: some who were weary of the inconveniences of war had left for home, some were desirous of peace, but there remained three who stood solidly in the way of agreement; however, being very greedy for money, they could easily be bribed. He reported the number of the enemy. He said that the King had paid out in salaries all his money and also that gotten from fines and did not think that he would fight in open warfare with the Venetians, since the vicissitudes of fortune had changed, but that he especially had the city of Novara at heart and would send aid shortly by night.

30. At these words the envoy hastened to Duke Lodovico to excuse himself. On 9 August Greek stratiotes advanced straight to Vercelli [30] and attacked it; they brought captive into camp four soldiers of Gian Giacomo Trivulzio, leaving eight slain. In addition Vitelli, the leader at Naples, was almost captured. The prisoners were questioned separately about the number of the enemy, and some, thinking they would be tortured, revealed secrets out of fear and said that there were then fifteen thousand French at Asti, Turin, and Vercelli. On 10 August the town Bulgaro [31] near Vercelli was burned with the approval of Duke Lodovico so that it would not fall into the hands of the enemy. On that day five hundred Teutons who had been in the service of the King deserted to the Venetians. A messenger from Gian Giacomo Trivulzio came to the commander announcing with feigned readiness for battle that shortly Trivulzio would test the opposing force with arms. On 12 August two hundred of a certain type of artillery which they call in military language harquebuses were received into the city because the roads were poorly guarded. On 13 August the people of Novara began to eat bran bread because food was very scarce,[32] and for this reason the Duke of Orléans drove out all those of the populace who were poor and useless. A great many suffered from fever and diarrhoea due to the poor quality of the food and drinking of water.

31. His diebus Pontificis nuntius [188] in castra venerat ad Regem Gallorum iturus qui dirum anathematis Pontificis et Concilii nomine discrimen deferebat Carolum Regem Gallorum nisi arma in Italia deposuisset sociosque infestare desiisset [189] horrendo fidei orthodoxae anathemate damnatum iri et omnis qui consilio aut armis eum sequerentur. Milites Comitis Achaiazani circiter C insalutato imperatore e castris discessere, quod legatus Venetus Melchior Trivisanus [190] in contione graviter conquestus est petiitque in ea ut milites lanceis inermes redditos ex pugna instrui curarent, rusticos item operarios qui exercitui ligone deserviant: satis laboris [191] hactenus quaesitum esse a rusticis Venetarum urbium. His diebus vigilias [192] et labore continuo fatigato corpore noctuque frigore correpto ventris fluxu quam diariam vocant imperator laboravit. XVIII Calendas Septembres suburbia penitus direpta sunt, exinde igne absumpta. Eo die Galli cum Venetis subitaria pugna dimicarunt in qua CC circiter Veneti cecidere et Aloisius Lancea tormento sublatus est.

32. XVII Calendas legati Veneti Petrus Marcellus et Georgius Emus imperatoria insignia clavam argenteam ac vexillum a Veneto Senatu ob res foeliciter gestas in castra maximo plausu detulere. Ea primum sub tentorio ante altare deposita sunt, quod hostilibus spoliis ornatum erat et regiis cortinis virgatis more patrio violaceo et croceo serico consutis aureis litteris Regis et Reginae nomina indicantibus. Convenere omnes duces legati Veneti ac exercitus totius principes. Tum sacrificio rite peracto [193] Georgius Emus Senatus [194] nomine insignia elargitus est his paucis verbis: "Magnanime Princeps, haec tibi imperatoria insignia Venetus Senatus animi tui [195] et fidei [196] memor praeter stipendia elargitur qui gubernatoris praefectura contentus Gallos ferocissimos hostes ad Italiae fines acriter fugasti. Ob id cunctis dignus visus est qui imperator eligereris. Tibi fideique tuae Senatus Venetus statum et rerum summam ita commendat ut in reditu de Gallis lauro [197] redimitus more patrio triumphes."

33. Tum imperator, ut audivimus, ita respondit. "Ego Senatus Veneti illustrissimi auspiciis ferociam superbiamque Gallorum praefecturae dignitate cohibere conatus sum. Nunc vero adepto [198] imperatorio nomine pro bene merentissimi [199] Senatus laude et gloria fortunas

---

[188] cius B     [189] desiisset infestare EF     [190] om. B     [191] laborum EF
[192] vigilia B vigiliis EF     [193] peracto rite EF     [194] Senatui B     [195] tamen
B     [196] fidei et animi tui EF     [197] laurae B     [198] adempto A ademto EF
[199] meritissimi EF

31. During this period a messenger from the Pope had come into camp on his way to the King of the French. He was carrying an ominous decision of excommunication in the name of the Pope and the College which stated that unless Charles, king of the French, laid down his arms in Italy and stopped attacking the allies he and all those who followed him in plan or arms would be condemned to awful excommunication from the orthodox faith.[33] About a hundred soldiers of the Count of Caiazzo departed from camp without notifying the commander, a thing of which the Venetian proveditor Melchiorre Trevisan complained bitterly in the assembly. And he asked in it that the soldiers who had returned unarmed from battle be equipped with lances, likewise the peasant laborers who were serving in the army with hoes: enough toil, he said, had been exacted of the peasants of the Venetian towns. In these days, since his body was weakened by continual toil by day and afflicted by cold at night, the commander suffered a flux which they call *diaria*.[34] On 15 August the suburbs were completely sacked and then consumed by fire.[35] On the same day the French fought with the Venetians in a sudden battle in which about two hundred Venetians were slain and Luigi Lancia was killed by artillery.[36]

32. On 16 August the Venetian legates Pietro Marcello and Giorgio Emo brought to the camp from the Venetian Senate, amid loud applause, the insignia of general, a silver staff and standard, for good conduct of affairs.[37] These were first put down in the tent before the altar, which was adorned with spoils from the enemy and royal curtains striped in the traditional manner, stitched with violet and yellow silk, and lettered in gold with the names of the King and Queen. All the leaders assembled, the Venetian proveditors, and the captains of the whole army, and when mass had been said, Giorgio Emo in the name of the Senate bestowed the insignia with these few words: "O noble Marquis, the Venetian Senate, mindful of your courage and faith, bestows these insignia of general upon you over and above your salary, on you who, satisfied with the office of governor, bravely put the French, a very fierce enemy, to flight to the bounds of Italy, for which reason you have seemed worthy in the eyes of all to be chosen general. To you and your good faith the Venetian Senate commends the state and the conduct of affairs in such a way that on your return you may be crowned with laurel for your victory over the French and celebrate a triumph after our country's custom."

33. Then the general, as I heard it, replied thus: "Under the auspices of the most illustrious Venetian Senate, I have tried in the dignity of my office of commander to check the ferocity and haughtiness of the French. Now indeed that I have acquired the title of general I shall

omnis et vitam maiore fide expositurus sum." [200] Hanc vocem tubarum clangor excepit, et congratulantium principum vicissim oscula imperatoremque ad tabernaculum magna militum caterva comitati sunt, ubi duces equitesque inter epulas lautissimas supra castrorum luxuriam pro maxima imperatoris libertate [201] magnam diei partem inter epulas consumpsere. Tum quidam ex [202] Mediolanensibus [203] retulit Ludovicum Ducem una cum uxore ea insignia videre voluisse. Legatis protinus annuentibus sceptrum et vexillum imperatorium [204] in arce media Mediolanensi ostendere. Tum "Auspicium foelix faustumque sit," ille inquit; idem optarunt plerique Mediolanensium.

34. XVI Calendas ex Germanis C a Rege ad Venetos transiere stipendiumque protinus accipere. Comes Petilianus qui huius belli anxius erat Vercellas urbem capi legatis et caeteris ducibus oportere suadebat, qua capta Novariam statim deditionem facturam occasionemque belli gerendi hostibus [205] ita [206] facile [207] adimi posse arbitrabatur [208] Allobrogumque Duci exinde restitui. XIIII Calendas per exploratorem edocti sunt imperator ac legati peditum octo millia apud Regem esse equites armatos mille octingentos Regemque Venetorum castra a triplici latere si opus fuerit aggredi velle, unde de mutandis castris rursus verba [209] habita sunt, Antonium Mariam praeterea Severinatem regia arma secuturum. Eo die imperator et reliqui duces in contionem [210] processere. Comes Petilianus paucis verbis haec locutus est. "Si pares hostibus sumus, principes,[211] in tutiora loca abeundum censeo, si vero superiores turpissima ignaviae nota discedemus, nam qui recedit fugere creditur." At Comes Acaiazanus dispersos milites recolligendos esse firmandaque castra munimentis [212] vallo fossa [213] ac flumine. Explorator alter bombardarum numerum ac vires ad unguem retulit, inter eas duas esse longitudinis pedum VIII cum dimidio quae pilas ferreas emittunt librarum XXXV (libra enim XVIII uncias continet),[214] quatuor vero quas colubrinas vocant longitudinis pedum XIIII (has alii passavolantes dicunt), quae pilas emittunt librarum XXII, item quos falcones vocant XIIII longos pedibus VII cum dimidio quae pilas plumbeas emittunt librarum XII.

---

[200] expositurus sum majori fide EF      [201] liberalitate EF      [202] om. EF
[203] Mediolanensium EF      [204] imperatorem B      [205] om. EF      [206] om. B
[207] hostibus add. EF      [208] arbitrabantur B      [209] verba rursus EF      [210] contione B      [211] princeps B      [212] om. EF      [213] fossis EF      [214] (libra —continet) om. EF

offer all my fortunes and my life with even greater loyalty for the renown and glory of this Senate which deserves the best." On these words followed the blaring of trumpets and the kisses of leaders congratulating the general in turn, and a great throng of soldiers accompanied him to his tent. Here by virtue of the great freedom accorded a general leaders and knights spent a large part of the day at table at a most sumptuous banquet which far exceeded the abundance of a camp.[38] Then one of the Milanese reported that Duke Lodovico and his wife wanted to see these insignia, and with the immediate approval of the proveditors they displayed the general's scepter and standard in the middle of the Milanese stronghold. "Let this be a happy and favorable omen," he said then, and a great many of the Milanese expressed the same wish.

34. On 17 August a hundred Germans deserted from the King to the Venetians and straightway entered their service.[39] The Count of Pitigliano, who was uneasy about this war, urged upon the proveditors and other leaders the necessity of seizing Vercelli; if this was captured, he thought that Novara would straightway surrender and that the opportunity of waging war could easily be removed from the enemy and the city restored to the Duchess of the Savoyards. On 19 August the general and proveditors were informed through a scout that the King had eight thousand foot soldiers and eighteen hundred armed cavalry, and that he was willing to attack the camp of the Venetians from three sides if necessary. Accordingly there was discussion again about changing the camp, and it was pointed out moreover that Antonio Maria Sanseverino would follow the royal arms.[40] On that day the general and the rest of the leaders went into conference, and the Count of Pitigliano spoke these few words: "If we are equal to the enemy, O leaders, I think we should withdraw to a safer place, but if superior, we shall withdraw under the most disgraceful brand of cowardice. For he who withdraws is believed to flee." But the Count of Caiazzo held that the scattered soldiers ought to be brought together again and the camp strengthened with fortifications, rampart, ditch, and the river. Another scout reported the number of hurling machines and their strength in detail, and that among them there were two eight and a half feet long which discharge iron balls weighing thirty-five pounds (a pound consists of eighteen ounces), four fourteen feet long called culverins (others call these *passavolanti*) which discharge balls weighing twenty-two pounds, and also fourteen seven and a half feet long which they call falcons and which discharge lead balls weighing twelve pounds.

35. Haec de [215] tormentorum numero ac magnitudine nuntiata sunt. XIII Calendas stratiotae quidam Graeca levitate XXV in urbem ad hostes transfugere, ex quibus duo capti sunt, alter vulneratus vix spirans alter protinus altissimo illo patibulo sublimatus est. His diebus Veneti legati Nicolaum Ursinum Petilianum comitem ad Senatus stipendia summo studio ducere curarunt, virum rei bellicae disciplinam callentem, qui in pueritia tyro deinde miles centurio primipilaris ductor ac imperator fuisset, ad quos Venetus Senatus respondit castrorum praefecturae tantum locum superesse, sed copiarum numerum se maiorem daturum liberalioraque [216] stipendia, satis ei esse pro tempore urbis Venetae gratiam inire illique maiora uberioraque non defutura si Deus vitam dederit. Quinquaginta igitur millia aureorum singulis annis pollicitus est Senatus nomine Melchior Trivisanus legatus et hortatus est ut oblatam pro tempore conditionem laetus acciperet. Tum Comes Petilianus se nihil illa hora posse respondere. Statuit autem prius a me Alexandro Benedicto physico pro accipienda conditione propitii syderis aspectum quaerere ut prosperam diem denunciarem,[217] cui respondi [218] XI Calendas ac sequentem diem prosperos eventus [219] indicare ex Iovis cum Luna coitu XII Librae gradu ac Veneris XV eiusdem signi ac Martis sextili contuitu peritorum iudicio.

36. XII Calendas Germani sub Venetorum stipendio de fuga consilium iniere et nisi Georgius Petraplanensis affuisset, qui feros animos mitigaverat, iam ad Regem defecissent. Nuntiatum est praeterea Regem XX millia peditum in summa collegisse exercitumque in dies augere et collatis signis propediem dimicaturum. Ea fama crebrior [220] erat ob urbis Novariae inopiam quae in maxima desperatione bombardarum ictibus auxilia signis datis petebat; Vercellenses paribus ictibus respondebant.[221] Ea nocte tabellarius Venetus a Gallis captus est cum litteris quae a legatis ad Senatum mittebantur quae publice [222] lectae sunt. Continebatur enim legatos conquestos esse CC equites copiarum Mediolanensium invito imperatore ob pecuniarum inopiam abiisse et ex Venetorum peditibus plurimos accepta pecunia distributorium [223] decoxisse, Regem deinde Gallorum in Galliam propediem recessurum. Dux Auriliensis easdem litteras et suas pariter tribus villicis ad Regem dedit. Hi rursus a nostris secundis vigiliis capti sunt, sed litterae Ducis

---

[215] om. B     [216] liberaliaque EF     [217] nunciarem EF     [218] respondit B
[219] eventos EF     [220] crebior EF     [221] respondebat B     [222] publicae B
[223] diributorium A distributorium A by MS. correction

35. Such was the report on the number and size of the artillery. On 20 August twenty-five stratiotes with Greek fickleness went to the city and deserted to the enemy; two were captured, one wounded so that he was scarcely breathing, and the other was shortly hung on that very high gibbet. At this time the Venetian proveditors gave the most zealous attention to bringing into the service of the Senate Niccolò Orsini, count of Pitigliano, a man experienced in the discipline of war, who had been a recruit in boyhood, then a soldier, centurion, captain, leader, and commander. To them the Venetian Senate replied that there remained only the office of prefect of the camp, but that they would grant a greater number of forces and a more liberal stipend to him, and that it was enough for him for the time being to have the gratitude of the Venetian city, and greater and wealthier recompense would not be lacking to him if God preserved him. So in the name of the Senate the proveditor Melchiorre Trevisan promised fifty thousand ducats a year [41] and urged him to accept joyfully these temporary terms. Then the Count of Pitigliano said that he could make no reply at that time, but he decided to seek first from me, the physician Alessandro Benedetti, an aspect of the stars propitious for accepting the terms, so that I might name the favorable day. I replied to him that in the judgment of the learned 22 and 23 August indicated a favorable outcome from the conjunction of Jupiter with the Moon at the twelfth degree of Libra, Venus being at the fifteenth in the same sign and Mars sixty degrees from this sign.

36. On 21 August the Germans who were in the pay of the Venetians made plans for flight, and had not Georg Ebenstein been at hand and calmed their wild minds they would soon have deserted to the King.[42] Moreover it was reported that the King had assembled twenty thousand foot soldiers in all, was increasing his army every day, and would shortly bring his standards together and fight. This rumor was the more frequent because of the scarcity in the city of Novara, which in the greatest desperation used blasts of artillery as signals in seeking aid, and the people of Vercelli replied with similar blasts. That night a Venetian courier was captured by the French with a letter from the proveditors to the Senate which was read in public. The content was that the proveditors complained because two hundred cavalry of the Milanese forces had departed against the will of the general on account of lack of money and because payment to a great many Venetian foot soldiers had impaired the funds at the distributing office, and also that the King of the French would shortly withdraw to France. The Duke of Orléans gave this letter and likewise one of his own to three peasants to carry to the King, and these in turn were captured by our men in

ad Regem protinus legi non poterant quae commutatis litteris et verbis scriptae erant. Mediolanum propterea missae sunt atque in nostratia verba translatae, mirandumque eo processisse ingenia ut nihil tam litteris reconditum sit quod humana industria non palam fiat. Conquerebatur in iis Auriliensis Dux Regem Gallorum in Galliam abiturum et Novariae urbis expeditionem foede relicturum eaque non sine regiae maiestatis dedecore iactari; rei frumentariae praeterea inopia et pecuniarum desperatione milites hostibus ultro sese dedituros auxilia irrita [224] spe in longum protrahi videntes; Germanos deinde [225] in castris Venetis seditionem cum Latinis internecivo odio commovisse et nisi Georgius Petraplanensis affuisset iam domos abituros; duces denique omnes inter se discordes esse. Hae litterae ad Senatum missae sunt. Tabellariorum deinde hora mutata est ne de caetero nocturna occasione interciperentur.

37. His diebus Vercellae urbs iam Gallorum diverticulum et contubernium facta est invita (ut dicunt) Domina, quod Ludovicus Dux aegerrime tulit conatusque exinde est Ducem Allobrogum a Gallorum studio avocare ut illa Vercellis Gallos excluderet,[226] penituitque Ducem Petiliani consilio Vercellas non occupasse,[227] significavitque nisi eos urbe expulisset agros omnes militibus diripiendos daturum. Illa respondit parva manu Gallorum Regem potentissimum ex sedibus suis non posse propellere, maximo [228] sibi damno esse alienos milites domi habere. Etsi imperator et legati Veneti non ut iniuriam vicinitati aut affinitati Ducis Ludovici inferrent omnia tamen igni ferroque devastanda militi permisere, ut alimenta Gallis adimerent seditioneque [229] omnia complerent. Tum Fracassius [230] Severinas ut prior praedae incumberet rem in posteram diem differre simulavit, Graecosque milites falsa cunctatione decepit. Itaque prior cum D militibus levius armatis in agrum sibi notum noctu irrupit ruraque Vercellensium populabundus vastavit. Armentorum circiter duo millia pecudes circiter mille abduxit. Hos secuti sunt Graeci stratiotae qui mille quoque armenta in castra duxere quae [231] trepidantes rustici in stabulis reliquerant, atque ita ager subito exinanitus est. His Fracassii milites inopiam et famem vicerunt. Reliqua si qua relicta erant armenta [232] iussu Ducis Allobrogum in vicina [233] oppida protinus missa sunt.

---

[224] inita B　　[225] in—deinde om. B　　[226] excluderetur B　　[227] occupavisse EF　　[228] maxima B　　[229] seditionemque A seditioneque A by MS. correction　　[230] Franciscus EF　　[231] qui B　　[232] jumenta EF　　[233] vicinia B

the second watch, but the letter of the Duke to the King could not be read at once because it was written with letters and words interchanged. Therefore it was sent to Milan and translated into our language. It is really a wondrous thing that talent has progressed to such a point that nothing can be hidden away in a letter which human industry will not reveal.[43] In this letter the Duke of Orléans lamented that the King of the French intended to depart for France and disgracefully abandon the campaign of the city of Novara and that these reports were being spread not without dishonor to the royal majesty; moreover, that from scarcity of the grain supply and desperation for money the soldiers would voluntarily surrender to the enemy when they saw aid long postponed and hope vain; and next, that the Germans in the Venetian camp had aroused sedition in internecine hatred with the Latins and if Georg Ebenstein were not there they would soon go home; and finally, that all the leaders were disagreeing with one another. This letter was sent to the Senate, and then the hour of the couriers was changed, lest they be intercepted again at night.

37. During this period the city of Vercelli became against the will of the Duchess, as they say, a refuge and stopping-place for the French, a thing which Duke Lodovico endured with the greatest difficulty. He tried then to draw the Duchess of the Savoyards away from her zeal for the French, so that she might drive them out from Vercelli, and repented that he had not seized Vercelli as Pitigliano had advised, and he indicated that unless she drove them from the city he would have the soldiers ravage the fields. She replied that with a small band she could not drive the very powerful King of the French from her territory and that it was a very great loss to her to have foreign soldiers at home. But the general and the Venetian proveditors nonetheless permitted the soldiers to ravage everything by fire and sword not to bring injury to the neighbors and relatives of Duke Lodovico but to remove food from the French and spread sedition everywhere. Then Fracasso Sanseverino, so that he might be first at the plunder, pretended to put off the affair to the next day and deceived the Greek soldiers by feigned hesitation, and thus, rushing out earlier by night with five hundred light-armed soldiers into territory which he knew, he was the first to devastate the fields of the people of Vercelli. He brought back to camp about two thousand cattle and a thousand sheep; [44] on him followed Greek stratiotes who led to camp a thousand more cattle which the frightened peasants had left in the folds, and so the territory was quickly stripped. With these animals the soldiers of Fracasso overcame their want and hunger. Any cattle which were left were sent immediately on order of the Duchess of the Savoyards to nearby towns.

38. XI Calendas pro adventu Ludovici Ducis magnifica in castris tentoria sub Tilia oppidulo disposita sunt novaque equitum armatorum supplementa sub Pesaurensi Principe in castra recepta sunt circiter CC. Nono Calendas Teutones et Latini milites pristinae seditionis memores pedestri pugna dimicavere, in qua Latinorum decem tormentis cecidere; caeteri instantes et fugientium Teutonum tergis inhaerentes L interfecere, ac nisi Comes Petilianus ea vespera praesto affuisset ad unum in tuguriis [234] caesi fuissent. In femore Marcus Ariminensis [235] centurio tormento parvo transsactus [236] est.

39. His diebus Novarienses fame tandem macerati instantemque expugnationem formidantes intercepta pristina nuntiorum occasione ex summis turribus arceque sublimi primis noctis vigiliis secundisque ac matutinis signi datione sublata ardenti face ac demissa per intervalla auxilia petere anxie coeperunt vel in conspectu hostium. Haec [237] exercitui alacritatem cognita hostium inopia attulere qui consumptis alimentis iumenta caedere [238] aggressi sunt nec equis quidem abstinuisse feruntur. Ea fames accedente aquae potu [239] perpetuae deinde vigiliae pavorque continuus varios vulgaverant morbos; ergo stratae erant viae aegrotis semivivis qui cibum implorabant, sed frustra surdas aures implebant eiulatibus, plures in dies cadebant. Dux Auriliensis dolore simul ac pudore anxius quia [240] causa tantae cladis ipse [241] esset litteras a Rege habuisse simulavit, quare per urbem campanas et tympana pulsantes adventantis Regis fiduciam irritam praeferebant. Caeterum noctu faces Galli longius refulgentes accendebant [242] auxilia expetentes. His diebus cum e castris egrederentur quidam ex amicis Novariensium et quaedam oppida visendi gratia adirent imposita super portis Severinatum insignia viderunt quae oppidanis impunitatem dedere; ob id ea nullus hostium aggredi ausus est. Oppidani illos magno honore domi [243] suscepere nullam belli calamitatem sentientes.

40. VII Calendas Septembris exploratores significavere Gallos mille et quingentos silente luna alimentis oneratos urbi auxilia laturos perdita securitate [244] singulis equitibus longiore distributo sacco. Imperator exercitus instructis secundis vigiliis duabus aciebus et equitibus levis armaturae ad viarum compita praecludenda ipse [245] agmina ducit albis funalibus accensis; bubulcos ducentes tormenta ardentes faces [246] anteibant. Dispositis militibus ac tormentis extinctis facibus explora-

---

[234] triguriis B     [235] Anninensis B     [236] transactus BEF     [237] Hac B     [238] cedere B     [239] potu aquae EF     [240] quod B     [241] om. EF     [242] accedebant B     [243] om. EF     [244] scuritate B     [245] ipsa EF     [246] tenentes add. EF

38. On 22 August for the arrival of Duke Lodovico magnificent tents were set up in the camp below the little town of Tiglia, and about two hundred new reinforcements of armed cavalry under the Lord of Pesaro were received into camp.[45] On 24 August the German and Latin soldiers, remembering the earlier rebellion, fought on foot, and ten of the Latins fell by artillery; the rest, pressing on the backs of the fugitive Teutons, killed fifty, and had not the Count of Pitigliano been at hand that evening, they would have been slain to a man in their huts. Marco of Rimini, a centurion, was hit in the leg by a small bullet.[46]

39. In this period the people of Novara were at length wasted away by hunger, and fearing an impending assault, since the previous means of messages had been intercepted, they anxiously began to seek aid using as a signal the device of raising and lowering a burning torch from the top of the towers and the lofty citadel in the first and second watches of the night and in the morning, even in sight of the enemy.[47] This circumstance awakened eagerness in the army when the straits of the enemy became known, for with their food consumed they prepared to slay baggage animals and were said to abstain not even from horses.[48] Hunger, along with the increased drinking of water, and then the unbroken wakefulness and continual fear, had spread many diseases; accordingly the streets were filled with people sick and only half-alive who kept begging for food, but in vain did they fill with their wails ears which were deaf, and more of them perished each day. The Duke of Orléans, overcome by a double sense of sorrow and shame, since he was the reason for such great destruction, pretended to have had a letter from the King, and at this they sounded bells and drums throughout the city and displayed a vain trust in the arrival of the King. But at night the French kindled torches which shone still farther off and they kept begging for aid. At this time when some of the friends of the people of Novara went out from the camp and approached certain towns for a visit they saw applied to the gates the insignia of the Sanseverino family, which gave safety to the townspeople, and on this account none of the enemy dared approach them. The townspeople took them in with great honor, for they experienced no distress in the war.

40. On 26 August scouts reported that in the dark of the moon fifteen hundred Frenchmen loaded with food would squander their safety and bring aid to the city and that a pack which was heavier had been assigned to each horseman.[49] At the second watch the general of the army drew up two lines and the cavalry of the light-armed forces to shut off the crossroads, and he himself led the lines with white tapers lit; glowing torches preceded the oxen which were pulling the artillery.

tores turmam equitum [247] hostilem [248] venientium longius audivere, qui cum se in medios hostes lapsos sensere abiectis protinus sarcinis fugam pecorum modo arripuere; multi capti sunt. Farina, vinum [249] et reliqua alimenta direpta, spoliati omnes in castra ducuntur praeter eos qui subito delituere. Die tamen reperti sunt qui pecuniis auro argento annulis monilibus et equis laetum militem plusquam verisimile sit reddidere. Duces capti sunt Statilianus et Pelizensis quidam natione Galli, atque Chion Prenethus Regis alumnus a Lazario Ariminensi captus est. Iacobatius Venetus peditum praefectus delitescentes inter vepres Gallos die [250] clamore terrefaciebat monendo stratiotas adventare utque cito exirent clamitabat. His vociferationibus [251] Galli quidam prae nimio metu supplices exiere veniam et salutem orantes; captivi qui Latinorum mores noverant [252] ac nativam in miseros clementiam auro se redimere studebant.[253] Legati Veneti praeconis voce ut omnes captivi ea die ad praetorium ducerentur edixere statueruntque ut ad belli ultima Mediolani ac Cremae in vinculis servarentur, deinde sua quisque pecunia captivitatem redimeret. Solebant enim qui capti fuissent post libertatem saeviores in Latinos esse. Dux Auriliensis qui hos in custodias mittendos audiverat illos a Venetis catenis vinctos [254] servari ad perpetuam triremium servitutem falso iactabat.[255] Ea saevitia ne in Turcis quidem unquam [256] usus est Senatus Venetus; argumentum fuerat quod militum calones et lixas Graeci milites vendere non poterant.

41. VI Calendas imperator et legati ob Germanorum saevitiam seditionemque continuam ac suspitionem statuerunt ne de caetero Germani ad militiam conscriberentur. Firmarunt praeterea ea die Fontanae arcem in qua equites C pedites CC collocavere ne facile in manus hostium deveniret. IIII Calendas Alobrogum legati ad imperatorem legatosque venere querelarum pleni, Ducem Mediolanensem affinitatis rationem non habuisse demirati quod milites contra veteris amicitiae iura agros amicorum depopulati essent. IIII Calendas Comitis Petilliani opera munimentum sub moenibus urbis ut protinus maiora tormenta

---

[247] om. EF    [248] hostium EF    [249] farina vinum om. EF    [250] diro EF
[251] vociferantibus EF    [252] non erant B    [253] statuebant EF    [254] junctos B
[255] jactitabat EF    [256] om. EF

When the soldiers and artillery had been arranged and the torches extinguished, scouts heard the enemy's band of cavalry coming at some distance, and when these saw themselves slipping into the midst of the enemy, they straightway threw down their packs and snatched at flight like sheep, and many were captured. Grain, wine, and the other foods were taken, and the despoiled soldiers were all led into camp except those who hid themselves quickly. But these were nonetheless found with daylight and gave joy almost incredible to the soldiers with their money, gold, silver, rings, bracelets, and horses. The French leaders Chatillon and one named La Palice were captured, and Chion Prenèthe, ward of the King, was taken by Lazzaro of Rimini. At daybreak the Venetian Jacopaccio, commander of the infantry, terrified by shouts the French who were hiding in the bushes and kept crying out that the stratiotes were approaching and that they should come out quickly. At these shouts some of the French did come forth as suppliants because of their excessive fear and begged for pardon and safety. The captives who knew the habits of the Latins and their natural clemency toward the wretched determined to ransom themselves with gold. The Venetian proveditors announced through a herald that all captives should be led to the judge's tent on that day, and they decided that until the end of the war they should be kept in bonds at Milan and Crema and that then each one should redeem himself from captivity with his own money. For those who had been captured were accustomed after being freed to be more savage against the Latins. The Duke of Orléans, who had heard that these prisoners were to be sent into custody, claimed falsely that prisoners were confined in chains by the Venetians and kept for perpetual slavery on the triremes. Such cruelty the Venetian Senate never used even against the Turks. Evidence of this was the fact that the Greek soldiers were not able to sell the servants of the soldiers and camp-followers.

41. On 27 August the general and proveditors decided that because of the cruelty of the Germans and their continuous mutiny, and distrust of them, no Germans should be enrolled in the future for the campaign. Moreover on that day they strengthened the citadel of Fontaneto,[50] in which they stationed a hundred horsemen and two hundred foot soldiers so that it might not fall readily into the hands of the enemy. On 29 August legates of the Savoyards came to the general and the proveditors with abundant complaints,[51] wondering at the fact that the Duke of Milan had had no respect for their close ties and that his soldiers had devastated the land of friends contrary to the rights of ancient friendship. Also on 29 August fortifications, the work of the Count of Pitigliano, were erected beneath the walls of the city so

ad murorum ruinam subducerentur constructum est. Verum prius suburbana igni ferroque devastata sunt templumque Divi Nazarii occuparunt, in quo ducentos equites CCCque pedites praesidio locaverunt duce Carolo Melitense.

42. Ea die in castris nunciatum est Florentinos cum Gallorum Rege foedera iniisse legatumque cum paciscendi auctoritate ad Regem misisse ut Pisas urbem dolo amissam restitueret ac oppida quae Petrus Medices tradiderat, C millia aureorum singulis annis pollicentes donec bellum inchoatum absolveretur, CC praeterea equites suo stipendio in Apulia alendos contra Regem Ferdinandum. Legatus a Mediolanensibus intercipitur. Patefacto foedere, Dux Mediolanensis copias in Pisanorum auxilium additis Venetorum pecuniis [257] mittit quibus Fracassium praeficit.[258] Ea nocte excubiis Nicolaus Savorgnanus ex Hunia gente patricius Venetus peditum dux terrefacto equo ac collapso armum [259] misere convellit Urbanoque filio militiae curam reliquit. Panis et avenae caritas quae semper in castris fuerat, qua causa proveniret quidam ex amicis patefecit qui oneratos currus ex principalibus horreis furnisque vehi affirmavit. In his maior pecuniarum pars impendebatur, nec in re alia maior quaestus fuit nec diuturnior. Peditum perpetuis dolis modus inventus est ut ii bis in mense recogniti bis stipendii dimidium acciperent etsi id quibusdam ducibus molestum fuit, Germanis praesertim nonnullis qui supposititiis [260] militibus distributorium [261] exedebant.

43. Interea ad expugnandam urbem multa ab imperatore parabantur, nec cessabat unquam ab opere modo hostium consilia explorare modo vigilias imperare, laboribus continuis novum militem fatigare. Sed fossae munimentaque eum sollicitabant. IIII Nonas Septembris Comes Nicolaus Petilianus Carolus Melitensis ad expugnationem cuncta [262] parabant etsi sociorum milites non exiguus livor excruciaret [263] ne gloria predaeque utilitas Venetorum copiis daretur. Dum igitur Comes Petilianus praefectus [264] expugnationem praepararet pilula plumbea sub renem dextrum tormento impacta est et ad sinistram scapulam infixa. E diruto enim munimento hostium ante portam urbis in caput toto corpore se ipsum devolvit visa tormenti flamma nec tamen subitum

---

[257] auxiliis EF     [258] praefecit B     [259] annum B     [260] suppositis BEF
[261] diribitorium AEF distributorium B     [262] omnia EF     [263] cruciaret EF
[264] om. F

that heavier artillery might shortly be brought up for the destruction of the walls. But first the suburbs were devastated with fire and sword, and they seized the church of San Nazzaro, in which they stationed two hundred cavalry and three hundred foot soldiers as a garrison under command of Carlo of Pian di Meleto.[52]

42. On that day it was announced in camp that the Florentines had made a compact with the King of the French and had sent an envoy to the King with authority to enter into terms for restoring the city of Pisa, which had been lost by treachery, and the towns which Piero de' Medici had handed over.[53] They promised a hundred thousand pieces of gold a year until the war which had been started was finished, and said moreover that at their own cost they would maintain two hundred horsemen in Puglia against King Ferdinand. The envoy was intercepted by the Milanese, and when the compact had been disclosed, the Duke of Milan sent forces to the aid of the people of Pisa; money was contributed by the Venetians, and Fracasso was put in charge.[54] On watch that night Niccolò Savorgnan, of the Hunnish race, a Venetian patrician and leader of the infantry, unfortunately dislocated a shoulder when his horse was frightened and fell; he left the responsibility of the campaign to his son Urbano. There was a scarcity of bread and oats, of which there had always been a sufficiency in the camp, and someone who was a friend disclosed for what reason this happened, for he asserted that loaded carts were carried off from the main storerooms and ovens. In this the greater part of the money was spent, and in no other thing was the expenditure greater or longer. For the continued treachery of the foot soldiers a way out was found, that those who were certified twice in one month were to receive half their salary twice, even though this was troublesome to certain leaders, especially some Germans who with supposititious soldiers exhausted the distributing office.

43. Meanwhile many things were being prepared by the general for storming the city, and he never stopped from the work now of spying out the plans of the enemy, now of ordering watches, now of wearying the new soldiers with continual labors. But the ditches and fortifications worried him. On 2 September Count Niccolò of Pitigliano and Carlo of Pian di Meleto were getting everything ready for the storming of the city, though no small envy tortured the soldiers of the allies lest glory and use of the booty be given to the Venetian forces. Then while the commander the Count of Pitigliano was preparing for the assault a lead ball struck him under the right kidney and passed to the left scapula.[55] For since the rampart of the enemy had been demolished before the gate of the city, he hurled himself down headlong when he saw

ictum evitare potuit. Socii manu praefectum excipiunt et in proximi coenobii cubiculum deferunt. Ingens protinus sollicitudo ac luctus in castra pervenit. Eiulantes milites querebantur in tanta rerum occasione clarissimum ducem extinctum esse desperatamque esse urbis expugnationem, Regem praeterea Gallorum non procul a castris signa fixisse.[265]

44. Huius enim consilio et industria imperator tanquam veterani militis et ducis utebatur. Me Veneti exercitus medicum subito nuntio evocari ad se iussit. Ego ut vulnus vidi interrogavi an concidisset evomuisset [266] sanguinemve [267] expuisset [268] urinam cruentam aut excrementa emisisset. Familiares qui eum pertulerant nihil horum vidisse affirmarunt. Urinam poposci quam ut claram vidi salvos esse renes et vessicam adiudicavi. Chirurgi omnes convocati sunt et medici reliqui, Petrus Franciscus Mantuanus militia ornatus Andreas Novariensis qui renum quoque salutem pronuntiavere. An salva essent intestina nisi iniecto clystere intelligi non potuit. Siliqua Aegyptia cum rore Syriaco summo mane pota et ventrem et intestina illaesa indicavit; mens item sana diaphragma sive praecordia integra ostendit. III Nonas praefectus in tabernaculum delatus est ubi cibi paululum assumpsit, somnum exiguum et per intervalla cepit.

45. Tum Regem Gallorum adventare certior fama erat. Hic vero tantam victoriam eripi sibi e manibus et ignobili morte in tabernaculo extingui querebatur gemens, et "Qui paulo ante," inquit,[269] "foede fugerat iam nos ultro provocat et superbos nuntios mittit. Fortunam meam," inquit, "in consilio habent Galli." His dictis a medicis quid spei superesset quaesivit. Omnes salutem large promisere, verum tardiuscule vulnus ad cicatricem perventurum, nam specillum aereum supra sesquipalmi longitudinem inditum [270] fuerat. Quidam vero non medicus sed circulator falsa artis ostentatione subitam salutem aquae medicatae potu polliceri ausus est fidemque medicamenti [271] dabat milii granum iniectum quod sequenti die ex ore vulneris prorumperet. Petilianus praefectus Ludovici Ducis suasu, ad quem circulator devolaverat,[272] potionem quae nihil venenati contineret moram perpeti nolens sumere statuerat. Inter has concertationes biduum consumptum est. Ego vero

---

[265] significavisse * E significavisse F    [266] evomisset EF    [267] sanguinemne B sanguinemque F    [268] exposuisset B    [269] om. EF    [270] indutum B [271] mendicanti B    [272] devolverat EF

the flaming shot, but he could not avoid the sudden blow. His comrades lifted up their commander in their arms and carried him into a cubicle of a nearby monastery. Straïghtway great anxiety and grief pervaded the camp, and the wailing soldiers lamented that at so favorable a point in affairs their most eminent leader had been killed, and that the storming of the city was despaired of, and that moreover the King of the French had fixed his standards not far from the camp.

44. Now the general used this man's wisdom and industry like that of a veteran soldier and leader, and he ordered me, physician of the Venetian army, to be summoned straightway by messenger, and when I saw the wound I asked whether he had fallen unconscious, or vomited, or spat out blood, and whether urine and stools were bloody. The servants who had carried him affirmed that they had seen nothing of this. I asked for urine and found that it was clear, and so I judged that the kidneys and bladder were intact. All the surgeons were summoned and the rest of the physicians, Pietro Francesco of Mantua, distinguished in the campaign, and Andrea of Novara, who also pronounced the kidneys intact. Whether the intestines were unharmed could not be determined except by injecting a clyster. Egyptian carob [56] drunk early in the morning with Syrian juice proclaimed the stomach and intestines uninjured; likewise the sound mind showed the diaphragm or heart intact. On 3 September the commander was carried into his tent, where he ate a little food and slept lightly and at intervals.

45. Then the report that the King of the French was approaching became more certain, and he complained, moaning, that so great a victory was snatched from his hands and that he would die an ignoble death in his tent. "The man who had disgracefully fled a little before," he said, "now challenges us wantonly and sends arrogant messengers. The French," he added, "have my misfortune in their plans." At these words he asked the physicians what hope remained. All abundantly promised him deliverance, but added that the wound would come to a scar somewhat slowly, for the bronze probe had gone in beyond the length of a palm and a half. However, someone who was not a physician but a quack dared with false display of skill to promise immediate deliverance by the drinking of some medicated water, and announced as guaranty of his remedy that if a grain of millet were put in it, on the following day the grain would make its appearance at the opening of the wound. The commander Pitigliano, on the urging of Duke Lodovico, to whom the quack had hastened, had decided to take the potion if it contained nothing poisonous, since he was unwilling to endure delay. In these disputes two days were consumed. But I who

qui chirurgi dolos et fraudem noveram facile circulatori persuasi qui
iam XV nummos aureos acceperat ut remedium in sequentem hebdo-
madem differret. Nobiles interea chirurgi [273] Ticino Mediolanoque acciti fuerant qui hominis temeritatem pariter damnavere. Pro Petiliani
salute vota a militibus suscepta sunt.

46. Pridie Nonas Septembres Dux Auriliensis aes pro argento signavit
pecuniarum inopia quam nemo renuere [274] ausus est. Nonis Georgius
Petraplanensis vir strenuus Germanorum peditum ductor, qui sub
Mediolanensi Duce merebat, ob eius fidem a Veneto Senatu pecunias
dono accepit. Ea die D rustici operarii ad munimenta acciti venerunt.
VII Idus Septembres Argentonus qui antea apud Venetum Senatum
legatus Regis fuerat sponte sua de pace cum Venetis legatis tractaturus
tubicinem praemisit qui legatis nuntiaret Regem Gallorum sociorum
foedera observaturum nec aliud in Italia praeterquam regnum quod
iure suum esset petiturum et pacem inprimis cum Venetis exoptare
quandoquidem sibi adversari [275] fortunam maximis discriminibus co-
gnovisset.

47. VI Idus Antonius Faber centurio ac Ioannes Feltrensis dum
strenue munimenta quaedam sub portis expugnarent graviter vulnerati
sunt. V Idus sub moenibus IIII mortaria in suburbio Divi Agapeti [276]
posita fuere ad tectorum ruinam, bombardae item longiores. Tum
Petrus Sclavus centurio sagitta vulneratus moritur. Aloisius Novellus
saucius [277] in tabernaculum defertur. Schalae in castra delatae sunt. III
Idus sacrae quaedam virgines urbem egressae in castra venere nuntian-
tes Gallos in urbe summa macie [278] ac squalore confectos esse, [279] no-
biliores frumento cocto vesci, privata domorum tecta [280] ad munimenta
corripi. Clandestino nuntio Brescius [281] inter regios proceres legatis
Venetis nuntiat Regiam Maiestatem cum Veneto Senatu pacem desiderare modo Senatus una cum Rege Ioannis Galeacii Mariae filium
puerum ad principatum promoveret Cremonam exinde urbem et alia
oppida propinquo accepturus. Legati vero ob fidem nuntium obiur-
garunt. Ea nocte bombardae duae ingentes in castra Mediolano delatae
sunt quae pilas lapideas librarum CC emittebant. Iis sequenti die
ingenti ruina turres et portam quatere coeperunt; una nocte totius
civitatis faciem mutatam esse videres.

---

[273] in add. B   [274] innuere B   [275] adversam B   [276] Agapidi B
[277] saucia EF   [278] in summa macie in urbe esse EF   [279] om. EF
[280] tuta EF   [281] Prescius EF

knew the wiles and deceit of the surgeon easily persuaded the quack, who had already accepted fifteen ducats, to put off the remedy to the next week. Meanwhile excellent surgeons were summoned from Pavia and Milan, who likewise condemned the temerity of that man. Vows were made by the soldiers for the deliverance of Pitigliano.[57]

46. On 4 September the Duke of Orléans because of the scarcity of money coined copper in place of silver, and no one dared to refuse it.[58] On the fifth Georg Ebenstein,[59] an active man, leader of the German foot soldiers who was serving under the Duke of Milan, received money from the Venetian Senate as a gift because of his loyalty. On that day five hundred peasant laborers were summoned and came to the fortifications. On 7 September Argenton,[60] who had earlier been ambassador of the King to the Venetian Senate, of his own accord sent ahead a trumpeter to treat of peace with the Venetian proveditors; [61] he was to announce to the proveditors that the King of the French would observe the terms of the allies and seek nothing else in Italy than the kingdom which was his by right, and that he desired peace especially with the Venetians, since he had learned that fortune opposed him at the greatest crises.

47. On 8 September Antonio di Fabri, a centurion, and Giovanni of Feltre were seriously wounded while strenuously storming some fortifications beneath the gates. On 9 September four mortars were put beneath the walls in the suburb of Sant'Agabio for the destruction of the houses, and likewise longer bombards. Then Pietro Schiavo, a centurion, was wounded by an arrow and died.[62] Luigi Novello was wounded and carried into his tent. Ladders were brought to the camp. On 11 September some nuns came out from the city to the camp and reported that the French in the city were afflicted with the greatest want and squalor: the more noble were eating cooked grain, and the roofs of private houses were being snatched away for fortifications. By secret messenger Bresse, one of the royal nobles, reported to the Venetian proveditors that His Royal Majesty wanted peace with the Venetian Senate provided the Senate together with the King would elevate the boy son of Giangaleazzo Maria to the principate, to receive then the city of Cremona and other neighboring towns. But the proveditors exhorted the messenger to keep the faith. On that night two huge bombards which discharged stone balls weighing two hundred pounds were brought into the camp from Milan. With these on the following day they began to batter the towers and the gate, and the destruction was enormous; in one night you could see the appearance of the entire city changed.

48. Tum Venetus Senatus ad praemia haud impiger expugnationis tempore primis moenia ascendentibus secundis ac tertiis pro legatorum exercitus arbitrio munera elargiri decreverat. In eo prospero successu exorta rursus inter socios milites invidia est ne Venetis armis urbs diriperetur praedaeque [282] Veneto militi [283] daretur. Tum Galeacius Severinas Mediolanensium copiarum praefectus ob Regis adventum quo [284] cum aperto Marte dimicandum esset ut tormenta moenibus amoverentur clamitabat deque damno ac iniuria si ab hostibus raperentur protestari legatis coepit. At Veneti duces summa desperatione tenebantur [285] cum urbem iam captam non posse capi [286] viderent frustraque pecunias profundi magni item exercitus instare ruinam et nisi praesto sit fortuna facile posse opprimi.

49. Fama fuit apud milites validissimum Venetorum exercitum hostes ac socios Mediolanenses si quid sceleris concepissent [287] ab insidiis terruisse. Facinoris suspicionem in castris augebant Severinatum fugiente Rege prompta salutatio Ducis Ferrariensis frequentes ac clandestini internuntii. Non ultra igitur legatis Venetis in expugnanda cura fuit sed in conservandis copiis sollicitudo duntaxat increvit. Fugae exitum plerique duces clam praetentavere, qui in magna rerum desperatione summa parte fluminis Ticini haud profundo [288] vado posse tranare nunciarunt.[289] Graviora etiam in dies iactabantur a Mediolanensibus militibus ut fit Venetos nisi annuente Ludovico Duce non posse discedere salutemque ac ruinam totius Italiae in sua haberi potestate et omnium rerum arbitrum esse. Maior ob [290] id Venetos milites cura subiit exercitus maioribus copiis amplificandi; propterea equites peditesque [291] undique conscribi petebant, famaque erat Gallorum Regem ab attiguis [292] Germaniae locis militum delectum habere, unde et a Veneto pariter Senatu iam delectus ubique haberi coepit. Tormentorum ingens numerus Venetiis Verona Brixiaque vehebatur, ductores alii ad stipendia conscribebantur, nec modus [293] erat in eo discrimine omnibus pro salute patriae sese accingentibus. De transportandis item pontibus cogitatum est. Nihil igitur omisere ut si opus esset ad Ticinum usque robur omnium virium processisset. Maior igitur atque periculosior belli moles superesse videbatur.

---

[282] praedaque EF    [283] militi Veneto EF    [284] qui ABEF    [285] tenebant EF    [286] capi non posse EF    [287] incepissent EF    [288] ptofundo A    [289] praetentarunt AB om. EF nunciarunt A by MS. correction    [290] od A    [291] pedites equitesque EF    [292] extiguis B    [293] mora B mens EF

48. Then the Venetian Senate, which was not indolent as regards rewards, decreed that in accordance with the judgment of the proveditors of the army gifts should be bestowed on those who were first, second, and third to scale the walls at the time of the assault. While matters were proceeding so favorably jealousy arose again among the allied soldiers from fear that the city would be torn asunder by Venetian arms and given to Venetian soldiers for sacking. Then Galeazzo Sanseverino, commander of the Milanese forces, kept shouting out that the artillery should be withdrawn from the walls because of the arrival of the King, with whom they would have to fight in open battle, and he began to protest to the proveditors about loss and injury if the artillery should be snatched away by the enemy. But the Venetian leaders were seized by the greatest desperation since they saw that a city already captured could not be captured, that money was being poured out in vain, and likewise that ruin of a large army impended and that the army could easily be overcome unless fortune assisted.

49. There was a report among the soldiers that the very powerful army of the Venetians had terrified the enemy and the Milanese allies against treachery in case they planned some villainy. Suspicion of crime was increased in camp by the readiness with which the Sanseverino family had greeted the King as he fled and by the frequent and secret messengers of the Duke of Ferrara. Accordingly the Venetian proveditors had no further concern for storming, but their anxiety merely for preserving their forces increased. A great many leaders secretly tested the expedient of flight, and in the extreme hopelessness of affairs they reported that it was possible to swim across the upper part of the Ticino where the channel was not deep. As often happens, worse things were said from day to day by the Milanese soldiers, that the Venetians could not depart without the consent of Duke Lodovico and that the safety or ruin of all Italy was in his hands and he was the arbiter of all things. For this reason the Venetian soldiers were more anxious to increase the size of the army with a larger number of troops, and therefore they tried to recruit foot soldiers and horsemen from all sides, and there was a report that the King of the French held a levy of soldiers in the neighboring regions of Germany, wherefore the Venetian Senate too began to recruit everywhere. A great number of artillery pieces were brought from Venice, Verona, and Brescia; other leaders were enrolled for the campaign, and in that crisis all armed themselves to the teeth for the protection of their country. There was thought also of transporting bridges, and they omitted nothing so that if there was need the forces might advance in full strength right up to the Ticino. Thus a greater and more dangerous military burden seemed to remain.

50. XVIII Calendas Octobres omnium ducum sententia fuit collatis signis cum Carolo Gallorum rege dimicare omniumque consensu emovenda esse tormenta saluti magis quam [294] aestimationi [295] consulentium. Sed Venetorum contatione [296] ea quoque ut dicemus restituta est. XVII Calendas imperator Venetus a pugna ad pacem quam variis nuntiis Rex praetentaverat animum convertit. Inter reliquos Comes Albertinus erat qui de pace plura procuraverat. Hic primum cum Philippo Argentono ac Ioanne Iacobo Triulcio de pacis conditionibus egit quem Gallorum Rex ad se acciri iussit, ad quem locutum esse accepimus legatos Venetos non posse satis admirari qui pacem totiens a se oblatam respuere videantur,[297] verum Senatum semper pacem [298] coluisse scire etiam a maioribus suis habere; eo primum annuente in Italiam venisse regnumque Neapolitanum recepisse sub antiquis pacis conditionibus; primum colloquia cum imperatore Veneto desiderare cum quo [299] paciscendi rationem [300] tractaturus esset; sed obsidione urbem levari prius velle, Camerianum exercitum ducere ubi de pacis conditionibus propius pertractandis facilior cura esset. Tum facta dicendi potestate Comes Albertinus omnia facilia esse respondit praeter duo, urbis obsidionem [301] amovere difficillimum esse cum L millia hominum adesse certum esset, et Camerianum oppidum occupandum esse ab hoste ne infecta pace tam prope haberetur hostis. Tum discessit omnia imperatori et legatis Venetis nuntiaturus. Venit cum caduceatore qui induciarum rationem attulit.

51. Forte sequenti die, hoc est XVI Calendas Octobres, Ludovicus Dux praeter omnium [302] opinionem cum carissima uxore Beatrice venit. Pridie Mediolano discesserat foelici horoscopo duce astrologo sine quo nihil aggredi consuevit, Iove in Libra, Luna in Leone, ac Mercurio in Libra pariter sextili contuitu, Marte quoque cum Luna ad trinum aspectum in Saggittario prosperos eventus significantibus. Induciae protinus indictae sunt tribus diebus hac conditione ut alimenta urbi necessaria permitterentur et ne quid in urbe Novaria interea construi posset. At nihil in re militari sine dolo inveniri potest. Dux quidem Auriliensis alimentorum magnam partem quae civibus et militibus debebatur in arcem transtulit, equos praeterea CC qui pabulo carebant Vercellas emisit. Galli qui in urbe erant fame iandiu macerati

---

[294] –que EF    [295] existimationi EF    [296] contractione B contestatione EF    [297] viderentur EF    [298] pacem semper EF    [299] de add. EF    [300] ratione EF    [301] obsidione EF    [302] omnem B

50. On 14 September it was the opinion of all the leaders that they ought to bring their standards together and fight Charles, king of the French, and that with the approval of all who considered safety rather than reputation the artillery ought to be moved out. But through the delay of the Venetians reputation also, as I shall relate, was restored. On 15 September the Venetian general turned his mind from battle to the peace which the King had earlier attempted by several messengers.[63] Count Albertino was among the others who had attended to various matters regarding peace. He first with Philippe of Argenton and Gian Giacomo Trivulzio acted on the terms of peace, and the King of the French ordered that he be summoned. I heard that the King told him that he could not sufficiently marvel at the Venetian proveditors, who seemed to scorn the peace so often offered by him, but that he knew the Senate had always cherished peace and had this even from his ancestors; that he had come to Italy first with the Senate approving and had received the Neapolitan kingdom under ancient terms of peace; that he desired a conference with the Venetian general first, with whom he intended to discuss the manner of the peace; that he wished the city to be relieved of the siege before that, however, and to take his army to Cameriano, where at closer hand they might discuss more readily the conditions of peace. Then when he was given opportunity to speak Count Albertino replied that everything was simple except two things: it was very difficult to lift the siege of the city, since it was certain that there were fifty thousand men there, and the town of Cameriano must be held by the enemy so that if peace was not concluded their enemy might not be stationed so close. Then he departed to report all to the Venetian general and proveditors. He came with a herald who brought the argument for an armistice.

51. On the following day, that is, 16 September, Duke Lodovico, as it happened, came contrary to the expectation of all with his very dear wife, Beatrice. He had left Milan the day before under a favorable horoscope from his astrologer, without which he was wont to attempt nothing; Jupiter was in Libra, the Moon in Leo, Mercury in Libra likewise in the sixth area, also Mars in Sagittarius one hundred and twenty degrees from the Moon, and all this indicated a prosperous outcome. A truce was declared for three days [64] on these terms, that necessary food be allowed the city and meanwhile nothing be erected in Novara. However, in military affairs nothing can be done without treachery. For the Duke of Orléans passed on to the citadel a large part of the food which was due the soldiers and citizens; moreover, he sent to Vercelli two hundred horses which were destitute of fodder. The French in the city, who for a long time had been wasted away by

squalidi in castra singulis diebus veniebant, cibo potuque saturi vesperi discedebant. Qui nunciarunt MDC Germanos procurante Vincentio Valerio castra Veneta subiisse. Caeterum in hoc bello militibus nihil magis adversum fuit quam equorum ingentium ante oculos ruinam videre.[303] Omnia cadaverum plena. Duo millia interiere. Nocte continuis excubiis, die fame vincebantur, nam muscarum taedio adeo cruciabantur ut contempto pabulo humi procumberent.

52. Inter has inducias Gallorum Rex militum abeuntium solicitudine perturbatus concione advocata exercitum in dies patriae desiderio magis exhauriri retulit, hostium vero increscere, verum quae de regibus Hispaniarum vulgata essent vana [304] procul dubio comperiri, in summaque tutum esse Venetos ac Mediolanenses ad pacis conditiones adducere ut regnum Neapolitanum labefactatum confirmari possit. Ea enim gens imbellis est quae quoruncunque bella minitantium imperata faciat,[305] stabilito eo imperio si Deus volet nihil obstabit quo minus ultra sinum Hadriacum copias traiiciat et terrarum spatia emensus maxima gloria minimo [306] periculo Hierosolymam quo Deus vocat perveniat. Sed talia iactando inprimis Venetorum fidem firmare opus esse, cum nulla natio sit [307] quae transire eos terminos prohibere possit,[308] sed suspectae ut [309] aiunt [310] vicinitatis [311] metus obstat.

53. His peractis legatos Principem Geensem ac Philippum [312] Argentonum mittit qui cum XV Calendas in conspectu Ludovici Ducis et imperatoris Veneti et legatorum essent [313] petiere ut facta abeundi facultate [314] Auriliensis Dux cum Maiestate Regis colloqui posset,[315] quibus Ludovicus Dux respondit nequaquam se id facturum sed prius de pacis conditionibus tractandum. Hic enim animo statuerat pacem omnino nutante imperio componere Genuam ac Savonam si opus esset traditurus, misitque Franciscum Bernardinum Vicecomitem cum quo imperatoris nomine Hieronymus Stanga [316] esset ut de conditionibus ageret, et cum in contione esset non ultra de bello inferendo sed deponendis [317] armis consilia habenda esse proposuit, amotis iam a moenibus tormentis, et conversus ad Hispaniae regum legatum quid ei videretur interrogavit. Aderant autem et reliqui legati. Ille "Nihil iure fieri potest," inquit, "sine regum suorum et sociorum omnium [318] con-

---

[303] om. B    [304] varia B    [305] faceret EF    [306] numero B    [307] esset EF
[308] potest EF    [309] om. EF    [310] iunt A om. EF    [311] vicinitis F
[312] Philippo B    [313] esset EF    [314] libertate EF    [315] potest EF
[316] Stranga EF    [317] deponendus A    [318] om. EF

hunger, kept coming to the camp from day to day in wretched condition, and when they were sated with food and drink in the evening
they would leave. They reported that a thousand six hundred Germans
in charge of Vincenzo Valiero had entered the Venetian camp. But in
this war there was nothing harder for the soldiers than to see the
disaster to mighty horses before their eyes.[65] Everything was filled with
their corpses. Two thousand died. By night they were overcome by
continual wakefulness, by day by hunger, for they were so tortured by
the pest of flies that they scorned their food and sank down on the
ground.

52. During this truce the King of the French was disturbed by concern over those who were departing; he summoned a conference and
reported that every day the army was being drained the more because
of longing for the native land, that the army of the enemy, however,
was increasing, that it was clear that the rumor concerning the King
and Queen of Spain was without doubt vain, and in short that it was
safe to bring the Venetians and the Milanese to terms of peace so that
the tottering realm of Naples could be strengthened. For they are an
unwarlike people, he added, who obey the commands of whoever
threatens war, and with French rule stabilized there, nothing, God willing, could hinder him from sending his forces across the Adriatic and
after measuring off great spaces of lands from reaching Jerusalem,
whither God had summoned him, with the greatest glory and the least
danger. But in making such claims he added that it was necessary first
to strengthen the faith of the Venetians, since there was no nation
which could prohibit him from crossing those bounds, but fear of
dangerous nearness, as they say, was a stumbling block.

53. This done, he sent as legates the Lord of Gié and Philippe of
Argenton, who on 17 September were received by Duke Lodovico and
the Venetian general and proveditors and who asked that the Duke of
Orléans be allowed to come and talk with His Royal Highness. Duke
Lodovico replied to them that he would by no means permit this and
that they must first discuss terms of peace. For he had decided in his
mind, since his power was faltering, to promote the peace in every
way, and he intended to surrender Genoa and Savona if necessary. He
sent Francesco Bernardino Visconti and with him in the name of the
general Girolamo Stanga to treat concerning the terms.[66] When he
was in the assembly he proposed that plans be made not to carry on
the war further, but to lay down their arms, since the artillery had
already been removed from the walls, and he turned to the ambassador
of the rulers of Spain and asked what he thought. The rest of the am-
bassadors were also at hand. "Nothing can be done legally," he said,

sensu." Ad quae commotus Ludovicus Dux et indignationis [319] plenus reges eius sociorum foedera non servasse respondit nihilque penitus tentasse sese verba tantum accepisse, verum imperium suum in maximo versari periculo, deliberandi igitur moram sibi plurimum obesse, se [320] pluris salutem imperii sui facere quam [321] sociorum dignitatem et gloriam, sed foederis iura praeterquam a Venetis a nullo hactenus servata fuisse constare.

54. Rediere nuncii eo die qui ad Regem ierant nunciantes Maclodiensem Cardinalem plures quam par erat conditiones regio nomine expostulasse sibique discedentibus re infecta Ioannem Iacobum Triulcium Regiam Maiestatem ad mitiores conditiones venturam [322] annuisse. De damno enim Regis incredibili Cardinalis ipse Gallus plura recensuerat. Ex [323] vultu tamen omnium circumstantium ad pacis desideria [324] ut in patriam redirent animos inclinare facilis coniectura erat in duobusque [325] tantum res versari videbatur [326] altero ut Senatus Venetus ab iniuria abstineret et ne Ferdinando Regi auxilia conferret. Ludovicus Dux pacis avidus descendere videbatur ad conditiones easque per tabellarios caduceatoresque praemitti [327] petiit.

55. XIII Calendas Octobres Sesia flumen citra Vercellas adeo increvit ut castra Regis citra [328] ripas copiae reliquae ultra divisis viribus non sine periculo essent. XII Calendas inter Ducem Mediolanensem ac legatum Hispanie rursus contentio orta est in ipsa contione ne quid sine sociorum consensu fieret. Foederis praeterea [329] conditio una palam lecta est in qua continebatur ne quid de pace cum hoste proponi posset insciis sociis. De consilio prius habendo legatus respondit, Ludovicus vero Dux ut litteris tantum significaretur interpretabatur.[330] Non sine rursus indignatione legato obiecit ex sociis neminem praeter sanctissimum Senatum Venetum foederis sacra iura servasse et se sociorum negligentia de finiendo bello invitum [331] tractare.

56. Eo extra contionem dimisso legati regii admissi sunt, Proimperator [332] Giensis et Praenensis ac Argentonus proceres. Ii petiere ut Auriliensis Dux facta abeundi potestate per medios hostes ad Regem proficisci posset rediturus ad Principis Mediolanensis arbitrium. Tum

---

[319] indignatiois A commotionis EF    [320] om. EF    [321] quem B    [322] venturum EF    [323] et B    [324] deputeria B    [325] duobus quoque B    [326] videbantur B    [327] promitti EF    [328] circa EF    [329] propterea EF    [330] interpretabat B    [331] inditum B    [332] proimperatore EF

"without the approval of my King and Queen and of all their allies." [67] Disturbed at these words and filled with indignation, Duke Lodovico replied that his King and Queen had not kept the pledge of the allies, that they had attempted nothing solid but given only words, that his power was plunged into the greatest danger, that delay in deliberating was a great hindrance to him, that he considered the safety of his kingdom of greater account than the dignity and glory of the allies, and that the rights of the league, it was clear, had been observed by no one except the Venetians.

54. On that day messengers who had gone to the King came back with the report that the Cardinal of Saint-Malo had demanded more conditions than was right in the name of the King, and that when they were departing with the matter unfinished Gian Giacomo Trivulzio had promised that His Royal Majesty would come to milder terms. For the French Cardinal himself had recounted many things concerning the incredible loss which the King had suffered. But it was easy to guess from the faces of all those standing around that their minds inclined to a longing for peace, so that they might return to their country, and the matter seemed to hinge on only two things, that the Venetian Senate abstain from injury and that it refrain from bringing aid to King Ferdinand. Duke Lodovico seemed ready to accept the terms, since he was eager for peace, and he asked that they be sent ahead by couriers and heralds.[68]

55. On 19 September the river Sesia on this side Vercelli swelled to such an extent that the camp of the King on the near side and the rest of the troops on the far side, with forces divided, were not without danger.[69] On 20 September a quarrel arose again between the Duke of Milan and the ambassador of Spain in the assembly itself, lest anything be done without the consent of the allies. Moreover one condition of the compact was read publicly, according to which nothing could be proposed about peace with the enemy without the knowledge of the allies. The ambassador talked about holding a council first. But Duke Lodovico interpreted that this meant only by letter and again not without indignation reproached the ambassador, saying that of the allies no one except the very sacred Venetian Senate had observed the sacred rights of the compact and that unwillingly, because of the negligence of his allies, was he discussing the ending of the war.

56. When the Spanish ambassador had been dismissed from the conference the royal envoys were admitted, Marshal de Gié and the nobles Piennes and Argenton. These asked that the Duke of Orléans be permitted to go out through the midst of the enemy and proceed to the King, with the understanding that he would return at the will

plura de conditionibus tractavere incassum. Legati regii commemorabant Romanorum Regem Regis sui amicum esse nec ab eo iniuriam reformidari.[333] At Ludovicus Dux inquit, "An Novariam urbem imperii occupatam esse ignoratis, meque ipsum ab imperio dependere vel magis ipsum Regem in territorio Imperatoris Caesaris Maximiliani bella gerere non sine maiestatis suae iniuria?" Ab his omnes discessere infecta re.

57. Postera die hoc est XI Calendas rursum in castra venere, in tabernaculum admissi sunt, iussi consedere. Ludovicus Dux sic orsus est, "Si Rex vester depositurus est arma ad pacis conditiones aequas [334] descendere opus est. Ego satis tutus sum Maximiliani Romanorum regis patrocinio et Veneti Senatus armis, cui ego et omnis posteritas semper debebit qui [335] statum imperii mei incolumem servavit. De pacis vero conditionibus classem in pugna captam iure belli restituendam esse non putamus deque damno immodico Regis resarciri impossibile est, vel iudex eligendus." De Francisco Secco ad imperatorem Venetum pertinere respondit.

58. His diebus nuntiatum est Maximilianum regem Romanorum maximo cum exercitu suadente Zaccharia Contareno Veneti Senatus legato in auxilium sociorum paratum esse bellumque cum Gallis maxime optare. X Calendas Octobres [336] Ludovicus Dux clandestino colloquio legatos Gallorum allocutus est non sine aliorum [337] suspitione. Interea loci dum haec in castris geruntur Venetus Senatus in dies supplementa mittere non cessabat, litteris tamen suadebat ut Ludovicus Dux Neapolitani regni difficultatem omnem inter Gallorum Regem et Ferdinandum cuiuspiam iudicis arbitrio dari [338] omni nixu [339] studeret. Ille mox legatis regiis, "Facile," inquit, "sine armis regno potiturus est si velit Rex vester," legatis modum rogantibus respondit,[340] "Pheudi titulo, ut quotannis ei tributa persolvantur," [341] maximumque decus esse regi regibus imperare. Argentonus respondit se super his sine Regis nutu quicquam [342] non audere. His ultro citroque acceptis abiere. Eo die Auriliensis Dux sine iniuria multis comitantibus ad Regem profectus est. VIII Calendas rursus Novaria Salucensis quoque Marchio Vercellas versus discessit induciaeque ad Calendas Octobres [343] Veneti Senatus causa protractae [344] sunt ut consultis patribus [345] quid de

---

[333] reformidari iniuriam EF    [334] om. EF    [335] quod EF    [336] Septembris ABEF    [337] proditionis EF    [338] dare EF    [339] omnino EF    [340] respondi EF    [341] persolvatur B    [342] quemquam B    [343] contract. B [344] protracta B    [345] partibus EF

of the Duke of Milan. Then they discussed other things about the terms in vain. The royal envoys called to mind that the King of the Romans was a friend of their King, and that no injury from him was feared. But Duke Lodovico said, "Do you not know that a city of the empire, Novara, has been seized and that I myself depend on the empire, or rather that the King himself fights wars in the territory of the Emperor Caesar Maximilian, not without injury to his own sovereignty?" After this they all departed with the matter unfinished.

57. On the next day, that is, 21 September, the envoys returned again to camp and were admitted to the tent and sat down as bidden. Then Duke Lodovico began in this fashion: "If your King intends to lay down his arms, he must come to just conditions of peace. I am safe enough under the protection of Maximilian, king of the Romans, and under the arms of the Venetian Senate, to which I and all my posterity will always be indebted, since it has kept the state of my power unharmed. As for the terms of peace, we do not think that a fleet captured in battle ought to be returned by right of war, and as for the immoderate loss of the King, restoration is impossible or a judge ought to be chosen." Concerning Francesco Secco he replied that it was a matter for the Venetian general.[70]

58. During these days it was announced that Maximilian, king of the Romans, was ready with a very large army to help the allies on the advice of Zaccaria Contarini,[71] envoy of the Venetian Senate, and that he very much wanted war with the French. On 22 September Duke Lodovico talked with the envoys of the French in a secret conference, not without suspicion on the part of the others. Meanwhile as these things were being done in camp, the Venetian Senate did not stop sending reinforcements daily, but it urged by letter that Duke Lodovico make every effort to hand over to the decision of some arbiter the entire difficulty between the King of the French and Ferdinand concerning the Neapolitan kingdom. "Without arms," he soon said to the royal envoys, "your King can easily gain possession of the kingdom if he wishes," and when they asked how, he replied, "By feudal title, so that each year tribute may be paid to him," and he added that it was the greatest honor for a king to rule over other kings. Argenton replied that with regard to these things he dared do nothing without the approval of the King. After these exchanges on both sides they departed. On that day the Duke of Orléans proceeded to the King without harm and with a large escort. On 24 September the Marquis of Saluzzo again departed from Novara in the direction of Vercelli. The truce was prolonged until 1 October for the sake of the Venetian Senate, so that

ineunda pace decretum fuisset rescriberent.

59. IIII Calendas inter Germanos et Italos seditio alia exorta est. Illi cum oberrantem per castra militem Latinum antea infestum viderent interceperunt et convocatis protinus militibus in mediam coronam obligatis post tergum manibus protraxere. Magnis enim [346] clamoribus circumstabant et Teutonum studia omnium [347] ad necem ferebantur. Una erat vox [348] Teutonica lingua pari [349] emissa consensu ut protinus trucidaretur, nec armata factio ab ullo compressa [350] est. Tum unus militum ilico caput abscidit. Cognita re Latini hunc carnificem perdita securitate obequitantem [351] observavere qui cum secus fossas Tiliae securus [352] cristis sublimis pertransiret lanceis subito confossus a pluribus equo concidit.[353] Vox illa ad tuguria Germanorum delata omnes ad arma excitavit. Hi coiere. Latini pariter equites ac [354] pedites [355] in aciem [356] protinus stetere, lanceis telis tormentis gladiis veluti collatis signis dimicare coeperunt intestina rabie. Germani subito cedunt, Latini instant. Tum imperatoris adventu socialis pugna repente dirempta [357] est.

60. His diebus circiter Germanorum XX millia in Regis auxilium venerunt, gens fera, sui iuris, qui insolenti petulantia pecunias ingentes exposcebant. Verum auri inopia Gallorum Regem Ludovicum [358] Ducem [359] metus ingens ad propalandam pacem praecipites trahebant illum ut confecta pace dimissis Germanis salarium non exolveret, eamque ob causam in castris seditionem oriri facile haud dubitabat, nam nec tantam Germanorum multitudinem expeti [360] speraverat. Hunc exhausto fere exercitu sub pacis spe numerus recentium hostium Germanorum perterrebat. Interea indies peditum ac equitum ingens numerus ex Latinis solutis veluti castris discedebant.[361] Ludovicus Dux non sine magna proditionis suspitione interdixit ne quis ex portitoribus fluviorium quemquam militum traiicere audeat capitali poena indicta.

61. Rex pacis conditionis [362] aucto exercitu meliores reddere curabat in biduumque induciae protractae fuere. Calendis Octobribus inter has inducias Ludovicus Dux veritus ne quid fraudis inferretur dimisso

---

[346] eum EF        [347] omnem B omnia F        [348] uxor EF        [349] proin EF
[350] comperta EF        [351] ob aequitatem EF        [352] sequuturus EF        [353] concidit equo EF        [354] om. EF        [355] om. EF        [356] acie EF        [357] direpta EF        [358] om. EF        [359] om. EF, et add. EF        [360] expes EF        [361] discendebant A descendebant EF        [362] conditiones BEF

after deliberating they might report what had been decreed about beginning the peace.

59. On 28 September another quarrel arose between the Germans and Italians when the former saw a Latin soldier who had earlier been hateful to them wandering through the camp; they intercepted him, and as the soldiers straightway assembled dragged him into the middle of the crowd with his hands tied behind his back. They stood around shouting loudly, and the Teutons all wanted him killed. With one voice and by common consent they shouted out in the Teutonic tongue that he should be slain at once, nor could the armed faction be repressed by anyone. Then one of the soldiers suddenly cut off his head and the Latins, when they learned what had happened, lay in wait for this murderer as he was riding along off his guard, and when he had crossed beyond the ditches of Tiglia, free from care and with the crest of his helmet standing high, suddenly he was pierced by several lances and fell from his horse. The report was carried to the tents of the Germans and aroused them all to arms. These assembled. The Latins likewise, both horsemen and foot soldiers, forthwith took their stand in battle line and began to fight with lances, javelins, artillery, and swords, just as if the standards had been brought together, and with inward rage. The Germans suddenly withdrew, the Latins pressed on. Then at the arrival of the general this fight between allies was suddenly stopped.

60. At this time about twenty thousand Germans came to the help of the King; they are a wild race, sui juris, and with insolent stubbornness they demanded much money. But scarcity of gold induced the King of the French,[72] and great fear Duke Lodovico,[73] to announce the peace quickly. The King wanted to be freed of expense by dismissing the Germans when peace was attained, and he was by no means doubtful that because of them sedition might easily arise in camp, for he had not expected the number of the Germans to rise so high. Lodovico, since his army was almost depleted because of hope of peace, was frightened by the number of hostile Germans who had recently arrived. Meanwhile every day a great number of foot soldiers and horsemen of the Latins departed, just as if the army had been disbanded. Duke Lodovico, not without great suspicion of treachery, prohibited all the ferrymen on the river from carrying any soldier across, under threat of death.

61. The King as his army grew endeavored to make better conditions of peace, and the truce was prolonged for two days. On 1 October, in the midst of this truce, Duke Lodovico, fearing that some trickery might be worked especially when the troops had been dismissed,

praesertim exercitu cum Novariensibus civibus res [363] clam composuit ut portam sibi aperirent in magna rerum desperatione qua universus exercitus admitteretur. VI Nonas [364] Octobres Senatus Venetus de pacis conditionibus nihil sine sociorum monitu agere velle ex iure foederis respondit; instantiore enim cura petebat Rex ut Senatus quoque pacis conditionis [365] amplecteretur. His auditis legati regii a fide Venetorum Ludovicum Ducem avocare contendunt clamque hortantur ut bellum Venetis [366] inferat cum Rege pacatus vel Regi cum Venetis dimicaturo viam bello aperiat.

62. Induciae iterum in octavum diem protractae sunt. Legati exercitus solicitudinis pleni a Senatu litteris petiere quidnam incompositis rebus de copiis agendum esset quoniam temporis iniquitate in castris contineri milites non possent. Respondit Senatus pecuniis datis eas in agrum Brixianum tuto subducendas. Legati interea rediere quorum animos cogitationes exedebant quod nullo modo Venetum Senatum pro eorum animo ad pacis conditiones iure foederis trahere potuissent, apud quos Ludovicus Dux Veneti Senatus fidem summopere collaudavit dolumque [367] aut fraudem nunquam in eo inventum esse commemoravit, cui vel infidi Turcae praecipue crederent.

63. Eo die Dux Brasinchensis [368] Germanus cum equitibus CCCC Ludovici Ducis stipendio magnifice instructis castra ingressus est. IIII Nonas captivus Barbontis [369] nothus Gallus [370] Mantua ad castra venit, quem Ludovicus Dux admonuit non finito bello illi Mantuam redeundum esse, alioquin vices subiret Cardinalis Genuensis filii qui tantumdem auri impenderet quantum ipse nothus pro redemptione promisisset. III Nonas Hercules dux Ferrariensis castra ingressus est arci Genuensi utriusque nomine imperaturus, qui una protinus cum exercitus imperatore Regem Gallorum adierunt, a quo [371] honorifice pridie Nonas suscepti sunt. Rex plura cum imperatore de Tarrensi pugna collocutus est, mox de pace et [372] deponendis armis mentio habita petiitque an sub eius stipendio contra Ferdinandum Regem militare vellet, cui se sacramento astrictum esse Veneto Senatui et imperatorio nomine se ornatum esse respondit. His dictis Rex extra urbem egressus equos sublimes et egregios adduci iussit omnesque ab imperatore Veneto

---

[363] om. B    [364] Octobribus inter—VI Nonas om. EF    [365] conditiones BEF    [366] Venetis bellum EF    [367] -que om. B    [368] Brunschwichensis B    [369] Barbontis captivus EF    [370] Regis Galliae EF    [371] quibus B    [372] om. BEF

secretly made an arrangement with the citizens of Novara that in the height of their desperation they should open a gate to him by which the whole army might be admitted.[74] On 2 October the Venetian Senate replied that in accordance with the rights of the alliance it was not willing to enter into any discussion of the terms of peace without advising its allies, for with more pressing anxiety the King kept asking that the Senate also embrace conditions of peace. On hearing this the royal envoys hastened to summon Duke Lodovico away from loyalty to the Venetians and secretly urged him to come to terms with the King and make war on the Venetians or to open a way for the King to war, since he intended to fight with the Venetians.

62. The truce was prolonged for eight days more. The proveditors of the army were filled with anxiety and asked the Senate by letter what ought to be done about their forces with affairs unsettled, since because of the poor weather the soldiers could not be kept in camp. The Senate replied that they should be paid and removed in safety to the territory around Brescia. Meanwhile the envoys returned, their minds gnawed by cares because in no way, on account of the rights of the compact,[75] could they induce the Venetian Senate as they wanted to terms of peace. Before them Duke Lodovico praised highly the good faith of the Venetian Senate and called to mind that never had deceit or treachery been discovered in it: even the faithless Turks could trust in it.

63. On that day the Duke of Braunschweig, a German, entered the camp with four hundred horsemen wondrously equipped at the expense of Duke Lodovico. On 4 October the French Bourbon bastard, who was a prisoner, came to the camp from Mantua,[76] but Duke Lodovico advised him that since the war was not finished he ought to return to Mantua; otherwise he might enter the service of the son of the Cardinal of Genoa, who would pay as much gold as the bastard himself had promised for his redemption. On 5 October Ercole, duke of Ferrara, who was to command the stronghold of Genoa in the name of both, entered the camp.[77] He together with the general of the army [78] straightway approached the King of the French, and they were honorably received by him on 6 October. The King spoke long with the general about the battle of the Taro and talked with them about peace and about laying down arms. He asked whether he was willing to campaign in his service against King Ferdinand, to which the general replied that he was bound by oath to the Venetian Senate and was honored by it with the name of general. At these words the King went outside the city and ordered tall and distinguished horses to be brought in, and when they were praised by the Venetian general he

laudatos elargitus est. Ille duos tantum dono accepit gratiasque Regi immortales egit quo salutato et omnibus proceribus in castra rediit. Tum Ioannis Iacobi Triultii filio protinus Ludovicus Dux oppida in integrum et proventus restituere promisit.

64. VIII Idus Octobres Proimperator Giensis regius in castra Venetorum venit quem sic locutum esse in contione ad legatos accepimus: "Rex noster scire [373] admodum cupit hostisne an amicus sit, Senatus vester an velit Monopolim restituere." Ad quem legati exercitus pluribus verbis non opus [374] esse responderunt, veterem Regis amicitiam Senatum [375] colere, bellum semper odisse, pacis conditiones non respuere verum insciis sociis nihil obfirmare posse. His dictis dimissaque contione legatus ad Regem rediit omniaque ordine nuntiavit.

65. VII Idus legatus Ludovici Ducis retulit se cum apud Regem esset pacis foedera specialius a Veneto Senatu desiderantem cognovisse eum diutine [376] anxium cum proceribus suis in secretis fuisse, stabilita tandem cum Ludovico Duce pace contionem dimisisse, ultra Alpes protinus equitaturum. Ea die Proimperator Giensis regius una cum aliis legatis in castra sociorum venit; aderant et legati Veneti et Hispaniensis orator. Tum coram omnibus has a Rege Gallorum conditiones datas accepit Ludovicus Dux: ut classem primum Rex in Genuensi portu ad praescriptum parare posset neve Ludovicus Dux Ferdinando Regi hosti auxilia mitteret, classemque Genuae retentam restitueret,[377] Genuensem arcem Herculi Ferrariensi duci in biennium traderet, Ioannem Iacobum Triultium revocaret restitueretque [378] eius oppida et captivos inter quos Miolensis Princeps ac magnus Barbontis nothus ac L millia nummum aureorum Auriliensi Duci penderet, omnes demum sibi foedere coniunctos observaret. A Ludovico vero legatus Regis has quoque conditiones accepit, quarum prima ut foedera priora inter Pontificem Maximilianum regem Romanorum reges Hispaniae Senatum Venetum imprimis servarentur, Novaria deinde restitueretur, item pecuniae hoc est circiter CC millia nummum aureorum Regi mutuo data redderentur. Reliquae [379] exigui momenti fuere. Tum Ludovicus Dux et legatus Gallorum auditis pacis conditionibus iureiurando se omnes [380] servaturos promisere ac legatus protinus discessit.

---

[373] om. B     [374] opus non EF     [375] om. B     [376] diutius EF     [377] classemque—restitueret om. F     [378] restitueret ac A restitueret EF revocaret restitueretque A by MS. correction     [379] reliqua BEF     [380] omness A

presented them all to him. He accepted only two as a gift, and gave everlasting thanks to the King,[79] and when he had saluted him and all the nobles he returned to camp. Then Duke Lodovico promised to restore towns and revenues intact forthwith to the son of Gian Giacomo Trivulzio.[80]

64. On 8 October the royal Marshal de Gié came to the camp of the Venetians, and I heard that in assembly he spoke as follows to the proveditors: "Our King wants very much to know whether he is friend or enemy, and whether your Senate wishes to restore Monopoli." The proveditors of the army replied to him that there was no need of further words: the Senate cherished the ancient friendship of the King, it had always hated war, it did not scorn conditions of peace, but it could sign nothing without the knowledge of its allies. At these words the assembly was dismissed and the envoy returned to the King and reported all things in order.

65. On 9 October the envoy of Duke Lodovico reported that when he was with the King, who desired pledges of peace especially from the Venetian Senate, he had learned that he had been for a long time anxious and in secret conference with his nobles; that at length, when peace with Duke Lodovico had been established, he had dismissed the conference; and that he would shortly ride beyond the Alps. On that day the royal Marshal Gié came to the camp of the allies with other envoys; there were present also Venetian envoys and the Spanish orator. Then in the presence of all Duke Lodovico accepted the following terms which the King of the French had offered: first that the King could prepare a fleet in the port of Genoa according to agreement; that Duke Lodovico would not send aid to Charles's enemy King Ferdinand; that he would restore the fleet held at Genoa and surrender the Genoese citadel to Duke Ercole of Ferrara for two years; [81] that he would recall Gian Giacomo Trivulzio and restore his towns and captives, among them Prince Miolans [82] and the great Bourbon bastard; that he would pay fifty thousand gold coins to the Duke of Orléans; and finally that he would respect all joined to him by the compact. From Lodovico the envoy of the King accepted in turn these conditions, that the former alliances between the Pope, Maximilian who was king of the Romans, the rulers of Spain, and the Venetian Senate should be kept above all; and next that Novara should be restored; and that the money given to the King in common, that is, about two hundred thousand pieces of gold, should be returned. The other terms were of small moment.[83] Then Duke Lodovico and the envoy of the French, after hearing the conditions of peace, promised by oath that they would preserve them all, and the envoy shortly departed.[84]

66. VI Idus imperator et legati exercitus concrematis tuguriis amotis tentoriis milites dimisere [381] quos Ludovicus Dux ac legati caeteri extra castra comitati sunt gratiasque imperatori et legatis exercitus egit statimque in castra rediit. Gallus eo die Vercellis in Galliam moestissimus [382] discessit pecunias et exercitum comparaturus. Imperator ad [383] vicum Granarolam exercitum Venetum duxit XII millia passuum a castris. Ea die Galeatius Severinas Novariam ingressus est et arci novum praesidium imposuit. V Idus imperator in Vegevenis [384] oppido [385] Ludovicum Ducem commoratus est ubi una cum legatis Venetis consumpto inter laetitiam regali prandio equos conscendere. Oppido egressis Ludovicus Dux ita locutus est: "Gratias immortales agimus Senatui vestro sanctissimo qui nutanti imperio magna fide magna constantia opem rebus dubiis attulerit, qui nunquam exercitum discedere passus sit donec firmatis rebus recepta Novaria ipse tutus in meo fuerim imperio vobisque legatis plura me debere fateor qui existimationem meam vel meis invitis tutati fueritis et tormenta a moenibus intempestive amovere nolueritis,[386] et nisi vestra affuisset fides consiliumque res nostrae ocyus quam Neapolitanae praecipites corruissent.[387] De quibus meritis ac laudibus ipsi [388] coram Serenissimo Principe vestro et Senatu universo gratias agentes [389] uberius referemus."

67. Post mutuos complexus discessere. Dux Vigevenas [390] rediit, imperator vero iunctis ponte [391] Ticini ripis cum omnibus copiis Ticinum versus iter aggressus est. Legati vero IIII Idus Mediolanum venere; ibi duobus diebus consumptis Laudem Pompeiam deinde Cremam pridie Idus venere unde Germani accepta pecunia discessere, hinc et Itali pedites domum abiere. Annuntiarunt [392] Carolum Melitensem militiae clarum consilio acrem manu strenuum principibus acceptissimum et militibus charum febre correptum Papiae obisse. Cremae stativorum ratio habita est. Equites fere omnes per Cremensem Bergomensem Brixiensemque agrum distribuli sunt. Legati Crema Idibus Urcios Novos venere Olio flumini ponte imposito. XVII Calendas Novembres [393] legati Brixiam iere ubi litteras a Senatu accepere quibus libera redeundi domus potestas data est. Hinc Mantuam venerunt quorum causa [394] XIII Calendas imperator Mantuanus ludos fecit. Consumptis aliquibus diebus Calendis Mantua discessere Padoque

[381] divisere B    [382] moetissimus A    [383] om. EF    [384] Vegenenis A    [385] apud add. EF    [386] noluerit AEF nolueritis A by MS. correction volueritis B    [387] corruissent praecipites EF    [388] ipsa EF    [389] agente B    [390] Vigenas B    [391] pontis EF    [392] Annuntierunt EF    [393] Novi EF    [394] ea EF

66. On 10 October the general and the proveditors of the army, after burning the huts and removing the tents, dismissed the soldiers, and Duke Lodovico and the other envoys escorted them outside the camp. He gave thanks to the general and proveditors of the army and straightway returned to camp. The Frenchman on that day mournfully set out from Vercelli toward France to get together money and an army. The general led the Venetian army to the village of Granerolo [85] twelve miles from the camp. On that day Galeazzo Sanseverino entered Novara and put a new garrison over the citadel. On 11 October the general awaited Duke Lodovico in the town of Vigevano and there, after merrily consuming a regal meal with the Venetian proveditors,[86] they mounted their horses. As they were going out from the town Duke Lodovico addressed them as follows: "I give everlasting thanks to your Most Sacred Senate,[87] which with great faith and constancy in doubtful affairs brought aid to my tottering power and which never allowed the army to depart until, with affairs stabilized and Novara recovered, I was secure in my own realm. And to you proveditors I confess I owe more, since you protected my reputation even against the will of my people and refused to remove artillery from the walls prematurely. Had it not been for your faith and wisdom my power would have fallen headlong even more quickly than did that of Naples. Concerning these merits and praises I shall speak and give thanks more abundantly before your Most Serene Doge and the whole Senate."

67. After embracing one another they departed. The Duke returned to Vigevano; the general, after spanning the river Ticino with a bridge, set out toward Pavia with all his forces. On 12 October the proveditors arrived at Milan, and after spending two days there came to Lodi and then on 14 October to Crema, where the Germans received their pay and departed. From here the Italian foot soldiers went home. Then came the news that Carlo of Pian di Meleto, eminent in campaign, keen in counsel, strenuous of hand, most acceptable to the leaders and dear to the soldiers, had been struck down by a fever and had died at Pavia.[88] At Crema an assignment of stations was held. Almost all the horsemen were distributed through the territory of Crema, Bergamo, and Brescia. The proveditors came from Crema to Orzinuovi on 15 October after a bridge had been thrown across the river Oglio. On 16 October [89] they arrived at Brescia, where they received a letter from the Senate in which free opportunity was given for returning home. From here they went to Mantua, and in their honor the Mantuan general held games on 20 October.[90] After spending some days there they

flumine Venetias venerunt.

68. VI Idus Novembres Augustinus Barbadicus princeps summae sapientiae et universus Senatus triumphalem navem pro more Bucentaurum dictam conscendere obviam imperatori de re publica bene merito ituri cum quo et legati exercitus erant. Tum Princeps cum universo Senatu cumque legatis omnibus Italiae principum et Maximiliani regis Romanorum et Hispaniae regum [395] imperatorem laetitia ingenti [396] in navem excepit eumque de victoria collaudando amplexus est triumphique imaginem per urbem more patrio dedit. Comitabantur navem regiam mimorum [397] uniremes civiumque naviculae innumerabiles. Hinc inde ab omni populo maximo excepti sunt plausu multiplicique Senatorum amplexu dies fere consumpta est. Caeteri cum patribus ad quotidiana colloquia dati; de bello de pace plura elocuti sunt. Idibus accepta a Senatu grata missione Patavium venit, inde Vicentia Verona domum rediit. Tum Lucas Pisanus praefectus designatus Veronam concessit. XVII Calendas Decembres Melchior Trivisanus alter legatus classis imperator in comitiis delectus est.

FINIS [398]

---

[395] om. EF    [396] laetitia ingenti EF    [397] numorum B    [398] om. B

departed from Mantua on 1 November and came by the river Po to Venice.[91]

68. On 8 November [92] Agostino Barbarigo, doge of the greatest wisdom, and all the Senate boarded the triumphal ship traditionally called Bucentaur to go and meet the general who deserved well of the republic, with whom were also the proveditors of the army. Then the Doge with all the Senate and with all the envoys of the princes of Italy, of Maximilian the king of the Romans, and of the rulers of Spain welcomed the general to the ship with great joy,[93] congratulated him on his praiseworthy victory, and gave a representation of triumph through the city in accordance with ancestral custom. Single banked galleys carrying actors and innumerable barks of citizens accompanied the regal ship. On all sides and by all the people they were welcomed with the greatest applause, and almost the entire day was consumed in the many embraces of the Senators. Additional days were given over to daily talks with the Senators, and they discussed many matters concerning the war and the peace. On 13 November, with welcome discharge received from the Senate, he came to Padua, and then by way of Vicenza and Verona returned home.[94] Then Luca Pisani, who had been designated prefect, withdrew to Verona, and on 15 November Melchiorre Trevisan, the other proveditor, was elected general of the army in assembly.

## THE END

## ALEXANDER BENEDICTUS VERONENSIS PHYSICUS
## SEBASTIANO BADUARIO EQUITI ET HIERONYMO BERNARDO
## CONSILIARIIS VENETI SENATUS CLARISSIMIS
## SALUTEM PERPETUAM DICIT

Belli Gallici libri excellentissimi consiliarii qui nuper studiosissime recogniti sunt in vulgus prodire audent nec popularem censuram languidae auctoritatis verentur, discussis rebus omnibus. Verum multa de industria praetermisimus periculis undique obviis quae tamen non sine magna quorundam nota dici potuissent etsi ad Senatus huius perennem gloriam pertinere non dubitaverimus. Vulgatissimum enim est veritatem odia parere et necem saepenumero maturare inde in plerisque rebus conscientiae vis illa elanguescit emoriturque abducuntque in diversum vel inclinant scriptorem praesentia [399] discrimina. Temerarii item animi esse putant hominem non sibi ignoscere. Connivere igitur paululum pro tempore opus fuit donec posteris alii confidentius apertiora [400] sine metu relinquant, quum ossa ac cineres iniquorum rabiem contemnunt. Nos tamen intentionem non occultamus quum strabonem quempiam petum vel claudum alium infirmum talis [401] parcius appellamus. Nostra igitur simplicitate contenti has ephemeridas contractius expeditiusque conscripsimus quas cum in castris essemus promisimus et ea tam diligenter quam libenter in tantis occupationibus collegimus ne omnino tanta Italiae clades quae subita Venetorum vi ultra Alpes propulsa est magna posteritatis iniuria supprimeretur. Verum haec multo aliter ac caeteri qui post nos scripturi sunt indicavimus, quae excellentissimi consiliarii qualiacumque sint aequo animo suscipietis si nihil tam parvum esse quod non gloriam parere possit existimaveritis. Vale. Venetiis MIIIID sexto Calendas Septembres.[402]

Impetratum est ab illustrissimo Senatu Veneto ne liceat cuiquam has ephemeridas imprimere nec Latino sermone nec vulgario etc. ut in privilegio.[403]

---

[399] praesentiae B     [400] aptiora B     [401] tales B     [402] FINIS add. B
[403] Impetratum—privilegio om. BEF

### ALESSANDRO BENEDETTI OF VERONA, PHYSICIAN, SENDS CONSTANT GREETINGS TO THE KNIGHT SEBASTIANO BADOER AND TO GERONIMO BERNARDO, MOST EMINENT COUNSELORS OF THE VENETIAN SENATE

The books on the French war, most eminent counselors, which have recently been edited with the greatest care, dare to appear in public and do not fear the popular censure of listless authority, since they discuss all events. But I have purposely passed over many points where dangers were at hand on all sides, points which could not be told without disgrace to certain individuals even though I did not doubt that they pertained to the everlasting glory of this Senate. For it is very common for truth to produce hatred and often hasten death,[95] whence in many matters that power of conscience languishes and dies and present dangers lead or incline a writer to the opposite of truth. Likewise they think it the mark of a rash mind for a man not to excuse himself. So it was necessary to connive a little in accordance with the circumstances, until others without fear may more confidently leave things clearer to posterity, since bones and ashes scorn the frenzy of the wicked. However I do not hide my intention when somewhat sparingly I call blink-eyed someone who squints, or weak in the heel someone who limps. So, satisfied with my simple style, I have drawn up rather briefly and simply in writing that diary which I promised when I was in camp and which, busy as I was, I gathered together as industriously as I did cheerfully so that the mighty destruction of Italy which by the sudden help of the Venetians was pushed beyond the Alps might not be suppressed with great injury to posterity.[96] But all this I have set forth far differently than will the others who write after me. These commentaries, such as they are, you will graciously accept, most excellent counselors, if you think there is nothing so small as not to acquire glory. Farewell. From Venice, 27 August 1496.

By decree of the most illustrious Venetian Senate no one shall be permitted to print this diary in Latin or in the vernacular etc. as stated in the privilege.[97]

# NOTES TO BOOK I

1. These elegiacs are one sample of the great flood of verse which the expedition of Charles VIII evoked before, during, and after the actual events. This verse appeared in Latin, French, and the various Italian dialects and was sometimes formal, sometimes informal. On the formal side suffice it to mention here two examples, the song of victory, *De neapolitana victoria*, of Charles's court poet Publio Fausto Andrelini, which was published in Paris by Félix Baligault about 1495, Goff A-704, and Panfilo Sassi's *De bello tarrensi*, which was published with his *Epigrammata* at Brescia by Bernardinus de Misintis, for Angelus Britannicus, in 1499, Goff P-24, and is carried in Pietro Giustiniani, *Rerum venetarum ab urbe condita ad annum M.D.LXXV. historia*, Argentorati, sumptibus Lazari Zetzneri, 1611, Appendix, I3b-K5a.

Specimens of popular verse are cited or quoted in Jules de La Pilorgerie, *Campagne et bulletins de la grande armée d'Italie commandée par Charles VIII, 1494-1495*, Nantes, Paris, 1866, 222-227; Alessandro Luzio and Rodolfo Renier, "Contributo alla storia del malfrancese ne' costumi e nella letteratura italiana del sec. XVI," in *Giornale storico della letteratura italiana*, 1885, 5, 418-432 (with particular reference to syphilis) and "Francesco Gonzaga alla battaglia di Fornovo (1495) secondo i documenti mantovani," in *Archivio storico italiano*, Serie 5, 1890, 6, 236-244; Emilie Herbst, *Der Zug Karl's VIII. nach Italien im Urteil der italienischen Zeitgenossen*, Berlin und Leipzig, 1911 (*Abhandlungen zur mittleren und neueren Geschichte*, Heft 28); and Nella Vichi Santovito, "Un cantare quattrocentesco sulla calata di Carlo VIII," in *Studi e ricerche sulla storia della stampa del quattrocento*, Milano, 1942, 5 p.

Two manuscripts, now *Monacenses latini* 716 and 952, which belonged to the physician Hartmann Schedel of Nuremberg include similar verses. See Antonio Casetti and Vittorio Imbriani, *Canti popolari delle provincie meridionali, 1*, Torino, 1871 (*Canti e racconti del popolo italiano* pubblicati per D. Comparetti ed A. D'Ancona, 2), 45-46; Munich, Bayerische Staatsbibliothek, *Catalogus codicum latinorum*, edd. Carl Halm and Georg Laubmann, *1*, pars 1, Monachii, 1868 (*Catalogus codicum manu scriptorum Bibliothecae regiae monacensis, 3*, 1), 137-138, 164; and Louis Thuasne, *Djem-sultan*, Paris, 1892, 359, 448-451.

2. On 31 December 1495 Marino Sanudo dedicated to Barbarigo Book I of his account of Charles's expedition; see *La spedizione di Carlo VIII in Italia*, pubblicata per cura di Rinaldo Fulin, Venezia, 1873, 15-17.

3. This sentence is quoted in the Latin by Apostolo Zeno, *Dissertazioni vossiane, 2*, Venezia, 1753, 44. The entire letter is reprinted in the Latin in *Bibliotheca Smithiana, seu catalogus librorum D. Josephi Smithii*

*angli per cognomina authorum dispositus,* Venetiis, 1755, Part 3, CCLXXX-VIII-CCLXXXIX.

4. The first three sentences of this paragraph are quoted in the Latin by Zeno, *loc. cit.,* and earlier in *Giornale de' letterati d'Italia,* 1713, *16,* 470.

5. A third tribunal of forty members, *Quarantia civil nuova,* was instituted in 1492. It handled cases arising on the mainland. On the government of Venice see, for example, Gaspare Contarini, *The commonwealth and government of Venice,* translated out of Italian into English by Lewis Lewkenor, London, 1599 and Abraham-Nicolas Amelot de la Houssaie, *Histoire du gouvernement de Venise,* Amsterdam, 1695, 3 vols., a work which at the time of its original publication in 1676-1677 aroused great resentment in Venice. Agostino Sagredo gives a succinct account of the government in his preface to Domenico Malipiero, *Annali veneti dall' anno 1457 al 1500, 1,* Firenze, 1843 (*Archivio storico italiano, 7,* Part 1), XXVII-XXXII.

6. Andrea del Verrocchio's marvelous equestrian statue, in bronze, of the condottiere Bartolomeo Colleoni was unveiled on the Campo Santi Giovanni e Paolo on 21 March 1496, the very date Benedetti wrote this letter. Marino Sanudo, *I diarii, 1,* pubblicati per cura di Federico Stefani, Venezia, 1879 (R. deputazione veneta di storia patria), col. 96, reports that everyone went to see it.

7. On 14 September a fire devastated the back part of the Palazzo Ducale from the cortile to the Rio di Palazzo. The work of reconstruction begun by Antonio Rizzo was still in progress in 1496. The ornate façade on the east side is his.

8. In his letter to Barbarigo, dated 31 December 1495, Sanudo, *La spedizione di Carlo VIII in Italia,* Venezia, 1873, 16 writes, "Havendo l'eterno Iddio posto le Alpe per termene, che barbari e tal generatione fusseno divise dalla italica gente, la qual parte de Italia secondo cosmographi et scriptori de siti è la più bella parte di la terra habitabile, et più fructifera."

9. From 1496 to 1509 the dominion of Venice included Trani, Mola di Bari, Monopoli, Brindisi, and Otranto in Puglia.

10. Giuseppe Cervetto, *Di alcuni celebri anatomici italiani del decimoquinto secolo,* Edizione seconda, Brescia, 1854, 74 reprints the Argument in the Latin. He owned a copy of the Aldine edition. An Italian translation occurs in Roberto Massalongo, "Alessandro Benedetti e la medicina veneta nel quattrocento," *Atti del Reale Istituto Veneto di Scienze, Lettere ed Arti,* 1916-1917, 76, Part 2, 232.

11. In a letter to Lodovico Sforza, 8 February 1494, Montils-les-Tours, he said, "Ce sera pour aller plus avant et faire quelque grant service à Dieu, à l'église et à l'exaltacion de la foy catholicque, qui est la chose en ce monde que plus j'ay à cueur"; see *Lettres de Charles VIII roi de France,* publiées d'après les originaux . . . par Paul Pélicier, *4,* Paris, 1903, 11.

Writing to Pope Alexander VI, 14 March 1494, Lyon, *ibid.*, 28-29 he mentions his "desiderium et affectionem . . . eundi contra Turcos pro servitio Dei, exaltatione fidei, et pro redimendo pauperes christianos qui sunt inter manus eorum in captivitate et miseria." Sanudo, *op. cit.*, 22 says, "Mosso *etiam* (come diceva) da zelo di la fede, per discacciar Turchi del suo dominio et recuperar la Terra Santa"; cf. *ibid.*, 30 and the pious manifesto of Charles in La Pilorgerie, *op. cit.*, 101-103, made to Europe just before he left Florence in November to enter the Papal States.

12. Henri-François Delaborde, *L'expédition de Charles VIII en Italie*, Paris, 1888, 315 suggests that this was the Calabrian monk Francis of Paola (1416-1507), who founded the Order of Minims, or Hermits of St. Francis of Assisi, and was canonized by Leo X on 1 May 1519. He had assisted Louis XI (cf. Philippe de Comines, *Mémoires*, édités par Joseph Calmette, *2*, Paris, 1925, 294 ff., 314; the reader will wish to consult also, for any references to the *Mémoires*, the edition by Bernard de Mandrot, Paris, 1901-1903, 2 vols., whose notes are helpful and who cites Benedetti occasionally from Domenichi's Italian translation of 1549) and was highly esteemed by both Charles VIII and Louis XII. Sanudo, *op. cit.*, 29-30 states that in particular certain "hermits" urged Charles to undertake the Italian expedition.

The physician Jean Michel published a vision of Charles as conqueror of Jerusalem and monarch of the world; see Étienne Lauréault de Foncemagne in *Histoire de l'Académie royale des inscriptions et belles-lettres*, 1751 (for the years 1741-1743), *16*, 241-245 and *17*, 544, La Pilorgerie, *op. cit.*, 46-47 and 431-433, Delaborde, *op. cit.*, 317, and Walter Arthur Copinger, *Supplement to Hain's Repertorium bibliographicum*, Part 2, *1*, London, 1898, no. 4028.

Jean Michel de Pierrevive occurs early in Charles's letters (29 April 1485, ed. Pélicier, *1*, 1898, 76-77 and 24 December 1486, *ibid.*, *5*, 1905, 202) and was one of the physicians whose advice Charles recommended in protecting the dauphin Charles-Orland (10 October 1492-6 December 1495) from an epidemic of "verolle" in course at Amboise, "pour savoir," said Charles in his letter of 17 August 1495, Turin (*ibid.*, *4*, 1903, 257-258) to the child's chamberlains, "si ladicte maladie de verolle procede par contagion ou influence de mauvais air." Michel is said to have died, however, on 22 August. Charles made him a gift apparently of land in Auvergne sometime before his death (Charles's letter, before 1495, *ibid.*, *5*, 1905, 280-281) and afterward ordered that special consideration be shown his son-in-law (12 July 1497, Moulins, *ibid.*, 142-143; this same letter is printed again, *ibid.*, 238-239 under date of 12 July 1490).

It may be added that Charles's concern for the health of the dauphin is clear also from a letter of 19 September 1495, Vercelli (*ibid.*, *4*, 1903, 293) in which he orders that only the apothecary Nicolas Bourgale be permitted to furnish the child sugars and spices. On the death of the dauphin see Comines, *op. cit.*, *3*, 1925, 256-257.

13. Ph. van der Haeghen, "Examen des droits de Charles VIII sur le royaume de Naples," *Revue historique*, 1885, *28*, 89-111 finds that the claim was not valid. The complicated history of the claim and of French

relations with Italy in earlier reigns is summarized by Delaborde, *op. cit.*, 1-151; see also Émile G. Léonard, *Les Angevins de Naples*, Paris, 1954. Charles said in a letter to the inhabitants of Troyes, 10 February 1494, Amboise, ed. Pélicier, *4*, 1903, 12, "Ledict royaume nous apartient tant par droicte succession que par testament de la maison d'Anjou"; cf. in Guillaume de Jaligny, *Histoire de Charles VIII roy de France*, Paris, 1694, 675-683 the "Traité des droits du roy Charles VIII. aux royaumes de Naples, Sicile & Arragon, mis par escrit en 1491. du commandement du roy, par Leonard Baronnat maistre des comptes." Comines, *op. cit.*, *3*, 1925, 1-10 also examines the claim.

14. Astrology aside, it is well to remember that the historian must often date from astronomical phenomena. This necessity has recently been demonstrated anew by William D. Stahlman and Owen Gingerich, *Solar and planetary longitudes for years −2500 to +2000 by 10-day intervals*, Madison, 1963. The tables furnished on p.489 therein include the years 1493-1495 and should be consulted also for Benedetti's remarks in II.35 and II.51.

15. Whoever from the loggia of the Biblioteca Capitolare has seen the impetuous Adige hurling itself through Verona on its way to the Adriatic will realize what power it could unleash for destruction until in 1889-1895 its turbulent force was confined within strong embankments. As Pietro Bembo, *Della historia vinitiana . . . volgarmente scritta, libri XII*, Vinegia, 1552, f. 15b tells the story, "Il fiume Adice, havendo gran parte di Verona allagata, & molte mura & case ruinate, portò via etiandio un ponte fermissimo posto in mezzo della Città." I owe to Dr. Mario Carrara, Director of the Biblioteca Civica at Verona, the information, in a letter of 5 June 1964, that the bridge severely damaged by the floods of 3-7 October 1493 was the Ponte delle Navi, which spans the river behind the apses of San Fermo Maggiore. Built of wood in 1153 and of stone in 1373-1375, it was reconstructed last after World War II. In this portent Benedetti as a native of the region of Verona had of course special interest.

16. At this time Girolamo Savonarola was also predicting the invasion; see Delaborde, *op. cit.*, 316, 439 and Comines, *op. cit.*, *3*, 1925, 144-146, 176, 184, 195, 203. He considered Charles the instrument of Divine Justice.

17. This prophecy is cited by Delaborde, *op. cit.*, 318. Myron P. Gilmore, *Humanists and jurists*, Cambridge, Mass., 1963, 46, discussing the humanist tradition on historical writing as it is set forth in Giovanni Pontano's dialogue *Actius*, reminds us that the historian of Pontano's time dared not omit, and in fact felt himself bound to report, "presages, oracles, prophecies, visions, and sacrifices." Gilmore also remarks, 49-50, on the fact that Comines is constantly aware of the hand of God in the French expedition and of the divine rule, in fact, over all human affairs and, 52-53, that Francesco Guicciardini was among those who followed the precepts of Pontano. Benedetti's classical precedent for such information as is provided in I.2 is of course Livy.

18. Negotiations and events in the years immediately preceding the descent of Charles into Italy are related by Delaborde, *op. cit.*, 214-391. Pages 153-213 cover the period from the death of Louis XI, 30 August 1483, when Charles was thirteen, to 1491.

19. See Sanudo, *op. cit.*, 484-486, on the feeling between Venice and Ferrara.

20. In a letter to Ercole dated 26 February 1494, Moulins, ed. Pélicier, *4*, 1903, 21, Charles states that he has received the son into his service "voulentiers et de bon cueur." This was Ferdinando, born in Naples in 1477. Ercole mentions his own pleasure in the affair in letters to Charles of 13 February and 3 April 1494, Ferrara, *ibid.*, 331-332 and 333-334.

21. For a recent review of the position of Alexander VI with relation to the expedition of Charles see Giovanni Soranzo, *Il tempo di Alessandro VI papa e di fra Girolamo Savonarola*, Milano, 1960 (Pubblicazioni dell'Università cattolica del Sacro Cuore, Serie terza, Scienze storiche, 1), 51-157.

22. Components of the fleet which sailed from Naples on 22 June 1494 under command of Frederick of Aragon, brother of Alfonso and prince of Taranto, are listed by Sanudo, *op. cit.*, 51-52.

23. See, for example, Pélicier's edition of Charles's letters, *4*, 1903, 73-74, 76-77.

24. Of convenience in following Charles's route is the article, in calendrical form, of Ernest Petit, "Séjours de Charles VIII (1483-1498)," in France, Comité des travaux historiques et scientifiques, Section de philologie et d'histoire, *Bulletin philologique et historique*, 1896, *15*, 629-690. Delaborde, *op. cit.*, 324-326, calculates 31,500 men for the land forces and 10,400 exclusive of the sailors manning the ships for the sea forces.

25. Francesco Gonzaga relates his interview with Charles's envoys in a letter of 23 April 1494, Marmirolo, to his wife Isabella d'Este Gonzaga, then in Urbino; see Luzio and Renier, *Archivio storico italiano*, Serie 5, 1890, *6*, 207-208. The important Gonzaga archives are catalogued in the publication *L'Archivio Gonzaga di Mantova*, Volume primo a cura di Pietro Torelli, Ostiglia, 1920, Volume secondo a cura di Alessandro Luzio, Verona, 1922 (Pubblicazioni della Reale Accademia Virgiliana di Mantova, Serie I, Monumenta, 1-2).

26. Charles was taken on 13 September with a high fever which his physician Théodore Gaynier or Guaynier of Pavia thought due, according to Delaborde, *op. cit.*, 404-405, to sunstroke. It was soon recognized, however, as a mild form of smallpox. Sanudo, *op. cit.*, 87 states that he had a high fever and that many physicians attended him, among them "Theodoro da Parma [Pavia?], al qual li prestava gran fede." On page 88 Sanudo adds that Lodovico Sforza on 17 September sent to Asti to see him

"Ambrosio de Rosate *(Rusciate)* suo medico et ottimo astrologo, et visto, conoscete esser varuole, le qual zà se discoverzivano su la persona; per la qual cosa tutti comenzono a star di bona voja, perchè saria mal breve, come fu." Charles got up on 21 September and in two weeks he was cured; see also Comines, *op. cit.*, 3, 1925, 46. A recent article on the appearance of the word "variola" in the medical vocabulary is Ernest Wickersheimer's in Deutsche Akademie der Naturforscher zu Halle, *Nova acta leopoldina*, N.F., 1963, 27, no. 167 (Beiträge zur Geschichte der Medizin und der Naturwissenschaften, Festschrift für Professor Dr. Rudolph Zaunick zum 70. Geburtstag am 26. VIII. 1963), 175-182. The following March, in Naples, Charles was afflicted with a rash which may have been measles (cf. Sanudo, *op. cit.*, 263-264). Writing to his brother-in-law the Duke of Bourbon, 28 March 1495, Naples, ed. Pélicier, 4, 1903, 187, he mentioned the earlier illness, saying, "Pour habillier mon visaige il ne suffisoit pas que j'eusse eu la petite verole, mais j'ai eu la rougeole, de laquelle, Dieu mercy, je suis guery."

27. On Piero's conduct, the sentiment in Florence, and Charles's entry 17 November 1494 and stay in the city see Sanudo, *op. cit.*, 131 ff. and Delaborde, *op. cit.*, 434-485. He departed 28 November. Events in and concerning Florence in this period are related also by George Frederick Young in *The Medici*, 1, London, 1909, 309-343, and Roberto Ridolfi, *Vita di Girolamo Savonarola*, 1, Roma, 1952, 107 ff., 116-135; see also the relevant references in Sergio Camerani, *Bibliografia medicea*, Firenze, 1964. Michelangelo had fled the city early in October, going first to Venice and then to Bologna.

28. In a letter to the city of Lucca, 29 November 1494, Florence, ed. Pélicier, 4, 1903, 342-343, Charles promises to repay 10,000 ducats lent by the city for his expedition to Naples. Cf. Sanudo, *op. cit.*, 111.

29. See Sanudo, *op. cit.*, 111 ff. and for Pisa's part in these and subsequent events the "Memoriale" of Giovanni Portoveneri in *Archivio storico italiano*, 1845, 6, Parte 2, 281-360.

30. For the series of events in Romagna see Sanudo, *op. cit.*, 60, 66 ff., 71 ff., 92 ff., 664 ff. Bernardo Dovizi da Bibbiena recounts many events of the campaign in his letters of August-31 October 1494 from the Casentino, the Aragonese camp, and Florence to his brother Piero and to Piero de' Medici; see the edition by Giuseppe L. Moncallero, *Epistolario di Bernardo Dovizi da Bibbiena*, 1 (1490-1513), Firenze, 1955 (Biblioteca dell' "Archivum romanicum," Serie I, 44), 79-237 and Moncallero's helpful notes. The war in Romagna, says Moncallero, 236, n.1, "era terminata senza che gli stessi protagonisti se ne fossero reso conto."

31. 21 October 1494; see Sanudo, *op. cit.*, 674 ff. "A'15 d'Ottubrio," says Malipiero, *op. cit.*, 1, 1843, 320, "se ha aviso che el Duca Zuan Galeazzo de Milan è morto da flusso; et è opinion comune, che Lodovico so zio l'habbia fatto morir per via de tosegho."

32. 22 October 1494. Lodovico received thus all the prerogatives of

power which he had already exercised in fact since 1479. Charles adds in a letter to Maximilian, 4 September 1495, Turin, ed. Pélicier, *4*, 1903, 280 that Lodovico "tolsi el ducato a lo figliolo del quale l'era tutore, et de queste cose ne volemo lassare el judicio a Dio. . . ." On the investiture granted in April by Maximilian and performed on 26 May see Sanudo, *op. cit.*, 312, 321, 330, 353-355 and Johann Christian Lünig, *Codex Italiae diplomaticus, 1,* Francofurti & Lipsiae, 1725, coll. 493-498. I have used the copy of Lünig in the Biblioteca Marciana which belonged to Apostolo Zeno.

33. Charles described on the day of his entry, 17 November 1494, the welcome accorded him; see his letter to the Duke of Bourbon, ed. Pélicier, *4*, 1903, 111-112.

34. On the enmity between Alexander VI and Giuliano della Rovere (cardinal 1471 and pope, Julius II, 1503) see Sanudo, *op. cit.*, 41-42. The Cardinal "le victuarie venivano per el Tevere in Roma non lassava intrar." On page 148 Sanudo quotes prices. Again in August 1495 provisions for Rome were blockaded at Ostia; see Charles's letter, 21 August 1495, Chieri, ed. Pélicier, *4*, 1903, 264-269, in which he requests the Pope to re-establish in his privileges the Cardinal of San Pietro in Vincoli, and *ibid.*, 269-270.

35. On 10 December the Duke of Calabria had arrived with most of the troops which he had commanded in Romagna; see Delaborde, *op. cit.*, 499. In a letter to Ercole, duke of Ferrara, 12 December 1494, Viterbo, ed. Pélicier, *4*, 1903, 126-127, Charles interprets their entry as an act of hostility toward himself. On 12 January 1495, Rome, *ibid.*, 143 he wrote to the Duke of Bourbon that when the Pope "a veu que j'approuchoye, avecques partie de mon armée, ceste ville de Romme, et que en icelle j'avoye bonne intelligence, il a donné chemin au duc de Calabre et à ses gens, et s'en est allé ledict duc de Calabre dedans le royaume de Napples." Cf. Sanudo, *op. cit.*, 160 ff. and Girolamo Priuli, *I diarii,* a cura di Arturo Segre, *1,* Città di Castello, 1912-1921 (*Rerum italicarum scriptores:* raccolta degli storici italiani dal cinquecento al millecinquecento, ordinata da L. A. Muratori. Nuova edizione, t. 24, p. 3), 13.

·36. Castel Sant'Angelo. Sanudo, *op. cit.*, 149 states that he had provisioned it for three years.

37. Actually the evening of 31 December. See Sanudo, *op. cit.*, 163 ff.; Johann Burchard, *Liber notarum ab anno MCCCCLXXXIII usque ad annum MDVI* a cura di Enrico Celani, *1,* Città di Castello, 1907-1910 (*Rerum italicarum scriptores.* Raccolta degli storici italiani dal cinquecento al millecinquecento, ordinata da L. A. Muratori. Nuova edizione, t. 32, p. 1, *1*), 558-559, who says, "Feria quarta, XXXI decembris, bono mane, de mandato ss. d. n. pape, equitavi obviam regi Francie sibi dicturus ordinem receptionis sue juxta ceremonialia. . ."; and La Pilorgerie, *op. cit.*, 112-115.

38. On 17 January 1495, Rome, Charles wrote to the Duke of Bourbon, ed. Pélicier, *4*, 1903, 150-151, that he had that day gone from the Palace of San Marco to the Vatican and met there the Pope who had come

from the Castel Sant'Angelo. He accompanied the letter with a copy of the
agreement negotiated on 15 January and ratified on 18 January; cf. Sanudo,
*op. cit.*, 185 ff. Guillaume Briçonnet was promoted cardinal on 16 January.

According to Arnaldo Cortesi in the *New York Times*, 14 May 1957,
1, 4, President René Coty's visit to Pope Pius XII on 13 May 1957 was
the first made to the Vatican by a French chief of state since that of Charles.
Charles's stay in Rome 31 December 1494-28 January 1495 is summarized
by Delaborde, *op. cit.*, 506-526, who mentions that on 20 January the King
touched for scrofula more than five hundred persons assembled in the
chapel of St. Petronilla near St. Peter's. Burchard, *op. cit.*, 565, 570 places
this chapel within the earlier St. Peter's. The remains of this saint, buried
originally in the cemetery of St. Priscilla, were transferred again, this time
to an altar in St. Peter's, when that church was rebuilt in the sixteenth
century. A mosaic copy of Guercino's "Saint Petronilla" adorns the chapel
of St. Michael in St. Peter's; the original has been transferred to the Pinaco-
teca Capitolina. St. Petronilla was special patroness of treaties concluded
between popes and Frankish emperors.

Lodovico Sforza's opinion of Charles's powers in touching for scrofula
was not high. According to a dispatch of the Venetian envoy Sebastiano
Badoer, 3 December 1494, published by Samuele Romanin, *Storia documentata di Venezia*, 5, Venezia, 1856, 58, he said to Charles, "Sire, per Dio voi
non guarirete più per miracolo quelli che hanno mal di scrofola alla gola,
perchè si dice che quando vien presentato alcun simile infermo a V.M. bi-
sogna che la si confessi e poi segnando la lo guarisce; voi avete commesso
e fatto commetter tanti mali in questa vostra venuta che se vorrete con-
fessarvi non troverete chi vi possi assolver e per conseguenza non siete più
per far miracoli." Sanudo, on the other hand, *op. cit.*, 245, speaking of
Charles's devoutness, says that he "varisse di mal di scrovole, secondo el
costume regio de Franza, disceso da Santo Ludovico re, et qui in Italia
molti del mal preditto segnando varite, *ut dicitur.*" In Fulin's edition of
Sanudo all Latin words are italicized; the italicizing here is not intended to
stress "ut dicitur," but the fact that the words were given in Latin may. In
the 1883 edition, 12, Fulin points out that Marco Guazzo, *Historie . . . ove
si contengono la venuta, & partita di Carlo ottavo, re di Franza*, Venetia,
1547, copies from this passage but does not catch the irony of "ut dicitur."

Sanudo, *op. cit.*, 189 informs us that three of the French died in
Rome, perhaps of the pest, which they did not fear or avoid; in Rome, in
fact, they stayed in houses which had not been inhabited since the pest of
1492.

39. Sanudo, *op. cit.*, 45-47 provides documents which passed between
Alexander VI and the Sultan in June and September 1494. The Sultan sug-
gested that Zizim "sia levato di travaglio a quello migliore modo apparerà
a Vostra Grandezza, e translatata l'anima sua ne lo altro mondo." On page
192 Sanudo describes the scene when the Pope consigned Zizim to Charles;
Zizim was to go only as far as Terracina (p. 190), but Charles took him instead to Naples. The departure of Charles is related on pages 195-196.
See also Burchard, *op. cit.*, 548 ff., 573 f.

40. Sanudo, *op. cit.*, 125.

41. The Spanish fleet was commanded by Galcerán de Requeséns, count of Trivento, in the province of Campobasso (cf. Sanudo, *op. cit.*, 203, 255, 290, 386); the land forces, by the conqueror of Granada, "El Gran Capitán," Gonzalo Fernández de Córdoba.

42. "Parve," says Lodovico Antonio Muratori, *Annali d'Italia dal principio dell'era volgare sino all'anno MDCCXLIX, 13*, Napoli, 1758, 382, "che il Cielo secondasse tutti i suoi passi, perchè quel verno fu così dolce, quieto e sereno, che sembrava una primavera, in guisa che all' esercito Franzese non riusciva d'incomodo o danno il far viaggio in quella stagione." Sanudo, *op. cit.*, 147 mentions that in December 1494, when Charles was still on his way to Rome, although it was winter, "tempi da star a li allozamenti, pur franzesi li piaceva guerrizar, et li pareva istade, per esser sotto un altro clima."

43. Cesare Cardinal Borgia was the second son of Alexander VI by Vannozza de' Catanei, on whom see Pietro De Angelis in *Atti e memorie dell'Accademia di storia dell'arte sanitaria*, Appendice alla *Rassegna di clinica terapia e scienze affini*, Serie 2, 1954, 20, 5 p. and Burchard, *op. cit.*, 562, n.2. Two days after Charles's departure from Rome he escaped from the French at Velletri. Charles gave the news to Lodovico Sforza on 6 February 1495 in a letter from Ferentino, ed. Pélicier, 4, 1903, 160. Sanudo, *op. cit.*, 197 states that the Cardinal "la notte, de Velitri si havea calato gioso de li muri de la terra" and that he went to Spoleto. He showed himself openly in Rome again on 25 March; see Sanudo, 279.

44. "Tutto el Reame," says Sanudo, *op. cit.*, 188, "era in combustione, non si obediva più comandamenti di re Alphonso, si udiva romori ne le cittade, cridando: Franza! Franza! *maxime* li Anzuini et cupidi di nove cose."

45. The date was 21 January 1495. On 3 February he sailed from the Castel dell'Ovo to Mazzarrà Sant'Andrea near Messina. See Sanudo, *op. cit.*, 192-195. Charles in a letter to the Parlement of Grenoble, 6 February 1495, Ferentino, ed. Pélicier, 4, 1903, 165 (see also page 175) wrote of having heard that "le roy Alphonce est en estat qu'il ne sçauroit faire ne bien ne mal." Alfonso died on 18 December 1495.

46. In a letter to the Duke of Bourbon from Pisa 20 June 1495, ed. Pélicier, 4, 1903, 218, Charles on his return trip from Naples states that he has ordered Terracina and other papal cities restored to the Pope.

47. Sanudo, *op. cit.*, 208.

48. Sanudo, *op. cit.*, 209 speaks of "grandissima inopia" of food.

49. In a letter to the Duke of Bourbon, 12 January 1495, Rome, ed. Pélicier, 4, 1903, 146, Charles said, "Ceulx de Laquille ne desirent que eulx mettre entre mes mains et n'attendent sinon que je leur envoye des gens pour ce faire"; cf. Sanudo, *op. cit.*, 187, 206, 217. On 6 February from

Ferentino, *ibid.*, 164, he announced to the Parlement of Grenoble that "La-quelle" had been taken. He mentions again in a letter to the Duke of Bourbon, 11 February, Veroli, *ibid.*, 169 the good will of its inhabitants.

50. Sanudo, *op. cit.*, 234 gives the number as five. From Procida he proceeded to Ischia and then to Messina. See also page 244.

51. His entry into Capua 19 February is described by Sanudo, *op. cit.*, 230.

52. Charles wrote to the Duke of Bourbon on the day of his entry into Naples, 22 February 1495, ed. Pélicier, 4, 1903, 176-178, and often thereafter. The date is given as 20 February in a letter to the archbishop of Embrun and to Jean Rabot, *ibid.*, 5, 1905, 265-266. Charles's stay in Naples is summarized by Delaborde, *op. cit.*, 558-578, 599-606; cf. Sanudo, *op. cit.*, 234 ff., 241 ff. An eyewitness account, richly illustrated in color, of Charles's entry and of subsequent events is contained in MS. M 801 in The Pierpont Morgan Library. Its author, whose surname alone we know, was Ferraiolo; the account is included in his Neapolitan chronicle, 1423-1498, which was edited, with commentary, by Riccardo Filangieri under the title *Una cronaca napoletana figurata del quattrocento,* Napoli, 1956 (Accademia nazionale di archeologia, lettere e belle arti di Napoli). See in particular pages 128-139. I owe this reference to Curt F. Bühler. Dr. Bühler cited the account in *Publications of the Modern Language Association of America,* 1952, 67, 584.

53. 16 February 1495; see Sanudo, *op. cit.*, 226. The citadel fell on 10 March according to Sanudo, 265, and on 27 March according to Charles's letter to the Duke of Bourbon 28 March, Naples, ed. Pélicier, 4, 1903, 185.

54. Sanudo, *op. cit.*, 226-227, 249.

55. Charles wrote to the Duke of Bourbon regarding Taranto on 28 March, Naples, ed. Pélicier, 4, 1903, 185.

56. They had been commissioned to accompany Charles only as far as Rome. On 21 January there, when they gave notice of their intention to depart, Charles, according to Sanudo, *op. cit.*, 189-190, expressed his unwillingness to lose them and obtained permission from Venice for them to remain. On 22 February, *ibid.*, 234, they visited Charles at Poggioreale; see also *ibid.*, 294-295 and for their return to Venice 17 May and the report they gave there *ibid.*, 340.

57. 25 February 1495. Sanudo, *op. cit.*, 243 states that he was taken ill before Charles reached Capua with "cataro, el qual li era disceso in uno ochio et nel stomego, o vero fusse reuma"; that he was carried to Aversa and then to Naples, where physicians bled him and used other remedies; that he improved somewhat, "pur la febbre li cressete, onde non volle provisione alcuna che, *ita volente fato,* in questa matina expirò, fermo e costante ne la fede soa." On pages 244-245 Sanudo stresses the great loss to the Pope of the forty thousand pieces of gold which the Sultan had been

paying annually (cf. I.12) and therefore considers poisoning *"non . . . credendum."* He reports, however, that the French charged poisoning because *"post mortem* li fu trovato alcuni segni di veneno sul corpo" and cites Petrus de Abano and other writers on poisons for the information that poison can be administered to take effect only at an appointed future time. Charles, "dolendosi molto di la morte dil fratel dil Turco," concealed news of the death for several days; even after burial the same guards and attendants were maintained at Zizim's residence, and the physicians continued their visits. See also Malipiero, *op. cit.*, *1*, 1843, 145-146. Louis Thuasne discusses the last phase of the life of Zizim, from 1 January 1495 on, and the various theories concerning the death on pages 347-375 of *Djem-sultan*, Paris, 1892. On pages 368-369 he cites from Johann Georg von Eckhart's edition of the *Diaria* in *Corpus historicorum medii aevi*, *2*, Lipsiae, 1723, col. 1582, Benedetti's statement concerning Charles's negligence, which he says was repeated word for word by Corio and by Giovanni Stella in his *Vite ducentorum et triginta summorum pontificum*, Venetiis, Bernardinus de Vitalibus, 1505.

58. Sanudo, *op. cit.*, 347.

59. In his letter to the Parlement of Grenoble, 6 February 1495, Ferentino, ed. Pélicier, *4*, 1903, 164 Charles says, "Avons si avancé que avons mis à nostre obeissance . . . la pluspart de la Poille et Prusse."

60. At Florence and Siena the French seem to have abstained from this violence; see Delaborde, *op. cit.*, 441-442, who on page 530, n.1 and page 575 accuses the Venetians in particular of spreading false rumors in this respect. Comines, *op. cit.*, *3*, 1925, 51 denies that the French raped women, but cf. Sanudo, *op. cit.*, 111, 267, 345. Most of Chapter 18 is quoted by John Seargeant Cyprian Bridge, *A history of France from the death of Louis XI*, *2*, Oxford, 1924, 330 from Benedetti in the 1863 edition of Lodovico Domenichi's Italian translation, *Il fatto d'arme del Tarro*, Novara, 36-37.

61. Chapter 18 is quoted to this point, from Eckhart's edition, in Louis Thuasne, *Le mal français à l'époque de l'expédition de Charles VIII en Italie*, Paris, 1886, 98.

62. See Delaborde, *op. cit.*, 544 and Sanudo, *op. cit.*, 207. The town, in the province of Rome, has been called Artena since 1870. Charles in his letter to the Parlement of Grenoble, 6 February, Ferentino, ed. Pélicier, *4*, 1903, 164 says simply, "Avons si avancé que avons mis à nostre obeissance la place de Montfortin." See also *ibid.*, 281.

63. See Delaborde, *op. cit.*, 547-548. Charles tells of the assault in letters to the Duke of Bourbon of 9 and 11 February, Veroli, ed. Pélicier, *4*, 1903, 166-169 (see also 173, 281). Cf. Sanudo, *op. cit.*, 209-210.

64. One episode of the Pope's relations with Charles, set forth in a let-

ter taken at Fornovo and dated by Delaborde 1 February 1495, is examined by the latter in *Bibliothèque de l'École des chartes,* 1886, 47, 512-524.

65. See Sanudo, *op. cit.,* 256-257.

66. The document was signed in Venice on the evening of 31 March 1495; the several envoys remained at the Doge's Palace until 2 a.m. Negotiations, which had begun during Charles's march on Rome, were longer and more difficult than the simple statement of Benedetti reveals; see Delaborde, *L'expédition de Charles VIII en Italie,* Paris, 1888, 530 ff. and 579-607 and Sanudo, *op. cit.,* 217 ff., 250 ff., 268 ff. Sanudo lists on page 283 the patricians present at the signing of the document and describes on pages 299-305 the ceremonies held in Venice on the occasion of its public announcement on Palm Sunday, 12 April; similar celebrations took place in Milan and Rome on the same day. The text of the announcement is given by Sanudo and by Malipiero, *op. cit., 1,* 1843, 336-337. See also Priuli, *op. cit.,* 20 and Lünig, *op. cit., 1,* 1725, coll. 111-118.

67. According to Sanudo, *op. cit.,* 181 *Battista* Trevisan, ambassador of the Signoria, had died at Milan 24 December 1494. Sebastiano Badoer, "rimaso privo del carissimo collega, non stette molto ben, et si ammalò, però di mal vecchio, per la sua gamba." He often discussed matters with Lodovico, adds Sanudo, and pointed out that Charles should not rule in Italy. Cf. Sanudo, 249, 251.

68. Some Turkish pashas, when they were informed of the league, expressed astonishment that each member of it had so diametrically changed position: Lodovico Sforza had brought Charles into Italy and now joined the league against him, Venice could have opposed his coming but refrained and now formed this league against him, etc.; see Sanudo, *op. cit.,* 374 and Fulin's comment in the 1883 edition, page 10, n.1, "Come si vede, c'era più buon senso a Costantinopoli che in Italia."

69. Philippe de Comines, *op. cit., 3,* 1925, 110, arriving in Venice on 2 October 1494, found it "la plus triumphante cité que jamais j'aye veüe et qui plus faict d'honneur à ambassadeurs et estrangiers et qui plus saigement se gouverne et où le service de Dieu est le plus sollempnellement faict." James Morris, to whom Comines was maternal ancestor, retains much of the spirit of this description of the city in *Venice,* London, 1960. The same spirit pervades the calendar of the Metropolitan Museum of Art for 1964, *Venice, views and echoes,* by Margaret R. Scherer, where part of the above passage is quoted in English on the plate facing the week of 24 May.

This "triumphant" city is pictured in the bird's-eye view in the great woodcut by Jacopo de' Barbari which was published in Venice by Anton Kolb in 1500; see Luigi Servolini, *Jacopo de' Barbari,* Padova, 1944, 48-54 and plates LXXXVII-LXXXIX.

70. Sanudo, *op. cit.,* 285-286. Comines "si buttò al letto," says Sanudo, "et la colera li mosse, et have alquanto di fastidio, benchè li fusse mandato medici per la Signoria, quali concluseno non harebbe mal niuno, ma era

alquanto contaminato; come cussì fo." For Comines' account of the formation of the league and his great concern about it, see his *Mémoires*, 3, 1925,
118-133. Malipiero, *op. cit.*, *1*, 1843, 334 says that he "restete sora de sè,
e disse che mai questa Signoria ha roto la so fede ad alcun, e come podeva
esser che la rompesse al so Re." "Cadaun," said the Doge, "ghe darà
libero transito, e la Signoria sarà la prima a darghe transito e vittuaria per
le so terre." Cf. *ibid.*, 341-342. The secret had been so well kept that according to Bembo, *op. cit.*, f.22a, Comines "andando a palazzo ogni giorno,
& ragionando co gli altri Ambasciadori; pure non potè mai di ciò cosa
veruna intendere: di maniera che essendo egli stato chiamato il seguente
giorno, che la lega fu terminata, dal Prencipe nel collegio, & certificato dal-
lui la lega esser fatta, & saputi i nomi de collegati: di poco il sentimento
non perdè." Comines left Venice 31 May.

71. Sanudo, *op. cit.*, 256 mentions the Pope's belief that "el cardinal
S. Piero *in Vincula* con ditto Re [de Franza] metteva grande odio con il
Pontifice, et sarebbe stato contento di nova eletione o di far scisma." See also
page 267, "El cardinal San Piero *in Vincula* voleva venisse [Soa Majestà]
a Roma a dismetter el Papa e farne un altro." On page 277 Sanudo relates
the Pope's fear that if he left Rome the cardinals remaining "havriano po-
tuto crear uno altro Papa, et poner scisma in la Chiesia de Dio."

Léon-G. Pélissier published in *Revue d'histoire moderne et contemporaine*, 1900-1901, 2, 386-393 three letters of 6 May 1495 to the Pope
which are preserved in the Biblioteca Marciana and according to which
Charles on his second visit to Rome did not wish to present himself as the
Pope's enemy. They are by Charles himself, signed "Rex Francie, Sicilie,
et Jherusalem" (also ed. Pélicier, 4, 1903, 202-203), assuring the Pope that
he "omni tempore inveniet nos filium obedientissimum ecclesie" and stating
confidently, "Sed Deus, qui est versus retributor, reddet unicuique juxta
merita sua"; by Jean de Bilhères-Lagraulas, cardinal of Saint Denis; and
by Guillaume Briçonnet, cardinal of Saint-Malo. Cf. Sanudo, *op. cit.*, 401.
Similar sentiments are expressed in Charles's letter to the Pope of 21 August,
Chieri, ed. Pélicier, 4, 1903, 264-269.

72. Some of Charles's later provisions in regard to the kingdom of
Naples are set forth in a letter to Menaud de Guerre, 21 August 1495,
Chieri, ed. Pélicier, 4, 1903, 272. See also *ibid.*, 276, 287, 313-315, and for
events of 1496 the relevant letters, *ibid.*, 5, 1905. Sanudo, *op. cit.*, 391-392,
606 lists the governors who were left in control.

73. He still held this post when on 31 December 1495 Sanudo, *op. cit.*,
297-298 dedicated to him Book III of his account of Charles's expedition. On
his efforts to persuade the Pope to leave Rome see Sanudo, 339, 356, 358;
on page 368 he is mentioned as being in Perugia with the Pope.

74. Sanudo, *op. cit.*, 356-358.

75. The Pope left Perugia on 22 June and returned on 27 June to
Rome by way of Orvieto and Viterbo; see Sanudo, *op. cit.*, 426, 439.

76. He had left Naples 20 May. For this second visit see Sanudo, *op. cit.*, 364-367. The correction of his route from Naples to Pisa is the most important among the manuscript corrections made in numerous copies in the shop of Aldus Manutius and recently discovered by Dr. Bühler; see the Introduction.

77. He entered Siena 13 June; see Sanudo, *op. cit.*, 392. On later relations of Charles with Siena see his letter to authorities there 13 December 1495, Lyon, ed. Pélicier, *4*, 1903, 325-327.

78. In a letter to the Duke of Bourbon, 20 June 1495, Pisa, ed. Pélicier, *4*, 1903, 216-220, Charles tells of his journey from Naples and of the flight of the Pope from Rome to Perugia. Charles's second stay in Pisa is related by Sanudo, *op. cit.*, 421-422, 429.

79. The victory of Louis, duke of Orléans, at Rapallo over Frederick of Aragon, prince of Taranto, is reported by Charles in letters of 10 and 11 September 1494, Asti, ed. Pélicier, *4*, 1903, 89-93. On 8 and 9 May 1495, Naples, *ibid.*, 204-210, Charles had urged the Duke of Bourbon to hurry aid to Louis at Asti against Lodovico Sforza. In the second letter, 207, he mentions "la ligue qui a esté faicte en ceste Ytalie." Louis' efforts in 1495 to incite the Swiss against Lodovico are set forth by Teodoro di Liebenau in *Archivio storico lombardo*, 1889, *16*, 607-624. For Swiss involvement with France and Milan 1495-1499 see Ernst Gagliardi in *Jahrbuch für schweizerische Geschichte*, 1914, *39*, 1*-283* and 1915, *40*, 1*-278*.

80. Sanudo, *op. cit.*, 382-383, 395-396 and Comines, *op. cit.*, *3*, 1925, 150-151; the city was taken on 13 June. La Pilorgerie, *op. cit.*, 309-314 reprints a letter, dated from Novara 15 June, which was sent to France by one of the members of Louis' suite and which describes the march from Asti to Novara and the surrender of Novara. The entry and surrender are described by Antonio Rusconi, *(1495) Assedio di Novara*, Novara, 1884, 7-9 from an eyewitness account by Cristoforo Gorizio of Novara which is preserved in a manuscript in the Archivio of the Cattedrale there; he documents in the pages immediately following the conspiracy against Lodovico Sforza.

81. From Giovanni Castiglione; see Rusconi, *op. cit.*, 10-12.

82. Sebastiano Badoer had finished his term of service; see Sanudo, *op. cit.*, 312, 321, 330, 354, 360. He finally left on 5 June and reached Venice on 13 June; see Sanudo, 371, 385. On Lioni's reports see Sanudo, 397, 425.

83. Contarini reached Milan on 21 June; see Sanudo, *op. cit.*, 410-411. The people flocked to see the stratiotes, who on the request of Lodovico Sforza demonstrated their prowess in running. Cf. I.27 and Malipiero, *op. cit.*, *1*, 1843, 351-352.

84. This is Benedetti's first mention of the man to whom he, or

possibly Aldus Manutius, probably presented a copy, on vellum, of the *Diaria*. It was King George III's copy and is preserved in the British Museum; see *Catalogue of books printed in the XV*[th] *century now in the British Museum, 5*, 1924, 555 (IA. 24420). Its capitals are illuminated in gold and colors, and the arms of the Trevisan family, illuminated, appear in the lower margin of f.2b. According to Curt F. Bühler, *Papers of the Bibliographical Society of America*, 1949, *43*, 372-373, it incorporates all the stop-press corrections and was therefore printed "after at least a majority of the paper copies had been produced. . . . [It] contains no manuscript corrections, perhaps because Aldus feared that they might disfigure the vellum leaves."

On 31 December 1495 Sanudo, *op. cit.*, 471-472 dedicated to Melchiorre Trevisan Book IV of his account of Charles's expedition.

85. See Sanudo, *op. cit.*, 423 for Charles's choice of this route. The French entered Pontremoli 26 June, *ibid.*, 435 and Comines, *op. cit.*, 3, 1925, 154-157.

86. Sanudo, *op. cit.*, 360.

87. Sanudo, *op. cit.*, 224-225 relates negotiations of February and on page 370 states that on 5 June Francesco Gonzaga was made "governador zeneral di tutte le zente sì da pie' come da cavallo"; the appointment was later changed, however, to that of "Capetanio zeneral . . . da terra," *ibid.*, 524 and cf. Benedetti, II.10, 32. Jacopo d'Atri, "Croniche del marchese di Mantova," ed. Carlo E. Visconti in *Archivio storico lombardo*, 1879, *6*, 43-44, furnished a letter from the Doge 21 June 1495 which requests of "tutti li prefecti de zentedarme, conductieri, stipendiarij" obedience to Gonzaga. On pages 58-59 he provides the letter of 27 July concerning the second appointment.

88. Cf. I.25. These horsemen, recruited in Greece and Albania, were fierce in battle, accustomed to every fatigue, and extremely fast; they ate sparingly and were satisfied with anything provided their horses fared well; see Luzio and Renier in *Archivio storico italiano*, Serie 5, 1890, *6*, 231-232. Sanudo, *op. cit.*, 313-314 states in addition that they were "vestiti con casacche et cappelli in capo: varii portano panciere, ma una lanza in mano, una mazoca et la spada da lai (*a lato*); . . . stanno continuamente sotto di loro cavalli, i qual non manzavano fieno come questi italiani. Sono usi a latrocinii, et continuamente esercitano in la Morea tal exercitii; stanno a l'impeto de Turchi, sono optimi a far corarie, dar guasto a paesi, investir zente, et fedeli sono al suo signor *ut plurimum* assà . . . ; et non fanno presoni ma taglia la testa." Comines, *op. cit.*, 3, 1925, 163-164 also describes the stratiotes; he had seen them at Venice.

89. D'Atri, *op. cit.*, 45 names four, "Phebo da Gonzaga, Marcho da Martinengo, el Conte Joan Francesco da Gambara et il Conte Alovisio Avogadro."

90. On the night of 22 June, according to Sanudo, *op. cit.*, 408, Doge

Agostino Barbarigo was afflicted with fever and colic pains, the result of overwork. The physicians Giovanni dall'Aquila and Girolamo dalla Torre, or Turriani, of Verona were summoned from the Studio at Padua, and he was shortly cured. But his illness is mentioned again *ibid.*, 436, where it is said to have been aggravated by bad news concerning Pontremoli, and also *ibid.*, 474 (6 July) and 500 (12 July). Comines, *op. cit.*, 3, 1925, 124 says that he was ill of "colicque" already in March. Cf. Malipiero, *op. cit.*, 2, 1844, 695.

91. Cf. Sanudo, *op. cit.*, 412

92. See Sanudo, *op. cit.*, 433.

93. This is Benedetti's first mention of the man to whom Aldus Manutius presented a copy of the *Diaria* which is now preserved in the Library of the San Francisco Medical Center of the University of California and which Dr. J. B. deC. M. Saunders and Mrs. Carmenina Tomassini, Administrative Librarian, graciously permitted me to mention here. It was described in E. Weil's Catalogue 28, item 14, and bears on f.68b an inscription to Pisani which is reproduced on Plate I there. In a letter of 18 June 1964 Dr. Weil assured me that the inscription was indeed in the hand of Aldus.

94. Mario Equicola, *Dell'istoria di Mantova libri cinque*, Mantova, 1607, 218 cites Benedetti for these distances.

95. On 4 July Gilbert de Nevers wrote to inform the Duke of Orléans that he and the Marshal of Gié had reached a point five miles from Fornovo with their forces and were awaiting there Charles and the artillery; see La Pilorgerie, *op. cit.*, 321-322.

96. I.42. Sanudo, *op. cit.*, 447-449 lists the leaders and the number of horsemen and foot soldiers assigned to each as of 1 July. See also Malipiero, *op. cit.*, 1, 1843, 349-351. On pages 469-470 Sanudo summarizes succinctly the state of affairs in Italy just before the battle, setting forth which side the various rulers and cardinals supported; see the Introduction.

97. His passage of the Apennines with his heavy artillery is related by Comines, *op. cit.*, 3, 1925, 160-162. See also the report of 26 July 1495 in René-Alphonse-Marie de Maulde La Clavière, *Procédures politiques du règne de Louis XII*, Paris, 1885, 667: "De la (le roi) passa lesdites montaignes et Alpes, qui ont de long bien IIII journées de mauvais pays, ou l'artillerie a esté passée par force de gens, pour ce que les chevaux n'y povoyent riens, tant estoient les montaignes droites et mauvaises, et a cables et engins a esté passée a grant faulte et sterilité des eaues pour les chevaux et hommes, pain, vin et autres victuailles; et ne se trouvera jamais que Cipion ne Hanibal de leur temps fissent ung tel passage."

98. Equicola, *op. cit.*, 218 cites Benedetti for this distance. The battle of Fornovo and the events immediately preceding it are related by De-

laborde, *op. cit.*, 608-651. On page 646, n.1 he states that he has not wished to interrupt his recital by continual reference to his sources, of which the best and clearest is Comines and among the Italians the most important Benedetti, whom he accuses, however, of falsification in certain details. He was using Domenichi's translation in the 1863 edition.

Comines, *op. cit.*, 3, 1925, 169-170 states that when the French arrived the people of the region sold black bread and wine which was three fourths water. From fear of poison he had them taste it first. "En ce pas, fault parler à l'honneur des Ytaliens, car nous n'avons point trouvé qu'ilz ayent usé de nulles poisons; et s'ilz l'eussent voulu faire, à grand peyne s'en feust-on sceü garder en ce voyage." Cf. I.66.

99. Cf. Sanudo, *op. cit.*, 445. This was on the principle "Nisi Dominus custodierit civitatem, in vanum vigilant qui custodiunt eam." Agostino Barbarigo was ill at the time. The order was given, says Bembo, *op. cit.*, f.24a, "che si facessero molte elemosine a monasteri di sacre vergini, & preghiere & orationi in tutte le chiese per la salute della patria."

100. Sanudo, *op. cit.*, 485 states that Ercole, disguised, had come himself to the French camp and said that the Venetians would not fight.

101. Cf. Sanudo, *op. cit.*, 444, 452.

102. Sanudo, *op. cit.*, 455-456 gives a slightly differing account; cf. *ibid.*, 475 and Comines, *op. cit.*, 3, 1925, 172-173. See also the letter of Francesco Gonzaga, 3 July 1495, in Luzio and Renier, *op. cit.*, 216-217. Bridge, *op. cit.*, 2, 1924, 251 cites Benedetti on this conference from Domenichi's translation in the 1863 edition, 54-55. Claude Joseph de Cherrier, *Histoire de Charles VIII roi de France*, 2, Paris, 1868, 219-220 quotes some of the dialogue from Corio, whom he uses also at other points; Corio, it will be remembered, was following Benedetti.

103. That it was not a usual practice at least in the camp of Lodovico Sforza is clear from André de La Vigne and Octavien de Saint Gelais, "Le vergier d'honneur," in *Archives curieuses de l'histoire de France*, 1, 1834, 412-413, where we are told that Charles showed his camp on 16 September 1495 to Venetian and Milanese envoys "pource que le duc de Millan ne voulloit jamais souffrir que on veist le sien, ne que personne estrange entrast dedans de paour que l'on sceust son ordre, estat et façon de faire; mais le Roy ne fist pas ainsi. . . ."

104. The services of Francesco Secco had been granted to Charles late in June by the Florentines; see Sanudo, *op. cit.*, 422.

105. Sanudo, *op. cit.*, 450 states that the proveditors gave one ducat for each head but that the first stratiote to present a French head to Francesco Gonzaga received ten ducats. Cf. Luzio and Renier, *op. cit.*, 214-215 and Sanudo, *op. cit.*, 464. The Venetians, says Gilbert Pointet in La Pilorgerie, *op. cit.*, 360, "se sont monstréz d'une mauvaise nature, car ilz nous ont fait la guerre ainsi que si nous estions Turcqs et come ilz font

faire aux Turcqs. Car en leur ost, ils ont fait venir des estradiotz grecz, albanois et esclavons. . . . Quant ilz ont tué ung homme des nostres ilz lui couppent la teste et la portent aux Venissiens qui leur en donnent ung ducat oultre leur solde. Ainsi le font aux Turcz. . . ."

106. Comines, *op. cit.*, 3, 1925, 163 relates that one of the stratiotes cut off the head of a "gentilhomme appellé Le Beuf."

107. Bridge, *op. cit.*, 2, 1924, 286, using Domenichi's translation in the 1863 edition, 57, cites these figures but gives "2,600 mounted arblasters" instead of 2,700.

108. What succeeding centuries have called the Battle of Fornovo was not of course fought at Fornovo. The probable site is Ozzano Taro, three kilometers down the right bank of the river and five minutes by modern train from Fornovo. For further particulars see Pierluigi Spaggiari, "Intorno alla battaglia di Fornovo," *Aurea Parma*, 1952, 36, 36-41. Sanudo's account of the actual battle begins on page 475. Angelo Pezzana, *Storia della città di Parma*, 5, Parma, 1859, gives a detailed account of the battle and of its geography and chronology, citing Benedetti and others often, now in agreement, now in disagreement; see in particular pages 274-312. On preceding pages he is helpful for earlier events. On both Fornovo and Novara and on the account in general of Comines see Bernard de Mandrot, *Revue historique* 1900, 73, 241-257 and 74, 1-38.

109. The fertile Lombard plain, where fields never had to lie fallow, is described by Comines, *op. cit.*, 3, 1925, 167, and the valley of the Taro at Fornovo, stony now as it was then, *ibid.*, 171. The traveler approaching from Borgo Val di Taro today can readily imagine with what emotions Charles must have looked upon the broad expanse which opened out before him after the narrow passages through the mountains. In the Taro's gravel the thickets and shrubbery described by Benedetti in I.44 still grow in profusion, and even when the river is a mere trickle it is not difficult to picture the obstacle it presented when swollen, the mud of its banks in which the men slipped and slid, the confusion wrought by the stratiotes as they ran down the hill, and, in fact, the confusion of the entire battle which followed. The Italians were encamped at Giarola, so named from the gravel of the valley, the French facing them on the right bank of the Taro near Fornovo.

110. As the story is told in La Vigne and Saint Gelais, *op. cit.*, 379, "Lundy matin, sixiesme de juillet,/ Sur les six heures il fist chanter sa messe/ Dedans son camp où pas n'estoit seulet,/ Puis disna, sans moleste ou presse,/ Et à huyt heures, avecque sa noblesse,/ Virillement il monta à cheval,/ Et comme preux, vertueux et loyal./ Quant son armée fut bien encouraigée,/ Il fist marcher tant d'amont que d'aval,/ Seigneurs et aultres en bataille rangée. . . ." There is also an account in prose on pages 383-397. On page 391 Charles is termed "vray fils de Mars, successeur de César, compaignon de Pompée, hardy comme Hector, preux comme Alexandre, semblable à Charlemaigne, couraigeux comme Hanibal, vertueux

comme Auguste, heureux comme Octovien, chevaleureux comme Olivier et délibéré comme Rolant." On the comparisons see I, note 118. The feats of Charlemagne were a constant spur to Charles; see Sanudo, *op. cit.*, 22 and Comines, *op. cit.*, 3, 1925, 45.

111. Comines, *op. cit.*, 3, 1925, 174 describes for the night of 5 July a heavy storm, with thunder and lightning: "sembloit que le ciel et la terre fendissent ou que cela signifiast quelque grant inconveniant à venir."

112. Similar sentiments are expressed in a speech put in the mouth of Charles by Leonardo Sfrenati; see Alberto Del Prato, *Archivio storico per le provincie parmensi*, Nuova serie, 1905, 5, 252-253. Sfrenati's work *De bello italico*, which covers the years 1494-1502, is discussed by Michele Lupo Gentile in *Archivio storico italiano*, Serie 5, 1903, 32, 423-430.

113. Cf. Sanudo, *op. cit.*, 476.

114. He was, says Comines, *op. cit.*, 3, 1925, 179, "homme jeune qui jamais n'avoit riens veü."

115. Del Prato, *op. cit.*, 242, n.5 points out that whereas the "Relazione" which he publishes, 239-251, mentions the father, who was "governatore ducale di Parma," Benedetti states that it was the son who fought against Charles.

116. Cf. I, note 109.

117. "Behaved rather as a common soldier than as a general," says Bridge, *op. cit.*, 2, 1924, 257, translating from Domenichi's version in the 1863 edition, 73. Equicola, *op. cit.*, 219 quotes from Benedetti as follows: "Francesco Gonzaga Prefetto, fece quel dì l'officio di Capitano, et di soldato. Primo di tutti gli altri Francesco turbò l'ordine, havendone morti molti, et pugnando fortemente, penetrò per mezo le genti d'arme Francesi, et essendogli ferito il cavallo, ritornò a' suoi."

118. Francesco, in fact, changed horses three times during the battle; see Sanudo, *op. cit.*, 478. An aide wrote to Isabella d'Este Gonzaga the next day that not since Hector of Troy had anyone fought on horseback as did he; see Luzio and Renier, *op. cit.*, 220, n.5. Priuli, *op. cit.*, 26 states that he attacked the French camp "cum tantto animo . . . quanto maj hebe Cexaro o Hanibale." For the comparisons see I, note 110. Francesco's friend Floriano Dolfi of Bologna, professor of jurisprudence at the Studio there (see Giovanni Fantuzzi, *Notizie degli scrittori bolognesi*, 3, Bologna, 1783, 256-258) in a letter of 19 July, Bologna, Luzio and Renier, *op. cit.*, 228-229, begged Francesco to play the part thereafter of general, not of captain of a squadron, and to avoid exposing himself to risk unnecessarily.

The importance of horses in this engagement is clear also from the account by Jacques de Mailles, in Joseph François Michaud and Jean Joseph François Poujoulat, *Nouvelle collection des mémoires pour servir à l'histoire de France*, 4, Paris, 1837, 503, of the exploits of "le bon Chevalier sans paour et sans reprouche," Pierre du Terrail, lord of Bayard, who "se porta triumphamment par dessus tous en la compaignie du gentil seigneur de Ligny son bon maistre, et luy fut tué deux chevaulx soubz luy le jour."

119. See also Chapter 66 for their concern with plunder. On 7 July, writing "Ex castris victricibus Sanctissime ac Serenissime Lige in Glarolis," Francesco Gonzaga gave his wife an account of the battle. The principal cause of disorder, he said, was the disobedience of the stratiotes, who "non atesero ad altro che robare, et quando fo il bisogno non fo alcuno che volesse comparere"; see Luzio and Renier, *op. cit.*, 221-222, and for Gonzaga's relations with Pietro Duodo, proveditor of the stratiotes, *ibid.*, 231-232. D'Atri, *op. cit.*, 50-51 says that the stratiotes "cupidi de guadagno se levorno da lo ordine loro et voltose a li cariagij de francesi, quali richi e de gran numero erano, attendendo solo a robare non se curorno fare quello gli era stato imposto."

120. Spaggiari, *op. cit.*, 38-39, adducing the "Relazione" which recounts the battle and which was published by Del Prato, *op. cit.*, stresses the point that it was not only the stratiotes who occupied themselves with plunder. The writer of the "Relazione," page 244, states that "nostri italianj che son povri et mal pagacti a li soy signorj vedendo circha cinque milia chariagi de franzosi esser abandonacti da essi, esperando levarsi li strazi dentorno arsalirno detti chariagi." Cf. Sanudo, *op. cit.*, 480, "Se'l non fusse stato la cupidità di la preda de molti italici homeni d'arme, oltra li Stratioti et fanti, tutti Franzesi erano da nostri malmenati." Note also, *ibid.*, 482, "Si tutte le zente nostre havesseno voluto far el dover era grandissima vittoria."

121. Cf. Sanudo, *op. cit.*, 480.

122. According to Sanudo, *ibid.*, he received twelve wounds.

123. In Sanudo, *op.* cit., 652 he is called "monoculo." On 5 November he was named "cavalier di San Marco" for his faithful services.

124. The capture of Mathieu, called "le Grand Bâtard de Bourbon," is mentioned by Charles in a letter to Menaud de Guerre, 21 August 1495, Chieri, ed. Pélicier, 4, 1903, 271. He was the natural son of Jean II, duke of Bourbon. Francesco Gonzaga mentions his capture in letters to his wife 7 July, Giarola, Luzio and Renier, *op. cit.*, 222 and to his sister Elisabetta, duchess of Urbino, 16 July, San Giorgio di Lomellina, *ibid.*, 224. Equicola, *op. cit.*, 219, quoting from Benedetti, says, "Francesco Gonzaga havendo mutato cavallo, con capati Cavalieri perseguitò i nimici, et fece prigione il Bastardo di Borbone, e'l Prencipe Miolense."

125. Many artists, contemporary and later, have depicted the battle scene. Cf., for example, the woodcut reproduced from *La mer des histoires*, Paris, Verard, 1502, by Delaborde, *op. cit.*, at page 640 and in much smaller size by Elizabeth Mongan in Carl Zigrosser, *Prints: thirteen illustrated essays on the art of the print*, selected for the Print Council of

America, New York, Chicago, San Francisco, 1962, 265; the woodcut reproduced from the same work, Lyon, Davost, 1506, by Miss Mongan, 267; the anonymous French engraving, 1495, now in the Lessing J. Rosenwald Collection, National Gallery of Art, which is reproduced entire and also in detail by Miss Mongan and is fully described in her article, 253-268, where additional representations are mentioned; and the two oil paintings by Pier Ilario Spolverini (1657-1734) at Parma which are listed in Armando Ottaviano Quintavalle, *La Regia Galleria di Parma*, Roma, 1939 (Ministero della educazione nazionale, Direzione generale delle belle arti, Le guide dei musei italiani), 283-284. Calmette in his edition of the *Mémoires* of Comines, *1*, 1924, XXIII, n.5 relates to Fornovo the miniature of the battle scene which precedes the second part of the *Mémoires* in a manuscript of the early years of the sixteenth century which belonged to Anne de Polignac, niece of the wife of Comines; this is now no. 20960 in the Bibliothèque Nationale, Nouvelles acquisitions françaises; see Léopold Delisle, *Mélanges de paléographie et de bibliographie*, Paris, 1880, 347-349, the edition of the *Mémoires* by Bernard de Mandrot, *2*, 1903, CIX-CXII, and Paris, Bibliothèque Nationale, *Catalogue général des manuscrits français*, par Henri Omont, Paris, 1918, 243. For other portrayals, including one by Tintoretto, see Del Prato, *op. cit.*, 232-233.

Miss Mongan mentions Benedetti on page 259 and quotes from Domenichi's translation of 1549, 32. On page 256 she reproduces a plan of the battle from Bridge, *op. cit.*, *2*, 1924, facing page 253, whose description of the battle on pages 263-266 and 285-287 is among the most detailed in English. Another plan is furnished by Eugenio Massa in his valuable analysis of the battle in *Rivista militare italiana*, 1912; I know this article through an offprint, numbering 25 pages, which was presented to me by Prof. Dott. Luigi Belloni in 1953. A third plan, a photograph of which is in my possession through the kindness of Francesco Reali of Fornovo, was made by Dante Guidetti, Tenente Colonello di Cavalleria, Reggimento Lancieri di "Aosta," Reggio Emilia.

Perhaps the best-known representation of Charles VIII is the terra cotta bust, by an unknown sculptor, in the Bargello at Florence; Delaborde used it for the frontispiece of his book and inserted in his text several other portraits. To these may be added, for example, those in MS. M 801 of The Pierpont Morgan Library, for which see Ferraiolo, *op. cit.*; the portrait by an unknown painter in the Uffizi Gallery, Florence; those in the Flemish tapestry "The Glorification of Charles VIII," about 1490, which was designed by Jan van Roome, is preserved in The Cloisters in New York, and is described by James J. Rorimer in *The Metropolitan Museum of Art Bulletin*, 1954, *12*, 281-299; and that in the fresco by Guido Ubaldo Abbatini, seventeenth century, in the sacristy of Santo Spirito in Rome. I owe to Pietro De Angelis, librarian of the Biblioteca Lancisiana, the information that the "signature" of Charles in the manuscript *Liber Confraternitatis S. Spiritus et S. Mariae in Saxia de Urbe* is not Charles's but was set down in his presence on 4 June 1495 by Costanzo Guglielmi; cf. Alessandro Canezza and Mario Casalini, *Il Pio istituto di S. Spirito e ospedali riuniti di Roma*, Roma, 21 April 1933, L. Another memorial of Charles in Rome is the church of Trinità dei Monti, which was begun on his order in 1495 and consecrated in 1585 by Sixtus V

126. Bridge, *op. cit.*, 2, 1924, 287 cites Benedetti's figures from Domenichi's translation in the 1863 edition, 82. Comines, *op. cit.*, 3, 1925, 192 states that most of those killed were killed "de coup de main, car je ne croy point que l'artillerie des deux costéz tuast dix hommes et ne dura point le combat ung quart d'heure." He adds that the pursuit lasted three quarters of an hour.

127. Del Prato, *op. cit.*, 247, n.1 points out that although Benedetti says twelve French nobles perished he enumerates by name only nine, and those "con nomi feudali assai alterati." In like manner Italian names proved disconcerting to French writers; Trivulzio, for example, becomes Toussy in the report published by Maulde La Clavière, *op. cit.*, 669. In the "Mémoire particulier fait par une personne d'esprit, *Archives curieuses de l'histoire de France, 1*, 1834, 190 Bembo is accused of being "si impudent, que, pour accroistre le nombre des morts de nostre costé, il forge des noms de seigneurs qui sont incognus en France." But Bembo, *op. cit.*, f.26a says only, "De Francesi morirono da mille: & tra questi il Capitan della guardia del Re, & quello de Balestrieri a cavallo, & quello officiale, che essi gran Maniscalco chiamano: & fino a diece altri Capitani di soldati. Il Bastardo poscia di Borbon, che d'auttorità peraventura appo il Re era il primo; & di gran nome tra Francesi ferito, & due figliuoli di gran Signori, & il Capellano del Re, & altri furono fatti prigioni; non essendo de Vinitiani venuto alcun vivo a mano de Francesi."

128. Guillaume de Villeneuve, "Mémoires," in Michaud and Poujoulat, *op. cit.*, *4*, 1837, 383 states that "n'y fut prins homme de renomée du party de France, que monseigneur le grant bastart de Bourbon, qui moult vaillament et vertueusement se pourta pour le jour, comme bon et hardy chevallier qu'il estoit."

129. The French, says Sanudo, *op. cit.*, 673, "portano gran pantoffe in piedi et molto, in questo tempo, large; et le sue stafe di le selle de li cavali sono longissime; portano li stivali di sopra le schiniere."

130. Luzio and Renier, *op. cit.*, 233 cite Benedetti on the plunder. Spaggiari, *op. cit.*, 38 suggests that it was purposely abandoned by the French to discourage pursuit, just as a man being chased by dogs will throw them a bone and so escape. Sanudo, *op. cit.*, 482 lists some of the plunder but passes over "molte altre cosse, di le qual scrivendo sarebbe tedioso"; cf. page 491.

131. Some of these riches went to followers of the French camp. Charles complains in a letter to the inhabitants of Lyon, 18 July 1495, Asti, ed. Pélicier, 4, 1903, 229-230 that "aucuns vagabonds, gens sans maistre ny adveu qui suivoient nous et nostre armée," had snatched silver, jewels, silks, etc., and he requests that they and their luggage be searched on arrival at Lyon.

132. On the amours of Charles at Lyon before the descent into Italy see Sanudo, *op. cit.*, 47, Pierre Desrey, "Relation du voyage du roy Charles

VIII pour la conqueste du royaume de Naples," in *Archives curieuses de l'histoire de France, 1*, 1834, 204, Delaborde, *op. cit.*, 342, 382-383; for one in Lucca Sanudo, 111; and for those in Naples Sanudo 261-262, 340, 345 and Delaborde, 576-577. On pages 661-662 Delaborde denies that Charles's failure to come to the aid of the Duke of Orléans, besieged in Novara, was due to an amour in Chieri. But cf. Sanudo, 551 and D'Atri, *op. cit.*, 65.

This passage, beginning "In summa praeda," is quoted by Cervetto, *op. cit.*, 108, n.2 from the 1496 Aldine edition, and beginning "Ex regio apparatu," by Gerolamo d'Adda, *Indagini . . . sulla Libreria Visconteo-Sforzesca*, Appendice, 1879, 98 from the same edition. It was used by Corio, Eugène Müntz, *La Renaissance en Italie et en France à l'époque de Charles VIII*, Paris, 1885, 513, Thuasne, *op. cit.*, 102, n.1, Delaborde, 649, n.3, and Bridge, *op. cit.*, 2, 1924, 263.

The whole question of the booty taken from the royal tent is a confused one. Already on 13 August Francesco Gonzaga, Luzio and Renier, *op. cit.*, 235, had returned to Charles "un libretto ed alcune carte de diverse picture, quale [*sic*] se sono retrovate qua." These are acknowledged by Charles in a letter of 17 August, Turin, ed. Pélicier, 4, 1903, 259-260, in which he asks that Gonzaga watch for any other "dessegni" lost by a painter of his and also for "certe reliquie poste in una pichola maiestà d'oro." On 7 December 1495, Lyon, ed. Pélicier, 4, 1903, 321-322, he alerted Gonzaga in addition to "plusieurs paintures de diverses façons et devises que l'un de mes paintres avoit tirées et portraictes où il y avoit aucunes villes et chasteaulx, quartes marines et autres nouvelles choses de pardelà, et semblablement les registres et papiers qui touchent le fait de ma despense." In reply Gonzaga assured him on 29 January 1496, Luzio and Renier, 236, that he had instituted inquiries and would certainly send whatever was recovered.

Other contemporary writers cite various and sometimes the same objects. Luca Pisani, for example, mentions in his letter of 8 July 1495, in Malipiero, *op. cit.*, 1, 1843, 363, "l'altar portabile del Re, l'ancona di zogie, la croseta zoielada che fu del Re Ludovico, il calese, il turibolo, et la campanella d'arzento"; Malipiero, 371, a helmet "tutto coverto dalle bande de cape d'oro con smalti, e de sora de squame d'oro smaltae, e ha in cima una corona con algune zoie," a "spada, fornia d'oro massizzo," a "cassetta massiza d'argento, tre quarte lunga; e do larga, fodrà di veluo celeste. Ghe era dentro un sigillo d'oro massizzo del Re de Franza moderno, e un altro mazzor, pur d'oro, che fo de so padre: e un retratto de so fio de età de tre anni"; and *id.*, 377-378, "un'anconeta d'oro, granda quanto è la palma della man: se avre in do fazze . . . ; ha del legno della Santissima Croce, del velo della vesta della Madona, della vesta del Salvator, della sponza e del ferro della lanza. . . . ; la è adorna de perle e de rubini e de balassi." The writer of the "Relazione," Del Prato, *op. cit.*, 249, speaks of a "colona lavoracta de intalij trasilij oro brustacto chera una bellissima cosa da vedere." Sanudo, *op. cit.*, 543-544, lists "una bellissima reliquia, zoè la anconeta [cf. II.16] che fo dil Re di Franza . . . con zoie et degnissime reliquie, zoè di la vesta di Christo et tutti li misterij di la Passione, cossa di farne grande extimatione; et uno subioto d'oro ch'el Re talhora sonava, chiamando certi chani." Priuli, *op. cit.*, 26 records the King's silver, "la soa chiexia, la sua spada et il suo elmetto."

On display in the Tesoro of San Marco today is an elegantly decorated box of gilded silver over wood which is thought to have been Charles's. My attention was first called to it by Dr. Luigi Gullini; Prof. Giuseppe Mazzariol of the Biblioteca Querini Stampalia provided further information. I quote the description from Antonio Pasini, *Il Tesoro di San Marco in Venezia*, *1*, Venezia, 1886, 85-86, to which the reader is referred for additional discussion and an illustration: "E desso [cofanetto] a base quadra (centimetri quattordici e mezzo per lato) ed alto otto centimetri e mezzo: è in solido legno, tutt'attorno elegantemente legato in argento dorato, e coperto di velluto azzurro [cf. Malipiero, 371, above], il quale fa spiccare cinquantasette fiordalisi dello stesso metallo. La parte superiore, che s'apre a cerniera, presenta nel mezzo un manico mobile, avente all'estremità testine d'animali; due simiglianti manichi sono ai lati. Sul dinnanzi, là dove esservi dovrebbe il pertugio per la chiave, sporge un quadrato, nella parte anteriore del quale veggonsi tre edicolette archiacute; nella centrale sta ritto un principe nimbato e coronato, collo scettro nella destra e coll'*acacia* nella sinistra; alla sua dritta nell'altra edicola una figura alata (che, a quanto pare, s'appoggia ad un albero) tiene disteso un brevi, in cui alcuni segni fatti a capriccio danno a prima vista lusinga di un'iscrizione: dall'opposta parte vedesi una donna." It is mentioned by Ugo Ojetti, *Cose viste*, *2*, Firenze, 1951, 652.

Charles was also concerned in the letter to Francesco Gonzaga, 7 December 1495, Lyon, about the loss at Fornovo of certain medical books which belonged to his physician Théodore Gaynier or Guaynier of Pavia. It may be added that Charles himself possessed at least one medical manuscript which was presented to him and his wife between January 1492 and September 1494 and is now no. 509 in The Pierpont Morgan Library; see Curt F. Bühler and Robert H. Bowers, *Bulletin of the history of medicine*, 1942, *11*, 69-86. It contains Petrus de Abano's treatise on poisons and the lapidary of Franciscus Pamoleus. The Biblioteca Nazionale of Naples has a manuscript of the *Horae B. Mariae Virginis* which was written for Charles, and the Fondazione Giorgio Cini in Venice another executed for him on order of Lodovico Sforza at the time of his expedition into Italy; see Italy, Ministero della Pubblica Istruzione, *Mostra storica nazionale della miniatura*, Palazzo di Venezia, Roma, Catalogo redatto dal Prof. Giovanni Muzzioli, Firenze, 1953, nos. 736 and 662.

133. For reactions in Venice see Sanudo (this time an eyewitness), *op. cit.*, 482-483 and letter of Nicolò Lipomano, 8 July, Malipiero, *op. cit.*, *1*, 1843, 355. It was thought that Charles had been captured. On 8 July 1495 the Senate formulated a letter "Provisoribus generalibus foelicissimi exercitus nostri" which began "El fortissimo et victorioso congresso de questo foelicissimo exercito nostro cum lo exercito inimico facto adi. 6 del Instante et significatone per le vostre del instesso zorno ad hore. 3 de nocte ne ha afferito singular piacer et jucundia de animo . . ."; see Venice, Archivio di Stato, Deliberazioni (1494-1495), Secreta, Senato, Reg. 35, ff. 134v-135 and also dispatches of 8, 9, and 10 July on ff. 137-138. For the announcement of the battle in Naples on 10 July see Ferraiolo, *op. cit.*, 154-155.

134. An early French report of the battle was that sent 7 July from

Medesano by Jacques de Thenray to the Duke of Orléans; see La Pilorgerie, *op. cit.*, 349-350 and cf. Pélicier's edition of Charles's letters, *4*, 1903, 83, n.

135. Comines, *3*, 1925, 197-202 relates the events of Chapter 62 in which he was chief actor. Cf. Sanudo, *op. cit.*, 487-488.

136. According to Villeneuve, *op. cit.*, 383 Charles "tousjours eust la face droit à ses ennemys, l'espée au poing, la bouche plaine de bonnes et vertueuses paroles à ses gens. Et le fait de mesme le cueur plus gros que le corps avecques la fierté de ung lyon, tant que la bataille dura, et après la victoire doulx et begnin comme ung ange, recognoissant la grant grâce que Dieu lui avoit faite." It was said that he was wounded, "mais il fust promptement secouru de bons et hardis cappitaines et autres gens de guerre . . . et aussi de plusieurs gentilshommes qu'il avoit nourris. . . ." According to the report reprinted in Maulde La Clavière, *op. cit.*, 669, "n'y eut homme qui se portast si vertueusement que fist le roy ne en si bonne contenance, et lui fut le clou de sa visiere couppé d'un coup d'espée: dont de tout est eschappé sain et sauve, Dieu mercy." Jean Bouchet, "Panégyric du chevallier sans reproche, Louis de la Trémoïlle," Michaud and Poujoulat, *op. cit.*, *4*, 1837, 437 writes that Charles was victorious "par le secours et bon service dudict seigneur de La Trimoille, et aultres vaillans princes, capitaines, et gens de bien de France."

137. Made "capitano zeneral di mar" 22 June 1494; see Sanudo, *op. cit.*, 61. On 31 December 1495 Sanudo, 129-130, dedicated to him Book II of his account of Charles's expedition.

138. See Sanudo, *op. cit.*, 492 ff. and the letter of Geronimo Contarini in Malipiero, *op. cit.*, *1*, 1843, 372-376.

139. Bembo's report to Grimani on operations in Sicily, dated 15 June 1495, is provided by Sanudo, *op. cit.*, 416-420.

140. Cf. Sanudo, *op. cit.*, 495.

141. Sanudo, *op. cit.*, 488, 489 states that they were burned. Cf. Priuli, *op. cit.*, 28 and Delaborde's statement, *op. cit.*, 654, "Les Italiens ne manquèrent pas de tirer parti de ces feux pour accuser les Français d'y avoir brûlé pêle-mêle leurs morts et leurs blessés." Piero Vettori in a letter to Guido da Montefeltro, duke of Urbino, 14 July 1495, Florence, in Abel Desjardins, ed., *Négociations diplomatiques de la France avec la Toscane*, *1*, Paris, 1859, 625 does not accept the story fully, stating that the "Francesi, si dice (questo non vi dò per cosa certa), che missero tutti li loro morti in tre case, cacciaronvi fuoco e arsenle. . . . Ammazarono tutti li loro prigioni, e tutti li feriti che non gli potevano seguitare."
Charles's journey to Asti is related by Comines, *op. cit.*, *3*, 1925, 202-208; cf. Delaborde, *op. cit.*, 652-657.

142. Cf. Sanudo, *op. cit.*, 489.

143. Sanudo, *op. cit.*, 507 states that the Count of Caiazzo later "andava parlando con quelli Signori per strata, et che quando andò driedo, andò più presto per confortar quei populi di Piasenza et Piasentina che per offender Franzesi." At Tortona Fracasso furnished provisions to the King and talked with him regarding the war. Charles gave him a horse. See also Comines, *op. cit.*, *3*, 1925, 207, Malipiero, *op. cit.*, *1*, 1843, 366, Priuli, *op. cit.*, 28 and n.3, and La Vigne and Saint Gelais, *op. cit.*, 400-401. Fracasso's movements during the Caroline War are recorded in letters to Lodovico Sforza and others dated 20 September 1494-22 August 1495 and published on pages 51-65 of Vittorio Adami's edition of his correspondence, *Miscellanea di storia veneta*, 4, Part 2, 1930. On page 33 Adami states that Fracasso "rappresenta la figura classica del grande capitano di ventura. Invano si cerca nella sua lunga carriera un sentimento di amor patrio; la sua principale ambizione è quella di compiere brillanti operazioni militari e di raccogliere onori e ricchezze."

144. Cf. I.30. Here again there was danger that food, wine, and water might be poisoned; the natives "aisement nous eussent empoisonnéz," says Comines, *op. cit.*, *3*, 1925, 209-210, "s'ilz eussent voullu; . . . mais il est de croire que Nostre Seigneur leur en oustoit le vouloir."

145. According to the "Relazione" published by Del Prato, *op. cit.*, 248-249, the people of Parma assisted the wounded in every way possible, "chi de denari chi de zuchari maniscrista, et coreandri, chi de una medecina chi de una altra, che in vero se li fusseno proprij filij non gli haverebbeno poctucti far magior demonstratione de conpassione."

146. His friend Floriano Dolfi reproved Francesco Gonzaga in the letter of 19 July, Bologna, Luzio and Renier, *op. cit.*, 228-229, for failing to pursue the enemy and acting instead like "el bon medico che cura lo infirmo che non vole guarire et cum ogni disordine et inobedientia mena in lungo la sua infirmitate." "Como può esser," he added, "che lo inimico converso in fuga per le terre del suo hoste a salvamento si conduca per uno grande viagio et ritrovi opportuna victuaria in via?"

147. Sanudo, *op. cit.*, 506.

148. Sanudo, *op. cit.*, 517 relates this incident as follows: "Partito el nostro exercito da Gierola, in campo fo amazà Lorenzo Avogaro, zentilhomo nostro et cittadino di Brexa, era lì in campo franzese, et venuto nel nostro per adatar el conte de Petigliano, et fo incolpà di. . . . et vero. Lo amazò do fratelli, *videlicet* Hannibal et Zuan Antonio Del Denedo."

149. Charles had reported himself victorious at Fornovo in letters of 12 July 1495, Crova, to his sister Anne de Beaujeu, duchess of Bourbon, and of 15 July, Asti, to the inhabitants of Lyon; see Pélicier's edition, *4*, 1903, 227-229. Writing to the Pope on 21 August, Chieri, *ibid.*, 265-266, he again spoke of Fornovo, "in el qual loco piacque a Dio a noi donar la victoria contra quelli che volevano impedir nostro pasazo." "Noi siamo stati malcontenti," he added, "de la effusione del sangue." See also *ibid.*,

275, 282-283. William Thomas, *The history of Italy (1549)*, edited by George B. Parks, Ithaca, New York, 1963, 57 summarized as follows: "But ere ever Charles returned out of the realm of Naples, which was within less than a year after, the Bishop had wrought a new league against him wherein the Emperor Maximilian, the King of Aragon, the Venetians, and the Duke of Milan were his colleagues, so that Charles in his return toward France was fought withal and sore handled." The lengthy letter written by Gilbert Pointet to his brother, 15 July, Asti, is reprinted by La Pilorgerie, *op. cit.*, 351-361; it describes in detail the events during and after the battle from the point of view of a civil servant connected with the baggage train.

150. On 4 September 1495, Turin, ed. Pélicier, 4, 1903, 279-284 Charles wrote to Maximilian complaining of Lodovico Sforza's conduct during the Italian campaign.

151. "Tout allait mal," says Delaborde, *op. cit.*, 657, where Charles was not present. For Ferdinand's return to Naples 7 July see Sanudo, *op. cit.*, 501-503 and cf. 517 ff. Francesco Gonzaga's letter of congratulation, 8 August 1495, Casaleggio, is provided by D'Atri, *op. cit.*, 62-64.

152. According to Sanudo, *op. cit.*, 507 Charles saw that Orsini "andava con lui di malavoia." Vincenzo Celletti in *Gli Orsini di Bracciano*, Roma, 1963, treats of this Virginio, really Gentil Virginio, "conte di Tagliacozzo, signore di Bracciano, Gran Connestabile del regno di Napoli," on pages 30 ff. and, for this period, 43-46. The sentence of excommunication against him, promulgated 2 June 1496 by Alexander VI, is furnished, in part, on page 225.

153. See Sanudo, *op. cit.*, 510-511.

154. For an account of one which occurred before the battle of Fornovo see Sanudo, *op. cit.*, 446, and for a report of Bernardo Contarini's, dated 5 July, Villa Pernate, *ibid.*, 466-468. Lodovico Sforza praises him on page 484 in a letter of 7 July, Milan. See also *ibid.*, 508-510.

# NOTES TO BOOK II

1. Cervetto, *op. cit.*, 74-75 reprints the Argument in the Latin. An Italian translation occurs in Massalongo, *op. cit.*, 232-233.

2. The arrival of the Italians is cited from Benedetti by Calmette in Comines, *op. cit.*, 3, 1925, 212, n.5. Cherrier, *op. cit.*, 2, 1868, 270-318 furnishes an account of the siege of Novara

3. Already late in June there had been scarcity of food in Novara; see Sanudo, *op. cit.*, 411.

4. Rusconi, *op. cit.*, 22 quotes this sentence and the two following sentences from Domenichi's translation in the 1863 edition. Galeazzo Sanseverino had reported to Lodovico Sforza on 7 July 1495 earlier efforts to divert water; see Rusconi, 22-24.

5. Cf. II, note 32.

6. Sanudo, *op. cit.*, 250 states that "secondo el consueto si dette el titolo dil Duca di Milano."

7. In a letter of 28 August 1495, Chieri, ed. Pélicier, 4, 1903, 274 Charles promised assistance to the inhabitants of Novara.

8. Such incidents were frequent. On 23 August, says D'Atri, *op. cit.*, 67, Germans in the service of the Venetians came to blows with Italians "per differentia de una femina," and many were killed. See also D'Atri, 348-349.

9. Sanudo, *op. cit.*, 86 and 88 mentions that already on 21 September 1494 the Duke of Orléans was afflicted with "doppia quartana." Sanudo himself, as he reveals on page 641, fell a victim to quartan fever even as he was writing his history of the expedition. Especially from the month of September 1495 he relied for details of events on Francesco Giorgio, son of Geronimo, who was at Rome; "alio modo, non poria haver compita la verità di questa opera, perchè non potendo inquerir le nove, quelle non poteva scriver."

10. This passage is cited by Delaborde, *op. cit.*, 660 from Domenichi's translation in the 1863 edition.

11. A letter of Benedetti's, written in camp 22 July 1495, is printed in Sanudo, *op. cit.*, 516-517. It reports on conditions in camp, mentions Pietro

Duodo and Luigi Valaresso, and refers to the *Diaria* in the words "In commentariis historiam redegimus, quam expectabis."

12. According to Sanudo, *op. cit.*, 571 a certain Bonino, "stafier di mons. di Serna" (Serva on page 558) was hanged on 31 August.

13. Briona inclined to the French both earlier and later; see the letter of Charles to Lodovico Sforza, 11 January 1496, Lyon, ed. Pélicier, 5, 1905, 1-3 and notes. D'Atri, *op. cit.*, 59 states that it was taken on 29 July.

14. He returned "verso Roma a li suoi castelli"; see Sanudo, *op. cit.*, 543.

15. The list of rewards "a molti benemeriti di la Signoria" is given in Sanudo, *op. cit.*, 524-528 and, at first hand, in the minutes of the Senate for 24 July with introduction "Proprium et ingenitum est institutum Dominii nostri debitis premissis afficere eos omnes, qui pro statu nostro arduum aliquid et laudabile effecerunt"; see Venice, Archivio di Stato, Deliberazioni (1494-1495), Secreta, Senato, Reg. 35, f.144.

16. See Luzio and Renier, *op. cit.*, 226. The Venetian Senate promoted Francesco from "governatore" to "capitano generale" on 27 July. Benedetti describes in Chapter 32 the later ceremony for presentation of the standard. Cf. I.27.

17. Sanudo, *op. cit.*, 480, 481 states that he was badly wounded and would have been killed had not "uno suo ragazo" pulled him away from the fighting. See also *ibid.*, 525-526. His wounds numbered twelve. He was treated in Parma by several unnamed physicians who said there was no hope and in addition by the surgeons Andrea Morandini of Padua and "Giovanni de Tristan" from Verona, who had been his physician for fourteen years, and by physicians from Bologna. Three pieces of bone were removed from his head. On 1 August he reached Venice, and "in brevissimo tempo varite, et andò molto alegramente in Collegio, et tutta la terra have piacer di la sua salute per la sua fideltà." Cf. his own account, Parma, 28 July, of the battle in Malipiero, *op. cit.*, *1*, 1843, 367-370.

18. She had written to Venice the day after her husband's body was brought to her a letter "la qual fece quasi tutti lacrimar"; see Sanudo, *op. cit.*, 524-525, and Malipiero, *op. cit.*, *1*, 1843, 366. She had five children.

19. Called "Zuan Bianco" by Sanudo, *op. cit.*, 527. The house was "in la citadella di Verona."

20. Anne de Bretagne, then aged nineteen.

21. On 4 August, Turin, ed. Pélicier, 4, 1903, 243-244, Charles wrote to the canton of Lucerne requesting 4000-5000 Swiss to assist him in Lombardy. On 12 August he informed the Duke of Bourbon, *ibid.*, 254 that

Swiss were constantly coming into his service. See also *ibid.*, 271, 285. For his relations with the Swiss in 1496 see *ibid.*, 5, 1905.

22. Sanudo, *op. cit.*, 528-530, carries events at Novara to 1 August. Finding then that his manuscript is becoming too long, he begins on page 547 to tell matters briefly day by day for the month of August, saying that although he was not present he will write "tutta la verità, *nil praetermisso che sia da conto.*"

Rusconi, *op. cit.*, 26, n.2 cites Domenichi's translation in the 1863 edition on the swamp, forest, double ditch, and stronghold.

23. Sanudo, *op. cit.*, 515-516 provides a list, 18 July 1495, of forces to be transferred from Vespolate.

24. Six lines sufficed Sanudo, *op. cit.*, 550 for an account of this review. It was "bellissima, et za molti anni non fo fatta simile." He dates it 5 August. The account of D'Atri, *op. cit.*, 61 is also succinct. According to him, "dal tempo de Romani in qua mai fo veduto el magior numero nè le meglio in ordine de zentedarme." Rusconi, *op. cit.*, mentions on page 34 Benedetti's account of the review and the fact that Cesare Morbio did an oil painting of it for the Municipio of Novara. I am indebted to R. Fumagalli, Secretary-Treasurer of the Società Storica Novarese, for the information, in a letter of 28 September 1964, that this painting is now neither in the offices of the Comune of Novara nor in the Musei Civici, but that there does exist a painting by Morbio of the later battle at Novara as a result of which Lodovico Sforza was captured on 10 April 1500 by the French.

25. Galeazzo had worn French dress on 17 April 1494 when he made official entry into Lyon to confer with Charles on behalf of Lodovico; see Delaborde, *op. cit.*, 341. Pezzana, *op. cit.*, 5, 1859, 310 cites this reprimand.

26. The science of deploying marching men with precision in parade or military maneuver is ancient. John Kinloch Anderson discusses an example of wheeling from Xenophon, *Respublica lacedaemoniorum*, 1.11.10, in *Classical Philology*, 1964, 59, 175-178.

27. This information on equipment sent by Lodovico Sforza is used by Rusconi, *op. cit.*, 34 from Domenichi's translation in the 1863 edition.

28. Charles in a letter to Menaud de Guerre, 21 August 1495, Chieri, ed. Pélicier, 4, 1903, 271, mentions that food did reach the city in spite of the blockade. Sanudo, *op. cit.*, 554 states that on the night of 15 August "alcuni cavalli" entered with flour from Vercelli. On 17 August a spy reported, *ibid.*, 555-556, that three hundred horse would come with flour; arrangements were made to intercept these, but they did not appear either that night or the next. Some food was intercepted on 21 August, *ibid.*, 562. Cf. II.40.

29. Rusconi, *op. cit.*, 33 used from Domenichi's translation in the 1863

edition this information on the single well in the stronghold and the fifteen hundred wells dug by the soldiers.

30. French forces at Vercelli on 19 August are listed by Sanudo, *op. cit.*, 558-559.

31. See Sanudo, *op. cit.*, 550: "A dì 9 ditto, nostri corsse et spianò uno castello chiamato Bulgaro, fra Novara e Verzei."

32. Sanudo, *op. cit.*, 551 states that they had only soured wine, which the French nobles drank sugared; grain was ground in five hand mills, but the bread made from this flour was "negrissimo et chativo"; there was only horsemeat, and little of that. When eggs were needed for a Frenchman who had been wounded, the price was thirty soldi each, "cossa incredibile, per non esser galine"; cf. *ibid.*, 554, 561, 565, Priuli, *op. cit.*, 34 and n.1 (where Benedetti is cited from Domenichi's translation in the 1863 edition), and Benedetti, II.2, 39.

On 14 August the Duke of Orléans issued an edict that within three hours all who had no money must leave. The hand mills in a day could grind only enough flour to feed a hundred men. Bembo, *op. cit.*, f.28a says that "gli assediati . . . furono sforzati a mangiarsi i proprii cavalli: & molti di farina corrotta & fracida, & di pane di semola si pascevano, & acqua beeano: la quale acqua da Francesi, & da Tedeschi meno, che da tutti gli altri huomini suole esser beuta volentieri: La onde molti di loro ne morivano."

33. For the letter of 5 August threatening excommunication see Sanudo, *op. cit.*, 547 and Malipiero, *op. cit.*, 1, 1843, 383-389. Malipiero, 391-393 provides the letter of 21 August in which the Pope thanked Venice for freeing Italy from the French.

34. Sanudo, *op. cit.*, 552, 555, 556 also mentions this flux. According to D'Atri, *op. cit.*, 66-67 the Venetian Senate urged him to leave the camp and seek treatment elsewhere, but he felt it his duty to remain.

35. This and the following sentence are quoted by Rusconi, *op. cit.*, 34 from Domenichi's translation in the 1863 edition. Charles in a letter to Menaud de Guerre, 21 August 1495, Chieri, ed. Pélicier 4, 1903, 272 mentions the burning of villages between Novara and the Ticino.

36. By a spingard, according to Sanudo, *op. cit.*, 553.

37. Cf. I.27, II.10. According to Luzio and Renier, *op. cit.*, 226 Francesco Gonzaga described the following ceremony in a letter to his wife dated 15 August. Sanudo recounts it on pages 552-553 and reports that Gonzaga, in replying to the presentation speech by Giorgio Emo, concluded with the statements "Nel corpo di mia madre era servidor de la prefata Illustrissima Signoria. Potrà haver uno capetanio più praticho de mi, ma di fede tale mai lo troverà al mondo." Cf. the accounts of D'Atri, *op. cit.*,

64-65, Malipiero, *op. cit.*, *1*, 1843, 381, Priuli, *op. cit.*, 35 and Segre's n.2 which describes the "dietroscena" which preceded.

Andrea Mantegna's great altarpiece, "La Madonna della Vittoria," which was vowed by Francesco during the battle, was triumphantly conveyed on the first anniversary of the battle, 6 July 1496, to the church constructed for it in Mantua, was removed from there in 1797, and is now preserved in the Louvre, is described, with bibliography, in *Andrea Mantegna, Catalogo della mostra* [Mantova, Palazzo Ducale] *a cura di Giovanni Paccagnini*. . . . Mantova, Comitato della mostra di Andrea Mantegna, Seconda edizione, 24 settembre 1961, 60, no.40 and plates 55-57; see also Alessandro Luzio, "La 'Madonna della Vittoria' del Mantegna," in *Emporium*, 1899, *10*, 358-374 and Luzio and Renier, *op. cit.*, 227.

The catalogue of the Mostra also describes busts of Francesco in terra cotta, possibly by Giancristoforo Romano and Giovanni Minelli respectively, on pages 151-152, nos. 108-109 and plates 126-127. The second bust was set in 1514 by the Mantuan physician Giovan Battista Fiera under the arch of the Porta Nuova in Mantua. Both busts are now in the Palazzo Ducale.

38. On 27 July Isabella d'Este Gonzaga had sent to Francesco provisions "quali pure goderà per mio amore: perchè se bene la dica non esser uso in campo a simili pasti, non dubito però che la manzi malvolentieri del bono quando gli ne viene mandato"; see Luzio and Renier, *op. cit.*, 226, n.4.

39. See Sanudo, *op. cit.*, **554**.

40. After the peace of 9 October 1495 Antonio Maria Sanseverino did indeed offer his services to Charles, who in a letter to Lodovico Sforza, 15 October, Crescentino, ed. Pélicier, 4, 1903, 305-306 wrote that he had accepted them and on 1 December, Lyon, *ibid.*, 319-320, thanked the Duke of Ferrara for his kindness to Sanseverino.

41. According to Sanudo, *op. cit.*, 561 this sum was agreed upon after Pitigliano had refused 44,000 and then 48,000, "dicendo meritava più."

42. This passage is cited by Delaborde, *op. cit.*, 665. Sanudo, *op. cit.*, 561 states that Ebenstein was "molto reverito" by the Germans and that "si questo non fusse, in campo non si poria governar todeschi."

43. See Sanudo, *op. cit.*, 563-564 and Malipiero, *op. cit.*, *1*, 1843, 382 for this episode. They differ in details.

44. Sanudo, *op. cit.*, 562-563 differs in details.

45. Sanudo, *op. cit.*, 560.

46. Sanudo, *op. cit.*, 565.

47. A similar device is mentioned by Sanudo, *op. cit.*, 557.

48. Cf. II, note 32.

49. Cf. II.28 and Sanudo, *op. cit.*, 565-566, 567. Comines, *op. cit.*, 3, 1925, 221 assigns these efforts to a certain Chastillon, "jeune gentilhomme de la maison du roy"; this was Jacques II, lord of Chatillon. See also D'Atri, *op. cit.*, 67-68.

50. Rusconi, *op. cit.*, 22 cites Domenichi's translation in the 1863 edition for the fact that on 28 August help was sent to prevent Fontaneto from falling into the hands of the French.

51. Sanudo, *op. cit.*, 568 and D'Atri, *op. cit.*, 68.

52. D'Atri, *op. cit.*, 334-335. This church, he says, was a monastery of the order of St. Francis.

53. The agreement, formally concluded in Turin 26 August and ratified in Florence 7 September, was announced to the Florentines by Charles in a letter of 16 August, Turin, ed. Pélicier, 4, 1903, 255-257; see *ibid.*, 272 for Charles's statement on 21 August concerning the Florentines, "Sono amici de' miei amici et nemici de' miei nemici." See also *ibid.*, 296-297, 310-311, 312, 323-325. For his relations with the Florentines in 1496 see the relevant letters, *ibid.*, 5, 1905. It would seem that the letter published there in the Supplement, 258-262, should be dated a year later, 29 August 1495.

54. This passage is cited by Delaborde, *op. cit.*, 663. Cf. Sanudo, *op. cit.*, 598-599.

55. Earlier he "si fece uno pocho di mal a una gamba," according to Sanudo, *op. cit.*, 568. D'Atri's account, *op. cit.*, 335-336 of the almost mortal wound is brief: "Essendoli andato il Conte de Pitigliano per sollecitare ch'el borgo [de San Nazario] se fortificasse, gli fo tracto da uno schiopetto voltandose in dreto lo accolse in la schena apresso la centura e passatoli el zuppone de piastre ch'el portava remanendoli la balotta dentro non senza periculo de morte, cum grande despiacere de Francesco." Malipiero, *op. cit.*, 1, 1843, 389 states merely that "'l Conte de Pitigian, Governador General, è stà ferio de schiopo in una cossa." See also the letter of Melchiorre Trevisan, 13 September, *ibid.*, 390. Guazzo, *op. cit.*, gives an account on f.213b.

56. Benedetti mentioned "siliqua Aegyptia" in the letter to Jacopo Contarini, 24 June 1493, which is prefixed to his *De observatione in pestilentia;* see, for example, the edition in Rhazes, *De ratione curandi pestilentiam*, Parisiis, 1528, f.Ela. Both Egyptian carob and Syrian scammony were in common use as purgatives.

57. This entire episode of Pitigliano's wound is quoted from the 1549 edition of the Italian translation by Francesco Pellegrini, *La medicina militare nel regno di Napoli*, Verona, 1932, 245-247 as an example of early

skill in diagnosis. A summary of it in German based on Eckhart's Latin edition of 1723 is provided by Heinrich Buess in *Vierteljahrsschrift für schweizerische Sanitätsoffiziere*, 1957, *34*, 316-317. According to Cervetto, *op. cit.*, 75-76 it puts Benedetti before Hieronymus Brunschwig, the first edition of whose *Cirurgia* was published at Strassburg 4 July 1497, Goff B-1225. But Pellegrini makes the point that Benedetti called himself *physicus*, not surgeon, that surgeons were summoned from Pavia and Milan, and that in I.56 he speaks of "vulnerum *medicis*."

About 14 September Pitigliano is said by Sanudo, *op. cit.*, 607 to have been in Milan for treatment of a "tumefaction." By 3 October, *ibid.*, 623 he was improving; "la ballotta era redutta do deda a presso la piaga." On 5 October, *ibid.*, 625 five hundred ducats were sent to him "per spender in curarse de la egritudine." The proveditors visited him on their way back to Venice, *ibid.*, 628. Late in October, *ibid.*, 649 and Malipiero, *op. cit.*, *1*, 1843, 399, he came by the Po to Chioggia, where he was received with honors and a Latin oration; since he did not understand Latin, this was repeated in the vernacular. Two physicians accompanied him, sent by Lodovico Sforza "per medicarlo *continue*." At Venice he lodged in a house near Sanudo's. Giovanni dall'Aquila and Girolamo dalla Torre, or Turriani, of Verona were again summoned from Padua, but the shot could not be located. He was sometimes in bed, sometimes not. On 6 November he visited the Arsenale, *ibid.*, 653, which Comines too, *Mémoires*, *3*, 1925, 112-113, had seen on his arrival in Venice, "et altre bellissime cosse si mostra a' forestieri quando veneno in questa terra." But he was not cured, and he remained under treatment. On 19 November, Sanudo, 656-657, which the astrologers considered a favorable day (cf. page 607), the insignia of "governador di le zente nostre" were conferred upon him in a ceremony at the church of San Marco. He departed from Venice on 24 November.

58. Rusconi, *op. cit.*, 37 cites this information from Domenichi's translation in the 1863 edition. According to Bembo, *op. cit.*, f.28a, the Duke of Orléans "havea fatto battere . . . una moneta di rame, per essernegli mancante le altre, laquale per una d'argento valesse." Rusconi, 45-47 points out that any coins struck under conditions of siege must have been poorly minted and that three elegant types reported by Carlo Morbio must therefore be spurious. He considers genuine, however, two medals of victory struck by Lodovico Sforza and described by Pietro Caire.

59. According to Sanudo, *op. cit.*, 570, he had been carried on 28 August to Vigevano to be cured of a high fever.

60. This passage is cited by Delaborde, *op. cit.*, 666.

61. The negotiations for peace are related by Comines, *op. cit.*, *3*, 1925, 224-243 and Malipiero, *op. cit.*, *1*, 1843, 395 ff.

62. D'Atri, *op cit.*, 335

63. *Ibid.*, 338 ff.

64. Delaborde, *op. cit.*, 667 refers the reader for the events immediately preceding to Domenichi's translation in the 1863 edition, 204-214, which is here II.46-51.

65. Sanudo, *op. cit.*, 571 mentions illness and death among both men and horses.

66. According to Sanudo, *op. cit.*, 608 they could not go to Vercelli because the bridge over the Sesia had been washed out; cf. Chapter 55.

67. The conduct of the Spanish ambassador as related here and in Chapter 55 is cited by Delaborde, *op. cit.*, 667-668.

68. Sanudo, *op. cit.*, 608 ff. treats in detail the making of the peace.

69. Sanudo, *op. cit.*, 607.

70. By a letter of 30 September 1495, Vercelli, ed. Pélicier, 4, 1903, 299, Charles sent a representative to discuss the matter of Francesco Secco with Francesco Gonzaga. Cf. Sanudo, *op. cit.*, 611.

71. He had been appointed 6 April; see Sanudo, *op. cit.*, 290.

72. Some of Charles's financial difficulties are related in letters to the Duke of Bourbon, 5 and 10 September 1495, Turin, ed. Pélicier, 4, 1903, 284-287, 289-292. See also *ibid.*, 5, 1905, 269-271.

73. The credentials empowering Philippe de Comines to discuss the peace with Lodovico Sforza were furnished by Charles in a letter to Lodovico 28 September 1495, Vercelli, ed. Pélicier, 4, 1903, 298. On events at Novara see also Ferraiolo, *op. cit.*, 155, 185, 188.

74. This information is quoted by Rusconi, *op. cit.*, 38 from Domenichi's translation in the 1863 edition.

75. The Senate's loyalty to the league as related here and in Chapter 64 is cited by Delaborde, *op. cit.*, 669.

76. Treated with all courtesy in the castle at Mantua since his capture, Mathieu was ordered released on 26 September by Francesco Gonzaga; see Luzio and Renier, *op. cit.*, 220, n.5.

77. Charles had written him 23 September 1495, Vercelli, 4, 1903, 295 requesting his assistance in the negotiations with Lodovico Sforza and the Venetians.

78. Anticipating this meeting Gonzaga on 21 September had asked his wife to send him specially fine clothes for the occasion; see Luzio and Renier, *op. cit.*, 246. Sanudo, *op. cit.*, 625 states that he was received "molto *honorifice.*" See also La Vigne and Saint Gelais, *op. cit.*, 419.

79. According to La Vigne and Saint Gelais, *loc. cit.*, Charles gave him "ung moult beau courcier qu'il avoit achapté du bastard de Liége." Sometime after Fornovo Francesco Gonzaga had requested of Charles the return of three horses. Charles replied 24 July 1495, Asti, ed. Pélicier, 4, 1903, 232, saying that he was sending one horse and would send the other two if they were found. D'Atri, *op. cit.*, 350-351 relates that to reciprocate Charles's gift Gonzaga sent two steeds, both bay, one of which "faceva salti cum tutti quatro li pedi ad un tempo." Good horses were of course valued highly in this period; cf. Comines' description, *op. cit.*, 3, 1925, 175 of the horse which Charles rode at Fornovo, "le plus beau cheval que j'aye veü de mon temps, appellé Savoye . . . et estoit noir et n'avoit que ung oeil."

80. Trivulzio's son came to the Venetian camp on 6 October with thirty horses.

81. The Genoese citadel is the subject of a letter to Charles from the Duke of Ferrara dated 8 and of two dated 12 November 1495, Genoa, ed. Pélicier, 4, 1903, 351-355. He took possession on 12 November. For his relations with Charles in 1496 see the relevant letters, *ibid.*, 5, 1905.

82. Prince Miolans had not yet been restored on 18 October, when Charles wrote Lodovico Sforza from Chieri, ed. Pélicier, 4, 1903, 306 urging his release. Charles was also concerned that terms regarding the fleet at Genoa had not been put into effect. Two days later, *ibid.*, 309-310, he thanked Lodovico for stopping at his request three carracks which had been chartered to Ferdinand, but on 2 November, *ibid.*, 316-317, he had to write again on the matter from Grenoble. Charles's letters of 1496, ed. Pélicier, 5, 1905, record additional infractions of the peace.

83. The French text of the treaty of 10 October 1495 between Charles and Lodovico Sforza is published, for example, in Jean Dumont, *Corps universel diplomatique du droit des gens*, 3, Part 2, Amsterdam, 1726, 331-333; cf. Jaligny, *op. cit.*, 722-727. For the Latin text see Lünig, *op. cit.*, 2, 1726, coll. 1303-1308.

84. On the next day, 10 October, Charles informed Lodovico Sforza in a letter from Vercelli, ed. Pélicier, 4, 1903, 301-302, that he had signed the treaty. In the same letter he expressed a desire to see Francesco Gonzaga before that general departed.

85. For the successive stops see Sanudo, *op. cit.*, 627 ff.

86. "Qui a Vegevene," says Sanudo, *op. cit.*, 628, "fece un bel pasto a ditti nostri Provedadori."

87. According to Sanudo, *op. cit.*, 645 he felt himself obligated to the Signoria "*dum spiritus regeret artus.*"

88. According to Sanudo, *op. cit.*, 629, "li manchava uno ochio [cf.

I, note 123 for Pietro Busichio, "monoculo"], era di età di zercha anni 50."
He had fallen ill in camp and was carried to Pavia.

89. On 17 October, at word of pest in Siena and Florence, it was announced on the Piazza and at Rialto that no one from those territories could enter Venice *"pro nunc"*; see Sanudo, *op. cit.*, 648.

90. Sanudo, *op. cit.*, 653 states that they arrived in Mantua 8 November. The games included a contest between a lion and a bull "ch'è bellissimo veder." D'Atri, *op. cit.*, 352 states that Gonzaga entered Mantua with the proveditors 1 November; he does not mention the games.

91. See Sanudo, *op. cit.*, 654.

92. Comines had come 4 November from Milan regarding the peace. The Doge, on greeting him, exclaimed that he had grown thin; see Sanudo, *op. cit.*, 651. Comines replied that this was the result of war, and that earlier, when he had been living in Venice as French ambassador, he had eaten heartily under her hospitality. See his *Mémoires*, 3, 1925, 106-115 for his impressions when he first arrived in Venice 2 October 1494 and cf. I, note 69. A year later, on 4 November 1495, *ibid.*, 248 he termed Venice "la plus reverente cité que j'aye jamais veü aux choses ecclesiastic-ques, et qui ont leurs eglises myeulx parées et acoustrées."

93. D'Atri, *op. cit.*, 353. Francesco "mai se recordava havere veduto tanta multitudine de zente, nè magiore demostracione de leticia." Cf. Priuli, *op. cit.*, 40 and Segre's n.1.

94. "Ben contento," says D'Atri, *loc. cit.*, "cum universale leticia et consolacione de tutti."

95. The passage "verum multa . . . saepenumero maturare" is quoted in the Latin by Apostolo Zeno, *Dissertazioni vossiane*, 2, 1753, 45, with the introductory words, "si scusa di aver taciute più cose, gloriose bensì per la Repubblica ma ignominiose per altri, e pericolose per lui." The entire letter is reprinted in the Latin in *Bibliotheca Smithiana* . . . , 1755, Part 3, CCLXXXIX-CCXC.

96. This sentence is rendered into Italian from the Latin by Massa-longo, *op. cit.*, 231: "Contento della mia semplicità, dettai più concisamente e speditamente che non avessi promesso quand'ero alla guerra; e le posi insieme con cura pari al diletto pur in mezzo a così gravi confusioni, perchè non perisse, con non lieve torto ai posteri, la notizia di tanto immane calamità, ricacciata oltr' Alpe dalla subitanea forza dei Veneziani."

97. Rinaldo Fulin, *Archivio veneto*, 1882, 23, 123-124 (no.50) documents this privilege from the Notatorio del Collegio in the Archivio di Stato at Venice under date of 26 June 1496: "Alessandro Benedetti; 'physico da Verona', compose 'la historia gallica'. Nel publicarla, e così per il latino come per il volgare, chiede ed ottiene un privilegio di dieci anni. I contravventori perdano i libri e paghino un ducato per copia."

# LITERATURE CONSULTED

Abano, Petrus de. See: Petrus de Abano.

Adami, Vittorio. See: Sanseverino, Gaspare.

Adda, Gerolamo d'. *Indagini storiche, artistiche, e bibliografiche sulla Libreria Visconteo-Sforzesca del Castello di Pavia.* Parte prima, Milano, G. Brigola, 1875. Appendice, Milano, Presso i principali libraj, 1879.

Adelmann, Howard B. The fence. *The American Scholar,* 1943, *13,* 14-25. The quotation in my Preface is from page 15.

Adria, Jacopo d'. See: Atri, Jacopo d'.

Ady, Cecilia M. The invasions of Italy. In: *The new Cambridge modern history, 1,* 1957,* 343-367.

Alessandro Benedetti, anatomo e medico militare del quattrocento. *Il giardino di Esculapio,* 1952, *21,* 41-52.

Allen, Don Cameron. *The star-crossed Renaissance.* The quarrel about astrology and its influence in England. Durham, North Carolina, Duke University Press, 1941.

Allut, Paul. *Étude biographique & bibliographique sur Symphorien Champier.* Lyon, Chez Nicolas Scheuring, 1859.

Amelot de la Houssaie, Abraham-Nicolas. *Histoire du gouvernement de Venise.* Amsterdam, Chez Pierre Mortier, 1695. 3 vols. The quotation in my Preface is from *1,* f. **6a.

Anderson, John Kinloch. Xenophon *Respublica lacedaemoniorum,* 1.11.10. *Classical Philology,* 1964, 59, 175-178.

Angiolgabriello di Santa Maria (Paolo Calvi). *Biblioteca, e storia di quei scrittori così della città come del territorio di Vicenza.* Vicenza, G. B. Vendramini Mosca, 1772-1782. 6 vols.

Aretinus, Leonardus. See: Bruni, Leonardo.

Argelati, Filippo. *Bibliotheca scriptorum mediolanensium.* Mediolani, in aedibus Palatinis, 1745. 2 vols. in 4.

*L'art de vérifier les dates.* Paris, Moreau, 1818-1844. 42 vols.

Astruc, Jean. *Mémoires pour servir à l'histoire de la Faculté de Médecine de Montpellier;* revus & publiés par M. Lorry. Paris, P. G. Cavelier, 1767.

————. *A treatise of venereal diseases, in nine books.* London, Printed for W. Innys and others, 1754.

---

* The year is given after the volume number with monographs; the practice is reversed for serials.

Atri, Jacopo d'. Croniche del marchese di Mantova, ed. Carlo E. Visconti. *Archivio storico lombardo*, 1879, *6*, 38-68, 333-356, 500-513.

Aubert, Félix. *Histoire du Parlement de Paris de l'origine à François I^er, 1250-1515*. Paris, A. Picard et fils, 1894. 2 vols.

Auton, Jehan d'. *Chroniques de Louis XII*. Édition pub. pour la Société de l'Histoire de France par R. de Maulde La Clavière. Paris, Librairie Renouard, 1889-1895. 4 vols.

Avesani, Rino and Peebles, Bernard M. Studies in Pietro Donato Avogaro of Verona. *Italia medioevale e umanistica*, 1962, *5*, 1-84.

Avicenna. *Liber canonis*. . . . Venetiis, apud Juntas, 1582.

Bartolotti, Gian Giacomo. See: Tortelli, Giovanni.

Barzini, Luigi. *The Italians*. London, Hamish Hamilton, 1964.

Baschet, Armand. *La diplomatie vénitienne*. Les princes de l'Europe au xvi^e siècle. François I^er, Philippe II, Catherine de Médecis, les papes, les sultans etc. etc. d'après les rapports des ambassadeurs vénitiens. Paris, Henri Plon, 1862.

Bayard, lord of (Du Terrail, Pierre). See: Mailles, Jacques de.

Becker, Felix. See: Thieme, Ulrich.

Belloni, Luigi. Storia della medicina a Milano. In: *Storia di Milano* della Fondazione Treccani degli Alfieri [Milano] *11*, 1958, 595-696 and *16*, 1962, 933-1028.

——. See also: Morgagni, Giovanni Battista; Tortelli, Giovanni.

Bembo, Pietro. *Della historia vinitiana . . . volgarmente scritta, libri XII*. Vinegia, appresso Gualtero Scotto, 1552.

Benedetti, Alessandro. De pestilentiali febre. In: Rhazes, *De ratione curandi pestilentiam*. Parisiis, 1528, ff. 17-42b.

——. De pestilenti febre. In: Schiller, Joachim, *De peste brittanica*, Basileae, 1531, pp. 25-60.

——. Diaria de bello carolino [Venice, Aldus Manutius, Romanus, after 27 August 1496.]

——. De bello venetorum, cum Carolo VIII. gallorum rege, anno M.CCCCXCVI. gesto. lib. II. In: Giustiniani, Pietro. *Rerum venetarum ab urbe condita ad annum M.D.LXXV. historia*, Argentorati, 1611, Appendix, ff.Glb-I3a.

——. De rebus a Carolo VIII. Galliae rege in Italia gestis. Libri duo. In: Eckhart, Johann Georg von, *Corpus historicorum medii aevi*, 2, Lipsiae, 1723, coll.1577-1628.

——. *Il fatto d'arme del Tarro fra i principi italiani, et Carlo ottavo re di Francia, insieme con l'assedio di Novara*, tradotto per Messer Lodovico Domenichi. In Vinegia, appresso Gabriel Giolito de Ferrari, 1549.

——. ——. Edizione precisa alla pubblicata dal Giolito in Venezia nel MDXLIX e dedicata ai Cittadini Novaresi. Novara, Antonio Crosa e Carlo Moscotti, 1863.

——. *Historia corporis humani sive anatomice*. Venetiis, Bernardinus Guerraldus Vercellensis, 1502.

————. *Anatomice sive historia corporis humani. Eiusdem collectiones medicinales seu aforismi.* Parisiis, Henricus Stephanus, 1514.

————. *Anatomice, sive de hystoria corporis humani, libri quinque. Eiusdem Aphorismorum liber. Aphorismi Damascaeni. Hippocratis iusiurandum.* Argentorati, apud Iohannem Hervagium, 1528.

————. *Omnium a vertice ad calcem morborum signa, causae, indicationes & remediorum compositiones utendique rationes, generatim libris XXX conscripta. Praeterea Aphorismorum lib.I. De pestilentiae causis, praeservatione, & auxiliorum materia lib.I. Humani corporis anatome, tractata lib.V.* Basileae, per Henricum Petrum, 1539.

————. Medicinalium observationum rara exempla. In: Dodoens, Rembert, *Medicinalium observationum exempla rara,* Coloniae, 1581, 294-306.

————, editor. See: Panteo, Giovanni Antonio; Plinius Secundus, C.

Biancolini, Giambatista. *Cronica della città di Verona,* descritta da Pier Zagata, ampliata e supplita da G. B. Verona, D. Ramanzini, 1745-1749. 2 vols. in 3.

Biblioteca Apostolica Vaticana. See: Vatican City.

Bibliothèque Nationale. See: Paris.

*Biografia universale antica e moderna.* Venezia, Missiaglia, 1822-1832. 65 vols. in 33.

Bisacco, Alfonso. *La chiesa di S. Pantaleone in Venezia.* Venezia, Grafiche Sorteni, 1933.

Bishop, Morris. *Petrarch and his world.* Bloomington, Indiana University Press, 1963.

Boerner, Friedrich. *Commentarius de Alexandro Benedicto medico.* Brunsvigae, 1751.

————. *Noctes guelphicae sive opuscula argumenti medico-literarii.* Rostochii et Wismariae, Apud Io. Andr. Bergerum et Iac. Boednerum, 1755.

Bolgar, Robert Ralph, *The classical heritage and its beneficiaries.* Cambridge, University Press, 1954.

Bonet, Théophile. *Bibliothèque de médecine et de chirurgie.* Genève, Compagnie des libraires, 1708. 4 vols.

Bongi, Salvatore. *Annali di Gabriel Giolito de' Ferrari da Trino di Monferrato, stampatore in Venezia.* Roma, presso i principali librai, 1890-1895. 2 vols. (Ministero della pubblica istruzione, Indici e cataloghi, 11.)

Bosatra, Andrea and Candiani, V. Note e commenti su Alessandro Benedetti, anatomico e medico dell'Ateneo padovano del XV secolo; con particolare riguardo per la rinoplastica. *Minerva medica,* 1955, *46* (2, n.54, 7 luglio). Reprint, 8 p.

Bouchet, Jean. Panégyric du chevallier sans reproche, Louis de la Trémoïlle. In: Michaud, Joseph François and Poujoulat, Jean Joseph François, *Nouvelle collection des mémoires pour servir à l'histoire de France,* 1. série, 4, Paris, 1837, 403-478.

Bowers, Robert H. See: Bühler, Curt F.

Boyd, Julian. *The first duty.* An address delivered at the opening of an exhibition of the Arthur H. and Mary Marden Dean Collection of Lafayette at Cornell University on April 17, 1964. The Cornell University Library, 1964. The quotation in my Preface is from page 4.

————. A modest proposal to meet an urgent need. *American Historical Review,* 1965, *70,* 329-349. (Presidential address before the American Historical Association, Washington, D.C., 29 December 1964.)

Brenzoni, Raffaello. *Fra Giovanni Giocondo veronese.* Firenze, Leo S. Olschki, 1960.

Bridge, John Seargeant Cyprian. *A history of France from the death of Louis XI.* Oxford, Clarendon Press, 1921-1936. 5 vols.

British Museum. See: London.

Bruni, Leonardo (Aretinus, Leonardus), *Epistolarum familiarium libri VIII.* [Venice, Damianus de Mediolano, de Gorgonzola, in part by Petrus de Quarengiis] 15 June 1495.

Bruno, A. See: *Nuovo dizionario.*

Bühler, Curt F. Aldus Manutius: the first five hundred years. *Papers of the Bibliographical Society of America,* 1950, *44,* 205-215. (Slightly revised version of the Trumbull Lecture delivered at Yale University 27 October 1949.)

————. Savonarola's arrest and the theft of a book: Libri impressi cum notis manuscriptis, VII. *Renaissance News,* 1954, *7,* 95-97.

————. Stop-press and manuscript corrections in the Aldine edition of Benedetti's *Diaria de bello carolino. Papers of the Bibliographical Society of America,* 1949, *43,* 365-373.

————. The thirteenth recorded manuscript of the *Cronaca di Partenope. Publications of the Modern Language Association of America,* 1952, *67,* 580-584.

———— and Bowers, Robert H. A medical manuscript presented to Charles VIII of France. *Bulletin of the History of Medicine,* 1942, *11,* 69-86.

Buess, Heinrich. Der Feldzugsbericht des Humanistenarztes Alessandro Benedetti (ca.1450-1512). *Vierteljahrsschrift für schweizerische Sanitätsoffiziere,* 1957, *34,* 313-319.

Bunnètt, Fanny Elizabeth. See: Grimm, Herman Friedrich.

Buonarroti, Michelangelo. *The letters.* Translated from the original Tuscan, edited & annotated in two volumes by E. H. Ramsden. Stanford University Press, 1963. 2 vols.

Burchard, Johann. *Liber notarum ab anno MCCCCLXXXIII usque ad annum MDVI* a cura di Enrico Celani. Città di Castello, S. Lapi, 1907-1942. 2 vols. (*Rerum italicarum scriptores.* Raccolta degli storici italiani dal cinquecento al millecinquecento ordinata da L. A. Muratori . . . Nuova edizione, t.32, p. 1, vol. 1.)


Calmette, Joseph. See: Comines, Philippe de.

*The Cambridge modern history.* Cambridge, University Press, 1902-1912. 13 vols. and atlas.

Camerani, Sergio. *Bibliografia medicea.* Firenze, Leo S. Olschki, 1964. (Biblioteca di bibliografia italiana, 45.)

Camerini, Paolo. *Annali dei Giunti.* Firenze, Sansoni, 1962, 1963. vol. 1, parts 1, 2. (Biblioteca bibliografica italica, diretta da Marino Parenti.)

Candiani, V. See: Bosatra, Andrea.

Canestrini, Giuseppe. See: Desjardins, Abel.

Canezza, Alessandro and Casalini, Mario. *Il Pio istituto di S. Spirito e ospedali riuniti di Roma.* Roma, Istituto editoriale di monografie illustrate di aziende, 21 April 1933.

Casalini, Mario. See: Canezza, Alessandro.

Casetti, Antonio and Imbriani, Vittorio. *Canti popolari delle provincie meridionali* raccolti da A.C. e V.I. Torino, Ermanno Loescher, 1871-1872. 2 vols. (*Canti e racconti del popolo italiano* pubblicati per cura di D. Comparetti e A. D'Ancona, vol. 2-3.)

Castiglione, Baldassare. *Il libro del cortegiano.* A cura di Vittorio Cian. Firenze, Sansoni, 1947.

Castiglioni, Arturo. The origin and development of the anatomical theater to the end of the Renaissance. *Ciba Symposia,* 1941, *3,* 826-844.

———. La scuola medica di Padova. *Rivista Ciba,* 1949, *19,* 606-640.

Catalano, Franco. La crisi politica e sociale di fronte al "barbaro." In: *Storia di Milano* della Fondazione Treccani degli Alfieri, [Milano], 7, 1956, 415-508.

Celani, Enrico. See: Burchard, Johann.

Celletti, Vincenzo. *Gli Orsini di Bracciano.* Roma, Fratelli Palombi, 1963.

Cervetto, Giuseppe. *Appendice ai Cenni per una nuova storia delle scienze mediche.* Verona, G. Antonelli, 1842.

———. *Cenni per una nuova storia delle scienze mediche,* letti alla sezione medica della seconda riunione degli scienziati italiani in Torino. Verona, G. Antonelli, 1841.

———. *Di alcuni celebri anatomici italiani del decimoquinto secolo.* Edizione seconda. Brescia, Tipografia di G. Venturini, 1854.

———. *Lettera al profess. Giacom'Andrea Giacomini relativa ad una orazione del prof. Francesco Cortese sul Teatro anatomico di Padova.* Verona, G. Antonelli, 1845.

Cestaro, Benvenuto. Domenichi, Lodovico. In: *Enciclopedia italiana, 13,* 1932, 114.

Champier, Symphorien. *Index librorum in hoc volumine contentorum.* Libelli duo primus de medicine claris scriptoribus . . . secundus de legum divinarum conditoribus. . . . De corporum animorumque morbis. . . . Collectiones medicinales. . . . Alexandri Benedicti veronensis Aphorismi sive collectiones. . . . Lyon, Jannot de Campis, c.1506.

———. *Que in hoc opusculo habentur.* Duellum epistolare: Gallie & Italie antiquitates summatim complectens. Tropheum Christianissimi Galliarum regis Francisci huius nominis primi. Item complures illustrium virorum epistole ad dominum Symphorianum Camperium. Venetiis, Jacobus Franciscus de Jonta, 1519.

————. See also: Allut, Paul.

Charles VIII. *Lettres de Charles VIII roi de France.* Publiées d'après les originaux pour la Société de l'Histoire de France par Paul Pélicier. Paris, Librairie Renouard, 1898-1905. 5 vols. (vol. 5 by P. Pélicier and Bernard de Mandrot.)

Cherrier, Claude Joseph de. *Histoire de Charles VIII roi de France.* Paris, Didier et C^{ie}, 1868. 2 vols.

Chevalier, Cyr Ulysse Joseph. *Répertoire des sources historiques du moyen age.* Bio-bibliographie. Nouv. éd. Paris, A. Picard, 1905-1907. 2 vols.

Chiocco, Andrea. *De collegii veronensis illustribus medicis.* Veronae, typis A. Tami. 1623.

Choulant, Ludwig. *Handbuch der Bücherkunde für die ältere Medicin.* Leipzig, Verlag von Leopold Voss, 1841.

Cian, Vittorio. See: Castiglione, Baldassare.

Ciapponi, Lucia A. Appunti per una biografia di Giovanni Giocondo da Verona. *Italia medioevale e umanistica,* 1961, 4, 131-158.

Cicogna, Emmanuele Antonio. *Delle inscrizioni veneziane.* Venezia, G. Orlandelli [and] l'Autore, 1824-1861. 6 vols. in 7.

————. *Saggio di bibliografia veneziana.* Venezia, dalla Tipografia di G. B. Merlo, 1847.

————. See also: Soranzo, Girolamo.

Colucci, Giuseppe. *Delle antichità picene.* Fermo, l'autore, 1786-1797. 31 vols.

Comines, Philippe de. *Mémoires.* Nouvelle édition, publiée avec une introduction et des notes . . . par B. de Mandrot. Paris, Alphonse Picard et fils, 1901-1903. 2 vols. (Collection de textes pour servir à l'étude et à l'enseignement de l'histoire, 33-34, 35-36.)

————. ————, édités par Joseph Calmette . . . avec la collaboration du chanoine G. Durville, Paris, Champion, 1924-1925. 3 vols. (Les classiques de l'histoire de France au moyen age publiés sous la direction de Louis Halphen, 3, 5, 6.)

————. See also: Prucher, Auda; Valerius Maximus.

Contarini, Gaspare. *The commonwealth and government of Venice.* Translated out of Italian into English by Lewis Lewkenor. London, John Windet for Edmund Mattes, 1599.

*Il contributo veronese alle scienze mediche,* edito in occasione delle Giornate Mediche Veronesi 29-31 luglio 1949. Verona, S. A. M. Bettinelli.

Copinger, Walter Arthur. *Supplement to Hain's Repertorium bibliographicum.* London, H. Sotheran, 1895-1902. 3 vols.

Corio, Bernardino. *Historia continente da lorigine di Milano tutti li gesti fatti, e detti preclari, e le cose memorande milanesi.* Mediolani, apud Alexandrum Minutianum, 1503.

————. *Storia di Milano,* riveduta e annotata dal Prof. Egidio De Magri. Milano, Francesco Colombo, 1855-1857. 3 vols.

————. See also: Güterbock, Ferdinand.

Cortesi, Arnaldo. Coty pays historic call on Pontiff. *The New York Times,* 14 May 1957, 1, 4.

Cosenza, Mario Emilio. *Biographical and bibliographical dictionary of the Italian humanists and of the world of classical scholarship in Italy, 1300-1800.* Boston, G. K. Hall & Co., 1962. 5 vols.

Davis, James Cushman. *The decline of the Venetian nobility as a ruling class.* Baltimore, Johns Hopkins Press, 1962. (Johns Hopkins University. Studies in historical and political science, Series 80, no. 2.)

De Angelis, Pietro. Vannozza de' Catanei, benefattrice dell'Arcispedale del Salvatore ad S. S. in San Giovanni in Laterano. *Atti e memorie dell'Accademia di storia dell' arte sanitaria,* Appendice alla *Rassegna di clinica terapia e scienze affini,* Serie 2, 1954, 20. 5 p.

De Bertolis, Glauco. Alessandro Benedetti: il primo teatro anatomico padovano. *Acta medicae historiae patavina,* 1956-57, *3,* 1-13.

Delaborde, Henri-François. Un épisode des rapports d'Alexandre VI avec Charles VIII. *Bibliothèque de l'École des chartes,* 1886, *47,* 512-524.

――――. *L'expédition de Charles VIII en Italie.* Paris, Librairie de Firmin-Didot et C$^{ie}$, 1888. Reviewed by J. Vaesen, *Revue des questions historiques,* 1889, *45,* 574-588.

Delfino, Pietro. *Epistolarum volumen.* Venetiis, arte et studio Bernardini Benatii, 1524.

――――. See also: Schnitzer, Joseph.

Delisle, Léopold. *Mélanges de paléographie et de bibliographie.* Paris, Champion, 1880.

Del Prato, Alberto. Contributo alla storia della battaglia di Fornovo. *Archivio storico per le provincie parmensi,* Nuova serie, 1905, *5,* 227-255.

Del Re, Giuseppe. *Cronisti e scrittori sincroni napoletani.* Napoli, dalla stamperia dell'Iride, 1845-1868. 2 vols.

De Magri, Egidio. See: Corio, Bernardino.

Desjardins, Abel, ed. *Négociations diplomatiques de la France avec la Toscane,* documents recueillis par Giuseppe Canestrini et publiés par Abel Desjardins. Paris, Imprimerie impériale, 1859-1886. 6 vols.

Desrey, Pierre. Relation du voyage du roy Charles VIII pour la conqueste du royaume de Naples. *Archives curieuses de l'histoire de France depuis Louis XI jusqu'à Louis XVIII,* 1. sér., 1834, *1,* 199-223.

*Dizionario biografico degli italiani.* Roma. Istituto della Enciclopedia italiana, fondata da Giovanni Treccani [1960-1963]. vols. 1-5.

Dodoens, Rembert. *Medicinalium observationum exempla rara.* Coloniae, Apud Maternum Cholinum, 1581.

Domenichi, Lodovico. See: Benedetti, Alessandro.

Dovizi, Bernardo, da Bibbiena. *Epistolario.* [Edited by] Giuseppe L. Moncallero. Firenze, Leo S. Olschki, 1955. vol. 1, 1490-1513. (Biblioteca dell' "Archivum Romanicum," Serie I, Storia, letteratura, paleografia, 44.)

Dumont, Jean. *Corps universel diplomatique du droit des gens.* Amsterdam, Chez P. Brunel, R. et G. Wetstein, les Janssons Waesberge, et L'Honoré et Chatelain, 1726-1731. 8 vols.

Durand, Ursin. See: Martène, Edmond.

Du Terrail, Pierre, Lord of Bayard. See: Mailles, Jacques de.

Eckhart, Johann Georg von. *Corpus historicorum medii aevi,* sive scriptores res in orbe universo, praecipue in Germania, . . . gestas enarrantes aut illustrantes . . . collecti et nunc primum editi. Lipsiae, apud Jo. Frid. Gleditschii, B. Fil., 1723. 2 vols.

Eloy, Nicolas François Joseph. *Dictionnaire historique de la médecine ancienne et moderne.* Mons, chez H. Hoyois, 1778. 4 vols.

*Enciclopedia italiana di scienze, lettere ed arti.* [Roma] Istituto Giovanni Treccani, 1929-1939. 36 vols.

Equicola, Mario. *Dell'istoria di Mantova libri cinque* scritta in commentari . . . riformata secondo l'uso moderno di scrivere storie per Benedetto Osanna. Mantova, per Francesco Osanna, 1607.

Fabricius, Johann Albert. *Bibliotheca latina mediae et infimae aetatis.* Hamburg, sumtu viduae Felgineriae ex officina Piscatoria, 1734-1746. 6 vols.

Facciolati, Jacopo. *Fasti gymnasii patavini.* Patavii, apud J. Manfrè, 1757. 3 pts. in 1 vol.

Fantuzzi, Giovanni. *Notizie degli scrittori bolognesi.* Bologna, stamp. di S. Tommaso d'Aquino, 1781-1804. 9 vols.

Ferraiolo. *Una cronaca napoletana figurata del quattrocento,* edita con commento da Riccardo Filangieri. Napoli, L'Arte Tipografica, 1956 (Accademia nazionale di archeologia, lettere e belle arti di Napoli).

Ferrari, Luigi. *Onomasticon,* repertorio bibliografico degli scrittori italiani dal 1501 al 1850. Milano, U. Hoepli, 1947.

Filangieri, Riccardo. See: Ferraiolo.

Fisch, Max H., *Nicolaus Pol Doctor 1494.* With a critical text of his guaiac tract edited with a translation by Dorothy M. Schullian. Published for The Cleveland Medical Library Association by Herbert Reichner, New York, 1947.

Florio, Giorgio. De expeditione Caroli VIII. in Neapolitanum regnum. In: Graevius, Joannes Georgius, *Thesaurus antiquitatum et historiarum Italiae,* 9, Part 6, Lugduni Batavorum, 1723, 6th columniation, 1-18.

Foncemagne, Étienne Lauréault de. Éclaircissemens sur la personne et les ouvrages de Jean Michel, premier médecin de Charles VIII. *Histoire de l'Académie royale des inscriptions et belles-lettres,* 1751 (for the years 1741-1743), *16,* 240-245.

————. Eclaircissemens historiques sur quelques circonstances du voyage de Charles VIII en Italie . . . *Ibid.,* *17,* 539-578.

————. Observations sur deux ouvrages historiques concernant le règne de Charles VIII. *Ibid.,* 579-606.

Fouquet, Jean. See: Valerius Maximus.

Freher, Marquard. *Rerum germanicarum scriptores.* Editio tertia, curante Burcardo Gotthelffio Struvio. Argentorati, Sumptibus Johannis Reinholdi Dulsseckeri, 1717. 3 vols.

Freher, Paul. *Theatrum virorum eruditione clarorum.* Noribergae, Impensis J. Hofmanni, 1688.

Fuchs, Leonhart. *Opera.* Francofurti ad Moenum, Impensis Sigismundi Feyrabend et Simonis Huteri, 1566-1567. 3 vols.

Fueter, Eduard, *Geschichte der neueren Historiographie.* München und Berlin, Druck und Verlag von R. Oldenbourg, 1911. (Handbuch der mittelalterlichen und neueren Geschichte, herausgegeben von G. v. Below und F. Meinecke, Abteilung 1, Allgemeines.)

Fulin, Rinaldo. Documenti per scrvire alla storia della tipografia veneziana. *Archivio veneto,* 1882, 23, 84-212.

————. See also: Sanudo, Marino.


Gabrielli, G. A., Notizie intorno a Filippo-Luigi Polidori da Fano. *Rivista delle Marche e dell'Umbria,* 1865, 1, 243-280.

Gagliardi, Ernst. Mailänder und Franzosen in der Schweiz, 1495-1499. *Jahrbuch für schweizerische Geschichte,* 1914, 39, 1*-283* and 1915, 40, 1*-278*.

Gentile, Michele Lupo. Sul "De bello italico" di Leonardo Sfrenati. *Archivio storico italiano,* Serie 5, 1903, 32, 423-430.

*Gesamtkatalog der Wiegendrucke,* herausgegeben von der Kommission für den Gesamtkatalog der Wiegendrucke, Leipzig, K. W. Hiersemann, 1925-1938. Vols. 1-7.

Ghilini, Girolamo. *Alcune biografie di medici illustri tratte dai volumi ine-diti del Teatro d'uomini letterati.* Per le nozze Tecchio-Sardi. Venezia, Gio. Cecchini, 1880.

————. *Teatro d'huomini letterati.* Venezia, per li Guerigli, 1647, 2 vols.

Gilmore, Myron P. Freedom and determinism in historians. *Studies in the Renaissance* (Publications of The Renaissance Society of America), 1956, 3, 49-60.

————. *Humanists and jurists.* Cambridge, Mass., The Belknap Press of Harvard University Press, 1963.

Gingerich, Owen. See: Stahlman, William D.

Giovio, Paolo. *Historiae sui temporis.* Basileae, 1567. 2 vols. in 3.

Giuliari, Giambattista. *Della letteratura veronese al cadere del secolo XV.* Bologna, tip. Fava e Garagnani, 1876.

Giustiniani, Pietro. *Rerum venetarum ab urbe condita ad annum M.D.LXXV. historia.* Argentorati, sumptibus Lazari Zetzneri, 1611.

Godefroy, Denis. See: Jaligny, Guillaume de.

Goff, Frederick R. *Incunabula in American libraries.* A third census of fifteenth-century books recorded in North American collections. New York, The Bibliographical Society of America, 1964.

Gonesse, Nicolas de. See: Valerius Maximus.

Graevius, Joannes Georgius. *Thesaurus antiquitatum et historiarum Italiae.* Lugduni Batavorum, sumptibus P. van der Aa, 1704-1725. 10 vols. in 24.

Grassi, Giuseppe, *Dizionario militare italiano*. Torino, A spese della Società tipografico-libraria, 1833. 4 vols. in 2.

Grimm, Herman Friedrich. *Life of Michael Angelo*. Translated by Fanny Elizabeth Bunnètt. New edition. Boston, Little Brown and Co., 1906.

Guazzo, Marco. *Historie . . . ove si contengono la venuta, & partita di Carlo ottavo, re di Franza. . . .* In Venetia, all'insegna di S. Bernardino, 1547.

Güterbock, Ferdinand, Die Urkunden des Corio, ein Beitrag zur Geschichte des Lombardenbundes. *Neues Archiv der Gesellschaft für ältere deutsche Geschichtskunde*, 1898, *23*, 213-227.

Guicciardini, Francesco. *La historia d'Italia*. Nuovamente . . . ristampata. . . . Venetia, appresso Niccolò Bevilacqua, 1568.

————. *Storie fiorentine dal 1378 al 1509*, a cura di Roberto Palmarocchi. Bari, Gius. Laterza & Figli, 1931. (Scrittori d'Italia, 134.)

Guignebert, Charles. *A short history of the French people*. Translated by F. G. Richmond. New York, The Macmillan Company, 1930.


Haeghen, Ph. van der. Examen des droits de Charles VIII sur le royaume de Naples. *Revue historique*, 1885, *28*, 89-111.

Hain, Ludwig. See: Copinger, Walter Arthur.

Halm, Carl. See: Munich. Bayerische Staatsbibliothek.

Hauser, Henri. *Les sources de l'histoire de France, XVI^e siècle (1494-1610). I. Les premières guerres d'Italie. Charles VIII et Louis XII (1494-1515)*. Paris, Alphonse Picard et fils, 1906. (Manuels de bibliographie historique, III. Les sources de l'histoire de France depuis les origines jusqu'en 1815. Deuxième partie.)

Heckscher, William S. *Rembrandt's ANATOMY OF DR. NICOLAAS TULP*. Washington Square, New York University Press, 1958.

Heiberg, Johan Ludvig. *Beiträge zur Geschichte Georg Valla's und seiner Bibliothek*. Leipzig, Otto Harrassowitz, 1896. (*Centralblatt für Bibliothekswesen*, Beiheft 16.)

Heraeus, Wilhelm. See: Martialis, M. Valerius.

Herbst, Emilie. *Der Zug Karl's VIII. nach Italien im Urteil der italienischen Zeitgenossen*. Berlin und Leipzig, Dr. Walther Rothschild, 1911. (*Abhandlungen zur mittleren und neueren Geschichte*, Heft 28.)

Hesdin, Simon de. See: Valerius Maximus.

Hesnaut. See: Thuasne, Louis.

Holweck, Frederick George. *A biographical dictionary of the saints*. St. Louis, Missouri, B. Herder Book Co., 1924.


Imbriani, Vittorio. See: Casetti, Antonio.

Italy. Ministero della Pubblica Istruzione. *Mostra storica nazionale della miniatura*. Palazzo di Venezia, Roma. Catalogo redatto dal Prof. Giovanni Muzzioli. Firenze, Sansoni, 1953.


Jaligny, Guillaume de. *Histoire de Charles VIII roy de France*, par Guillaume de Jaligny, André de la Vigne, & autres historiens de ce temps-là. . . . Enrichie de plusieurs memoires, observations, contracts de mariage, traitez de paix, et autres titres et pièces historiques non encore imprimées. Le tout recueilli par feu Monsieur [Denis] Godefroy. Paris, Imprimerie Royale, par Sebastien Mabre-Cramoisy, 1684.

Justinianus, Petrus. See: Giustiniani, Pietro.

Kickartz, Hans Dieter. *Die Anatomie des Zahn-, Mund- und Kieferbereiches in dem Werk "HISTORIA CORPORIS HUMANI SIVE ANATOMICE" von Alessandro Benedotti.* Diss., Institut für Geschichte der Medizin der Medizinischen Akademie in Düsseldorf, 1964.

Kilburn, K. See: Lucianus *Samosatensis.*

Koestermann, Ericus. See: Tacitus, P Cornelius.

Kristeller, Paul Oskar. *Iter italicum.* London, The Warburg Institute, Leiden, E. J. Brill, 1963. Vol. 1.

Lacroix, Paul. *Louis XII et Anne de Bretagne.* Paris, Georges Hurtrel, 1882.

Lambeck, Peter. *Prodromus historiae literariae.* Lipsiae et Francofurti, ex officina C. Liebezeit, 1710.

Lancetto, Vincenzo. *Memorie intorno ai poeti laureati d'ogni tempo e d'ogni nazione.* Milano, A spese di Pietro Manzoni, 1839.

La Pilorgerie, Jules de. *Campagne et bulletins de la grande armée d'Italie commandée par Charles VIII, 1494-1495,* d'après des documents rares ou inédits, extraits, en grande partie, de la bibliothèque de Nantes. Nantes, Paris, Didier et Cie, 1866.

Lask, Thomas. Speaking of books. *The New York Times Book Review,* 8 December 1963.

La Trémoïlle, Louis de. See: Bouchet, Jean.

Laubmann, Georg. See: Munich. Bayerische Staatsbibliothek.

La Vigne, André de and Saint Gelais, Octavien de. Le vergier d'honneur. *Archives curieuses de l'histoire de France depuis Louis XI jusqu'à Louis XVIII,* 1. sér., 1834, *1,* 315-435.

Leathes, Stanley. Italy and her invaders. In: *The Cambridge modern history, 1,* 1903, 104-143.

Léonard, Émile G. *Les Angevins de Naples.* Paris, Presses Universitaires de France, 1954.

Leonardo da Vinci. *Leonardo da Vinci on the human body.* The anatomical, physiological, and embryological drawings. With translations, emendations and a biographical introduction by Charles D. O'Malley and J. B. deC. M. Saunders. New York, Henry Schuman, 1952.

———. *Selections from the notebooks,* edited with commentaries by Irma A. Richter. London, Oxford University Press, 1953 (The World's Classics, 530.)

Lewkenor, Lewis. See: Contarini, Gaspare.

Liebenau, Teodoro di. Il Duca d'Orleans e gli svizzeri nell'anno 1495. *Archivio storico lombardo,* 1889, *16,* 607-624.

Liruti, Gian-Giuseppe. *Notizie delle vite ed opere scritte da' letterati del Friuli.* Venezia, M. Fenzo, 1760-1780. 3 vols.

Litta, Pompeo. *Famiglie celebri italiane*. Milano, presso l'autore, 1819-1874. Vols. 1-10.

London. British Museum. Department of Printed Books. *Catalogue of books printed in the XV^th^ century now in the British Museum*. London, Printed by order of the Trustees, 1908-1962. 9 vols.

———. ———. *General catalogue of printed books*, London and Beccles, printed by W. Clowes and Sons Ltd., 1931———.

Longhena, Mario; Solari, Arturo; Picotti, Giovanni Battista. Fornovo di Taro. In: *Enciclopedia italiana*, *15*, 1932, 719-720.

Longo, Francesco. See: Malipiero, Domenico.

Lucchetta, Francesca. *Il medico e filosofo bellunese Andrea Alpago.* . . . Padova, Editrice Antenore, 1964. (Comitato per la storia dell'Università di Padova. Contributi alla storia dell'Università di Padova, 2.)

Lucianus Samosatensis. *Lucian*, with an English translation by K. Kilburn. Vol. 6, London, William Heinemann Ltd., Cambridge, Mass., Harvard University Press, 1959. (Loeb Classical Library.)

Lünig, Johann Christian. *Codex Italiae diplomaticus*. Francofurti & Lipsiae, Impensis haeredum Lanckisianorum, 1725-1726. 2 vols.

Luzio, Alessandro. Una fonte mantovana del Guicciardini. *Atti della Reale Accademia delle Scienze di Torino*, 1923, *58*, 284-293.

———. La "Madonna della Vittoria" del Mantegna. *Emporium*, 1899, *10*, 358-374.

———. See also: Mantua. Reale Accademia Virgiliana.

——— and Renier, Rodolfo. La coltura e le relazioni letterarie di Isabella d'Este Gonzaga. 7. Gruppo meridionale. *Giornale storico della letteratura italiana*, 1902, *40*, 289-334.

——— and ———. Contributo alla storia del malfrancese ne' costumi e nella letteratura italiana del sec. XVI. *Ibid.*, 1885, *5*, 408-432.

——— and ———. Francesco Gonzaga alla battaglia di Fornovo (1495) secondo i documenti mantovani. *Archivio storico italiano*, Serie 5, 1890, *6*, 205-246.


Maffei, Scipione. *Verona illustrata*. Verona, per J Vallaroi e P. Berno, 1731-1732. 4 vols.

Mailles, Jacques de. La très-joyeuse, plaisante et récréative histoire . . . des faicts, gestes, triomphes et prouesses du bon chevalier sans paour et sans reproche, gentil seigneur de Bayart [Pierre Du Terrail]. In: Michaud, Joseph François and Poujoulat, Jean Joseph François, *Nouvelle collection des mémoires pour servir à l'histoire de France*, 1. sér., *4*, Paris, 1837, 479-607.

Malgaigne, Joseph François. See: Paré, Ambroise.

Malipiero, Domenico. *Annali veneti dall'anno 1457 al 1500* . . . ordinati e abbreviati dal senatore Francesco Longo con prefazione e annotazioni di Agostino Sagredo. Firenze, Gio. Pietro Vieusseux, 1843-1844. 2 vols. (*Archivio storico italiano*, 7.) The quotation in my Preface is from *1*, xxvi.

Mandrot, Bernard de. L'autorité historique de Philippe de Commynes. *Revue historique*, 1900, *73*, 241-257, *74*, 1-38.

————. See also: Charles VIII; Comines, Philippe de.

Manget, Jean Jacques. *Bibliotheca scriptorum medicorum veterum et recentiorum*. Genevae, sumptibus Perachon et Cramer, 1731. 4 vols.

Mantua. Mostra di Andrea Mantegna. *Andrea Mantegna. Catalogo della mostra* [Mantova, Palazzo Ducale] *a cura di Giovanni Paccagnini.* . . . Mantova, Comitato della mostra di Andrea Mantegna, Seconda edizione, 24 settembre 1961.

Mantua. Reale Accademia Virgiliana di Scienze, Belle Lettere ed Arti. *L'Archivio Gonzaga di Mantova*. Volume primo a cura di Pietro Torelli, Ostiglia, 1920. Volume secondo a cura di Alessandro Luzio, Verona, Mondadori, 1922. (Pubblicazioni della Reale Accademia Virgiliana di Mantova, Serie I, Monumenta, 1-2.)

Martène, Edmond and Durand, Ursin. *Veterum scriptorum et monumentorum historicorum, dogmaticorum, moralium, amplissima collectio*. Parisiis, apud Montalant, 1724-1733. 9 vols.

Martialis, M. Valerius. *Epigrammaton libri*, recognovit W. Heraeus. Lipsiae, in aedibus B. G. Teubneri, 1925. The quotation in my Preface is from II.8, line 8.

Massa, Eugenio. La battaglia di Fornovo, 6 luglio 1495. *Rivista militare italiana*, 1912. 25 p.

Massalongo, Roberto. Alessandro Benedetti e la medicina veneta nel quattrocento. *Atti del Reale Istituto Veneto di Scienze, Lettere ed Arti*, 1916-1917, *76*, Parte seconda, 197-259. Reviewed by Alberto Chiapelli, *Archivio storico italiano*, 1917, *75*, Parte 1, 245-247.

Maulde La Clavière, René-Alphonse-Marie de. *Procédures politiques du règne de Louis XII*. Paris, Imprimerie nationale, 1885. (Collection de documents inédits sur l'histoire de France, publiés par les soins du ministre de l'instruction publique. 1. sér. Histoire.)

Mazzatinti, Giuseppe and Sorbelli, Albano. *Inventari dei manoscritti delle biblioteche d'Italia*. Firenze, Leo S. Olschki, 1890-1963. Vols. 1-85.

Mazzuchelli, Giammaria. *Gli scrittori d'Italia*. Brescia, presso G. B. Bossini, 1753-1763. Vols. 1-2 in 6.

Mémoire particulier fait par une personne d'esprit et bien instruite des affaires touchant Charles VIII, les personnes principales de son temps, et celles par lui eslevées, les actions plus considérables et dicts plus mémorables. *Archives curieuses de l'histoire de France depuis Louis XI jusqu'à Louis XVIII*, 1. sér., 1834, *1*, 159-198.

Mensi, Luigi. *Dizionario biografico piacentino*. Piacenza, A. Del Maino, 1899.

Metropolitan Museum of Art. See: New York.

Michaud, Joseph François and Poujoulat, Jean Joseph François. *Nouvelle collection des mémoires pour servir à l'histoire de France*. Paris, Chez l'éditeur du Commentaire analytique du code civil, 1836-1839 (1854). Three series, 34 pts. in 32 vols.

Missirini, Melchior. *Degli illustri italiani e loro scoperte nelle scienze nelle lettere nelle arti*. Siena, 1838.

Mittarelli, Giovanni Benedetto. *Bibliotheca codicum manuscriptorum monasterii S. Michaelis Venetiarum prope Murianum una cum appendice librorum impressorum seculi XV*. Opus posthumum. Venetiis, ex typ. Fentiana, 1779.

Molinier, Auguste. *Les sources de l'histoire de France des origines aux guerres d'Italie (1494). V. Introduction générale. Les Valois (suite), Louis XI et Charles VIII (1461-1494)*. Paris, Alphonse Picard et fils, 1904. (Manuels de bibliographie historique. V. Les sources de l'histoire de France depuis les origines jusqu'en 1815. Première partie.)

Molmenti, Pompeo. *La storia di Venezia nella vita privata*. Quinta edizione. Bergamo, Istituto italiano d'arti grafiche, 1910-1912. 3 vols.

Moncallero, Giuseppe L. See: Dovizi, Bernardo, da Bibbiena.

Mongan, Elizabeth. The battle of Fornovo. In: Zigrosser, Carl, *Prints: thirteen selected essays on the art of the print*, selected for the Print Council of America. New York, Chicago, San Francisco, 1962, 253-268.

Morelli, Jacopo. *Operette*. Venezia, Alvisopoli, 1820. 3 vols.

Morgagni, Giovanni Battista. *De sedibus, et causis morborum per anatomen indagatis libri quinque*. Venetiis, ex typogr. Remondiniana, 1761. 2 vols.

———. *Gli inventori anatomici italiani del XVI secolo nel carteggio col medico milanese Bartolomeo Corte*, a cura di Luigi Belloni. Pel XV Convegno Nazionale della Società Italiana di Anatomia, Milano, 1-4 ottobre 1953. Milano, Industrie Grafiche Italiane Stucchi.

Morris, James. *Venice*. London, Faber and Faber, 1960.

Mosto, Andrea da. See: Venice. Archivio di Stato.

Müller, Karl Konrad. Neue Mittheilungen über Janos Laskaris und die Mediceische Bibliothek. *Centralblatt für Bibliothekswesen*, 1884, *1*, 333-412.

Münster, Ladislao. Alcune considerazioni e precisazioni a proposito di un lavoro su Alessandro Benedetti, con riguardo per la rinoplastica. *Rivista di storia delle scienze mediche e naturali*, 1955, 46, 274-279.

Müntz, Eugène. *La Renaissance en Italie et en France à l'époque de Charles VIII*. Paris, Firmin-Didot, 1885,

Munich. Bayerische Staatsbibliothek. *Catalogus codicum manu scriptorum Bibliothecae regiae monacensis*. Monachii, sumptibus Bibliothecae, 1858-1912. 5 vols. in 11. Tom. 3-4: *Catalogus codicum latinorum*. T.1, pars 1, num. 1-2329 composuerunt C. Halm et G. Laubmann, 1868.

Muratori, Lodovico Antonio. *Annali d'Italia dal principio dell'era volgare sino all'anno MDCCXLIX*. Vol. 13: Napoli, presso Tommaso Alfano, 1758.

Muzzioli, Giovanni. See: Italy. Ministero della Pubblica Istruzione.

*The new Cambridge modern history*. Cambridge, University Press, 1957—. Vols. 1, 2, 5, 7, 10, 11, 12.

Nolhac, Pierre de. Inventaire des manuscrits grecs de Jean Lascaris. *Mélanges d'archéologie et d'histoire publiés par l'École française de Rome*, 1886, 6, 24 p.

New York. Metropolitan Museum of Art. *Venice. Views and echoes*. Margaret R. Scherer. Calendar for 1964.

*Nuovo dizionario dei comuni e frazioni di comune.* 26ª edizione, a cura di A. Bruno. Roma, Società editrice Dizionario Voghera dei Comuni, 1964.

Ojetti, Ugo. *Cose viste*. Firenze, Sansoni, 1951. 2 vols.

Okey, Thomas. *Venice and its story*. London, J. M. Dent & Co., 1904.

Olivieri, Dante. *Dizionario di toponomastica lombarda*. Seconda edizione, riveduta e completata. Milano, Casa editrice Ceschina, 1961. (Biblioteca italiana di opere di consultazione, diretta da Ferdinando Palazzi.)

——. *Toponomastica veneta*. Seconda edizione, riveduta e aggiornata. Venezia-Roma, Istituto per la collaborazione culturale, 1962. (Civiltà veneziana. Dizionari dialettali, 2.)

O'Malley, Charles Donald. *Andreas Vesalius of Brussels, 1514-1564*. Berkeley and Los Angeles, University of California Press, 1964.

——. See also: Leonardo da Vinci.

Omont, Henri. See: Paris. Bibliothèque Nationale.

Osanna, Benedetto. See: Equicola, Mario.

Paccagnini, Giovanni. See: Mantua. Mostra di Andrea Mantegna.

Palmarocchi, Roberto. See: Guicciardini, Francesco.

Panteo, Giovanni Antonio. *Annotationes . . . ex trium dierum confabulationibus ad Andream Bandam. . . . De thermis caldarianis quae in agro sunt veronensi*. Venetiis? c.1505?

Panzani, Giulio. *De venetae anatomes historia, et claris Venetiarum anatomicis prolusio habita in veneto anatomico theatro . . . VIII. Kal. Martii anno MDCCLXIII*. Venetiis, Apud Dominicum Deregni, 1763.

Panzini, Alfredo. *Sei romanzi fra due secoli*. [Milano] Arnoldo Mondadori, 1954.

Papadopoli, Nicolaus Comenus. *Historia gymnasii patavini*. Venetiis, apud S. Coleti, 1726. 2 vols. in 1.

Paré, Ambroise. *Oeuvres complètes*, ed. Joseph Françoise Malgaigne. Paris, J. B. Baillière, 1840-1841. 3 vols.

Paris. Bibliothèque Nationale. Département des Imprimés. Auteurs. *Catalogue général des livres imprimes*. Paris Imprimerie Nationale, 1897—.

——. Département des Manuscrits. *Catalogue général des manuscrits français*, par Henri Omont. Nouvelles acquisition françaises. IV. Nos. 10001-11353 et 20001-22811. Paris, Editions Ernest Leroux, 1918.

Parks, George B. See: Thomas, William.

Pasini, Antonio. *Il Tesoro di San Marco in Venezia.* Venezia, Ferdinando Ongaria, 1886-1885. 2 vols.

————. *Il Tesoro di San Marco in Venezia dal 1797 al presente.* Seconda edizione. Venezia, 1881.

Peebles, Bernard M. See: Avesani, Rino.

Pélicier, Paul. See: Charles VIII.

Pélissier, Léon-G. Le retour de Charles VIII à Rome. *Revue d'histoire moderne et contemporaine*, 1900-1901, *2*, 386-393.

Pellegrini, Francesco. Appunti per una storia del pensiero medico veronese. In: *Il contributo veronese alle scienze mediche*, edito in occasione delle Giornate Mediche Veronesi 29-31 luglio 1949. 63 p.

————. *La medicina militare nel regno di Napoli dall'avvento dei Normanni alla caduta degli Aragonesi, 1139-1503.* Verona, R. Cabianca, 1932.

Peroni, Vincenzo. *Biblioteca bresciana.* Brescia, Nic. Bettoni e soci, 1816-1823. 3 vols. in 1.

Perret, Paul-Michel. *Histoire des relations de la France avec Venise du XIIIᵉ siècle à l'avènement de Charles VIII.* Paris, H. Welter, 1896. 2 vols.

Petit, Ernest. Séjours de Charles VIII (1483-1498). France, Comité des travaux historiques et scientifiques, Section de philologie et d'histoire, *Bulletin philologique et historique*, 1896, *15*, 629-690.

Petrus de Abano. *Il trattato "De venenis"* commentato ed illustrato dal Prof. Alberico Benedicenti. Firenze, Leo S. Olschki, 1949. (Biblioteca della "Rivista delle scienze mediche e naturali," 2.)

Pezzana, Angelo. *Storia della città di Parma continuata da Angelo Pezzana.* Parma, Reale Tipografia, 1837-1859. 5 vols.

Picotti, Giovanni Battista. Nuovi studi e documenti intorno a Papa Alessandro VI. *Rivista di storia della chiesa in Italia*, 1951, *5*, 169-262.

————. Replica al Prof. Giovanni Soranzo. *Ibid.*, 1952, *6*, 107-110.

————. See also: Longhena, Mario.

Pieri, Piero. *Il rinascimento e la crisi militare italiana.* Torino, Giulio Einaudi, 1952. (Biblioteca di cultura storica, 45.)

Plinius Secundus, C. *Historiae naturalis libri XXXVII aptissimis figuris exculti ab Alexandro Benedicto Ve. physico emendatiores redditi.* Venetiis, per Melchiorem Sessam, 1513.

Poggiali, Cristoforo. *Memorie per la storia letteraria di Piacenza.* Piacenza, 1789, vols. 1-2 and continuation by Leop. Cerri, vol. 3, 1895.

Pol, Nicolaus. See: Fisch, Max H.

Portoveneri, Giovanni. Memoriale come il re di Francia passa in Talia per aquistare il reame di Nappoli col braccio della Signoria di Milano e dello Duca di Ferrara. *Archivio storico italiano*, 1845, *6*, Parte 2, 281-360.

Priuli, Girolamo. *I diarii*, a cura di Arturo Segre. Città di Castello. S. Lapi, 1912-1921, vol. 1. (*Rerum italicarum scriptores*. Raccolta degli storici italiani dal cinquecento al millecinquecento, ordinata da L. A. Muratori. Nuova edizione, riveduta. ampliata e corretta, t.24, p.3.)

Prucher, Auda. *I "Mémoires" di Philippe de Commynes e l'Italia del quattrocento.* Firenze, Leo S. Olschki, 1957. (Biblioteca dell'Archivio Storico Italiano, 6.)

Puccinotti, Francesco. *Storia della medicina.* Livorno, M. Wagner, 1850-1866. 3 vols. in 4.

Quintavalle, Armando Ottaviano. *La Regia Galleria di Parma.* Roma, La libreria dello stato, 1939. (Ministero della educazione nazionale. Direzione generale delle belle arti. Le guide dei musei italiani.)

Reali, Francesco. La battaglia di Fornovo avenne fra Oppiano e Giarola? *La Gazzetta di Parma,* 5 febbraio 1959.

————. Il Conte Bernardino de' Sanvitale massacrato nella battaglia di Fornovo. *Ibid.,* 2 agosto 1959.

Reichenbach, Giulio. Sassi, Panfilo. In: *Enciclopedia italiana, 30,* 1936, 890.

Reichmann, Felix. Historical research and library science. *Library Trends,* 1964, *13,* 31-41.

Renier, Rodolfo. See: Luzio, Alessandro.

Reuter, August. Berichte und Urkunden aus dem italienischen Feldzuge Karls VIII. in einem Wiegendruck. *Centralblatt für Bibliothekswesen,* 1903, *20,* 172-182.

Rhazes. *De ratione curandi pestilentiam. . . . Item . . . De pestilente febre.* Parisiis, apud Simonem Silvium, 1528.

Richter, Irma A. See: Leonardo da Vinci.

Ridolfi, Roberto. *Vita di Girolamo Savonarola.* Roma, Angelo Belardetti, 1952. 2 vols.

Romanin, Samuele. *Storia documentata di Venezia.* Venezia, Pietro Naratovich, 1853-1861. 10 vols.

Rorimer, James J. The glorification of Charles VIII. *The Metropolitan Museum of Art Bulletin,* 1954, *12,* 281-299.

Roux-Devillas, C. & F. *Catalogue 29,* Nouvelle Série. Paris [1951].

Rusconi, Antonio. *(1495) Assedio di Novara. Documenti inediti.* Novara, Premiata Tipografia dei Fratelli Miglio, 1884.

Sagredo, Agostino. See: Malipiero, Domenico.

Saint Gelais, Octavien de. See: La Vigne, André de.

Sanseverino, Gaspare. *Il carteggio di un capitano di ventura—Gaspare S. Severino d'Aragona detto Fracasso, 1475-1518.* [A cura di] Vittorio Adami. Venezia, La R. Deputazione Editrice, 1930. (*Miscellanea di storia veneta,* edita per cura della R. Deputazione di storia patria per le Venezie, 4, 2.)

Sansovino, Francesco. *Venetia città nobilissima, et singolare;* descritta già in XIIII. libri . . . et hora con molta diligenza corretta, emendata, e più d'un terzo di cose nuove ampliata dal M. R. D. Giovanni Stringa. In Venetia, Presso Altobello Salicato, 1604.

Sanudo, Marino. *I diarii (MDCCCCXCVI-MDXXXIII)* dall'autografo Marciano ital. cl. VII codd. CDXIX-CDLXXVII; pubblicati per cura di Rinaldo Fulin, Federico Stefani, Nicolò Barozzi, Guglielmo Berchet, Marco Allegri; auspice la R. Deputazione veneta di storia patria. Venezia, F. Visentini, 1879-1903. 58 vols.

———. *La spedizione di Carlo VIII in Italia,* raccontata da M.S. e pubblicata per cura di Rinaldo Fulin. Venezia, Marco Visentini, 1873.

———. ———. Venezia, Visentini, 1883.

Sassi, Panfilo. De bello tarrensi. In: Giustiniani, Pietro, *Rerum venetarum ab urbe condita ad annum M.D.LXXV. historia,* Argentorati, 1611, Appendix, ff. I3b-K5a.

Saunders, J. B. deC. M. See: Leonardo da Vinci.

Scherer, Margaret R. See: New York. Metropolitan Museum of Art.

Schiller, Joachim. *De peste brittanica commentariolus vere aureus.* Basileae, Excudebat Henricus Petrus, 1531.

Schnitzer, Joseph. *Peter Delfin, General des Camaldulenserordens (1444-1525).* Ein Beitrag zur Geschichte der Kirchenreform, Alexanders VI. und Savonarolas. München, Verlag von Ernst Reinhardt, 1926.

Schottenloher, Karl. *Die Widmungsvorrede im Buch des 16. Jahrhunderts.* Münster Westfalen, Aschendorffsche Verlagsbuchhandlung, 1953. (Reformationsgeschichtliche Studien und Texte, 76/77.)

Schullian, Dorothy M. *External stimuli to literary production in Rome, 90 B.C.-27 B.C.* A dissertation submitted to the graduate faculty in candidacy for the degree of doctor of philosophy, Department of Latin Language and Literature. Private edition, distributed by the University of Chicago Libraries, Chicago, Illinois, 1932.

———. A manuscript of Dominici in the Army Medical Library. *Journal of the History of Medicine and Allied Sciences,* 1948, *3*, 395-399.

———. The plague at Como, 1486. *Ibid.,* 1946, *1*, 174.

———. See also: Fisch, Max H.; Tortelli, Giovanni.

——— and Sommer, Francis E., *A catalogue of incunabula and manuscripts in the Army Medical Library.* Published for The Honorary Consultants to the Army Medical Library by Henry Schuman, Inc., New York, 1950.

Segre, Arturo. See: Priuli, Girolamo.

Servolini, Luigi. *Jacopo de' Barbari.* Padova, "Le tre Venezie," 1944.

Simeoni, Luigi. *Le signorie.* Milano, Francesco Vallardi, 1950. 2 vols. (Storia politica d'Italia.)

Smith, Charles Forster. See: Thucydides.

Smith, Joseph. *Bibliotheca Smithiana, seu catalogus librorum D. Josephi Smithii angli per cognomina authorum dispositus.* Venetiis, 1755.

Solari, Arturo. See: Longhena, Mario.

Soranzo, Giovanni. Pietro Dolfin, generale dei Camaldolesi e il suo epistolario. *Rivista di storia della chiesa in Italia,* 1959, *13*, 1-31, 157-195.

————. Risposta al Prof. Giovanni Picotti. *Ibid.*, 1952, *6*, 96-107.

————. *Studi intorno a papa Alessandro VI (Borgia)*. Milano, Vita e pensiero, 1950. (Pubblicazioni dell' Università cattolica del Sacro Cuore, N.S., 34.)

————. *Il tempo di Alessandro VI papa e di fra Girolamo Savonarola.* Milano, Vita e pensiero, 1960. (Pubblicazioni dell'Università cattolica del Sacro Cuore, Serie terza, Scienze storiche, 1.)

Soranzo, Girolamo. *Bibliografia veneziana in aggiunta e continuazione del "Saggio" di Emmanuele Antonio Cicogna.* Venezia, Prem. Stabil. Tip. di Pietro Naratovich, 1885.

Sorbelli, Albano. See: Mazzatinti, Giuseppe.

Spaggiari, Pierluigi. Intorno alla battaglia di Fornovo. *Aurea Parma,* 1952, *36*, 36-41.

Stahlman, William D. and Gingerich, Owen, *Solar and planetary longitudes for years −2500 to +2000 by 10-day intervals.* Madison, University of Wisconsin Press, 1963.

The stars foretell. Review in *The Times Literary Supplement,* 15 October 1964, of Louis MacNeice, *Astrology.*

*Storia di Milano.* [Milano] Fondazione Treccani degli Alfieri per la storia di Milano [1953-1962]. 16 vols.

Stringa, Giovanni. See: Sansovino, Francesco.

*Studi e ricerche sulla storia della stampa del quattrocento.* Omaggio dell'Italia a Giovanni Gutenberg nel V centenario della sua scoperta. A cura del Ministero dell'Educazione Nazionale e della Associazione Italiana per le Biblioteche. Milano, Hoepli, 1942.

Sudhoff, Karl. *Mal Franzoso in Italien in der ersten Hälfte des 15. Jahrhunderts.* Giessen, Verlag von Alfred Töpelmann, 1912. (Zur historischen Biologie der Krankheitserreger. Materialen, Studien und Abhandlungen gemeinsam mit V. Vossel, T. v. Györy, W. His herausgegeben von Karl Sudhoff und Georg Sticker, 5. Heft.)

Symonds, John Addington. *Sketches and studies in Italy and Greece.* London, Smith, Elder, & Co., New York, Charles Scribner's Sons, 1898-1900. 3 vols.

Tacitus, P. Cornelius. *Libri qui supersunt;* post C. Halm—G. Andresen denuo curavit Ericus Koestermann. Tomus posterior, *Historiarum libri, Germania, Agricola, Dialogus de oratoribus.* Lipsiae, in aedibus B. G. Teubneri, 1936. The quotation in my Preface is translated from the *Dialogus de oratoribus,* 21.2.

Thieme, Ulrich and Becker, Felix. *Allgemeines Lexikon der bildenden Künstler.* Leipzig, W. Engelmann, 1907-1950. 37 vols.

Thomas, William. *The history of Italy (1549).* Edited by George B. Parks. Published for The Folger Shakespeare Library, Cornell University Press, Ithaca, New York, 1963.

Thompson, Henry Yates. See: Valerius Maximus.

Thuasne, Louis. *Djem-sultan, fils de Mohammed II, frère de Bayezid II (1459-1495)* d'après les documents originaux en grande partie inédits. Paris, Ernest Leroux, 1892.

————. (_anagr._ Hesnaut). _Le mal français à l'époque de l'expédition de Charles VIII en Italie d'après les documents originaux._ Paris, C. Marpon et E. Flammarion, 1886.

Thucydides. _Thucydides,_ with an English translation by Charles Forster Smith. London, William Heinemann, New York, G. P. Putnam's Sons, 1920-1928. 4 vols. (Loeb Classical Library.)

Tiraboschi, Girolamo. _Storia della letteratura italiana._ Firenze, Molini, Landi e Co., 1805-1813. 9 vols. in 20.

Torelli, Pietro. See: Mantua. Reale Accademia Virgiliana.

Tortelli, Giovanni. _De medicina et medicis._ Bartolotti, Gian Giacomo. _De antiquitate medicinae._ Edited and translated by Dorothy M. Schullian and Luigi Belloni. [Milano, 1954.] (Omaggio della CIBA ai membri del XIV Congresso Internazionale di Storia della Medicina, Roma-Salerno, 13-20 IX 1954.)

Touring Club Italiano. _Guida d'Italia._ Milano, 1934—.

Tytler, Alexander Fraser. _Essay on the principles of translation._ London, J. M. Dent & Co., New York, E. P. Dutton & Co., 1907? (Everyman's Library.)


Valeri. Nino. _L'Italia nell'età dei principati dal 1343 al 1516._ [Milano], Arnoldo Mondadori, 1949. (Storia d'Italia, 5.)

_Valerius Maximus, miniatures of the school of Jean Fouquet._ Illustrating the French version by Simon de Hesdin and Nicholas de Gonesse contained in a MS. written about 1475 for Philippe de Comines. Reproduced in photogravure with frontispiece in color for Henry Yates Thompson, with an introduction by George F. Warner, Keeper of MSS., British Museum. London, Quaritch, 1907.

Valla, Giorgio. See: Heiberg, Johan Ludvig. The quotation in my Preface is from page 69.

Vatican City. Biblioteca Apostolica Vaticana. _Norme per il catalogo degli stampati._ Seconda edizione. Città del Vaticano, Biblioteca Apostolica Vaticana, 1939.

Venice. Archivio di Stato. Mosto, Andrea, _conte_ da, _L'Archivio di Stato di Venezia._ Indice generale, storico, descrittivo, ed analitico. Roma, Biblioteca d'arte editrice, 1937-1940. 2 vols. (Bibliothèque "Annales Institutorum," 5.)

Le vergier d'honneur. See: La Vigne, André de.

Vermiglioli, Giovanni Battista. _Biografia degli scrittori perugini e notizie delle opere loro._ Perugia, presso Vincenzio Bartelli e Giovanni Costantini, 1828-1829. 2 vols.

Vichi Santovito, Nella. Un cantare quattrocentesco sulla calata di Carlo VIII. In: _Studi e ricerche sulla storia della stampa del quattrocento._ Milano, 1942. 5 p.

Villeneuve, Guillaume de. Mémoires. In: Michaud, Joseph François and Poujoulat, Jean Joseph François, _Nouvelle collection des mémoires pour servir à l'histoire de France,_ 1. sér., 4, 1837, 377-402.

Visconti, Carlo E. See: Atri, Jacopo d'.

Voltaire, François Marie Arouet de. *Dictionnaire philosophique.* Amsterdam, Marc-Michel Rey, 1789. 8 vols.

Vossius, Gerardus Joannes. *De historicis latinis libri III.* Ed. altera. Lugduni Batavorum, ex officina Ioannis Maire, 1651.

————. See also: Zeno, Apostolo.

Warner, George F. See: Valerius Maximus.

Weiss, Roberto. The castle of Gaillon in 1509-10. *Journal of the Warburg and Courtauld Institutes,* 1953, *16,* 1-12, 351.

Welsch, Georg Hieronymus. *Sylloge curationum et observationum medicinalium centurias VI. complectens.* Ulmae, Impensis Gottlieb Goebelij, Typis Christiani Balthasaris Kuhnii, 1668.

Wickersheimer, Ernest. L'apparition de "variola" dans le vocabulaire médical. Deutsche Akademie der Naturforscher zu Halle, *Nova acta leopoldina,* N.F., 1963, *27,* no. 167, 175-182. (Beiträge zur Geschichte der Medizin und der Naturwissenschaften. Festschrift für Professor Dr. Rudolph Zaunick zum 70. Geburtstag am 26. VIII. 1963.)

Williams, Franklin B., Jr. *Index of dedications and commendatory verses in English books before 1641.* London, The Bibliographical Society, 1962.

Young, George Frederick. *The Medici.* London, John Murray, 1909. 2 vols.

Zagata, Pier. See: Biancolini, Giambatista.

Zanotto, Francesco. *Il Palazzo ducale di Venezia.* Venezia, G. Antonelli, 1853-1861. 4 vols.

Zeno, Apostolo. Giunte, ed osservazioni intorno agli storici italiani, che hanno scritto latinamente, registrate da Gherardo-Giovanni Vossio nel Libri III. de historicis latinis. *Giornale de' letterati d'Italia,* 1713, *16,* 414-474.

————. *Dissertazioni vossiane.* Venezia, G. Albrizzi q. Gir., 1752-1753. 2 vols.

Zigrosser, Carl. *Prints: thirteen illustrated essays on the art of the print,* selected for the Print Council of America, New York, Chicago, San Francisco, Holt, Rinehart, and Winston, 1962.

Zorn, Wolfgang. *Historischer Atlas von Bayerisch-Schwaben.* Augsburg, Verlag der Schwäbischen Forschungsgemeinschaft, 1955.

# INDEX OF
# PROPER NAMES
# AND PLACES

# INDEX OF PROPER NAMES AND PLACES

This index contains proper names and places occurring in the Preface, the Introduction and its notes, and the English translation, together with its notes, of Benedetti's *Diaria De Bello Carolino*. Groups of people representing nations or cities, like French, Italians, Venetians, Sienese, and government bodies are not included. Libraries, art galleries, churches, and the like are indexed under the city where they are located. Proper names occurring in book titles are not indexed, but translators and editors are brought out wherever possible. Publishers and places of publication are indexed only when they occur in narrative.

Forms and spellings are ordinarily adjusted to the vernacular, though not necessarily to the dialect concerned. When an Anglicized form is common it is usually adopted.

An entry may occur more than once on the page cited.

263